Immigrants in Turmoil

Modern Jewish History

Henry L. Feingold, *Series Editor*

Other titles in Modern Jewish History

Immigrants in Turmoil

Mass Immigration to Israel and
Its Repercussions in the 1950s and After

Dvora Hacohen

Translated from the Hebrew by Gila Brand

Syracuse University Press

First Edition 2003
03 04 05 06 07 08   6 5 4 3 2 1

This book was first published in Hebrew, in a slightly different version,
by Yad Izhak Ben-Zvi, Jerusalem, under the title *Olim be-Se'ara*
(Immigrants in turmoil).

All photographs courtesy of the Government Press Office of the State of Israel.

The paper used in this publication meets the minimum requirements
of American National Standard for Information Sciences—Permanence
of Paper for Printed Library Materials, ANSI Z39.48–1984.∞™

Library of Congress Cataloging-in-Publication Data

Hakohen, Devorah.
['Olim bi-se'arah. English]
Immigrants in turmoil : mass immigration to Israel and its
repercussions in the 1950s and after / Dvora Hacohen ; translated from
the Hebrew by Gila Brand.
        p. cm.—(Modern Jewish history)
Includes bibliographical references and index.
ISBN 0–8156–2969–9 (hardcover : alk. paper)—ISBN 0–8156–2990–7
(pbk. : alk. paper)
1. Israel—Emigration and immigration—Government policy. 2. Immigrants—Israel—
Social conditions—20th century. I. Title. II.
Series.
JV8749.I8H3413 2003
304.8'5694'009044—dc21
                        2003004556

Manufactured in the United States of America

Contents

Illustrations

Dvora Hacohen is professor of modern Jewish history at Bar-Ilan University, Ramat-Gan, Israel, specializing in the history of Zionism, the Yishuv (prestate Jewish community in Palestine) and the State of Israel, and Jewish immigration and absorption in Israel. In 2002, she was a visiting professor at Rutgers University in New Jersey.

She is the author of *From Fantasy to Reality: Ben-Gurion's Plan for Mass Immigration, 1942–1945* (Hebrew, 1994), *The Grain and the Millstone: The Settlement of Immigrants in the Negev in the First Decade of the State* (Hebrew, 1999), *The Ingathering of Exiles: Myth and Reality,* and numerous articles on these subjects. *Immigrants in Turmoil* was published in Hebrew in 1994.

Preface

"ONCE I THOUGHT to write a history of the immigrants in America. Then I discovered that the immigrants are American history." With these words Oscar Handlin opens his well-known book, *The Uprooted.*

I underwent a similar experience. While attempting to understand the social developments that took place in Israel upon the establishment of the state, I realized that the history of the State of Israel is tantamount to that of the great waves of immigration that flooded into it during the fifty years of its existence. Through this process there came into being not only a new state but also a new society. As I proceeded with my research, it became clear to me that the roots of the new Israeli society are to be found in the great wave of immigration of the first years of the state.

During that period, immigrants poured into Israel from dozens of countries and hundreds of communities all over the world, doubling its population within three years. In investigating the events of this mass immigration, I became aware of the extensive archival material revealing the great drama that took place in Israel during that time.

The discussions within the government and in the Jewish Agency Executive had been kept secret, including numerous arguments between the advocates of unrestricted mass *aliyah* (immigration of Jews to Israel) and its opponents. The great immigration simultaneously excited and repelled the old-timers. It was accompanied by stormy political struggles as well as by discussions concerning the future sociocultural shape of Israel.

For years sociologists and anthropologists have attempted to clarify various issues concerning the course of absorption of immigrants in Israel. Whereas the social scientists set out to clarify the new phenomenon while it was still at its height, the historians held their reserve, waiting for the dust to settle and for the picture to become clear, requiring as they did a longer perspective.

In my study I attempted to provide a systematic documentation of the mass immigration using the methods of the historical discipline. Because this is the first historical study of this subject, I attempted to relate to various aspects of the cognate problems of immigration and absorption in order to clarify the variety of contexts and mutual influences among them, of which it is difficult to take note while focusing upon one specific issue. The broad panorama allows one to understand the picture in its entirety and is likely to ease the penetration to depth of specific problems.

In the English version of this book, I have added an additional chapter that surveys the nature of the waves of immigrants that reached Israel during the first fifty years of its existence (1948–98), which contributed additional hues to Israeli society, a society still very much in the process of formation.

During the course of my research I had the privilege of becoming acquainted with dozens of individuals who took part in the project of immigration and absorption during the 1950s. Some of these people played central roles in the Jewish Agency, in local government, in the kibbutzim and *moshavim,* and participated in different circles spanning the entire gamut of the political spectrum. I wish to thank them for giving me generously of their time and patiently answering my questions; some of them also allowed me to examine private archives in their possession. Their help was invaluable.

I also met many immigrants and read some of their testimonies, which enabled me to focus more sharply on the problems of absorption from the perspective of the immigrant. Due to their lack of mastery of the Hebrew language and the hardships they suffered, at the time they arrived not many of the immigrants documented in writing the travails of absorption. Some of them expressed their feelings years later in various kinds of literary expression. This subject may serve as the basis for an interesting study that remains to be written.

My research was primarily based upon the extensive documentary material available in the public archives. I spent many days there and am deeply grateful to the directors and staff of these archives who opened to me their storehouses and assisted me willingly and graciously.

This study had its origins in my doctoral dissertation, written at Bar-Ilan University under the guidance of professors Shlomo Deshen and Ernest Y. Krausz. I am grateful to them for their guidance and their sage advice.

I am deeply indebted for his encouragement to my colleague Professor Moshe Lissak, a devoted scholar and a faithful friend. I also acknowledge the valuable comments and suggestions of my university colleagues. My writing was also enriched by the intellectual stimulation arising from seminars with my students at the university, for which I extend my thanks.

It is my pleasant duty to express my appreciation to Professor David Patterson, former director of the Oxford Centre for Hebrew and Jewish Studies, where

I was a visiting scholar during the writing of this book. The gracious help and cooperation of the director and staff of the Centre made my sojourn there a true pleasure. I am also grateful to the Memorial Foundation for Jewish Culture for assistance in my research.

Finally, I extend my gratitude to Professor Henry L. Feingold, series editor of the Modern Jewish History Series of Syracuse University Press, the members of the editorial staff there, the advisers who recommended and supported the publication of this book, and the devoted staff of the press.

Last but not least, I want to express my deepest gratitude to my husband and children for their encouragement and sustaining support.

August 2000   Dvora Hacohen

Immigrants in Turmoil

Introduction

I will bring them in from the northland
Gather them from the ends of the earth—
The blind and the lame among them,
Those with child and those in labor—
In a vast throng they shall return here.
                                            —Jeremiah 31:8

THE GREAT WAVE of immigration reaching the shores of Israel in the early days of statehood dramatically changed the demographic configuration of the Jewish people worldwide and transformed the Jewish Yishuv (prestate community). The State of Israel differed from other countries that threw off the yoke of foreign dominion and won their independence during the 1940s and 1950s; it grappled not only with the establishment of a new government but also with the creation of a new society. During its first three years as a sovereign state (1948–51), its Jewish population was doubled by the massive influx of immigrants—a record that remains unmatched even by the world's largest countries of absorption. Jews from all corners of the globe, from every country and every culture, streamed to Israel during this period, making it one of the most turbulent and difficult times in the nation's history.

From the start, the response to mass immigration gravitated between excitement and grave concern—an ambivalence that was to remain for years to come. Immigration, one must remember, was the heart and soul of the Zionist movement; it was perceived as the progenitor of the Jewish state. With the "ingathering of the exiles" as an ideological cornerstone and political independence as a goal, immigration became the spearhead of the Zionist battle. It was also through immigration that the Zionists hoped to realize their dream of social reform. *Aliyah* was thus an ideal; it was both the goal and the means toward that goal.

1

After the establishment of the state—the climax of Zionist achievement—it was expected that the "ingathering of the exiles" would be a top priority for the state, constituting its major mission and challenge. This was especially so in view of the fact that immigration had been a burning issue throughout the British Mandate. Toward the end of this period, the battle to open the gates intensified to the point that it became synonymous with the fight for independence.

Nevertheless, serious problems ensued as a result of the timing, scope, and composition of the wave of immigration. The timing was particularly difficult. The establishment of the state set off a bloody war with the Arabs, both those resident in Israel and those in the countries around it. The national effort thus focused on the battlefield. From the start the toll of the dead and wounded was very high. The moment Israel declared independence, it was invaded by Arab forces from all sides. From the standpoint of ammunition and manpower, the fledgling country could not hope to compete with the military might of the Arabs.

Israel was also in dire economic straits. Upon their withdrawal, the British had left behind them a state of financial chaos. Foreign currency reserves had been frozen and the hostile policies of the Mandatory government made it difficult to obtain credit. A wartime economy was in force and the situation was precarious indeed.[1] Under these circumstances, any wave of immigration, particularly an influx of such proportions, would be destined to hardship.

Myth Versus Reality

Given their gloomy prospects in Israel, the fact that masses of Jews from dozens of countries chose to leave their homes and resettle there seems nothing less than astonishing. Over time a myth grew up ascribing this phenomenon to two factors: (a) the unexpected fervor aroused by the declaration of a Jewish state, which led hoards of Jews to pack their bags and set sail for their new homeland; and (b) the single-mindedness of the leaders of the Yishuv and the Zionist movement, who insisted that mass immigration was a necessity upon the establishment of the state.

A careful reading of this episode brings to light a discrepancy between myth and reality. For one thing, it seems highly unlikely that hundreds of thousands of Jews from all over the world would have immigrated spontaneously on such short notice. Secondly, the attitude of the Yishuv leaders toward mass immigration at this particular interval was not unqualified. Hence our interest in ascertaining the true forces at work behind the surge of immigration in 1948.

Here we must distinguish among the various potential sources of mass *aliyah.* The Jews of the free world (notably the United States, Western Europe, and South America), constituting the vast majority of the Jewish people, were in no rush to depart for Israel. While they greeted the news of a Jewish homeland with excitement, this was not translated into practical moves toward immigration. Even before World War II, it was understood that Europe and the Muslim countries constituted the greatest pool of Jewish migrants. Indeed, it was the ratio between these two groups that determined the course and character of immigration to Israel in the early years of the state.

Eastern Europe was the cradle of the Zionist movement; Jews from Russia and Eastern Europe had been emmigrating to the Yishuv in waves since the end of the nineteenth century. On the eve of Israel's independence, this group made up 90 percent of the Jewish Yishuv.[2] However, the Holocaust severely reduced the number of potential immigrants from this part of the globe. Before World War II, nearly half the world's Jews resided in Russia and Eastern Europe. This was the world's largest regional concentration of Jews as well as the best-defined and most creative group from a national-cultural standpoint. The annihilation of European Jewry was thus seen as a death sentence for the Zionist movement and the Jewish Yishuv. As Chaim Weizmann, then president of the World Zionist Organization, declared: "We can count the bodies of our dead but the loss in values cannot be counted. The values that enrich human thought and human emotions—these are inestimable . . . Today we are fewer in number and impoverished in spirit."[3]

Approximately one million survivors were left in Europe after the Holocaust. Certain groups were singled out as potential candidates for immigration:

• Displaced persons: Tens of thousands of Holocaust survivors and refugees interned in DP (Displaced Persons) camps in Germany, Austria, and Italy.

• Detainees in Cyprus: Illegal immigrants picked up on the shores of Palestine and deported to Cyprus by the British.

• Jews of Eastern Europe and the Balkans: Jews from these regions who had survived the war or returned after the war, as well as those who had fled to Western Europe.

It ought to be remembered that, in addition to the havoc and physical destruction wreaked by the war, the countries of Eastern Europe were now occupied by Communist regimes. As a result, the Jews, like other inhabitants of the Communist bloc, could not leave freely.

The Jews in Muslim countries were another source of large-scale immigration. Hundreds of Jewish communities, numbering close to one million souls, were scattered throughout the Middle East, North Africa, and Asia.[4]

The activities of the Zionist movement also extended to the countries of the

East, but they were less successful there than in Europe. While branches of the movement operated in certain Arab countries, modern Zionism failed to capture the imagination of these Jews. A trickle of immigrants made their way to Palestine throughout the years, but most were motivated by religion rather than by Zionism and were taken in by Jews from their hometowns already residing in the country. Beginning in the 1940s the ties between the Jewish Yishuv and the Jews in Arab countries grew stronger.[5]

In general, the Jews of the East began to feel more secure once the European powers established a foothold in their countries. However, as Arab nationalism began to take shape in the 1920s and 1930s, the status of the Jews declined. Most of the Arab nationalist movements were affiliated with radical Muslim parties, some of them clearly anti-Jewish. The inclination of the Jewish elite and the intellectuals to embrace European culture, which put them on a closer footing with the government, also triggered Arab hostility. As nationalist zeal increased and gave rise to anticolonialism, the Jews found themselves in a shaky position that deteriorated further when their countries won independence. The state of affairs in Palestine had an effect, too. As the tension increased between Jews and Arabs, the Muslim movements declared their identification with the Arabs of Palestine and intervened in the politics of the Middle East. In consequence, the Jews were no longer perceived as a religious minority but were seen as a national minority associated with the Zionist movement—the enemy of the Muslim Arab world.[6]

The Jews of the East were not a homogeneous group. They did not constitute a unified segment within the Arab world but rather were composed of dozens of communities scattered throughout the region, each with its own social and cultural features, its own class structure, and its own ideology. Urbanization and secularization were at their height in many Muslim countries, and the Jews, too, were affected by these trends. Political and economic conditions were also in a constant state of flux, a situation that altered the financial and civil standing of the Jews depending on where they lived.

That the Jews in Arab countries would immigrate into Israel en masse was far from certain. When Israel became a state, these people were firmly rooted in their home countries; notwithstanding the problems confronting some communities, they were not expected to simply pack up and leave. True longing for Zion was anchored in the religious ethos. Many Jews from Arab lands had departed for Palestine over the years, but no such initiative was taken as a group—nor could it have been—after the establishment of the Israeli state.

The popular myth that hundreds of thousands of Jews from all corners of the earth dashed off in a frenzy to settle in the Jewish state is simply false. The much smaller number who stood at the gates included Jews from the DP camps in Europe, the deportees in Cyprus—a total of 24,500 people—and about 5,000 Yemenite Jews in Aden awaiting the opportunity to emmigrate from Yemen. The deportees, the Yemenites, and some of the DPs were under the jurisdiction of the British, whose hostile policies hindered immigration even after the declaration of statehood.[7] We may thus say that the great tide of immigration in 1948 was not a spontaneous, self-initiated rush upon the Jewish homeland.

It was the Jewish Yishuv, Palestine's long-standing Jewish community, which was responsible for bringing masses of immigrants to Israel and taking charge of the logistics involved. Assembling hundreds of thousands of people from dozens of far-flung places, arranging for their passage, and transporting them to Israel within a brief period of time required considerable organizational skill and an enormous outlay of money and manpower. It was the hosts themselves—that is, the Jewish Yishuv—who were saddled with this demanding mission. Thus the veteran Jewish community and its institutions played a decisive role in organizing the immigration enterprise and determining its timing, scope, and composition.

The declarations of policy issued by Israel's statesmen and Zionist leaders on various occasions perpetuated the myth of mass immigration. In public they spoke of their commitment to immigration, but the protocols of dozens of meetings of the Jewish Agency and Israeli government indicate that they were highly concerned about the timing and the large number of immigrants. These views were not aired publicly and great pains were taken to keep them confidential. That official statements and actual positions tended to diverge was nothing new in government and Zionist circles; in this sense, immigration was not handled differently. Immigration was a complex issue, and attitudes toward it had been formed long before the establishment of the state. In consequence, much may be learned by retracing our steps and examining the ambivalence of the Zionist leadership during the prestate years.

Mass Immigration Versus Selectivity

As a movement that embodied both the ideological and the practical, Zionism was characterized by a constant pull between ideals and activism, between utopianism and reality. Zionism emerged as a solution to the distress of the Jews; it combined redemption of the people with redemption of the land. But a simple combination of the two elements was impossible, and the leaders of the movement were forced to make a choice. The "ingathering of the exiles" was recognized as an important Zionist mission, but it was not always perceived as the immediate goal.[8] From its inception, the Zionist movement had been ambivalent toward mass immigration. It wrestled with the question of whether Israel was capable of being a refuge to so many at this preliminary stage or whether there were priorities insofar as building a new country and a new society were concerned. To what extent could the Zionist dream of social renaissance in the Jewish homeland be carried out if the country was flooded with indiscriminate immigration? These issues continued to be pondered throughout the history of the Zionist movement. During the early 1920s, as a great wave of East European Jews set sail for America and a quarter of the Jewish people were searching for a new home, Zionism finally gained headway in Eastern Europe, creating an opportunity for deflecting a certain amount of migration to Palestine. The Zionist leadership, however, was reluctant to admit large numbers into the country even though the Zionist Congress had proclaimed territorial concentration the only solution to the Jewish problem. These leaders maintained that "concentrating our national forces in Palestine is at present only a theoretical solution. There is no place for mass migration to Palestine. Zionism has yet to provide an answer to the burning issue of the masses who cannot wait."[9] This was likewise the position of those entrusted with Palestine's development at the time. Arthur Ruppin, director of the Palestine Office, set up in 1908 to oversee economic development and *aliyah,* favored slow, planned immigration in keeping with the country's absorptive capacity. Some Zionist leaders argued on behalf of a large-scale enterprise, but the majority felt there was no need for haste. Gradual development of the country at a pace compatible with economic opportunity was deemed preferable.

Together with the development of Palestine as the first priority and basis for realizing the Zionist dream, much thought was given to the issue of proper human resources. It was feared that, unless an immigrant met certain requirements, he or she would become an impediment and a burden to those who toiled. Much of the opposition to mass immigration was grounded in the belief that absorption difficulties would cause many immigrants to leave the country, subsequently harming the reputation and future of the Zionist enterprise. Many who made the move to Palestine during the Second Aliyah period remember being advised against it by Zionist leaders in the Diaspora: "When we went to see Mr. Broide, chairman of the Jewish National Fund Committee in Warsaw, and told him we would soon be immigrating to Palestine, he admonished us: 'Children! What do you think you will do there? You would be better off staying in Warsaw. Listen to those who are older and wiser than you and know what needs to be done in Eretz Israel.' "[10]

Potential immigrants to Israel from Arab countries also complained that they were turned down or prevented from going to Palestine. Some believed that they were rejected only because they were Asian Jews.[11]

The majority of the Zionist leaders felt that preference should be given to those who owned capital; those with needed skills, such as doctors and administrators; and the young and able-bodied, who could work as agricultural laborers. The Palestine Office was reluctant to accept responsibility for this last category. It did not encourage the *aliyah* of young people or cover travel expenses to Palestine. The growing rate of emigration offered further reason for wariness. One precaution, for example, was asking families interested in immigration to Palestine to send their children first. In the eyes of the Zionist leadership, the "ingathering of the exiles" was perceived more as a messianic dream than as a rational and realistic policy. After the Balfour Declaration, when the dream seemed to be coming true, the Zionist Organization swiftly issued a statement cautioning against the hasty immigration of multitudes.[12]

The debate over the ultimate goal of Zionism, the optimal pace of national development, and the type of activities that should be pursued began to sharpen in the mid-1920s. As the plight of the Polish Jews worsened and the United States severely tightened its immigration laws, a new wave of immigrants—a total of 82,000—turned toward Palestine. Known as the Fourth Aliyah, this was the first influx of major proportions.[13] Financially, it was quite solid and seemed headed for rapid growth and prosperity. However, the economic crisis that struck toward the end of the decade prompted many of the newcomers to leave, confirming the fears of those who called for a limit on immigration.[14] A few years later, when the Nazis rose to power in Germany and anti-Semitism became increasingly widespread in Eastern Europe, Palestine was again inundated with immigrants. The Fifth Aliyah, which commenced in the early 1930s, brought in 217,000 persons and constituted the second major wave of immigration.[15] This wave also aroused serious controversy in the Jewish Yishuv.[16]

At the forefront of the demand for selective, elitist immigration were the Socialist Zionists, who were bent on revolutionizing Jewish society and instituting a new code of values and way of life. To accomplish this, immigration had to be of the pioneering type. At the 1933 Zionist Congress, David Ben-Gurion, one of the prominent leaders of the movement, declared, "Eretz Israel today needs not ordinary immigrants but pioneers. The difference between them is simple: The immigrant comes to take from the land while the pioneer comes to give to the land. Therefore we insist on granting priority to pioneering *aliyah*. We see *aliyah* of this kind as a prerequisite for Zionist fulfillment."[17] It would not be amiss to say that support for selective immigration was the leading view during that time.

This approach was to change in the 1930s and especially the 1940s, when immigration became the focal point of the Jewish national struggle. The leadership of the Yishuv and the Zionist movement devoted endless effort to convincing the world of the necessity and urgency of throwing open the gates of Palestine, both as a vital means of rehabilitating Jewish refugees and as the free world's moral obligation toward the victims of the Nazis. These ideas gradually penetrated the consciousness of the Jewish Yishuv. As the battle for the Jewish homeland gathered strength, unrestricted immigration was increasingly seen as an integral part thereof. After the United Nations decision to partition Palestine passed on 29 November 1947, large-scale immigration began to be discussed as a matter of course. In planning the transition to statehood, the Labor Party (Mapai) addressed *aliyah* as one of six major items on the agenda; the subject also figured prominently in the deliberations of the Jewish Agency Executive and the National Council (Va'ad Haleumi).[18] Despite pessimistic reports on the state of the Holocaust survivors in Europe and the news that the Communists in Eastern Europe had blocked all exits, the matter continued to be spoken of as if the immigrants were poised and waiting at the door. Nor did the estimate regarding the number of potential immigrants change: the figure remained at two million, half from Arab countries and half from Eastern Europe, even though it was clear that not all those targeted would actually come.

On the eve of the establishment of the state, Israel's political and Zionist leadership regarded to the anticipated tide of immigration as if it were an irresistible force of nature. The debates on this topic included no concrete planning or probing of the problems involved in absorbing such a large body of newcomers; rather, the talks seemed to proceed on the principle of inertia.

After Israel's declaration of independence, a broad consensus emerged in most circles over the immigration issue, particularly when foreign elements began to question Israel's right to open its gates without restriction. Support for immigration continued to grow, both in the Jewish Yishuv and among the leadership, as the issue became the subject of an international dispute. However, this position was more fundamental than it was operative. It must be remembered that the main problem confronting the heads of the Yishuv during the early months of independence was the need to bolster the country's military strength. Immigrants who could contribute to the war effort were awarded priority; the matter of numbers was considered less pertinent and was not dealt with at the time.

Caught up in the war and its aftermath, the leaders of the Yishuv did not take the trouble to look closely at various aspects of mass immigration, such as its impact on the political system (which was by nature shaky and fragile) during a period of transition. During the Mandate period, this system was a web of parties and movements. It was an age of heightened political awareness, when most members of the Yishuv were affiliated with one party or another. The political struggle over the future of the country was thus accompanied by ideological infighting among various movements and loyalty to the point of zealousness over outlooks and beliefs. In the joint fight against the British, a national consensus emerged. On the whole, the Yishuv rallied around the prestate institutions and agreed to cooperate on matters connected with the struggle for nationhood. However, the old rivalries and political tensions returned with even greater vigor after the establishment of the state, as the new government took shape. Against this backdrop, the arrival of a large body of immigrants of unknown political affinity was a daunting prospect indeed.

Research Objectives

Israel's immigration policies were shaped by various institutions and organizations as well as by individuals who left an indelible mark on the enterprise as a whole. These are discussed at length in chapter 1, which probes their character and motives. As we have noted, there was a general consensus with regard to the inherent value of large-scale *aliyah,* but many were skeptical about the country's ability to organize and absorb immigrants under the prevailing conditions. Time and again, the question arose as to whether Israel should assume such a responsibility when its coffers were empty and even basic amenities could not be assured. This concern was considered legitimate by both national and Zionist leaders and could no longer be avoided after the state was declared and immigrants began streaming in. Let us reemphasize that it was not *aliyah* to which they objected but *aliyah* that was disproportionate to the country's absorptive capacity, especially when the masses were not yet converging on Israel's doorstep. The immigration enterprise placed a heavy burden on the fledgling country; careful organization and an intensive effort were needed to carry it out. Hence the call to refrain from a scheme that appeared overly hasty and unplanned.

The problem was not merely theoretical. Israel found itself in a serious dilemma when exit restrictions were relaxed in several countries at once, so that suddenly hundreds of thousands of Jews were free to be brought to Israel. It was then that Israel's mass immigration policy was put to the test. The country had to decide whether to allow all the immigrants in at the risk of overtaxing the absorption network, to set quotas for immigration from each country, or to give preference to immigrants from one country over those from another. These and other questions are dealt with in chapter 2. The financial crisis in Israel and its implications on immigration policy are examined in chapter 3.

Chapter 4 dwells on the physical and organizational aspects of absorbing this great influx of immigrants at a time of severe economic hardship and budgetary deficit. The unique features of the incoming population, as well as health problems and a shortage of housing and jobs, all influenced the type of programs that were adopted.

The deliberations on immigrant absorption raised fundamental Zionist issues that were reawakened by the establishment of the state. What, for example, were the goals of the Zionist movement in the social and cultural sphere? This issue had been a controversial topic since the earliest days of the Zionist movement, pitting the Socialist Zionists in particular against the others. Should Zionism devote itself to attaining political sovereignty or concentrate on social reform? Once the former had been achieved, the spotlight invariably turned toward social, cultural, and economic advancement. The prospect of large-scale immigration added fuel to the fire. In light of its dimensions and demographic composition, the wave of newcomers was expected to cause immediate and far-reaching change in the sociocultural landscape. For this reason, special attention was paid to drawing up and implementing programs that would serve as blueprints for the inauguration of a new society. Heading these efforts was David Ben-Gurion, who worked tirelessly to steer the country and supervise its social development in keeping with his philosophy. Ben-Gurion was accused by his opponents of being primarily interested in the political development of Israel.

Considerable space has been devoted to the political furor that accompanied the arrival of these immigrants. Apart from upsetting the political status quo, which was foreseen, the influx divided the Yishuv over certain moves that were capable of either rocking the system further or exerting a moderating effect. One pivotal issue was the granting to all newcomers of immediate civil rights, including the right to vote. Doing so was likely to alter the balance of power entirely, posing a threat or opening up possibilities for each party. Consequently, the 1948 wave of immigration set off a wild political scramble, with an endless round of confrontations and crises. Such was the conflict over education. This will be the subject of chapter 5.

The problems relating to absorption were so numerous that the Jewish Agency and the government were constantly improvising and seeking temporary solutions. Among those that left a lasting mark was the *ma'abara,* the transitional camp or quarter that was designed as a social bridge between the newcomers and residents of the towns. Envisioned as a breakthrough in the realm of absorption, the *ma'abara* program went awry from the very outset and became a serious impediment. As described in chapter 6, the dramatic confrontation between the established Jewish community and the *ma'abara* immigrants affected the newly emerging relationship between them, leaving profound implications for years to come.

Chapter 7 describes those policy changes that took place after four years of mass immigration. An uprising of the immigrants compelled the government and the Jewish Agency to take a closer look at their handling of immigrant absorption and consider the introduction of greater selectivity.

The study ends in 1953, when the first tidal wave of immigration to the Jewish state subsided. It documents the first stage of the process of the absorption and the approach adopted by their hosts in its early, formative years, which were vitally important and had a major impact on Israeli society in the making.

Chapter 8 presents an account of the waves of immigrants arriving in Israel between 1954 and 1998—the fiftieth anniversary of the State of Israel—and their effects on Israeli society.

Over the years, Israel's absorption policies have triggered an enormous amount of public debate and provided abundant material for social scientists, sociologists, and anthropologists. However, a thorough historical documentation of this period has never been attempted. The current study sets out to document and examine immigrant absorption from various perspectives in order to shed light on mutual influences and relationships that might be overlooked by a single perspective. In a description of the complex network of institutions, organizations, and personalities dedicated to the task of absorption, many issues cry out for further study and elaboration. It is hoped that others will take up that challenge.

Israel's ingathering of the exiles, with all the pain and suffering entailed, nevertheless remains one of the most miraculous events in the history of the state and the Jewish people. As Chaim Weizmann, Israel's first president, once said: "Miracles do occur in history, but we must work hard to make them happen." The heroes of the great immigration—the ones who made it happen—were no doubt the immigrants themselves. Their dramatic story remains to be told.

CHAPTER ONE

Policy in the Making

ON 17 MAY 1948, two days after the declaration of the State of Israel, a pair of steamers, *Lanitzahon* and *Medinat Yisrael*, stood anchored in Tel Aviv harbor as Egyptian fighter planes flew above, bombarding Camp Yonah, a Haganah base in northern Tel Aviv. These ships were a poignant symbol of the drama being played out in the region. Just ten days earlier, they had left Italy with their holds full of "illegal" immigrants; by the time they reached Tel Aviv, they and their human cargo were welcome newcomers to a sovereign Jewish state. The great tide of immigration, however, had not yet begun.

Numerous problems, each one more pressing than the next, faced the foreign and domestic policymakers of the nascent State of Israel. Along with the fundamental challenges of defining the character of the Jewish state and guiding its social development, there were prosaic matters to be dealt with. Among the issues that never seemed to leave the stage was immigration.

Until that time, immigration had served as the chief strategy for expanding and strengthening the infrastructure of the Jewish Yishuv under British rule. After the founding of the state, the wisdom of bringing in more immigrants began to be questioned. While the issue was not always admitted openly, there were many who feared that continued immigration would upset the country's social balance. Primarily, however, the controversy revolved around the question of whether Israel was in a position to absorb large numbers of immigrants at a time when serious problems loomed on both the economic and military fronts. In principle, there was broad public consensus regarding the importance of immigration, but opinions were divided on matters of volume and timing.

Immigration could not be approached in a vacuum; it was bound up with many other problems confronting the nation and was nearly always in the headlines. Concerns went far beyond the organizational and financial aspects of immigrant absorption. Mass immigration clearly had long-range implications for the social, economic, and political advancement of the country. In addition to pragmatic considerations, decisions in this sphere were invariably affected by the complex emotional response to the Holocaust. Consequently, the immigration issue was accompanied by much doubt and uncertainty; it touched off volatile debates that often strayed from the subject to expose sensitive nerves in the delicate social fabric of the Jewish Yishuv.

Caught in the Web of War and Diplomacy

The decision to terminate the British Mandate did not end the battle over immigration. On the contrary, the urgency of immigration became all the more apparent following the United Nations resolution of November 1947. The British, who did not anticipate this outcome, tried desperately to block implementation of the partition plan and spare themselves humiliation. They believed that, by drastically curbing immigration and preventing the Yishuv from preparing for the inevitable showdown with the Arabs, they would force the Jews and their political advocates to withdraw support for partition and consider alternate plans. Various formulas were proposed by the British, one after another, and these eventually produced the desired effect. On 19 March 1948, the U.S. State Department announced that it no longer supported the UN partition plan, favoring instead a UN trusteeship over Palestine.[1] The idea was to halt immigration and resettle displaced Jews in countries other than Palestine in the hope of forestalling a military confrontation between the parties and reaching a compromise in the interim.

The United States did not wait for the two sides to agree. On 30 March it asked the Security Council to impose a cease-fire on the fighting that had broken out on the morrow of the UN vote in November, calling for a special meeting of the General Assembly to reevaluate the political future of Palestine. The Arabs would not hear of a cease-fire, and the proposal brought before the General Assembly on 16 April was turned down both by the Soviet Union and by the Arabs. At this point, the U.S. State Department again attempted to postpone the declaration of the establishment of a Jewish state, urging the parties to negotiate an armistice agreement, which would halt the hostilities for three months and introduce international trusteeship. To lessen opposition to this plan, the Americans promised to support the release of the Jews interned in Cyprus and the monthly immigration to Palestine of fifteen hundred European Jews. In spite of the frightening prospects on the military front and the sense of dread that pervaded the Yishuv, the Jewish leadership refused to give in.

Meanwhile, all the parties geared up for the final battle over Palestine. Britain's announcement that it would withdraw its forces on 15 May set the country in a flurry. The Mandatory authorities stepped up their efforts to create economic and military chaos and encouraged the Arabs to intensify their attacks on the Jewish Yishuv. At the same time, they exhorted the U.S. State Department to pressure the leaders of Jewish organizations in America and in the Zionist Movement to embrace a postponement of the declaration of statehood. The Arabs terrorized the countryside, driving home the seriousness of their threat to turn Palestine into a bloodbath, and prodded the Arab countries to become more involved in political and international affairs.

Tension also mounted in the Jewish Yishuv between those who advocated the declaration of a Jewish state and those who opposed it. Those in the opposition urged the leaders of the Yishuv to accept the trusteeship proposal and to postpone statehood for the time being. The Zionist Executive and Moetzet Ha-Am (the People's Council) were split over this issue. When Moetzet Ha-Am met on 12 May 1948, the decision to go ahead with the establishment of the state was clinched by a single vote.[2] Resonating in the air were the warnings of the United States, the UN policy reversal, and the war cries of the Arabs. It was clear that the future of the state would be determined on the battlefield. In a race with time, the provisional government devoted its energies to the purchase and transport of arms and the consolidation of a defense force.

The battle over immigration continued even after the proclamation of the Jewish state. During the early months, all attention was focused on repelling the Arabs. There was no time to engage in policymaking that was not directly connected with the war effort. The immigration issue was only addressed insofar as it was useful for military and political purposes. The Arab countries were true to their word: the moment the state was born they invaded from all sides. Israelis believed that the British, too, did all they could to insure that the fledgling state would soon wither and die. Whereas arms were shipped to the Arabs in broad daylight and the Arab armies advanced upon Israel unimpeded, Britain and the United States carefully abided by the military embargo declared on Israel. Even after the termination of the Mandate, the British tightened supervision along the coasts to prevent the infiltration of ships carrying guns and ammunition. None of the displaced Jews in the camps under their jurisdiction—in Germany, Cyprus, Aden, and Tripoli—were allowed to immigrate. The United Nations dispatched observers (650 in July compared with 160 in June) to insure that no army-age immigrants were admitted who might be conscripted.

The immigration issue remained in the public eye throughout the War of Independence. Although Israel was now a sovereign nation, legally entitled to formulate its own policies, its international standing was still shaky. Moreover, its dependence on other countries for basic supplies—ammunition, fuel, food, and raw materials—was a source of unrelenting pressure. The great powers tried to intervene in Israeli affairs via the United Nations, particularly in the matter of immigration, on the assumption that this would appease the Arabs and move them to reach some kind of agreement. Israel thus found itself in a bind. Soon after the declaration of statehood and the invasion of the Arab armies, the UN Security Council decided to appoint a mediator to promote a peaceful solution between the parties. On 20 May, Count Folke Bernadotte of Sweden was asked to assume this task. After protracted negotiations, he declared that immigration was the main obstacle to obtaining a cease-fire. The accord drawn up between Bernadotte and Moshe Sharett, Israel's foreign minister, stated that immigration would be subject to supervision as long as the truce was in force.

During the first truce, which lasted from 1 June to 8 July 1948, Bernadotte worked on a formula that he hoped would provide the basis for a permanent peace treaty between the Jews and the Arabs. Here, again, the matter of immigration was pivotal; Bernadotte felt that it should be severely limited. According to his plan, each party would have the right to challenge the immigration policy of the other by means of a joint Jewish-Arab council. If no agreement could be worked out within the span of two years, the United Nations would intervene. The outcome would be a solution imposed on Israel, which would have implications for the future of Jewish immigration.[3]

Wartime Immigration

Attempts to halt immigration only stimulated the Yishuv to further action, the main consideration at this time being the importance of immigrants for the war effort. In the midst of the political struggle over Palestine after World War II, it became clear that security was a paramount problem. A campaign was launched to recruit young people in Palestine and Europe in anticipation of the establishment of a Jewish defense force. During the course of their work on behalf of the *ma'apilim* (illegal immigrants), *shelihim* (emissaries) of the Haganah organized military training in this sector. In February 1946, Nahum Shadmi was sent to Europe by David Ben-Gurion to instruct the young people in self-defense. He was assisted by *shelihim* from Palestine and those among the survivors who had belonged to pioneer youth movements before the war. In this way, the new immigrants would be in a position to join the armed struggle when they reached Palestine.[4] Such training was carried out in the DP camps in Germany, Austria, and Italy, and in the transit camp in Marseilles, where most of the recruits were Jews from North Africa. The Haganah also worked among Jewish youth in Eastern Europe, generally encountering no opposition from the authorities. In March 1948, Shadmi estimated the number of potential recruits in Europe at close to ten thousand.[5]

Military drilling of the *ma'apilim* was also conducted in the Cyprus detention camps, the source of another ten thousand able-bodied men and women. Palmah instructors, in collaboration with *shelihim* from Palestine, managed to smuggle in guns for training purposes right under the nose of the British. As the military situation in Palestine deteriorated, a cadre of young instructors was developed and the drills became more intense. After the establishment of the state, an Israel Defense Forces (IDF) delegation led by Zeev Aharon (later the chief education officer of the IDF) was dispatched to assess the number of military-age immigrants and to report to the IDF manpower division on how the training was progressing.

Gahal—Overseas Enlistment

Ma'apilim trained by the Haganah in the prestate period along with new immigrants taken straight from port to battlefield during the early months of the War of Independence were called *Gahal* (abbreviation of *giyyus hutz la'aretz;* "foreign recruits"). This group was an indispensable addition to the country's fighting forces. On 11 June 1948, when the first UN truce went into effect, Israel found itself in a precarious position. Within three weeks of declaring independence, there was no question of its inferiority in the military sphere. Israeli troops were confronted with column after column of heavily armed Arab regulars. With enormous determination, the Israelis succeeded in pushing back the enemy on several fronts, but the cost was bitterly high. During the first round of fighting, Israel counted 1,126 dead and more than 1,000 wounded, at a time when the entire army comprised fewer than 30,000 men and only 23,000 combatants.[6] The mood in Israel was grim, and the weary fighters, some of whom had gone for days without sleep, were in desperate need of relief.

The manpower division of the IDF announced that an additional 25,000 soldiers were urgently required to man the borders; consequently, it was decided to step up enlistment efforts in Israel and overseas. Immigration was eyed as a particularly valuable source of recruits, Ben-Gurion demanding that first priority be given to bringing over army-age immigrants and providing them with military training prior to departure. Indeed, the pace of immigration accelerated rapidly during the cease-fire, with nearly 11,000 newcomers arriving between 11 June and 8 July. Many came as part of the *Gahal* program and constituted an important reinforcement for the IDF.

Immigration did not cease after the expiration of the truce. During the ten days of fighting before the second truce went into effect (8–17 July), another 3,000 immigrants reached Israel's shores, some of whom were deployed straight off the boat. The IDF was able to report major successes during this interval, but casualties were high and included a substantial number of new immigrants.[7] The proportion of immigrants at the front increased steadily from the second truce onwards. By the end of July, 6,000 *olim* from the camps in Cyprus and Europe had joined the IDF, and the plan was to double that number over the coming weeks. There were thousands of army-age immigrants still interned in these camps, and arrangements were also under way to secure exit permits for thousands of young Romanian Jews. Meanwhile, military training of potential immigrants continued in Czechoslovakia and Poland.[8]

Like Britain, the United States declared that it would abide by the Security Council decision to withhold assistance to Israeli forces. The Americans were strict in enforcing the embargo on arms purchase and shipment but exhibited greater flexibility in the matter of immigration. At the DP camps in Europe under American administration, *aliyah* emissaries were asked to present lists so that the UN representatives could ferret out any draftable adult males among those bound for Israel. In practice, however, there was a tendency to look the other way. The Americans preferred to see the camps emptied after scathing attacks on the conditions prevailing there attracted considerable media attention in the United States. *Aliyah* activists took advantage of this situation to ignore the official ban and continue organizing groups of immigrants.

Throughout the summer of 1948, the IDF absorbed a steady stream of immigrants to the point where newcomers to Israel accounted for one-third of its new recruits.

Mahal—Foreign Volunteers

During the early weeks of the war, it became apparent that many of the new recruits sorely lacked military training. As the number of casualties mounted, there was a desperate need for skilled manpower and expertise. A partial answer was offered by Mahal (an abbreviation of *mitnadvei hutz la'aretz*, meaning "foreign volunteers"), a program in which foreign volunteers with military experience in their home countries enlisted in the IDF. Many of them were veterans of the air force, navy, armored corps, and artillery units. On the whole, Mahal volunteers were Jewish; however, there were also non-Jews who were inspired by the idea of a young country struggling for independence and came to lend a hand. Most of Israel's first pilots were Mahal volunteers. The total number of Mahal servicemen was not high, but their professional contribution was enormous.[9]

Immigrants Versus Refugees

In his recommendations to the United Nations, Count Bernadotte placed special emphasis on the right of Arabs who had fled their homes during the fighting to return to Israel and have their property restored to them.[10] The link between the Arab refugee problem and *aliyah* was obvious: the Arab countries insisted that immigration was a major factor behind the expropriation of land from the Arabs of Palestine, and Bernadotte drew up his proposal accordingly.

The Arab refugee issue did not cease to occupy Bernadotte during his term as UN mediator. Many of the Arab inhabitants had taken to their heels in March when the attacks began in the center of the country; this trend intensified as the war progressed, with the Arabs fleeing or being expelled from Tiberias, Haifa, and Safed in addition to the Arab villages captured by the IDF.

When the government met in June, it decided against allowing the refugees to return. Instead, the volume of immigration was to be increased and the abandoned property resettled by Jews. Ben-Gurion called for "the founding of new settlements at a quicker pace and over a wider area."[11] The government completely rejected Bernadotte's proposal to curb immigration and on 5 July voiced its opposition to any infringement on Israel's newly acquired sovereignty. The decision was that complete freedom to determine the scope and makeup of immigration lies at the very heart of the Jewish people's quest for statehood and has enhanced the import and urgency of this quest.[12]

The Arabs also rejected Bernadotte's plan and on 8 July, two days before the cease-fire officially ended, fighting resumed on the Egyptian front. The Security Council urgently convened and worked out an agreement for a second cease-fire, which began on 17 July. In the ten days between the first and second truce, bitter battles were fought all over the country, in which each side rushed to create new facts on the ground. This second truce, imposed on the parties from outside, was unlimited in duration but failed to ease the military tension. Both sides were eager to consolidate their positions and violations of the cease-fire were frequent on every front—in the North, in the Jordan Valley, in Jerusalem, and in the Negev. There was a sense that the country had been dragged into a war of attrition. As Ben-Gurion saw it, war was intended to break the enemy's spirit, whereas a cease-fire was "one of the ways of breaking ours."[13] All the while, Bernadotte toiled busily on his peace proposal, which he hoped to lay on the desk of the UN Assembly in Paris at the end of September. On 16 September he flew from the island of Rhodes to Israel; the following day he was assassinated in Jerusalem by members of the Lehi.[14]

Support for the Bernadotte Plan grew even stronger after his death, and increasing pressure was applied on Israel to accept it. Israel was threatened with sanctions, which it was hardly in a position to ignore given its shaky standing in the international arena. Steadfast in its opposition to narrower borders and the return of the Arab refugees, the Israeli government decided on the immediate establishment of ninety-six settlements in those parts of the country under dispute and the resettlement of Jews in former Arab villages. Responsibility for this undertaking was delegated to the pioneering movements—the kibbutzim in particular. Within months, thirty-two new settlements existed on the ground, and the plan was to double and even triple that number. It was around this time that the idea of Nahal, a program combining military service and agricultural work, began to take shape.[15] All eyes were once again turned toward the immigrants, many of whom were sent to live in urban neighborhoods and villages once occupied by Arabs.

Bernadotte had recommended turning Jerusalem into a UN stronghold in the spirit of the UN partition plan of 29 November, leaving the Galilee to the Jews and relinquishing the Negev to the Arabs from the Majdal-Faluja line southward. This plan placed particular emphasis on safeguarding the rights of the Arab refugees, which, as we have said, had a direct bearing on the issue of Jewish immigration. When the UN General Assembly convened in Paris on 21 September, the "will and testament" of Count Bernadotte hovered over the proceedings. In an atmosphere that was clearly hostile to Israel, the British and the Americans were inclined to accept his proposal, and the debate aroused considerable uneasiness in the Middle East. Israel braced itself for a confrontation as it awaited the verdict that would emerge from the corridors of the United Nations.[16]

The Arab Refugee Memorandum

Meanwhile, in August 1948 Israel's foreign minister, Moshe Sharett, appointed a committee of three to study the Arab refugee issue and come up with a solution.[17] From the earliest days of the British Mandate, there had been talk of transferring Arabs from Palestine to the neighboring countries as a means of solving the demographic problem and generating more land for Jewish settlement.[18] In the summer of 1948, however, this idea bore a different slant. The question was whether to permit the repatriation of Arabs who had left the country. Most members of the Israeli government and the Zionist Executive regarded the Arab exodus as irreversible.[19]

The memorandum drawn up by the above committee, headed by Joseph Weitz, cautiously proposed an exchange of Jews living in Arab countries with Arabs resident in Israel, although it did not maintain that the absorption of Arab refugees by the neighboring countries was linked to this happening: "The Jews who reside in Arab lands are loyal citizens . . . They are entitled to all the rights of Arabs who live there. Should they wish to leave and immigrate to Israel, they must be free to do so and take their property with them. If the Arab governments demand that the Jews leave as part of a population exchange, Israel will consent on condition that they be allowed to depart with all their possessions." [20]

This lengthy memorandum was presented to Ben-Gurion, who failed to attribute much importance to it.[21] He made a note of certain points in his diary, but his overriding concern was preventing the return of the refugees:

> They must not be brought back for they will constitute a Fifth Column . . . Rehabilitating them will require massive sums beyond the ability of the state. Arabs who remained in the country must be treated as equal citizens. Those who fled should be resettled by the governments of Syria, Iraq, Transjordan . . . [and] the Christians, by Lebanon . . . What if we are forced to take them back? Under no circumstances can we permit them to return to villages on the frontier; to the cities, only a certain percentage . . . to reunify families.[22]

By the committee's estimate, some 258,000 villagers and 248,000 city dwellers left their homes—a total of 506,000 people.[23]

Ben-Gurion already had in mind a solution to the refugee problem. Summoning to his office Joseph Weitz and Levi Eshkol, he ordered them to repopulate vacant Arab villages and neighborhoods as hastily as possible, using new immigrants for this task.

Immigrants on the Frontier

While the refugee question was being debated, war was raging in the Negev and the Galilee. IDF conquests in these regions led to the abandonment of another sixty-nine Arab villages. Ben-Gurion demanded that these, too, be resettled immediately. His orders for Beersheba, which had just been captured, were the same: "We must act as if we are certain that [Beersheba] will remain in our hands, otherwise it most assuredly will not."[24] He was particularly concerned about the Galilee: "We cannot hold on to a Galilee that is barren and empty. If we do not hurry to settle it . . . we shall incur political defeat. A chain of settlements should be established . . . We must take new immigrants there and ask the settlement bodies for instructors; if they are in the army, they ought to be released, for this endeavor has military significance."[25]

Large-scale settlement along the borders and in regions where Jewish presence was sparse was perceived by Ben-Gurion as the only way to guarantee the survival of the state. In his eyes, settlement was scarcely less important than military victory. "Our boundaries," he said, "will not be made secure by peace treaties but by a chain of settlements from one end of the country to the other"—and these dozens of new settlements were to be inhabited by immigrants.[26]

The Bernadotte Plan was unacceptable to both Jews and Arabs; hostilities resumed in mid-October. The United Nations put pressure on the parties to agree to a truce. Israel's self-confidence had been buoyed by its successes on the battlefield; its existence had become a fact that others were compelled to recognize. The armistice agreement with Egypt, signed in February 1949, was the first to be reached with an Arab nation at war with Israel. There were no limits imposed on immigration.

Foreign Policy and Immigration: Between the Blocs

In terms of its foreign policy, Israel walked a tightrope between East and West. As the Cold War intensified, this balancing act became increasingly difficult. One of the central motives behind Israel's dealings with the Communist bloc and its policy of "non-identification" was to secure the release of Jews from Eastern Europe. It was this goal that shaped Israel's foreign relations in general.[27]

At the time, Eastern European Jewry was believed to number more than eight hundred thousand persons. Foreign Minister Moshe Sharett, his top aides, and Israeli diplomats in the capitals of Eastern Europe began to negotiate for the release of the Jews. They were assisted by activists of Mossad le-Aliyah Bet, an immigration organization that had secretly initiated contact with East European governments prior to Israel's independence. Some of these activists came out in the open and joined the foreign service when Israel established diplomatic relations with the countries in question, but as often as not they continued to operate clandestinely as they had during the prestate period.

Negotiations with the Communist authorities were complicated and highly sensitive. Pushing aside the Iron Curtain was no simple task. The fact that a Cold War was in process further increased the need for caution. All talks between the parties were carried out secretly, and any agreements regarding the release of Jews were deliberately disguised and vaguely worded. In consequence, they were not always reliable. Such agreements were not worked out for the entire Communist bloc but rather separately for each country.

"Trade" Agreements

The issue of immigration was often addressed in the context of trade agreements. These were drawn up to disguise the fact that ransom was being paid to free the Jews. There were some countries where the release of Jews was approached as a purely financial transaction and it was not beneath them to bargain over the price per capita.

In negotiations with the Bulgarian government, Mossad operatives offered $100 for every immigrant and $300 for a Prisoner of Zion. Bulgarian Jews were among the first to reach Israel after the establishment of the state, in the summer of 1948. A total of $3 million was paid for their release—an immense sum in those days.[28]

The Hungarians demanded $80 per capita, which amounted to $2 million for 25,000 Jews. The figure set by the Romanians was $100 per capita, or a total of $5 million for 50,000 Jews. Meanwhile, the Hungarians raised their price to $100 per capita and insisted that they would only let older people go. The tone of the negotiations throughout was strictly businesslike. Accordingly, Israel's response to the Hungarian offer was that it was "(a) Too costly; (b) insufficient quantity (c) inferior merchandise."[29]

Rather than arranging for direct payment in the form of a head tax, the Israeli envoy to Poland, Yisrael Barzilai, preferred a straightforward trade pact. In May 1949 Israel signed an agreement with Poland in which it promised to purchase $16 million worth of Polish goods each year; in exchange, Poland would import $3.2 million worth of Israeli goods. This imbalance in favor of Polish commercial interests was a way of paying off Poland for the release of its Jews. Barzilai was involved in a whole series of financial and organizational arrangements connected with the exodus of the Jews and attempts to speed up its pace.[30]

Such agreements, requiring the outlay of astronomical sums of money, would have been inconceivable without outside funding. Israel's major source was the American Jewish Joint Distribution Committee (JDC), an organization that worked to alleviate Jewish suffering in Europe. However, even this organization did not have a limitless budget, and the transfer of such enormous sums from the West to the countries of Eastern Europe was interpreted by the United States as aid to the Communist governments at a time when the Cold War was at its height. Although they supported *aliyah*, American Jews were extremely sensitive on the subject of "dual loyalty," and their opposition was anticipated on these grounds. Furthermore, it was not only money that was being transferred. Some of these so-called "trade" pacts provided a hidden channel for delivering raw materials and basic supplies to the Communist bloc. The United States and its allies could not openly maintain commercial ties with the Communists, and it was here that Israel could be of assistance. Obviously, every precaution was taken to keep this activity under wraps, and most of the settlements with Eastern Europe were made far from the public eye.[31]

Again, these agreements were not always reliable and were subject to frequent alteration. For fear that the government might change its mind, Israel would arrange for the departure of the Jews almost as soon as the ink was dry. Under the circumstances, there was no time to think about absorption conditions in Israel. Even if the system was not ready, these people had to be rescued. Indeed, the gates soon closed. The countries of Eastern Europe maintained an inconsistent policy toward Israel and could not be relied upon as had been hoped for strategic, military, or economic assistance. Nevertheless, Israel continued to abide by its policy of neutrality in foreign relations and maintained diplomatic ties with all the countries in question.

The summer of 1950 constituted a turning point. There were several reasons for this, the main one being the outbreak of the Korean War. On 25 June 1950, when the Communists of North Korea invaded South Korea, U.S. President Harry Truman was quick to respond by sending American troops into the region to halt the Communist advance. The tension rose to new heights as China entered the fray on the side of the Communists. By the end of 1950, World War III seemed imminent and Israel felt that it could remain neutral no longer.

This shift in foreign policy was also a consequence of internal affairs. As immigrants flooded the country in the summer of 1950, the Jewish Agency and the government plunged deeper and deeper into debt.[32] Loans from the United States were the only hope, but these would not be forthcoming unless Israel made its position clear. The inevitable alliance with the West was certain to affect relations with the Communist bloc and hence the future of immigration.

During the first three years of statehood, while the agreements with the Communists were in force, some 300,000 Jews were allowed to leave Eastern Europe. The first wave was from Bulgaria. By the end of 1949, Israel had absorbed more than 35,000 Bulgarian Jews—almost the entire community; only 7,000 Jews remained. All told, the largest group of immigrants from the Communist bloc hailed from Romania (120,000 persons), followed by Poland (104,000) and Czechoslovakia (18,000—nearly half of the country's Jews). Only a small proportion of Hungarian Jews (14,000) reached Israel, with more than 100,000 left behind. In 1952 immigration activists estimated that more than half of East European Jewry would choose *aliyah* if the authorities let them go.[33]

The work of the Foreign Ministry in Islamic countries was of a different character entirely. These countries identified with the Arabs and saw themselves as partners in the struggle against Israel. Because there were no diplomatic ties or visible intercourse with these nations, any appeals regarding the exodus of North African Jewry were addressed to the British and French administrations in the region. These contacts were conducted in secret so as not to provoke the wrath of nationalist groups and Muslim fundamentalists. In independent Islamic countries, the Foreign Ministry was unable to operate and other Israeli elements had to be called in.[34]

Immigration to Israel continued without a stop through the harrowing days of the War of Independence. From the moment the state was declared on 14 May 1948 until year's end, a total of 103,000 immigrants made their way to Israel. During the war's most critical phases, the pace was slower. From May to August, a total of 33,000 newcomers arrived, mainly young people who could contribute to the war effort. During the last three months of the year, the flow increased to 20,000 and more per month. This was the start of the Great Aliyah, which was to gain in velocity in the weeks to come.

When the war was over, *aliyah* became Israel's foremost preoccupation. It was the concern of one and all, from the country's leaders to the man on the street. The "ingathering of the exiles" that had been spoken about endlessly was taking place before their eyes. Nevertheless, the price—political, strategic, and economic—was heavy. Large-scale immigration involved an enormous financial commitment that was to affect the country's growth for many years. Policies regarding immigration and absorption tended to be inconsistent, and political considerations, as we shall see, were often overriding.

A Race for Power

The shift from Mandatory government to sovereignty became official on the day the State of Israel was declared. However, the practical aspects of independence were shunted aside until after the war. As the fighting died down, it was incumbent upon Israel to determine its form of government, set up the necessary organs, and delineate national policies. During this time, immigration was the burning issue and its character was determined in no small measure by the people involved in government.

Israel's governing institutions did not appear out of the blue. The infrastructure laid during the prestate period had a tremendous influence. While the British were in power, the Jewish Yishuv operated as a distinct entity, a "society within a society" that strove for maximum autonomy especially in sensitive, nationally relevant spheres such as immigration, defense, international politics, and education. The Mandatory authorities handled those affairs that were less volatile from a political and ideological-national standpoint: organizing a police force to patrol the streets, enforcing civil and criminal codes of law, operating a court system, introducing technical services (postal service, trains, ports, and public works), and supervising foreign-currency exchange. Economically, the Jewish Yishuv relied on the Jews of the Diaspora. Foreign investment from this sector enabled the community to develop rapidly without having to seek resources at home. The World Zionist Organization and the Jewish Agency fought Israel's political battle for independence in the global arena. With the help of immigration, the country could look forward to a larger Jewish community with a solid economic foundation and greater security.

While the Mandate was in force, the leadership of the Yishuv pursued its activities on a voluntary basis. When the British departed, it was clear that the organs of self-government would play a critical role in molding the new nation. As a result, considerable rivalry developed between the functionaries of these institutions.

The Zionist Executive Versus the Government

During the period of the British Mandate, the Executive of the World Zionist Organization, which functioned as the government of the Jewish state in the making, was the highest-ranking national institution. The members of the Executive, elected by the Zionist Congress, headed the WZO's Political Department, Aliyah Department, Settlement Department, and so on. In April 1948, when the Minhelet ha-Am (People's Administration) was established, these officials continued to carry out their responsibilities as they had previously. On 14 May this people's administration became Israel's provisional government and its members were appointed ministers. However, they remained part of the Zionist Executive and worked simultaneously in both institutions. The head of the Jewish Agency's Aliyah Department, Moshe Shapira, one of the leaders of Ha-Poel ha-Mizrachi, also held the immigration portfolio in the provisional government; Moshe Shertok (who later changed his name to Sharett), head of the agency's Political Department, was Israel's foreign minister; Jewish Agency treasurer Eliezer Kaplan became minister of finance; and so on.[35]

Only Zionist Executive members living in *Eretz Israel* were elected to the people's administration. Members of the Executive in the United States and England, who had played an important role in the struggle for independence during the 1940s, were not included. While these figures were highly respected politically and socially in their home countries because of to their activism and government contacts, it seemed, as Israel's battle neared its end, that they were being denied a share in the new country's leadership. In Ben-Gurion's words, they were anxious about whether there would still be a need for "scaffolding" when the building was complete.

The World Executive saw itself as more than a political arm of the world Zionist movement. Its members felt it was their due to participate actively in leading the state and reaching decisions on national and foreign affairs. This was one of the issues deliberated by the Zionist Actions Committee when it convened on 6–12 April 1948. The World Executive called for a clear division of duties between the Zionist Executive and the Israeli government. Rose Halprin of the United States suggested that a select committee of overseas members meet every evening with the people's administration. Emanuel Neumann, also of the United States, proposed the establishment of a war cabinet composed of members of the Zionist Executive. The World Executive demanded a special meeting of the Actions Committee to discuss this matter.[36]

Israeli leaders were in no rush to hold such a meeting; in their eyes, there were more pressing items on the public agenda. The war and Israel's grave political and economic situation took precedence, they said, over the standing and duties of the World Zionist Organization. However, their major reason—unspoken—was probably their unwillingness to share authority with others. The Israelis sought to postpone the meeting until after the war on the grounds that the World Executive would not be able to enter the country anyway while the fighting was going on. This argument was suspect in the eyes of the overseas group as well as in those of a number of Israeli members who had been excluded from the government. They took it as a deliberate slight: "Now that we have a state, cooperation is no longer needed."[37] They insisted that the Actions Committee be convened without delay, and even set a date, August 1948, the first item on the agenda being "the division of tasks between the government of Israel and the Executive Committee of the Jewish Agency."[38]

Ben-Gurion refused to address this question. He advised his colleagues to concentrate on concrete issues such as security, immigration, and settlement and to "stop philosophizing." His plan was to make fund-raising on behalf of Israel the chief, if not only, mission of the Zionist movement, whereas policymaking would remain the prerogative of the Israel government. The World Zionist Organization Executive did not accept this plan. It maintained that the relationship between the State of Israel, the Zionist Organization, and the Jewish people should be given valid expression; it demanded a say in national affairs and pictured itself as a senate that would take an active part in formulating both foreign and domestic policy. Above all, it sought control over issues relating to immigration and immigrant absorption. Rose Halprin, Emanuel Neumann, and Yitzhak Gruenbaum warned that divesting the Zionist movement of all its responsibilities with the exception of finance would lead to its collapse.[39]

Ben-Gurion fiercely objected to this approach. "This state is a sovereign entity that cannot be subject to outside constraints," he declared. He emphasized that Israel had no intention of compromising the rights of the Zionist movement. However, as the central instrument for implementing Zionist goals, the Jewish state must enjoy precedence. At the same time, Ben-Gurion promised that no harm would come to the Jewish Agency and that it would be legally recognized as the juridical body of the Jewish people. To this, Yitzhak Gruenbaum responded cynically, arguing that the proposal amounted to granting the Zionist movement a charter, like Herzl once asked for, the only difference being that the charter Herzl sought was from a foreign country—not the State of Israel.

Neumann's complaint was that Israel's representatives in the United States never thought to consult with the Zionist movement there, leaving American Zionists with the sense of having no influence whatsoever. The Americans, he said, were not willing to be equated with the JDC, which provided money alone; they desired responsibility and partnership. Neumann threatened to resign if his demands were not met.[40] The clash between Ben-Gurion and the American Section of the Zionist Executive was not surprising. The two sides had already differed over the objectives and operational tactics of the Zionist movement. Now personal and political rivalry entered the picture, mingling with the fundamental debate over the structure of government in Israel and the country's relationship with world Jewry and its leadership.[41]

Ben-Gurion, as we have said, preferred to wait until after the war to discuss the division of authority between the government and the Zionist movement. He was supported on this issue by Golda Meyerson (Meir) and members of several other political parties. However, most of the Executive was opposed, including Moshe Kolodny (Kol), Yehuda Leib Fishman (Maimon), Shlomo Zalman Shragai, and Yitzhak Gruenbaum. Even such party colleagues as Eliyahu Dobkin disagreed with him and demanded that the problem be addressed immediately. Aaron Zisling and Yitzhak Ben Aharon of Mapam (acronym for Mifleget Po'alim Meuhedet, or United Workers Party) took advantage of the Actions Committee forum to attack Ben-Gurion publicly and settle scores with him on other controversial issues of the time.[42]

Berl Locker, who became chairman of the Jewish Agency Executive after Ben-Gurion's election as prime minister, pointed out that there were also practical reasons for separating the Zionist movement from the government: "There are legal restrictions on the actions of a sovereign nation within the borders of another nation . . . Will we be permitted to organize the exodus of Romanian Jewry? . . . Who will work to abolish the ban on emigration?"[43]

One of the questions asked was whether the membership of government ministers in the Zionist Executive served to strengthen or weaken that body. There was no agreement on this matter among members of the Executive, with the differences crossing party lines. Those who held cabinet posts, such as Gruenbaum (minister of the interior), Fishman (minister of religion), and Bernstein (minister of commerce and industry), maintained that ministerial membership in the Executive would lend more force to its decisions and would obligate the government to pay heed. Those members of the World Executive who were not in the government took the opposite stand. They feared that the ministers would dictate to the Zionist Executive and not the reverse. Abba Hillel Silver of the United States proposed that certain departments of the Jewish Agency be transferred to the Diaspora (mainly the United States), where they would operate independently. This motion was seconded by Rose Halprin, Emanuel Neumann, and Selig Brodetsky of Great Britain.[44]

Ben-Gurion again objected violently. He acknowledged that the Zionist Congress had been established in the Diaspora to defend Jewish rights there, but a central Zionist institution belonged in Israel and there was no room for two such institutions. Another idea was to impose specific tasks on the Zionist Executive and abolish the Jewish Agency. Members of the Executive continued to insist on the principle of *hafrada,* formal separation of the Executive from the Israeli government. Brodetsky drew attention to the problem of dual loyalty often cited by anti-Zionists in England. Neumann claimed that identifying between the two would affect fund-raising and tax exemption on donations in the United States. He also called for a financial separation between the Executive and the government; Eliezer Kaplan was both treasurer of the Jewish Agency and Israel's finance minister. Members of various Israeli political parties were among those who fought to strength the Zionist Executive and push out the ministers—S. Hirsch of Aliyah Hadashah and Rabbi Meir Berlin of the Mizrachi Party, to name a few. After a heated debate, it was decided that all cabinet members would resign from the Executive apart from Eliezer Kaplan, who stayed on as a member without portfolio.[45]

In his memoirs Neumann wrote, "I suspect that opposition to the *hafrada* was caused at least in part by nervousness about who would take charge of monies coming from the Diaspora. These fears were allayed by our agreeing to leave uncontested control over Jewish Agency funds to Kaplan."[46] New members of the Executive were elected to replace the ministers, and American Zionist leader Israel Goldstein became Jewish Agency treasurer.[47] However, separation from the Israeli government failed to strengthen the Zionist Executive. On the contrary, replacing the ministers with political leaders of lower rank detracted from its prestige, and the government became the seat of authority. Nevertheless, granting the Executive well-defined duties and autonomy in important spheres, in compliance with its demands, brought it closer to the foci of political power in Israel. The distribution of portfolios in the Zionist Executive generated much excitement, with a particularly vigorous battle over posts in the Immigration and Absorption Department.

Tug-of-War over Immigration and Absorption

With Ben-Gurion determined to prevent the Zionist Executive from participating in national affairs, the Actions Committee pushed for the adoption of the principle that the Zionist movement was responsible for all activities taking place outside Israel's borders. This included immigration, youth *aliyah*, Zionist propaganda, pioneer training, and so on. The debate revolved around those immigration-related tasks carried out inside the country, such as settling the newcomers in towns or agricultural villages. A majority of Executive members were inclined to link absorption and settlement together with immigration. They argued that the state would not be compromising its sovereignty by allowing the Executive to handle these issues, in view of the fact that the settlement enterprise was to be implemented by the Zionist movement following government directives.

Members of the government disagreed. Moshe Shapira, the immigration minister, insisted that all affairs related to *aliyah* should be dealt with by the state. He maintained that it was the job of the ministry to determine the scope and pace of immigration, quotas for various countries, etc. He also felt that absorption should be within his jurisdiction: "Absorption is linked to many government ministries and cannot be turned over to outside forces." He included the work of the Youth and He-Halutz Department in the same category.

Moshe Sharett, the foreign minister, agreed that the government should handle immigration in the Diaspora but only under the aegis of the Ministry of Foreign Affairs, whereas immigrant absorption would be dealt with by the Jewish Agency. Sharett's concern was that, because most of the power in the Zionist movement was concentrated in the hands of Western countries (the United States and Great Britain), Israel's contacts with Eastern-bloc countries in Europe might be affected. From a financial viewpoint, Sharett felt that the state was in a better position than the Zionist movement to mobilize international funding. Finance Minister Eliezer Kaplan advised that all issues related to *aliyah*, immigrant absorption, and settlement be handled by the Zionist Executive. He pointed out that the state was incapable of bearing the cost of mass immigration and called upon the Executive to assume financial responsibility in this sector. The majority voted in favor of Kaplan's proposal. At the close of the Actions Committee conference on 3 September 1948, it was resolved that the Zionist Executive would take charge of *aliyah,* absorption and settlement, Zionist propaganda in the Diaspora, fund-raising, and advancement of the Israeli economy.[48]

Paradoxically, the very argument that clinched support for Kaplan turned out to be baseless. The Jewish Agency did not have the resources to cover the immigration budget. A dispute among its fund-raisers in the United States further exacerbated the problem, so that a large proportion of the expenditure fell on Israel's shoulders. This shortage of funding was to have a critical impact on the country's immigrant-absorption system. The duties devolved on the Zionist Executive, important as they were, did not elevate its standing or enable it to function as an autonomous body. In practice, the Jewish Agency became an extension of party politics in Israel and operated under the same leadership.[49] The race for control over Israel's national institutions widened to the point where it went beyond the departments of the Jewish Agency and literally ran wild.

When the Actions Committee met again in September 1948, it decided to restructure the Jewish Agency, adding new departments and changing the function of others. The Jewish Agency now had twelve departments, five of which were directly concerned with immigration and absorption.[50] Particularly notable was the reorganization of the Aliyah Department. The management of immigrant hostels and care of immigrants during the initial stages of absorption, formerly within the domain of the Aliyah Department, now became the responsibility of the newly created Kelitah Department. The Actions Committee did not spell out the precise duties of this body, but it was soon to have a decisive influence on the manner in which new arrivals were resettled in Israel.

In keeping with the resolutions of the Actions Committee, five separate Jewish Agency departments were entrusted with the task of bringing in and absorbing immigrants: Aliyah, Kelitah, Land Settlement, Youth Aliyah, and Youth and He-Halutz. The function and areas of jurisdiction of these departments were far from clear; as a result, they were constantly fighting among themselves.

When portfolios were handed out in the Zionist Executive, all eyes were on those considered most prestigious, the Aliyah and Kelitah departments clearly being among them. Mapam immediately claimed Aliyah for itself on the grounds that its members were the guiding force behind Mossad le-Aliyah Bet. Until that time, the department had been headed by Moshe Shapira (Ha-Poel ha-Mizrachi), who vehemently opposed its relinquishment to any other party. In the end, the Aliyah portfolio went to Yitzhak Raphael (Werfel) of Ha-Poel ha-Mizrachi. In compensation, Mapam was given a section of the Aliyah Department devoted to Jews in Arab lands, the "Division for the Affairs of Jews in the Middle East." However, members of Mapam objected to working under Yitzhak Raphael and exerted such pressure that the division eventually split from the Aliyah Department and became an independent entity under Yaakov Zerubavel (Mapam).[51]

The assignment of portfolios and delegation of departmental duties did not end the competition in the Jewish Agency. Each department tried to broaden its sphere of activity even if this encroached upon the work of other departments. A case in point was the Department for Jewish Affairs in the Middle East under Zerubavel, which began to operate in Arab lands even in those areas that were under the aegis of the Aliyah Department. During its first year of existence, this department organized an administrative mechanism and a staff of emissaries and counselors that paralleled that of the Aliyah Department. It had two overseas branches: one in Paris to handle North Africa and Egypt, and an office in Teheran to handle Iran and the Middle East. Its Jerusalem headquarters initiated contact with Libya, Yemen, Aden, and India. The seventy-six persons in its employ worked in close cooperation with the activists of Mossad le-Aliyah Bet, many of whom belonged to the Palmah and were supporters of Mapam.[52] The activities of this department took place in the Diaspora; once the immigrants reached Israel, the Kelitah Department assumed responsibility for them.

Mossad le-Aliyah Bet

Aside from the various Jewish Agency departments, a significant contribution to *aliyah* was made by Mossad le-Aliyah Bet, an organization that chalked up a glorious chapter in the history of "illegal" immigration activities during the final decade of the British Mandate.[53] The Mossad operated through a prodigious network of dedicated and efficient activists stationed throughout Europe and the Middle East, especially in those countries where Zionist affiliation and *aliyah* were prohibited. Its work was done clandestinely for fear of provoking hostility among the local inhabitants or of attracting the attention of the authorities. Mossad le-Aliyah Bet played a central role in organizing groups of immigrants in their home towns, arranging for transportation, and getting them to their destinations. After the redistribution of portfolios in the Jewish Agency, this body continued to handle the transport of immigrants with the endorsement of the

Aliyah Department, but it insisted on financial independence and refused to become part of the Jewish Agency. Funding for its activities was received directly from the JDC, a fact its adversaries exploited to back up charges that the organization was not reporting income and expenditure.[54] Yitzhak Raphael was in favor of canceling the Mossad's budgetary autonomy. Mapam, however, fought mightily against any change in status. Raphael was forced to sanction the Mossad's Paris office as representing the Aliyah Department but not bound to its operations. The powers of the Mossad were never formally defined, a fact that served as a source of constant argumentation.

The Actions Committee resolved that "the Mossad will continue to function for the time being as the chief instrument for implementing mass immigration of Jews to Israel, albeit not the one and only instrument."[55] Years before the state came into being, Ben-Gurion had expressed dissatisfaction with the excessive freedom exercised by the Mossad. Moreover, many of the Mossad activists were members of Kibbutz Hame'uhad and had a direct connection to Mapam. The rift between Ben-Gurion and this camp widened further after the disbanding of the Palmah.[56] Ben-Gurion was not happy with the resolution of the Actions Committee, but neither was he interested in strengthening Raphael. He believed that the army should be in charge of bringing over immigrants: "A special service for transporting *olim* should be established by the Navy and headed by a special person."[57] This idea was not taken further; the Mossad continued to operate in many different spheres without change of status—a tribute, in no small measure, to the support it enjoyed in the political arena.

In addition to the Mossad, many other parties and movements had overseas representatives busily organizing groups of Jewish emigrants in their countries of origin. All these bodies were anxious to increase their activities and become more powerful. This tension found expression in the tug-of-war over Zionist Executive portfolios and, later, in the course of their work.

The Aliyah Department

In September 1948, Yitzhak Raphael of Ha-Poel ha-Mizrachi was appointed head of the Aliyah Department. Young and ambitious, Raphael was the son-in-law of Rabbi Yehuda Leib Hacohen Maimon (Fishman), a leader of the Mizrachi Party. Raphael soon realized that the department was losing strength: "Aliyah has many landlords—Mossad le-Aliyah, Briha, He-Halutz, delegations of emissaries, Palestine Offices, political parties."[58] Even the Palestine Offices, which had previously functioned as an important arm of the Aliyah Department in the immigrants' home countries, were no longer under his supervision. After the severe limits imposed on free immigration during the Mandate, these offices were in fact taken over by operatives of Mossad le-Aliyah Bet, who used underground channels to further illegal immigration under the sponsorship of the Jewish Agency. In many areas, it was the Mossad that was in basic control.[59]

Raphael was displeased with this state of affairs. He was determined to reorganize the Aliyah Department, revamp the Palestine Offices, and reinstate his authority: "In our first overseas contacts we found divided leadership and a state of grave indecision and disputation. There were conflicts and confrontations between the Palestine Offices, in the event that they were still somehow operative, and Mossad le-Aliyah, which was chiefly active and influential during the *ha'apala,* and also between the Israeli delegations in the camps and centers for Holocaust survivors."[60]

The problem was compounded by the fact that immigration and absorption were not the sole prerogative of the Jewish Agency. The government had established a Ministry of Immigration under Moshe Shapira, who had previously headed the Aliyah Department. The Ministry of Immigration appointed "immigration officers" to issue visas to private capitalists, those dependent on relatives in Israel, students at Israeli institutions, and experts who did not arrive under the aegis of the Jewish Agency.[61] These officers were generally former Palestine Office directors. At the time Shapira was serving simultaneously as head of the Aliyah Department and minister of immigration, he felt no need to define the tasks of the Palestine Offices more clearly. However, the reallocation of portfolios prompted his successor in the Jewish Agency, Yitzhak Raphael, to try to regain those powers that had been lost and to expand his power further. His first step was to sort out the various officials and assign them definite duties.

Raphael's major difficulty lay in the confrontation with Mossad le-Aliyah Bet. The Mossad still predominated in many important areas and the presumption was that it would continue to do so. The Aliyah Department would tend to official and peripheral matters, every so often granting "honors" to the head of the Mossad, as had been the practice when Shapira and Dobkin were partners in running the Aliyah Department.[62] Meanwhile, various political parties were waging a secret battle over the fate of the Mossad. Mapam activists in the Zionist Executive were struggling to preserve its independence and exclusivity in the field of immigration; Mizrachi and Ha-Poel ha-Mizrachi demanded that Zionist Executive activities be curbed. In consequence, the work of this organization emerged in a somewhat clearer light.[63] As the influence of Mapam declined, so did the power of the Mossad. Yitzhak Raphael was insistent; he wanted its responsibility limited to arranging the passage of immigrants by ship from Europe to Israel. Gradually, Raphael had his way and the Mossad enjoyed free rein only in those countries where emigration could not be organized openly.[64]

Another body that had a crucial impact on immigration was the Ministry of Foreign Affairs. Israeli diplomats in Eastern Europe negotiated endlessly with the authorities for permission for the Jews to leave. Raphael tried to participate in these talks, too, although he never questioned the ministry's right to engage in such activity.[65]

The friction that developed over immigration was not only external; there was also interdepartmental rivalry within the Jewish Agency. When portfolios were distributed, the Kelitah Department claimed housing. Raphael, however, objected to relinquishing this sector; an agreement was reached whereby the housing division would remain part of the Aliyah Department with a General Zionist at its head. In practice, housing was placed in the hands of a company named "Amidar," rendering the division superfluous.[66] Among the department chiefs, there were many who coveted the responsibilities of the Aliyah Department. Eliyahu Dobkin, formerly head of the Aliyah Department, was presented with both the Youth and He-Halutz and the Information portfolios. This did not stop him from issuing totally unauthorized statements about developments in his old department. Other departments attempted to intervene in the work of the Aliyah Department as well.[67]

Immigrant Health Care

During the prestate period, the health care of new immigrants had been the responsibility of the Jewish Agency's Aliyah Department. The newcomers obtained medical attention through existing institutions—Hadassah and Kupat Holim. In December 1944 it became necessary to create a broader framework to provide adequate care for the Holocaust survivors who arrived with a multitude of ills. The new service was headed by Dr. Grushka, who took orders from a committee composed of delegates of the Jewish Agency, Va'ad Leumi, Hadassah, and Kupat Holim. By means of this service, new immigrants received Kupat Holim health insurance for their first few months in the country and were covered for hospital expenses and ambulatory care. From October 1946, Hadassah assumed responsibility for all health and medical treatment in immigrant hostels and transit camps. The Aliyah Department and Hadassah thus became partners in the provision and funding of medical services for immigrants.

Mass immigration brought with it an unending stream of health problems. Concentration camp survivors and immigrants from Arab lands were diagnosed with a broad array of diseases, both chronic and infectious, requiring the medical profession to ready itself quickly. At this point, the Ministry of Health stepped in. From then on, immigrant health care became another point of controversy between the various bodies involved in immigrant absorption.

The Absorption Department

The problem of absorbing new immigrants loomed up in all its severity during World War II, when survivors of the Holocaust reached Israel's shores in a state of utter destitution. They initially arrived at the port of Haifa, where they were met by workers of the Aliyah Department. Later, when Italy joined the war, civilian ships stopped calling at Mediterranean ports and the immigrants disembarked at Istanbul. From there they traveled onwards by train, passing through Syria. The *aliyah* officials would meet them at Rosh Haniqra, the border station between Syria and Palestine. The British set up a clearance camp for the immigrants at Atlit, where papers were inspected and other arrangements were made. The camp was run by workers of the Jewish Agency Aliyah Department, who handled maintenance, food supply, medical care, and job referrals. Upon leaving the camp, where they spent only a few days, the immigrants were given a sum of money to cover immediate expenses. During 1939–45, a total of 33,065 immigrants passed through Jewish Agency camps in Atlit, Haifa, and Tel-Aviv.

After the war ended, in November 1945, an absorption unit was created within the Aliyah Department to coordinate such matters as the upkeep of immigrant hostels, supply of clothing and utensils, arrangements for health insurance, housing and job referrals, Hebrew language instruction, and cultural activities. By 1946 two new immigrant hostels had been built, in Kiryat Shmuel and Hadera, in addition to those in Haifa and Tel-Aviv, bringing the absorption capacity up to 1,750. As the number of immigrants grew, more hostels were built and the absorption capacity reached 4,750.

In August 1948, following the declaration of statehood and the impending arrival of large numbers of immigrants, the Zionist Actions Committee decided to establish a Jewish Agency department that would supervise the absorption process from beginning to end: setting up reception camps, making housing arrangements, providing food and vital services, and attending to all the immigrants' needs during the initial stages of absorption. Several parties fought tooth and nail for the leadership of the Kelitah Department; with its extensive powers, this body was bound to wield considerable influence over the immigrants and their political outlook.

After lengthy deliberations, the Kelitah Department was awarded to the General Zionists. The alignment of forces in the Zionist Congress, it should be pointed out, was not identical to the political constellation in the Jewish state. The General Zionists enjoyed considerable weight and were duly represented in the Zionist Executive: Dr. Israel Goldstein was Jewish Agency treasurer, while Moshe Kol was head of Youth Aliyah. Zvi Herman was the party's nominee for director of Kelitah,[68] but under pressure from Mapam another candidate, Yehuda Braginsky of Mapam and Mossad le-Aliyah Bet, was asked to share the position. Dr. Giora Josephthal of Mapai was appointed department administrator.

Josephthal, a German Jew and one of the founders of Kibbutz Gal'ed, had been active in immigration and absorption long before the state was established. Indignant at not being appointed head of the department, he submitted his resignation several weeks later on the grounds that he could not work under so many superiors (Raphael, Herman, and Braginsky): "They do not understand; they try to interfere in small matters and create conflict."[69] Eventually Josephthal submitted to party pressure and withdrew his resignation. Within a short while he became the life and soul of the Kelitah Department. Through his dynamic personality and the support of the government, he became an increasingly influential figure in the department even without being the first in command. Over time the Kelitah Department amassed far-reaching powers in the sphere of absorption and became a Mapai stronghold.

Beginning in 1949 the camps that were set up to receive the immigrants ceased being merely temporary shelters. Newcomers stayed there for longer and longer periods; by the end of the year, the reception camps held as many as one hundred thousand persons who had been quartered there for a number of months. The fact that the majority of immigrants were almost totally dependent upon the absorption authorities meant that even lower-ranking officials, such as camp administrators and employees, of whom there were close to three thousand, were invested with great power. Hence these jobs were also fought over and used as bargaining chips by the political parties.[70]

The Land Settlement Department

The Jewish Agency's Land Settlement Department likewise participated in the absorption of new immigrants: it referred immigrants to agriculture, designed and established new settlements, provided farm training, and financed all such activities. The Ministry of Agriculture handled only the veteran agricultural sector.[71] The Land Settlement Department was headed by Levi Eshkol (Shkolnik), a long-standing member of the Labor Movement, founder of Kibbutz Degania, and director-general of the Mekorot Water Company. A man of enormous vitality and capacity for work, Eshkol was initially nominated for the position of Jewish Agency treasurer. Ben-Gurion, however, argued that agricultural settlement was of critical importance for the absorption of immigrants and that a man of Eshkol's caliber was needed to give this sector the required push. In consequence, Eshkol was voted head of the Land Settlement Department.[72] Ben-Gurion's judgment soon proved sound. Under Levi Eshkol, the department lay the groundwork for more than 250 new settlements within the span of three years—an unprecedented feat in the history of the state and the Zionist movement.[73] Eshkol's impact on immigrant absorption went far beyond his duties in the Land Settlement Department. It was he who proposed the establishment of *ma'abarot,* transit camps where the new arrivals were housed until a permanent answer could be found. Initially, Eshkol was also responsible for setting up the system. In later years, as the treasurer of the Jewish Agency, he had an even greater influence on the manner in which immigrants were integrated into Israeli society.

Youth Aliyah

Youth Aliyah began its work in Germany in 1933, when the Nazis rose to power. This movement, devoted to the transfer of children and young people to Israel, was headed by Henrietta Szold. Youth Aliyah established educational institutions and youth villages for thousands of young immigrants and organized the placement of youngsters on kibbutzim. Special educational and study frameworks were developed to turn these adolescents into constructive, independent adults. After World War II, Youth Aliyah was active in rescuing children whose parents had perished in the Holocaust. Between 1945 and 1948, more than fifteen thousand youngsters were brought to Israel, the majority of them Holocaust survivors. Youth Aliyah was likewise successful in rescuing large numbers of young people from Asian countries.[74]

After the establishment of the state, Youth Aliyah opened its doors to young people in Israel. Many children whose parents were living in immigrants' camps and *ma'abarot* were enrolled in its institutions. Within the first two years of statehood, Youth Aliyah had six thousand youngsters in its care. In light of the large body of young people under its aegis, the Youth Aliyah Department was considered among the most influential in the Jewish Agency. A special division was set up to handle religious youngsters, who were sent to separate schools. As mentioned earlier, the Youth Aliyah Department was headed by Moshe Kol.[75]

The American Jewish Joint Distribution Committee

The American Jewish Joint Distribution Committee (JDC) was an overseas relief association that cooperated with the Jewish Agency and the Israeli government in organizing and financing the large-scale rescue of Jews from Europe and Islamic countries. This organization was founded in the United States after the outbreak of World War I to assist Jews in various countries whose lives had been disrupted by the war. The JDC helped Jewish communities to repair their damaged educational and economic institutions, and arranged for refugees to return to their home countries or settle elsewhere.

After World War II the JDC went into refugee and DP camps in Germany and the liberated areas. Surviving Jewish communities were provided with material assistance, and a concerted effort was made to alleviate the suffering of the sick and disabled. The JDC was a non-Zionist organization; it received funding through the United Jewish Appeal, and its relations with the authorities in Israel and the Zionist movement were problematic. When immigration to Israel was at its peak, the JDC assumed responsibility for maintaining transit camps in France, Italy, Aden, and elsewhere, and covered the bulk of the cost of transporting the immigrants to Israel.

The race to control Israel's immigration and absorption institutions reflected the tension surrounding the advent of the Great Aliyah. During its first years of independence, Israel was in the throes of molding and shaping its government and policies. It was a stressful era: public bodies and political parties pushed and jostled for a niche in the absorption process in the knowledge that the political views of the immigrants could be influenced in this way. The debate over immigration en masse versus slow, selective immigration was a fundamental one and pointed up sharp differences among the country's policymakers. Throughout Israel's first year, the future of *aliyah* lay on the scales, waiting to be tipped this way or that. Only in March 1949, when the government was formed, was the doubling of the population within four years declared official policy, and even then, paradoxically, without the endorsement of a government majority. By this time, however, a major immigration operation was in full swing, composed of organizations that had been doing such work in the prestate years, each going its separate way and not always cooperating. More often than not they were suspicious of one another, their relationship being based on competition and political rivalry. Because of the sensitivity of the issue and the great problems involved, Israel's immigration policy was far from well rounded or uniform. There were many snags and inconsistencies, with decisions affected by national and economic considerations as well as by internal politics. It was the great respect held for David Ben-Gurion and his staunch support of unrestricted immigration that determined the outcome.

Ben-Gurion and the Great Aliyah

After declaring independence, the State of Israel was not guaranteed to escape the political and social turmoil that had been the fate of other countries newly freed from foreign domination. The political reality of Mandatory Palestine, in which the Jewish national institutions were permitted to operate with a large measure of independence, no doubt facilitated the country's transition to full sovereignty. Nevertheless, not all sectors of the public accepted the authority of these institutions, and it was far from certain that the elected leadership of the Yishuv would exercise the same power once the political system was reorganized.

The continued influence of the social, cultural, and political configuration that emerged during the prestate period was only assured if there were no dramatic changes in that configuration. A major demographic shift, such as that which took place with the onset of mass immigration and produced a sociocultural entity very different from that of the Yishuv, could be expected to signal a turning point. Let us emphasize that no one doubted the importance of *aliyah* per se; it was regulating the quantity and insuring absorption that were sources of concern. Success on both counts would enable newcomers to be maximally integrated into the sociocultural fabric of the Yishuv and to forestall violent shocks to the system.

With the state born in a period of military, financial, and political distress, and with the leadership anxious to avoid severe internal strife over political and social matters, the debate concerning mass immigration was put on hold. This habit of postponing discussions of fundamental importance was to be repeated during the next years, becoming a salient characteristic of Israel's handling of issues in the social sphere. As the institutions of government took shape, the process by which they were built and the persons who built them were to have a tremendous impact. Israel's overall policy, and especially its long-term immigration and absorption policy, were a product of both factors working together: the system and those who ran it.

Paradoxically, the nation that arose in defiance of the United Nations and the great powers derived the formal legal structure for its government from the UN resolution of 29 November 1947 on the partition of Palestine. This resolution lay the guidelines for two governing bodies: a Provisional Council of State, which would operate as the legislative authority until democratic elections could be held, and a Provisional Government, which would act as the executive arm, both under international supervision. But these plans were disrupted by the rejection of the UN decision by the Arabs and the British. However, the Yishuv decided to proceed on its own. At its session in April 1948, the Zionist Actions Committee voted for the establishment of a National Council (Moetzet ha-Am) consisting of thirty-seven representatives of the Yishuv and the Zionist movement, and a thirteen-member National Administration (Minhelet ha-Am). These two bodies functioned as the country's national leadership during the period of transition. They chose the date for the establishment of the state, planned whatever administrative and legislative measures were deemed necessary, and proposed an outline of governance summarized in the Proclamation of Independence issued on 14 May 1948.

On the day of independence, the National Council became the Provisional Council of State (legislature) and the National Administration became the Provisional Government (executive). These two bodies were to take the helm until elected authorities were set up in accordance with a constitution adopted by the Constituent Assembly "no later than October 1, 1948." However, this deadline could not be met because of the war. In preparation for the elections, a national census was conducted on 8 November. The total population was recorded as 782,000, including 731,000 Jews.

On 25 January 1949 elections were held for the Constituent Assembly. The prestate Council of State, whose members belonged to a wide spectrum of political parties and movements, avoided fundamental decision-making in the legislative and political spheres so as not to arouse old controversies. Thus the electoral system employed by the institutions of Jewish self-government during Mandatory times, based on national-proportional representation, was considered the best choice for these elections, too.[76] Like other emergency decisions taken during the first months of statehood, this decision has remained in force for more than four decades and has in many respects determined the shape and character of Israeli governance. The electoral system also had much to do with the way the Great Aliyah became intertwined in Israeli politics.

On 16 February 1949 the Constituent Assembly enacted the Transition Law, defining the duties of the legislative and executive authorities. At this forum, Dr. Chaim Weizmann was elected president of the State of Israel. A week after his inauguration, Weizmann called upon David Ben-Gurion, head of the largest Knesset faction, to form the first government. In view of Ben-Gurion's indelible imprint on the outlook, goals, and priorities of the Jewish state, especially in its early years, we shall devote several pages to his social philosophy.

Ben-Gurion: On the State and its Goals

Ben-Gurion's leadership career was launched many years before the establishment of the state. As one of the pillars of the socialist Zionist labor movement, his thinking and political activities were firmly anchored in the philosophy of that movement. The challenges of Jewish national redemption and social reform colored all that he did.

In Ben-Gurion's eyes, 1949 was not the start of a post-war era in which life would return to normal. As far as he was concerned, the fight continued—not on the battlefield, but in the social and cultural domain, a fight that he perceived as no less demanding and critical for Israel's future. Ben-Gurion held that the establishment of a state was not a one-time act but an ongoing process. These were times of emergency that would require great sacrifice on the part of individuals and society. As he understood it, the coming years would be a continuation of the national and social struggle begun during the British Mandate. Israel's political victory did not mark the end of a period; it brought the Jews one step closer to their goal. The present was merely a stage, a path, that would lead to a transformation in the realm of society and nationhood. Hence, Ben-Gurion saw each person as a participant in a national and social mission.

Jewish Nationhood as a Revolution

Ben-Gurion frequently used the term "revolution" to describe the period of Israel's establishment. He referred to it as "the greatest revolution in the history of our people," and emphasized that the creation of a state was just the first phase: "Our generation has achieved great things, but we must not sing our own praises for the work is not yet done. In fact, it has scarcely begun." [77]

He further stated, "In the near future, we must lay foundations that will last scores if not hundreds of years. We must mold the character of the State of Israel and ready it to fulfill its historic purpose." [78] Ben-Gurion maintained that it was not possible to change the face of Jewish history in more than a political sense: "The independence we have tried to establish in the tumult of war must not end with politics . . . This revolution will have failed to achieve its aim if it is only political and military. The decisive revolution is yet before us—we must alter the country, the people, our entire way of life." [79] The main goal, he believed, was the complete transformation of the way people thought and lived, an overhaul of social and cultural norms.

Ben-Gurion saw before him the entirety of the Jewish people, not only those living in Israel. For a sweeping change in Jewish history, it was not enough to address the population of the Jewish state. Founding a tiny country on a small strip of land was not the ultimate aim; it was part of a broad revolution that would encompass all Jews. Herein lay the importance of the "ingathering of the exiles," of bringing as many Jews as possible to the Jewish state. For Ben-Gurion, *aliyah* was not only a means of rescuing Jewish communities in distress; nor was it simply a response to the country's pressing security and settlement needs, however high they may have figured on his scale. Ben-Gurion believed that the place of Jews was in Israel because it was here that social and cultural reform would alter the course of Jewish history.

Ben-Gurion utilized every opportunity to make his views known. He tried to inspire his listeners, to touch their core, to convey to them the grandeur of the national-historical mission: "Two revolutionary and glorious historical episodes are behind us today: the renaissance of the State of Israel and the victories of the Israel Defense Forces. However, these episodes have not exhausted the revolutionary content of modern times; they are no more than an opening and a preliminary for the main thing, which is the return of the exiles." [80]

Ben-Gurion worried about a drop in the level of ideological conviction, a common phenomenon in postrevolutionary societies. The continuous tension in the political arena, together with the War of Independence, had indeed triggered a desire for relief, a tendency to evade responsibility and full commitment to the national goal. Ben-Gurion sought to reengage all sectors of the community and encourage them to respond to the challenges confronting them. Time and again he emphasized that Israeli society was being tested:

> Now that the "Great Days" are over—the period of heroism and triumph on the military and diplomatic fronts which have transformed the face of Jewish and Israeli history and restored us to our former glory—we have come to the "Ordinary Days"—a period of plain hard work needed to build our economy and organize the state. While the flash and drama may be gone, this period is no less significant than the previous one. The economic and administrative test we now confront is no less crucial than the test of war in its seriousness or importance; on the contrary, it is longer and, in some respects, harder." [81]

These were trying times indeed; Ben-Gurion firmly believed in the need for patterns of government that could cope with the enormity of the tasks at hand. He perceived these tasks as a battle to be fought and tended to compare the institutions of government to an efficient military command with a clear-cut hierarchy of officers and subordinates. Ben-Gurion's admiration for strongly centralized leadership and his belief in the concentration of economic and political power in the hands of a few were well-known from his earlier days in public office.[82] These preferences were evident in the organizational and operative structure he sought to impose on the Israeli government.

On the eve of the elections for the Constituent Assembly, Ben-Gurion set out some of these ideas in his diary. Above all, he stressed the need for stability. He wished to see the provisional government, which was no more than a "federation of offices," replaced by a new government guided by collective responsibility and a central theme, and founded on a stable majority.[83] Furthermore, he wanted that majority to follow his lead. This was the philosophy behind his efforts to put together a government coalition, as well as his relations with organizations and kibbutzim. He believed that the elite—especially the intellectuals, of whose public and moral support he felt sure, and the kibbutz movements, which he saw as the executive arm of the social revolution and the chief absorbers of mass immigration—could be persuaded to undertake social missions.

Ben-Gurion was upset by the sharp criticism of his ideas in intellectual circles; the kibbutz movements, too, were hesitant to back him, particularly in the area of tactics. He was disappointed at the reaction of the intellectuals, but he was certain that he could change their minds and continued to woo them.[84] The kibbutz movements, on the other hand, were harshly attacked. Ben-Gurion found it difficult to accept their adoption of an independent stance on social issues. To his mind, pluralism and the avant garde contributed to the anarchy he so hated; they were the very opposite of order, discipline, and obedience, which were essential in these "times of emergency." He maintained that undertaking an investigation of fundamental issues at this point was both impossible and undesirable. Such discussions were an idle game and luxury Israel could ill afford when so many urgent affairs needed attention. Ben-Gurion's dispute with the kibbutz movements, intellectuals, and writers was exacerbated during the course of 1949. All the while, he pursued a stubborn campaign to force his beliefs on others and garner support in the political and ideological arenas. His choice of coalition partners was similarly motivated.

The Coalition

On 8 March 1949, after several weeks of negotiations, Ben-Gurion presented his cabinet to the Knesset—a coalition government of seventy-three members consisting of Mapai, the United Religious Front, the Progressives, and the Sephardim. Mapai had twice as many seats as all the other parties combined.[85] Thus, Ben-Gurion remained unchallenged in terms of strength and influence.

The General Zionists and Mapam were excluded, both because of old disputes and because of lack of agreement on current economic, social, and ideological issues. The chief reason, however, was Ben-Gurion's desire to neutralize the "civilian camp" that had dominated local government in the days of the Mandate, and Mapam, which had won nineteen mandates and constituted the largest party after Mapai. This rivalry was not specifically focused on allocation of portfolios or matters of foreign policy.[86] It hearkened back to the bitter controversies on the eve of Israel's independence and the establishment of the IDF, which culminated in the dismantling of the Palmah.[87] Yet above all, Ben-Gurion feared a challenge to his authority that would endanger the stability of the government. As far as he was concerned, a new era meant the end of power struggles and ideological bickering from the days of the Yishuv.

The United Religious Front was brought into the coalition by Ben-Gurion despite the fact that he had differed strongly with the religious camp since the inception of the Zionist movement. This partnership seemed to him more viable than any other. For the time being, both groups set aside their differences on such fundamental issues as the Jewish character of the state from a national and religious standpoint. As part of the coalition agreement, an accord was reached regarding Jewishness in the public domain. It was decided that the Sabbath would be a mandatory day of rest, public eating places would be kosher, and the principles of equality and personal freedom would be safeguarded. Only in one sphere, family law, did Ben-Gurion bow to religious pressure. The Chief Rabbinate and the religious courts were given exclusive jurisdiction in all matters pertaining to matrimony.

From the start, the partnership between Mapai and the religious camp was perched on a keg of dynamite. The explosion, when it came, was triggered by disagreement over the Great Aliyah, plunging the state into its first government crisis. When Ben-Gurion first put together the cabinet, he was totally confident in his ability to steer matters his way. Addressing the Knesset on 8 March 1949, Ben-Gurion spoke of the joint responsibility of all members and factions. He emphasized the obligation of the coalition to act in accordance with the plans it had endorsed as well as in future government decisions. Ministers were accountable not only to themselves but also to their parties. In this way Ben-Gurion was able to concentrate executive authority in the hands of the Knesset majority and prevent the minority from demanding that resolutions be put up for public debate.[88] Members of the coalition still had the right to criticize the government if it "deviated from the policy determined by the Knesset or the coalition," but ministers belonging to the minority bloc could not lobby as they had during the prestate period.[89] This seems to have been one of the reasons why the religious parties appealed to their supporters in the United States and elsewhere to become involved in the *aliyah* issue.

"A Shortage of Jews"

Throughout the final decade of British rule, immigration had been the spearhead of the Ben-Gurion's tireless battle for a sovereign state. His rivals accused him of using immigration as a tool to further his political aims. His true stand and motives were only to become clear after the state was established.

As soon as the UN partition plan was announced in November 1947, Ben-Gurion hastened to sketch his ideas for the future Jewish state; immigration formed an intrinsic part of his program. Four days after the UN decision, Ben-Gurion delivered an impassioned speech before a large Mapai audience. Barely able to contain his excitement, he declared,

> The state has not yet arisen. The United Nations has reached a great decision and, without a trace of exaggeration or rhetoric, an historical decision. *But this decision awaits implementation,* and implementation means more than an executive committee set up by the United Nations, the inauguration of a Jewish provisional government, the election of a constituent assembly, and the writing of a constitution. More even than declaring independence and being accepted as an equal partner in the United Nations. *These alone will not create a state . . .* The Jewish state is missing quite a number of things: a name, a capital, a government, an anthem, a constitution, a budget, a currency, an army, a police force, and so on and so forth. All these deficiencies can be easily remedied . . . However, the state lacks one basic thing, the most serious of them all: *it lacks Jews.* This deficiency cannot be rectified so easily. It has almost nothing to do with the United Nations; it depends solely on us. It cannot be done before the establishment of the state, but only afterwards, and so long as this lack is not made up for, at least minimally, there is no guarantee that the state will continue to exist beyond its establishment . . . To insure not only the birth of a Jewish state, but also its viability and national mission, we must bring one and a half million Jews to Eretz Yisrael and settle them here. Only when there are at least two million Jews here, can we speak of a state.[90] [*emphases in the original*]

In Ben-Gurion's view, a rapid increase in Jewish population was essential for the Jews to remain a majority in the Jewish state. According to the findings of the UN Partition Commission, the Arabs accounted for 40 percent of the country's inhabitants. Ben-Gurion hypothesized that a Jewish minority could conceivably join the Arab bloc and take over the government together. However, even ruling out such a threat, Ben-Gurion maintained that a Jewish state would have no future without massive immigration.

Ben-Gurion did not stop there. As the uncontested leader of Mapai, his opinions were the basis for all party discussions. In December 1947, when Mapai began to draw up plans for activity after independence, Ben-Gurion's influence was evident throughout. Six committees were set to work on social and economic programs to be presented at the Mapai convention in early 1948. In this way, the party hoped to lay the infrastructure for the new state. The committee dealing with immigration and absorption formulated a proposal for the first three years of statehood founded on the assumption of approximately 100,000 arrivals per year.[91]

It was not difficult to see the correspondence between this program and the views of Ben-Gurion. He had spoken of the need for a decade of immigration and absorption during which the real building of the state would be accomplished. After independence, the government presented the Knesset with a plan to double the Jewish population within four years. This meant bringing in 600,000 immigrants in a four-year period, or 150,000 per year. Absorbing 150,000 newcomers annually under the trying conditions facing the new state was a heavy burden indeed. Opponents in the Jewish Agency and the government of mass immigration argued that there was no justification for organizing large-scale emigration among Jews whose lives were not in danger, particularly when the desire and motivation were not their own.

Paradoxically, it was the knowledge that hoards of Jews were not knocking on the gates that made Ben-Gurion embrace the idea of mass immigration with such fervor. He coaxed everyone, from the Ministry of Foreign Affairs and the Jewish Agency Immigration Department to Mossad le-Aliyah Bet, to step up their activity and bring in more immigrants. His estimate was that the establishment of the state and the upswing in *aliyah* would create the dynamics for mass immigration. Ben-Gurion believed that only an unusual coincidence, in terms of the willingness of the Jews to come and the political timing, could create the kind of immigration he sought. If that moment were lost, large-scale *aliyah* and the "ingathering of the exiles" would never materialize and Israel would remain a tiny Mediterranean country of no consequence. Ben-Gurion's position was this: "Considering that our population in this country will very soon reach two million, a Jewish government whose concerns, plans, and activities are not centered around the immigration and settlement enterprise will be reneging on its chief responsibility and endangering the greatest historical achievement of our generation. For thousands of years we have been a people without a state. The great danger now is that we shall be a state without a people."[92]

. . .

Ben-Gurion clung fiercely to his policy of nonselective mass immigration in the face of opposition from both Right and Left. He called upon Jews from all corners of the globe to settle in Israel as soon as possible, and time and again repeated that immigration would determine the country's fate. At every forum, he explained the importance of *aliyah* for Israel's political and military strength and made a point of stressing its national significance.

Opinions on unrestricted immigration varied widely in government circles. Among the leading opponents was Eliezer Kaplan, the minister of finance and a senior cabinet member, who was highly respected for his financial expertise and sound judgment. Kaplan maintained that the scope of immigration should be determined in a pragmatic manner, taking into account the economic and absorptive capacity of the state. As one who had been involved for years as treasurer of the Jewish Agency, Kaplan was aware of the complexities of the absorption process. Because Holocaust survivors constituted the chief body of potential immigrants after the establishment of the state, the debate initially revolved around them. Many of the survivors in the DP camps reportedly were ill or crippled. Kaplan knew how difficult it would be to absorb such people. He was familiar with the inadequacies of the medical establishment in Israel, and he anticipated the serious problems they would encounter upon arrival. Moshe Shapira, who held the immigration and health portfolios, was of a similar mind. He, too, had had years of experience in *aliyah* as head of the Jewish Agency Immigration Department, and as minister of health he well understood the implications of bringing in disabled immigrants. The voices of these two were frequently heard whenever the subject of mass immigration arose for debate.

Members of another party in the coalition, the Progressives, were similarly hesitant about large-scale *aliyah*. They felt that organized, well-planned immigration, keeping apace with the country's economic and social capacity, would be more appropriate.

But as head of the government, entrusted with choosing the cabinet and steering its activities, Ben-Gurion had tremendous power over the country's social development. His prestige soared to new heights after the founding of the state and the impressive victory of the IDF in the War of Independence. As prime minister and minister of defense in Israel's first administration, as well as the uncontested leader of the country's largest political party, his opinions carried enormous weight. Thus, despite resistance from some of his cabinet members, he remained unflagging in his enthusiasm for unrestricted mass immigration and resolved to put this policy into effect.

Conditional Immigration

Because no deliberations had been held to hammer out the precise details and character of Israel's immigration policy, the government took its cue from two official documents: the Declaration of Independence (14 May 1948), which determined that "the State of Israel will be open for Jewish immigration and for the ingathering of the exiles," and the position paper of the first government, which spoke of "doubling the population within four years" (March 1949). There was no doubt as to where the Jewish Agency stood. When the Zionist Actions Committee met in Jerusalem from 22 August to 3 September 1948, it loudly proclaimed the basic right of every Jew to leave the Diaspora and settle in the Jewish homeland. All this made a theoretical debate on the subject quite superfluous. In the same spirit, the Provisional Council of State promulgated the Law and Administration Ordinance–1948, swiftly canceling all prohibitions and restrictions on immigration imposed by the British Mandate. The right to settle in Israel was only formalized two years later, through the Law of Return–1950, which, unlike immigration laws in other countries, treated *aliyah* as the natural right of every Jew. This point was illustrated by the use of the word "return" and was made clear by Ben-Gurion: "This is not a Jewish state simply because Jews constitute the majority of inhabitants; this is a state for Jews wherever they be, for every Jew who may desire it." During the Knesset hearings prior to the passage of this law, a general consensus reigned regarding the right of all Jews to return to their homeland.[93]

As we have said, Israel's immigration policy during the period immediately following independence derived from the declarations of the government and the Zionist Actions Committee. These statements were very broad and inclusive, and they offered no definitions or specifications with regard to immigrants. There were no limitations, preferences, or special directives, such as those stipulated at a later date by the Law of Return. Before legislation was passed, the *aliyah* activists were the ones who made the decisions—and not only in the administrative domain. There were also fundamental and sensitive issues to be addressed, such as those pertaining to religion. These matters were left to the discretion of persons directly involved in immigration, primarily employees of the Jewish Agency and the ministry who acted as they saw fit; officially, however, there was an Aliyah Committee established by the Provisional Council of State and representing different parties that exercised supervision.

After the Jewish Agency and the government were separated in August 1948, Yitzhak Raphael was appointed head of the Jewish Agency Immigration Department and Moshe Shapira became Israel's minister of immigration. During his trips to Europe and North Africa, Raphael closely studied the problems connected with *aliyah* and the work of emissaries sent overseas by the Immigration Department. He carefully distinguished between the duties of his staff and those of the government, and he continually sought to increase the responsibilities of his department.[94] From this point on, the government immigration officers were mainly in charge of issuing immigrant and tourist visas.

The Jewish Agency and the government essentially handled two different groups: the masses of impoverished immigrants who depended on the administrative and financial assistance of the Jewish Agency, and a smaller group of immigrants who arrived independently and paid their own way. From the outset, Moshe Shapira was against giving the Jewish Agency control over *aliyah* and was disturbed by the expansion of Raphael's department at the expense of his own. The competition between the two bodies was further heightened by personal rivalry. Shapira, an old-timer in the Zionist movement and the immigration enterprise, was reluctant to let go of any of the powers he enjoyed in the sphere of *aliyah* and to allow Raphael room to maneuver. Within months of Israel's establishment, his subordinates received a compilation of "aliyah regulations" to guide them in their work. For the first time, certain conditions were imposed that were to cause a great stir in the years to come. Shapira's personal outlook on *aliyah* was embedded in the "instructions on the issuance of immigrant and tourist visas" distributed to government offices overseas. In these instructions Shapira provided guidelines for selective immigration based on economic, medical, religious, and other criteria. This document was prefaced by an exposition of Israel's immigration policy: "This policy is currently founded on a genuine desire to hold the gates open for any Jew who wishes and is able to immigrate. In contrast to the position of the Mandatory authorities, it is the task of all those who work for the immigration services or in their name, to encourage the aliyah of elements that will contribute to the upbuilding of the state."[95]

The phrase "contribute to the upbuilding of the state" was not meant rhetorically; Shapira's intention was made clear in the subsequent paragraphs. It should be noted that some of these instructions were a carryover from the Mandate, for example the guidelines used by the Jewish Agency in granting legal immigration certificates, which took into account the candidate's financial situation. Persons in possession of no less than LP1000 (an enormous sum in those days), skilled workers, and free professionals with invitations to work in Israel were considered preferred categories whose immigration was to be encouraged. There were also special directives pertaining to matters of relevance after the establishment of the state. One specified the need for "especial caution during this time of emergency to prevent persons who are undesirable from a moral standpoint and persons who are liable to hinder our war effort from infiltrating the state." Another directive drew attention to the importance of keeping a watchful eye on the immigrants' health. There was nothing vague about these two orders. Their purpose was to collect pertinent data about the immigrants and convey them to the ministry.[96]

Spies and Communists

The statement pertaining to persons liable to hinder the war effort referred to potential immigrants suspected of being Communist spies. Israel had been warned that Communist authorities might try to plant spies among the immigrants, especially those from Eastern Europe. Mahal volunteers, both Jews and non-Jews, were also under suspicion. Those handling *aliyah* and army enlistment were advised to be on the alert.

In the debate that ensued over the definition of the word "Communist," the chief target were Romanian immigrants. As mentioned earlier, the Romanian government, after lengthy negotiations, had agreed to allow the controlled emigration of 5,000 Jews a month. However, it was rumored that the Romanian government had added another condition to the agreement through the intervention of political elements in Israel close to the Communists: namely, that the "Democrats" within the Romanian Jewish community would draw up the list of immigrants. Furious, the Romanian Zionists called for a boycott of this list; of the 3,600 candidates, not one was a member of the Zionist movement. The implication was that their first allegiance was to the Communist regime. In those days, the Communists in Israel were an active force and, in spite of their small representation in the Knesset (a total of four seats), were able to make their voice heard due to the pro-Soviet stance of Mapam, Israel's second-largest party. They propagandized on a broad scale and were active among the immigrants. The directors of *aliyah* in Israel were in a quandary: Should they admit the Romanians in spite of their alleged political affiliation or bar their entry?

Israel had consistently maintained a neutral stance toward the parties in the cold war; great caution was needed if the balance was to be preserved. The minister of immigration knew that one false step could ruin the relationship with the Romanian government that had been built up with such care. Hence his decision to be flexible in this case. "There is no danger that these immigrants will join the Communist Party in Israel," he explained. "They will strike roots here like any other Jew." Most members of the Aliyah Committee supported the minister's handling of the issue. Some criticized the Romanian Zionist movement and branded its boycott a dangerous game. The whole episode aroused controversy in Israel and triggered a spate of mudslinging between the *aliyah* activists of Mapam and other parties who accused Mapam of dealings with the Romanian government.[97] There were also charges that Mapam was in contact with additional Communist countries, Poland in particular, for the purpose of influencing the selection of *aliyah* candidates.[98]

Non-Jews, Gentile Women, and Uncircumcised Children

One of the orders received by *aliyah* officers was to bar the entry of non-Jews, even those planning a temporary stay. They were told to exercise extreme caution lest "undesirable elements" find their way into the country and to prohibit the entry of "persons presumed to be enemies of the state, even if they were formerly citizens of Palestine and hold Palestinian passports." This was, of course, a thinly veiled reference to Arabs and aroused no opposition considering that the War of Independence was then in process. The orders with respect to Gentile women married to Jews and uncircumcised children were not accepted with the same equanimity. These women were expected to convert and circumcise their children, causing an immediate outcry. Most of the Aliyah Committee members agreed with the minister that this procedure would eliminate complications in the sphere of marital law, but they refused to condone a regulation that was undemocratic and detrimental to the principle of *aliyah*. They urged the minister not to include it among the official regulations and to instead employ an "informational-persuasive" approach. However, the problem of non-Jewish women continued to preoccupy the Immigration Ministry. Its *aliyah* officers reported the arrival of a considerable number of mixed couples from Europe, sparking concern over the emergence of a Christian community and the prospect of family tragedies at some future date. Yisrael Barzilai, Israel's minister to Poland and a member of Mapam, was instructed not to hold up the immigration of non-Jewish women and their offspring but to be alert to such cases and report them to the ministry. There were also a number of Gahal soldiers who sought permission to bring their non-Jewish fiancées to Israel.

As an observant Jew, Moshe Shapira found it difficult to accept the notion of bringing so many Gentile women into the country. To make his argument more incisive, he focused on the problem of German women. He had been informed by his *aliyah* officers that there were cases of former SS officers who had married Jewish men and planned to immigrate to Israel. According to Shapira, "the Rabbinate and various religious groups are pressing for a strict ruling because they see such incidents as a stain on the lineage of our people." However, the matter of the German women went beyond purely religious concerns, especially with the Holocaust still so fresh in mind.

Uncircumcised children also posed a problem. Apart from the offspring of Gentile women, there were Jewish parents who had been unable to circumcise their sons during or after World War II. Some parents refused; in the wake of the Holocaust, they were reluctant to have their children bear a distinguishing Jewish mark and believed that keeping them uncircumcised was a form of "insurance" in the event of another war.

As anticipated, the religious parties welcomed the restrictions on Gentile women. Zerah Warhaftig of Ha-Poel ha-Mizrachi, later minister of religious affairs, noted that after World War II the United States also balked at admitting German women married to American soldiers. He was certain that Israel would not be denounced for doing the same; on the contrary, it would be ridiculed by the world if it took in these women. Warhaftig was opposed to the immigration of intermarried couples except in certain special cases and in favor of circumcising children prior to their arrival.

On the whole, the representatives of the nonreligious parties—Mapai, Mapam, and Revisionists—were inclined to support restrictions on the immigration of non-Jews but, out of concern for Israel's image, felt that these should be in-house rules rather than official government policy. Among the few who opposed limitations on Gentile women was Idov Cohen (General Zionists), who argued that this tiny group posed no risk to Israeli society. In the United States, he pointed out, there were many intermarried couples, and it would be wrong to cut them off from the possibility of *aliyah* in the future. As for uncircumcised children, nearly everyone, apart from the religious representatives, favored admitting them freely and having them undergo circumcision at some later date in Israel.

The minister of immigration, like the rest of his religious colleagues, tried to convince the Aliyah Committee to approve restrictions both on Gentile women and on uncircumcised children, returning repeatedly to this subject. In the camps, he said, Jews who married German women were ostracized from the community, and the rabbis in Germany had ruled against converting even those who were willing. Warhaftig also cited cases of Nazi murderers who managed to escape Germany through intermarriage. His position was unflinching. No visas would be issued to intermarried couples, and it would be up to the Jewish partner to decide whether to leave his spouse or forego *aliyah*. Shapira was willing to be flexible only in the case of Gentiles of special standing, such as those who saved Jews during the Holocaust. His *aliyah* officials were ordered to forward such requests to the ministry in Israel; an immigrant visa would be awarded to those who converted. With regard to the children, Shapira insisted that they must be circumcised before coming. If this were impossible for medical reasons, the officers would list the children's names to insure them the necessary attention in Israel. The Aliyah Committee eventually gave its consent, on condition that these regulations remained internal.[99]

On the whole, the press maintained a conspiracy of silence on the proceedings of this meeting. *Ha-Aretz* and *Ha-Tzofeh* reported matter-of-factly that the meeting was partly devoted to the serious problem of Gentile women and uncircumcised children arriving among the immigrants, and the committee reached a certain decision in this regard. Not another word was written on the content of this decision.[100] *Ha-Mashkif,* the newspaper of the Revisionists, added a bit of interpretation: The committee reached a decision to permit the immigration of Gentile women married to Jews, with the exception of German women.[101]

The Sick and the Disabled

The Immigration Ministry's *aliyah* officers were instructed to grant visas only to those in good health. Shapira, who served simultaneously as minister of health, explained that more than 10 percent of the displaced persons in the camps in Germany and Austria required continuous medical attention. The reports indicated a total of 2,300 cripples, 100 cases of tuberculosis, and a host of other chronic and contagious diseases. Shapira maintained that medical care for the immigrants was a very expensive proposition, whereas the state could barely cover the cost of absorption.[102] A debate raged between the Jewish Agency and the Ministry of Health as to the question of financing. Shapira claimed that it was the Jewish Agency's responsibility to finance absorption, including medical services; the Ministry of Health was prepared to supply the administrative and medical staff on condition that the Jewish Agency handled funding.[103]

From November 1948 on, medical supervision was introduced in the DP camps to prevent the immigration of persons who were seriously ill. Here, too, the Ministry of Health and the Jewish Agency clashed. The ministry accused the Jewish Agency of laxity in its supervision because its policy was to organize the *aliyah* of as many people as possible.[104] In the end, it was decided to establish a joint committee of physicians to determine criteria for the immigration of the sick and disabled; the committee was instructed to keep the number of sick *olim* to a minimum. Nevertheless, many diseased, sick, and elderly persons in need of medical attention and welfare found their way to Israel. Giora Josephthal claimed that they constituted close to 9 percent of the immigrant community.[105]

In December 1948 it was decided to tighten the medical selection. A review board under the joint auspices of the Ministry of Health and the Jewish Agency was asked to prepare a list of diseases that would bar a person from immigrating. Instructions were also given to halt the immigration of crippled people.[106] Yitzhak Raphael, who had just returned from a trip to Europe, affirmed that the DP camps in Germany were full of people with such handicaps. He told the Jewish Agency Executive that he had ordered officials there to stop granting them visas in compliance with the Executive's decision in this regard.[107]

As an increasing number of immigrants began arriving from Islamic countries, dismal reports were received about the health of this population. According to Raphael, during the medical examination of prospective *olim* in a certain North African country, thirty-four cases of venereal disease, trachoma, and other contagious illnesses were diagnosed in one day.[108]

Despite the orders to cut back on the number of sick and disabled immigrants, they continued to arrive in Israel. The *aliyah* activists either looked the other way or were tricked into believing these people were well. The burden of these immigrants' care fell on the Jewish Agency's Immigration Department. Its director, Zvi Herman, raised an outcry about the seriousness of the situation, claiming that elderly and handicapped persons accounted for nearly 18 percent of all newcomers and demanding that immigration from the DP camps in Germany and North Africa be reduced in view of the poor health that prevailed there.

Nevertheless, immigration swelled rather than diminished, and the medical situation worsened. The dilemma was greatest in those areas where it was planned to liquidate the Jewish community, such as the DP camps in Europe and countries like Bulgaria and Libya, where nearly the entire population had been transplanted to Israel. The question was what to do with the many sick, handicapped, and elderly people who remained. The Jewish Agency asked the JDC to take these people under its wing, and indeed, the willingness of this organization to help somewhat eased the hardship. However, the overall problem was not solved, and as the months went by the difficulties mounted. In the stormy debate over Israel's immigration policy, the plight of the old and suffering became a pivotal issue.

Karaites

Among those groups that the *aliyah* institutions tried to keep out of the country were the Karaites, a sect that rejected the Talmudic development of Judaism. The intention was to bar their entry as a separate community, not as individuals, as in the cases cited above. The restrictions pertained chiefly to the Karaites in Egypt, whose status differed from that of their brethren in Eastern Europe. In these countries, the Karaites lived apart from the Jewish community, whereas the congregation in Egypt maintained contact with "Rabbinate" Jews (those who accepted the authority of Talmudic law) and many of its members belonged to the Zionist movement. When they learned of the ban on their community, they called upon the Zionist leadership in Egypt and well-known figures in Israel, the Knesset, and the Zionist movement, to intercede on their behalf. The Aliyah Department would not budge from its position. When a group of Karaite families gained permission to leave Egypt on its own and headed for Israel, workers of Mossad le-Aliyah Bet cabled Raphael from France, asking what to do. Raphael's reply was curt: "The matter of the Karaites in Egypt was brought to my attention by Ephraim Shilo, who is in Israel now and was informed of our negative answer." [109]

The Karaites did not give up. They appealed to Yitzhak Ben-Zvi, then a Knesset member, who was known for his warm feeling toward this sect; Ben-Zvi spoke to Raphael, urging him to let them in. In addition to contacting Zionist leaders in their country, the Karaites approached the Egyptian branch of Torah va-Avoda—the movement to which Raphael belonged. All these people praised the Karaites for their Zionist affiliation and participation in the battles of the Jewish public.[110] Seeking a way to extricate himself from this predicament, Raphael asked Berl Locker, chairman of the Zionist Executive, to raise the issue at the Executive's next meeting.[111] Having thus provoked the rage of the Orthodox, who wanted to keep the Karaites out, he sought the advice of Rabbi Meir Uziel, Israel's chief rabbi, and Rabbi Zvi Frank, the chief rabbi of Jerusalem.

Rabbi Frank's letter of response explained the status of the Karaites from the vantage point of Jewish law and drew the following conclusion: "Heaven forbid that we should allow such pernicious leprosy into the society of Israel." [112] Rabbi Uziel adopted a far more moderate stance: "We have decided to permit their entry into Israel as sons of the Bible." To reassure his colleagues, Raphael declared that he had no intention of letting them in "for the time being." [113]

The controversy, however, would not subside. Yaakov Zerubavel of Mapam, head of the Jewish Agency's Department for Jewish Affairs in the Middle East, announced his objection to the rabbinate being the sole decision maker in matters of Jewish identity, and called for the Karaites to be admitted without restriction. At a closed meeting of the Jewish Agency Executive, Zerubavel confided that the Karaites not only were members of the Zionist movement but also had been active in the Jewish underground. He felt that Mossad le-Aliyah Bet should be the authority with regard to Karaite immigration.[114] Raphael, fearful of losing his grip, proposed that the matter be settled in conjunction with the rabbis. In response Zerubavel quipped, "That should be interesting—to see us partners." Nor did the episode end there.

During the course of 1949, the situation of the Jews in Egypt further deteriorated, so that the community of forty-four thousand confronted severe hardship. Nearly one thousand Jews had been arrested and some had been sent to concentration camps. All Jews holding government posts had been dismissed, and Jews were forbidden to open their stores and factories. Anyone who could find the opportunity to escape did so; upon reaching Rome, most of them applied for *aliyah*.[115] The Immigration Department emissary in Rome cabled Raphael to report a group of twenty Karaites among the fleeing Jews. He wanted instructions on how to handle them. Raphael cabled back, "Do not arrange the immigration of the Karaites until further notice."[116] Meanwhile, hundreds of Egyptian Jews converged on Rome and Marseilles. Mossad and Immigration Department officials were told to delay their immigration in view of the new restrictions, but the officials pleaded with their superiors to increase the quota: "We are being flooded in Marseilles and Italy by waves of escapees from Goshen [a code name for Egypt]. The JDC absolutely refuses to handle any more of them."[117]

As the stream of refugees from Egypt grew, together with the pressure to admit the Karaites, such families did end up settling in Israel. About this time the first immigrants from Poland began to arrive after the signing of an agreement with the Polish government in the fall of 1949. Among them were several Karaites, but no attempt was made to detain them so as not to anger the Poles; Israel had promised that it would not limit emigration from Poland in any way. The Immigration Department thus had its hands tied. Ironically, as soon as Yitzhak Ben-Zvi heard of the arrival of the Polish Karaites, he rushed to congratulate Raphael "on the aliyah of these forsaken brothers."[118]

Mass Immigration Versus Selectivity

During the first months of statehood, no legislation in the sphere of immigration was brought before the Knesset; Israel's open-door policy was taken for granted. However, members of the government and the Zionist Executive did have views on the subject. The issue was first broached in August 1948, when restrictions on immigration proposed by the Ministry of Immigration upset certain members of the Aliyah Committee. The bone of contention was Shapira's bid to select candidates for *aliyah* on the basis of not only religion but also financial standing. Shapira argued that he was not violating Israel's commitment to admit all Jews; he was "organizing" immigration to insure the welfare of those who came. He was even prepared to grant visas to sick and handicapped persons if a family member living in Israel would take responsibility for them. All these measures,

Shapira maintained, were intended to ease the burden on the state and regulate the flow of newcomers in keeping with the country's "absorptive capacity."[119]

Israel's immigration policy was not shaped by ideology alone. Security needs, foreign relations, and economic constraints also exerted considerable influence. Furthermore, there were external factors over which Israel had no control. The architects of this policy were Israel's leaders, but many different bodies took part in executing it, not always in collaboration: Mossad le-Aliyah Bet, the Ministry of Immigration, the Ministry of Foreign Affairs, the Ministry of Health, and others. The result was a complex bureaucratic mechanism that somehow dealt with immigration in its lumbering way.

In some cases, the fate of *aliyah* was determined by global events. The onset of the Great Aliyah plunged Israel into a severe economic crisis that compelled it to seek loans and financial assistance from the United States. The Korean War was then being fought, and approaching the United States meant the end of Israel's policy of neutrality. This immediately affected the relationship Israel had built up with the Communist bloc, primarily for the purpose of freeing its Jews.

The Israeli government and the Jewish Agency often worked at cross purposes concerning the question of *aliyah*. Making decisions and implementing them were hampered by infighting and jealousy, by disagreements both theoretical and practical about what needed to be done. In addition to this, there were social and political tensions resulting from the transition from British rule to independence and the changes in population makeup. Typical of the *aliyah* enterprise was the lack of clear distinctions between one authority and the next, between those who formulated policy and those who carried it out, between the categories of immigration and absorption. In the absence of solid administrative traditions, the implementation process fell into the hands of persons who did not agree and therefore featured many contradictions.

From May 1948 to March 1949, more than two hundred thousand persons immigrated to Israel; the following year, the number was higher.[120] Even advocates of mass immigration were stunned by the flood of newcomers who poured in unexpectedly from every direction. The major problem was to absorb them all. The absorption network was financially and organizationally unprepared for an undertaking of such magnitude, a fact which placed the economic structure of the country in genuine danger of collapse. While the test of Israel's immigration policy was not at the negotiation table and its fate was ultimately determined by a combination of factors, the conclusive voice in the debate over mass immigration versus selectivity was that of the prime minister, David Ben-Gurion.

CHAPTER TWO

Policy Put to the Test

Immigration: Free or Restricted

THE GREAT SURGE of immigration in 1949 took both Israel's leadership and its public by surprise. Even those who worked in immigration did not anticipate the enormity of the influx. The preliminary work had been done by several different bodies: the Foreign Ministry, which negotiated endlessly with the Allied powers and overseas governments; the Joint Distribution Committee, which provided financial backing for the accords that were reached; and Mossad le-Aliyah Bet and the Jewish Agency's Aliyah Department, which encouraged the Jews to make the move and organized them for departure. However, the actual flow could not be planned in advance by any of these groups. With talks in progress in dozens of countries, it was impossible to predict when and where the gates would open to Jewish emigration or how many Jews would be allowed to leave.

The turn of events was unforeseen. It seemed as if East and West were competing over who would let its Jews out first. Within a year, beginning in mid-1949, four countries—Yemen, Poland, Romania, and Iraq—lifted their ban on Jewish emigration. The Jewish population in these countries totaled seven hundred thousand persons and more, posing an unprecedented challenge to the Zionist movement and the State of Israel. This challenge was one to which Israel was forced to respond immediately and unconditionally, in spite of the fact that the immigrants of 1948 had not yet been properly absorbed due to the chronic lack of resources.

The major problem underlying the current tide of immigrants was not so much in the decision-making process as it was in the dynamics of the organizational period before their arrival. The government should have been able to regulate the number of immigrants with the help of its overseas emissaries, but these activists, sensing the historic nature of their mission, devoted all their energies to mobilizing as many *olim* as possible. When the response exceeded all expectations, there was no turning back. The emissaries fought mightily to complete the

European immigrants arriving at Haifa Port aboard the SS *Negba* rejoice upon reaching Israel. *Photograph by Teddy Brauner*

cycle they had begun and to assure that the Jews they had uprooted reached their destination. In Israel, however, the absorption workers were furious. The paradox was that success in mobilizing immigrants was perceived as an obstacle to the immigration enterprise. The country was both unprepared and incapable of absorbing the hordes of newcomers who converged upon it from all corners of the globe.

The authorities in Israel thus found themselves in a quandary: Should they permit immigration to continue without hindrance, or should they hold it back and limit the number of *olim* in accordance with the absorptive capacity of the country? On the one hand, the sight of the masses disembarking at Israel's ports was exhilarating; on the other, there were horrifying scenes of overcrowding and poverty at the immigrant camps. The whole question of quotas, however, was rendered hypothetical in the face of entire communities packing their bags and leaving for Israel.

Liquidated Communities

In certain countries, Jewish communities were "liquidated" and transplanted to Israel in their entirety. The circumstances surrounding their departure prevented

Israel from imposing any kind of schedule. The choice was between permitting free passage or risking a complete halt in the emigration process. This was the situation in Communist and Arab countries. The first Jewish communities transplanted to Israel were those of the Balkan states—Bulgaria and Yugoslavia. Immigration from Bulgaria began in October 1948; within three months, 15,700 Jews had reached Israel. From January to April 1949, another 15,000 arrived, and an additional 3,000 came during the weeks that followed. Of Bulgaria's 43,000 Jews, some 30,000 resettled in Israel in less than a year.

The bulk of the Jewish community of Yugoslavia relocated to Israel during the first wave of immigration in 1948. During the month of December alone, 4,200 persons made *aliyah;* 2,500 more immigrated in 1949. Of the 11,000 Jews remaining in Yugoslavia after World War II, a total of 7,000 left for Israel.[1] Immigration from the Balkan states continued in 1950, albeit at a slower pace; the result was that nearly all of Bulgarian and Yugoslavian Jewry resettled in Israel.[2]

As we have noted, the exodus from the Communist bloc was the product of tireless negotiations conducted with the utmost caution and secrecy; the slightest interference was liable to endanger it. Organizing *aliyah* from Arab nations was even more complicated. Of the Jews in all the countries of North Africa, only those from Libya participated in the first wave of immigration. The British administration in Libya, which had prohibited *aliyah* prior to the establishment of the state, allowed the Jews to leave in early 1949. Before that, a few hundred managed to slip out in secret. According to the Jewish Agency Aliyah Department, the British declaration had an "electrifying effect" on the Jews of Libya.[3] In March 1949, a Palestine Office was opened in Tripoli to handle the direct transfer of Jews to Israel. The majority of Libya's 32,000 Jews signed up, and that year some 14,000 were transported, mainly by boat. Meanwhile, organizational activity continued. Jews from small villages in Libya were sent to transit camps in the capital, where they underwent registration, medical screening, and treatment (financed by the Joint Distribution Committee). The scope and rate of immigration were largely influenced by the perseverance of the emissaries but other factors contributed. Rumors of the impending departure of the British and the declaration of Libyan independence increased the hostility of Muslim nationalists. This sparked panic among the Jews, who began to pressure the Aliyah Department to speed up its procedures.

Turkey was an unusual case. Because the Jews there seemed to be in no apparent danger, the Jewish Agency and the Joint Distribution Committee did not rush to organize their exodus. Moreover, the Turkish government refused to allow the opening of a Palestine Office to formally handle immigration. Without waiting for outside assistance, the Jewish community took steps on its own. The proximity of Turkey to Israel, as well as the fact that there were no impediments to maritime travel, made things easier. During the first year of statehood, more than 20,000 Turkish Jews made their way to Israel, largely unaided. When Turkey recognized Israel, the Aliyah Department began to operate on a regular basis. By the end of 1949, a total of 30,000 Jews had immigrated, a trend that continued into 1950.[4]

During the summer of 1947, some 200,000 Jews were in German DP camps awaiting permission to immigrate. There were one hundred such camps scattered throughout the four liberated zones in East and West Germany. It was these survivors who were targeted as the main source of *aliyah* when the State of Israel was born. The great powers openly encouraged them to leave so that the camps could be liquidated. The first group of 1,000 Jews was brought to Israel in June 1948, and the numbers steadily increased as the months went by.

The high point was March 1949, when 9,000 Jews were evacuated; these were sent to Israel on seventeen direct flights and nine train convoys through France. That summer, those survivors who had not opted for *aliyah* were assembled in seven camps. As the date approached for the closure of these camps, there was growing pressure on the inmates to register as prospective immigrants.[5] The detention camps in Cyprus were also liberated in January 1949. After the establishment of the State of Israel, 24,500 illegal immigrants were still being held there by the British, who refused to allow the release of military-age internees. Now they too were permitted to leave Cyprus, and within several weeks they were all in Israel.

During the first year of statehood, nearly 200,000 *olim* reached the Jewish state. Their absorption was encumbered by the large percentage of elderly, sick, and disabled persons requiring special attention, manpower, and budgets. The Kelitah Department of the Jewish Agency was helpless, its coffers continually empty. Toward the middle of 1949, when it seemed that the pressure of transplanted communities had begun to lift, Yemen and Poland suddenly agreed to release tens of thousands of Jews. Israel was particularly emotional over the news from Yemen, which had been venomous in its denunciation of the Jewish state. From the onset of Yemenite immigration in the late nineteenth century, the Yishuv in Israel had harbored special ties with the Jews of Yemen.

The consent of the Polish government came as another surprise. Poland had been the home of the largest concentration of Jews and a bustling center of Zionist activity before World War II; the Holocaust had transformed it into a giant graveyard. The announcement that the survivors would be allowed to emigrate aroused strong feelings in Israel, especially among former Polish Jews, many of whom held senior positions in the Israeli government and Jewish Agency. Here,

Immigrants arriving from Europe aboard the SS *Aktan* await disembarkation at Haifa Port.

too, emotions were mixed: on the one hand, there were fears of an inability to cope with their absorption and, on the other, Israel was anxious to expedite their arrival in every possible way.

The dilemma that arose at this point was whether or not Israel should introduce priorities in the sphere of immigration. The question was not raised outright, but it hovered in the air whenever the Jewish Agency executive met. It also crept into discussion when several countries relaxed their ban on Jewish emigration at the same time—for example, in the summer of 1949, when Yemen and Poland opened their gates; and again in 1950, when Romania and then suddenly Iraq declared similar intentions. Israel's policymakers were hard pressed to decide whether to establish immigration quotas for all countries or to give priority to one at the expense of another. In the end, as we shall see, it was reality that dictated government policy.

Immigration from Yemen: Operation Magic Carpet

Immigration from Yemen resulted in the liquidation of one of the oldest Jewish communities in the Diaspora. Yemenite Jewry had maintained solid ties with the

A Yemenite family walking through the desert to a reception camp set up by the JDC near Aden. *Photograph by Zoltan Kluger*

Yishuv in Palestine for hundreds of years. On the eve of the establishment of Israel, fifty thousand Jews resided in dozens of villages, towns, and cities throughout Yemen. With the Yemenite government radically supportive of the Arab struggle against Zionism and the Jewish state, the exit permit issued in the summer of 1949 was completely unexpected.

Toward the end of 1948, a group of five thousand Yemenite Jews reached Israel. These were refugees who had been intercepted in the British protectorate of Aden while en route to Palestine in 1945.

The Hashed Camp where they were interned was known by the Jews as "Camp Geula" (camp of redemption). The refugees were forbidden to continue their journey, and in keeping with British policy, were detained even after Israel's independence to prevent them from strengthening the country's military force. Although permission to leave was granted in November 1948, the British delayed the departure of 800 young people of army age. In the absence of a land route to Aden, Israel arranged an airlift to bring the group to Israel. The first plane landed in Lod on 16 December 1948. The timing of the operation added much to the magical atmosphere accompanying the rescue of Yemenite Jewry. The transports flew over the Negev while the Israel Defense Forces were still in combat with the Egyptian army. By 12 March 1949, a total of 5,250 Yemenite refugees had been evacuated.

When the last Yemenites left Hashed, the British authorities decided to shut down the camp, possibly to prevent another influx of Jews. The relationship between the British and the Yemenite government was a complex one. The British administration feared that its actions might be interpreted as assistance to Israel, the arch enemy of the Muslim world, and there were rumors that it was secretly encouraging the Imam to halt the exodus of Jews from Yemen. The British also ordered workers of the Joint Distribution Committee in Aden to stop handling Yemenite refugees.[6]

The Jews of Yemen came under the legal jurisdiction of three government networks. While the vast majority were subjects of the Imam, there were also some who lived in the sultanate between Yemen and Aden, and some in Aden itself, which was a British crown colony. *Aliyah* emissaries in Aden worked to penetrate Jewish enclaves and generate interest in immigration. With the help of intermediaries, they also tried to persuade the Yemenite authorities to permit the Jews to leave, or at least to turn a blind eye to their clandestine departure. In March 1949, a group of immigrants was stopped at the border. After much arguing and pleading, as well as the payment of a hefty bribe, the sultan allowed them to continue on their way. The British, however, prevented their admission into Aden. Only after feverish negotiations were the Jews admitted, on condition that their stop in Aden last no more than a few hours.[7] This preliminary trickle of immigrants turned into a torrent after the Imam sanctioned Jewish emigration in May 1949. Thus began Operation Magic Carpet or, as the Yemenite Jews preferred to call it, Al Kanfei Nesharim (on eagles' wings). During this operation, tens of thousands of Jews were airlifted to Israel with the utmost haste lest Yemen's leaders change their minds and reinstate the ban on emigration.

The British authorities in Aden were willing to cooperate, but they insisted that the Jews remain outside the city to avoid the spread of epidemics. Camp Geula—built, financed, and supervised by the Joint Distribution Committee—was set up for them not far from Camp Hashed and was meant to accommodate six hundred to one thousand persons for short stopovers. There were tents but virtually no sanitary facilities. The first immigrants began to arrive in June, but within weeks the place was teeming with a population of thousands.[8] The journey from Yemen was long and tortuous. Setting out from dozens of villages in Yemen, the Jews made their way to Aden by foot or riding on donkeys. The rough terrain, highway robbers, greedy local officials, and attacks of hostile villagers sapped their strength and emptied their pockets. The few *aliyah* emissaries

Jewish Yemenite immigrants brought on the Magic Carpet airlift from Aden to Israel. *Photograph by David Eldan*

who managed to enter Yemen could do little to help. Only when they reached Haj, near Aden, were they approached by workers of the Joint Distribution Committee and taken to Camp Geula. They were often stopped as they crossed the border, stranded between Yemen and Aden. Short on food supplies, thousands of refugees, among them women, children, and old people, nearly died of starvation. Nevertheless, the Jews of Yemen continued their trek to Israel via Aden.

The Jewish Agency and absorption authority had no control over the exodus from Yemen. During the early months, there was no clear data on the overall size of the Jewish community nor of the number of people on their way to Israel. Even information about the refugees in Camp Geula, such as the number of inhabitants, the size of families, and their state of health, remained vague. The work of the emissaries in Yemen was complicated by the dispersal of Jews over a wide area. In the absence of a communications network, it was difficult to relay and receive messages. The secrecy surrounding their work, necessary to avoid antagonizing the government and local populace, also minimized contact with institutions in Israel. Most activities were improvised on the spot in accordance with changing conditions. Not a word was said to the media about the rescue of

Yemenite Jewry lest news of the operation arouse opposition in Yemen and other Arab countries.

Birth Pangs of the Messiah

Caring for the Yemenite Jews in Aden was the sole responsibility of the Joint Distribution Committee. This organization built and financed the Geula transit camp and also made all the arrangements connected with flying the refugees to Israel. The British authorities consented to this arrangement because they wished to keep Israeli representatives out of Aden. The absorption network in Israel knew very little about what was happening in Yemen. Unlike the situation in other countries, contact with the JDC in Aden was tenuous at best. The director of JDC activities in Aden refused to cooperate with the Jewish Agency; he avoided meeting with its delegates and would not supply updated figures on the number of arrivals in Aden. In July 1949, when large groups began to reach the colony, Jewish Agency officials in Israel were in a quandary about how to proceed for lack of information about the size of the Yemenite Jewish community and how many immigrants were involved.

Giora Josephthal, who supervised the Jewish Agency absorption network, assumed that the number would not exceed 20,000 people; no one knew how quickly they would arrive. Absorption officials offered various speculations as to the rate and volume of Yemenite immigration. In July, Zvi Herman, head of the Kelitah Department, even hoped that the flow would slow down. Like other absorption workers, he saw the misery in the camps to which the newcomers were sent and looked forward to thinning out the population. "I think the standard in our camps will now begin to exceed that of the camps in Germany," Herman said. For the first time, the personal welfare of the immigrants became an issue. Herman went on to describe the efforts being made to organize immigrant camps according to country of origin, both for cultural and educational reasons and out of respect for different culinary traditions.[9]

However, the forecasts of a slowdown in immigration were not long-lived. The Jewish Agency began to receive word that huge numbers of immigrants were congregating in Aden and that their physical condition was poor. Nearly 70 percent of Yemenite Jews were said to be carrying infectious diseases such as trachoma and tuberculosis. However, the agreement with the British did not allow for prior selection, and it was feared that thousands would require medical treatment upon arrival in Israel. At this point, the immigration estimate for the next five months was still twenty thousand.[10] Even so, Jewish Agency officials were anxious and called for a reconsideration of the proposal to proceed more slowly.

Yitzhak Gruenbaum opposed unlimited immigration from Yemen. "Why liquidate the Yemenite Diaspora and transport people to this country who are more hindrance than help?" he asked. "By bringing in persons, seventy percent of whom are sick, we harm both them and ourselves . . . We are moving them to an alien environment where they will wither." However, the majority of executive members rushed to support this *aliyah*. As Rabbi Wolf Gold explained, "For the Jews of Yemen it is a matter of life and death. However difficult the situation in Israel may be, it is better for them to be here than to remain in Yemen." Berl Locker agreed with him: "We are dealing here with *pikuah nefesh* [saving an endangered life]." Gruenbaum stood firm in his opposition, and not only toward the immigration of Yemenite Jews. "We have no business liquidating Diaspora communities," he admonished his colleagues.[11]

In August 1949, the flow of Jews from Yemen increased. Moshe Shapira, who was both minister of immigration and minister of health, summoned the representative of the Joint Distribution Committee in Israel[12] and officials of the two ministries to an urgent meeting.[13] By September, Camp Geula, which had been designed to hold fewer than one thousand persons, was bursting at the seams with nearly thirteen thousand. The physicians who were sent to Aden to examine the prospective immigrants were stunned by what they saw. Dr. Sternberg described "a broad field covered entirely by masses of people lying closely together on the desert sand. Protruding from the sea of human beings were many spots of white. As we approached, we saw low benches upon which the dead had been laid out in their shrouds; they had not yet been buried."[14]

While in Aden, the medical delegation was informed that the British had sealed off the Yemenite border in light of the typhus epidemic in that country. Closure of the border was literally a death sentence on those Jews who were en route to Aden. The British authorities announced that they would bar the entry of more refugees until those currently at Camp Geula were evacuated. Dr. Joseph Meir, director-general of the Ministry of Health and a member of the delegation, reported on the seriousness of the situation and recommended that Israel's immigration authorities act more quickly.[15]

Medical screening of the immigrants in Israel also produced worrisome results. In early September, Josephthal told Ben-Gurion that conditions in the immigrant camps were catastrophic. The number of prospective *olim* from Yemen was still unknown but was presumed to be 30,000 at most. As far as the absorption network knew, there were 10,000 Jews waiting in Aden and another 14,000 in Yemen. With the authorities in Aden turning away newcomers until the backlog was eliminated, the departure rate was accelerated to 500 persons a day. Six

Habanim immigrants at
Lod Airport, stepping down
from the plane laden with
bundles, cooking pots, and
thermo flasks.
Photograph by Fritz Cohen

Skymaster planes were commissioned to fly the immigrants to Israel, 130 passengers aboard each flight.

During its first phase, Operation Magic Carpet was a well-kept secret, the media refraining from publishing the story. However, news of the operation broke at the beginning of November 1949.[16] *Aliyah* emissaries in Yemen found the publicity distressing and even Ben-Gurion was taken aback, but the planes kept landing. Sometimes there were as many as seven flights a day, and with each one came fresh reports of the suffering in Aden. Again Ben-Gurion urged the Aliyah Department to do its utmost to speed up immigration from Yemen. At the opening of the Knesset's second session, Ben-Gurion stated that the government would not waver from its mission to double the Jewish population of the state within four years. "Despite all the difficulties," he said, "we will continue to oppose any restrictions on immigration. We cannot congratulate ourselves on having found the answers to all the problems of aliyah or finding them in the near future . . . yet even if we must work desperately to maintain the rapid pace of mass immigration, we shall not flinch."[17]

When those involved in immigrant absorption continued to insist that the flow must be contained, Ben-Gurion decided to investigate personally. At Ben-Gurion's request, Yisrael Yeshayahu (Sharabi), a Yemenite Jew active in Mapai (later a Knesset member, minister, and Speaker of the Knesset), visited Yemen and returned with a discouraging account of the problems facing the Jewish community. Precise figures for the number of Jews remaining in Yemen were unknown, but Yeshayahu's estimate was 15,000–20,000. He told of enormous pressure put on the Joint Distribution Committee by the British governor of Aden to speed up the airlift. The governor warned that the Arab leaders were agitated over the emigration of Yemenite Jewry and fully blamed the JDC for the closure of the border. He maintained that this organization failed to stand by its word to supply enough planes to transport the people. When severe overcrowding developed, endangering the lives of the immigrants themselves and the health of the city of Aden, there was no choice but to close the borders.[18] Yeshayahu advised Ben-Gurion to allow immigration to proceed as quickly as possible.

As a result of these conflicting appeals—from absorption and health officials to slow down and from Aden and Yemen to move faster—Ben-Gurion became increasingly involved in the problems of the Yemenites. After a visit to Tel Hashomer Hospital, he noted in his diary: "Shocking scene of Yemenite children, genuinely starving. Not enough nurses to care for them. I do not know if any hospital is performing a more humane and Zionist service."[19] He later described his experience to the Knesset:

It was one of the most horrifying sights I have ever seen . . . In the wing set aside by the army for the children of Yemen, there were children and babies who were more like skeletons than living human beings, too weak to cry, many of them unable to absorb food. Only their eyes still shone with the light of life; they were the eyes of Jewish children . . . I understood at that moment what it means to "rejoice with trembling." I shuddered with excitement at this great and terrible sight. Yes—these are the birth pangs of the Messiah.[20]

Ben-Gurion demanded that the rescue of Yemenite Jewry be implemented with greater haste; indeed, the number of immigrants reaching Israel continued to swell. By the end of 1949, more than thirty-five thousand Yemenite Jews had arrived, with more to come in the following months. The final transport landed on 24 September 1950. All told, forty-seven thousand Jews immigrated to Israel from Yemen and another two thousand from Aden, Asmara, and Djibouti.

Immigration from Poland

As the exodus from Yemen reached its peak, Poland opened its gates to Jewish emigration. With great excitement, Yisrael Barzilai, the Israeli envoy to Poland, announced that, after lengthy negotiations with the Polish government, the Jews were free to leave. Aware of the difficult conditions in the immigrant camps and the Jewish Agency's consideration of proposals to limit immigration, Barzilai urged the Agency Executive to consider the Polish issue separately, using a different yardstick. The fate of the remnant of Polish Jewry, he said, was now in the hands of the Jewish Agency and the Israeli government. Moreover, immigration from Poland was likely to have consequences for other countries of Eastern Europe, where nearly half a million Jews resided. Hence the need for a special approach and incentives in the absorption of *olim* from Poland.

Barzilai wrote long letters to members of the Knesset and the Jewish Agency Executive on the subject of *aliyah* from Poland. He emphasized the need to bring these Jews to Israel quickly, lest the great opportunity that had presented itself over the last few weeks be lost:

> My assumption is that Polish Jewry, numbering some 70,000 to 80,000 souls, can be divided along general lines into three categories. First, a small minority that has made up its mind to remain in Poland. Second, a small minority that has made up its mind to immigrate. Third, a large or small majority that fits into neither category and can be influenced one way or another. The fate of aliyah from Poland depends upon the choice of this bloc. The decision could be an historical one. First of all, for Polish Jewry itself, because those who do not go to Israel immediately may never be able to . . . Secondly, for the Jews of other countries, because the broad consent granted by the Polish government may set a precedent for East European countries where emigration is now forbidden . . . The extent to which this permission is utilized may thus be the deciding factor for the path eventually chosen by Romania and Hungary.[21]

Barzilai's reason for demanding better absorption conditions for Polish immigrants was as follows:

> The most serious impediment to an atmosphere conducive to aliyah is the flood of reports from Israel about economic hardship and severe absorption difficulties—unemployment, housing shortages, overcrowded camps, high living costs . . . The official newspapers [in Poland] exaggerate and distort these reports . . . This has been turned into a form of propaganda against aliyah and may well in-

dicate the cross purpose of Polish policy—on the one hand, to permit emigration in principle and, on the other, to insure that only a few actually leave. The
ordinary Jew finds himself wedged between a rock and a hard place. If he does
not emigrate, he may miss the opportunity . . . If he does so, he immediately
loses his Polish citizenship, and should he arrive in Israel and find it impossible
to acclimatize, he will have nowhere to return . . . Feedback about the absorption of the first groups will have a crucial impact on the overall dimensions of
this aliyah. The far-reaching consequences of the decision which now faces the
Jews of Poland should make the government of Israel and the Jewish Agency
think carefully about handling the absorption of Polish Jews in a different manner so as to expedite their adjustment in Israel and spare them the suffering, dis-
appointment and setbacks experienced by North African immigrants.[22]

Barzilai had heard the stories about one hundred thousand *olim* being packed
into camps where they lived in tents and huts under insufferable conditions, and
he wished to save Polish Jews from this fate if he possibly could. In light of the
momentous decision they had to make, he came forward with his proposal for
preferential treatment and asked that the issue be dealt with urgently by the government and the Jewish Agency.

Privileges for Polish Immigrants

The debate over Polish Jewry revolved, not around the need to bring them to Israel, but around the idea of granting them special privileges. There were former
Polish Jews in the Jewish Agency who were moved by Barzilai's words and agreed
that preferential treatment was justified.[23] Yitzhak Raphael, director of the Immigration Department, spoke with pride of his Polish upbringing, and there was
no better advocate for Polish Jewry than Gruenbaum, who had been a leader of
the community and represented its interests in the Sejm before the Holocaust.
Gruenbaum's position as treasurer of the Jewish Agency lent extra weight to his
opinion.[24] Barzilai's proposal was also supported by such important figures as
Berl Locker, executive chairman of the Jewish Agency. As Eliahu Dobkin bluntly
put it: "We must grant this aliyah privileges, and the word does not scare me."[25]
    Some of those who attended the meeting at which Barzilai's proposal was dis-
cussed openly opposed such a bias. They argued that it would create bad feeling
among immigrants from other countries. Levi Eshkol commented, "If we have
camps populated by 100,000 people and suddenly the *Ashkenazim* are given
privileges, one can easily imagine the shouts that would erupt: 'The *shiknaz* gets

it all.' " Zvi Herman added, "I fear that not one of us would be left alive . . . Can you imagine the implications of special arrangements for 20,000 people?"[26]

As with other sensitive issues, it was decided to appoint a committee to probe the matter in depth. However, over the coming months it came up for discussion repeatedly at meetings of the Jewish Agency Executive and Yitzhak Gruenbaum was always at the head.[27]

After Gruenbaum stepped down as treasurer, he continued to lobby for superior conditions for Polish immigrants and to impress on all concerned the importance of making an extraordinary effort to ease their absorption. Raphael explained that "Polish immigrants are not like those of other countries . . . Among them are professionals who are needed by this country and will bring a blessing to the economy." In his eyes, there was nothing unfair about giving them preference: "For a long time, the immigrants from other countries who are making demands did not want to come here and delayed their aliyah. Thus we have no obligation towards them . . . The Jews of Poland did not immigrate because they had no opportunity to do so."[28] This was a veiled reference to those interned in the camps in Germany who had not hastened to leave for Israel yet had no compunction about presenting the Jewish Agency with a list of requests. Raphael further contended that the Jews of Poland were accustomed to a high standard of living. For them, he argued, camp life was a much greater hardship than for the Jews of Yemen, for whom the camp itself was a deliverance.

The Polish lobby tried to convince Ben-Gurion, also born in Poland, to take their side, but Ben-Gurion refused. In his diary, he wrote, "A question has arisen regarding aliyah from Poland. Absorption problems may frighten off many of them. A proposal was made to introduce special arrangements for Polish Jews. Out of the question. However, absorption procedures must be thoroughly reexamined, and large development projects planned and implemented."[29]

This topic arose continually at meetings of the Jewish Agency Executive. On one occasion, after hearing about the suffering of the immigrants who inhabited tents throughout the harsh winter season, Ben-Gurion began to think that perhaps an exception ought to be made for the Polish Jews. The following day, however, he changed his mind and quickly dispatched a letter to Gruenbaum: "I have reached the conclusion that it would be a mistake. We must not discriminate between immigrants, and no basis exists for granting benefits to Polish Jews. Whoever does not wish to come—let him not come. A person who immigrates to this country is not doing the Jewish people a favor. We must not spend on one *oleh* the amount we could spend on two. Preferring one type of *oleh* over another is certain to create demoralization among those who are preferred."[30]

Nevertheless, Gruenbaum continued his fight to rescue the Polish survivors and assure their absorption into Israeli society. He warned that *aliyah* from Poland could end up like *aliyah* from Czechoslovakia, which was hindered and even interrupted for a time because of letters full of bitter complaint about the conditions prevailing during the absorption of the first immigrants. Many of those who had registered for *aliyah* reversed their decision and stayed where they were. Under incessant pressure from Gruenbaum, the Jewish Agency agreed to appoint a special committee to handle Polish immigration; the committee consisted of representatives of the Association of Immigrants from Poland and Polish Jewry activists from different parties. Gruenbaum was elected president and a four-man council was established to oversee its operation.[31]

In November 1949 the first group of *olim* left Poland. The Polish government allowed these Jews to take their belongings with them, but later it imposed restrictions on the amount of property and money (fifteen dollars per person) that could leave the country. After a while, this allowance too was canceled and the emigrants could only take with them goods purchased from a special list drawn up by the government. While the Polish authorities had given the Jews permission to go, their ambivalence showed: Virulent propaganda was spread to dissuade potential emigrants from acting on their plans. Nonetheless, some forty thousand Jews signed up to leave. The government prevented the departure of two thousand of them, mainly physicians and clerical workers, on the pretext that they were vital to the economy. It also announced that the exit permits would be valid for one year, until September 1950.

From December 1949, immigration from Poland proceeded steadily, although the volume was smaller than that predicted by Barzilai. The operation was organized by the Aliyah office in Warsaw in cooperation with the government travel agency, Orbis. As requested by the Poles, the work was done quietly and without any publicity. Every week, two or three trains left for Italy with five hundred to seven hundred immigrants aboard. The immigrants disembarked at the ports of Bari or Venice, where Israeli ships were waiting to transport them to Israel. When the pressure increased, the Polish vessel *Protea* and the Israeli *Artza* sailed directly from Gidinia, Poland to Haifa, but these occasions were rare.[32]

The committee headed by Gruenbaum thought of conducting a special fund-raising campaign in the United States, but this plan was thwarted by Berl Locker, who argued that it would set off a spate of appeals on behalf of other Jewish communities such as Romania, Hungary, etc., and create chaos in the sphere of Jewish fund-raising. Moreover, if Polish Jews in the United States were asked to support their countrymen in Israel, what would become of the Jews of Morocco and Yemen? However, Gruenbaum persisted and found other channels of activity. He was able to mobilize loans and grants from various sources, using the money to secure better housing for Polish immigrants.[33]

Toward the second half of 1950, there was an increase in the number of Polish Jews reaching Israel. By September, however, only half of those who had expressed an interest in *aliyah* had left Poland, and time was running out. The Polish government submitted to Israeli pressure and extended the time limit until the end of February 1951. From that point on, Israel absorbed three thousand Polish immigrants every month. In all, twenty-eight thousand Polish Jews settled in Israel between December 1949 and March 1951.[34] After the time limit expired, the gates were closed and, according to the Aliyah office in Poland, some twenty thousand Jews were left behind.[35]

More Immigrants, More Dilemmas

Faced with the difficulty of absorbing so many newcomers, the Israeli government and the Jewish Agency grappled with the question of whether to proclaim a general slowdown of immigration or to give preference to one Diaspora community over another. This issue again rose to the fore in 1950, when Iraq and Romania simultaneously lifted their bans on Jewish emigration. The immigrant camps were overflowing and the basic resources to handle newcomers were depleted. Israel's decision-makers were at their wit's end, their dilemma compounded by the many twists and turns in the course of *aliyah* from different countries.

In May 1948 more than 350,000 Jews were living in Romania, constituting the largest Jewish community in Europe after the Holocaust. When Romania joined the Communist bloc that year, anxiety increased among the Jews. Economically, they were faring poorly, and their memories of war and anti-Semitism were still fresh. The majority of Romanian Jews were thus ripe for *aliyah*. Emissaries from Israel worked to pave the way through diplomatic and other channels, but at the end of 1948 the Romanians blocked all the exits. Only a handful of Jews, most of them old or sick, were allowed to leave the country.

In mid-November 1949 the authorities relented somewhat, issuing several thousand exit permits each month and as many as twenty-three thousand by May 1950. According to the Aliyah Department, 35 percent of those who received permits were elderly. A further policy shift became evident in the spring, apparently in response to the social unrest in Romania and the growing incidence of anti-Semitism. The government and the Communist Party, fearing an upset of the delicate political balance, considered measures to defuse the situation. Romania's foreign minister, Anna Pauker, herself of Jewish extraction, proposed rounding up the Jews in camps, but the idea was vetoed by the prime minister, Giorgio Dej. Eventually it was decided that emigration was the best solution; in this way, the Communist regime would be able to rid itself of negative elements and trouble—the Jews. There were even some who envisaged an end to Romania's economic difficulties: Eastern European countries such as Bulgaria and Hungary had received payment for every Jew allowed to leave.

The decision of the Romanian government required the approval of Moscow, which was secured after a round of talks with Soviet diplomats in Bucharest. As soon as the signatures on the agreement were dry, the authorities rushed into action. The Ministry of Interior hung notices on the walls of every police station in the country, and Jews interested in emigrating to Israel were asked to present the necessary documentation. Within days, dozens of registry offices were opened throughout Romania. Twenty-two offices opened in Bucharest alone, drawing 60 percent of the city's 120,000 Jews. Seventy-five percent of Iassi's 35,000 Jews registered for emigration, and the figures reached 90 percent in other areas. All this was accomplished in less than a month. Thousands of passports were issued as people lined the streets outside the Israel office in Bucharest. By the end of May, 10,000 Romanian Jews were waiting for ships to take them to Israel.[36]

The Jewish Agency executive had received a steady flow of information about the mood in Romania, contacts with the government, and the financial arrangements that had been worked out. It dared not call a halt or even a slowdown on immigration. The Romanian government was eager to get the Jews out before a commotion erupted over their release. The SS *Transylvania* sailed regularly between Romania and Israel at the fare of fifty-five dollars per passenger—twice the real cost of the trip—and the Joint Distribution Committee paid. At first, the line operated twice a month, carrying six hundred passengers each time; soon departures increased to four a month (in June) and six a month (in July). The number of passengers also increased at a steady rate, with as many as fifteen hundred persons aboard at one time.

Schemes to Diminish Romanian Immigration

During the summer of 1950 Israel's desperate pleas to release the Jews of Romania gave way to the embarrassing realization that it could not cope with the tens of thousands who were expected to come. In June, July, and August 1950, the government and the Jewish Agency pondered how to achieve more manageable numbers without provoking the Romanians into locking their gates as had happened in 1948.[37] Nobody was prepared to take that risk. At the insistence of the absorption authorities, immigration quotas had been established for other countries, but in the case of Romania this was deemed too hazardous. Instead, Israel searched for ways of manipulating the Romanians in order to achieve this end.

At a joint meeting of Jewish Agency and government officials, Minister Shapira proposed that Romania be asked to reduce the serious overcrowding on the Romanian ship that transported *olim*. Israel could claim that the passengers suffered greatly from the cramped conditions and that the level of hygiene was very poor. Most of the officials, including Ben-Gurion, thought the idea was a good one, but Yitzhak Raphael opposed it. "None [of the *olim*] are complaining; they are happy to come to Israel," Raphael said. Furthermore, Shapira's scheme contradicted the request of Israel's envoy in Bucharest to hasten the unloading of passengers and baggage so that the ship could return to Romania that same day to transport another group.

An alternate suggestion was to do the very opposite: to hold up the ship in port, disembark slowly, and delay baggage unloading. Shapira had his doubts. "I have the feeling that another ship is about to be added to this line," he said. "In that case, none of our ideas will be effective and the tempo of *aliyah* will reach 10,000 persons a month." The Romanians also began to separate passengers and baggage, sending the latter by freighter so that more people could fit on board their ship. In July the number of *olim* rose to 7,182.

When the Foreign Ministry heard the talk about reducing immigration from Romania, it warned against measures that might stop *aliyah* altogether. The Jews of Romania were very tense; some 15,000 were awaiting transport and feared that their passports would be confiscated if they did not leave soon. Savage propaganda and horror stories about the conditions in the immigrant camps began to appear in the press in order to intimidate those seeking permission to emigrate. All this contradicted the efforts of the Romanian government to speed up the departure of the Jews. Such ambiguity in a Communist regime, where newspapers were controlled from above, was strange indeed. The Foreign Ministry in Jerusalem speculated that the Romanians had not correctly assessed the number of people who desired to leave and were startled by the tens of thousands who applied for papers. The ministry was not at all certain that emigration from Romania would be allowed to continue.[38]

This assessment proved correct. In July most of the leaders of the Zionist movement in Romania were incarcerated. The Jewish community was shocked. Again there were speculations about why the Romanian government acted as it did: Was it trying to frighten applicants for emigration? Did this predict an end to Israel's diplomatic activity? There was a growing fear that emigration would be halted or drastically curtailed.[39]

Israel's immigration authorities were relentlessly pulled in two directions: the need to alleviate the crush in the immigrant camps and the inability to stave off outside pressures to absorb more immigrants. Time and again, these authorities resolved to slow down immigration, only to cancel their resolution in the next breath. Yitzhak Raphael transmitted the data he received from Romania and other countries to his colleagues in the Jewish Agency, laying the decision in their laps: "A verdict must be reached about the number of immigrants [from Romania]," he said. "If it is 5,000 [a month], then we must decide in favor of no immigration from Iraq, no immigration from Poland, no *olim* from other countries. If I also want immigration from other countries, then I must regulate *aliyah* from Romania so that it does not drown me."[40]

Activists of Mossad le-Aliyah Bet favored limiting immigration from Romania, but again not at the expense of crippling the entire enterprise. Another consideration was financial. In August, Israel had paid the Romanian government $412,500 for the release of Jews. The Romanians were now demanding an increment of $35 per head, which would increase the monthly outlay by $262,000.

"Dealing with Robbers"

In 1950 money became an even greater problem. The Joint Distribution Committee usually handled payments connected with the immigrants. However, by August its annual budget for this purpose was depleted and all immigration expenses would now fall on the Israeli government. Frantic, Eliezer Kaplan, the minister of finance, insisted that some way be found to restrict *aliyah* from Romania. He fiercely opposed paying more for the transport of the immigrants. Most of the others, however, recognized the risks involved in tampering with the current arrangements. Even Shapira, who in the past had joined Kaplan in calling for controlled immigration, agreed that in this instance it was too hazardous.

The debate revolved around cost. In August the Romanians raised their charge per passenger to ninety dollars. Israeli vessels could make the trip for one-third of that price, but the Romanians insisted on using their own ships. Kaplan and other members of the Jewish Agency Executive were indignant. Avraham Granott advised the Jewish Agency to stand firm: "The fear of stopping *aliyah* is not irrational, but the question is how far one should give in . . . We must not consent to blackmail," Granott said. Shapira disagreed with him, arguing that the state had no choice: "We must pay ransom," Shapira argued. "We are dealing with robbers. This is robbery in the disguise of a ticket."[41] Even though it might spell the end of emigration from Romania, Shapira favored negotiating with the Romanians. Golda Meir had harsh words for those who would turn them down:

"Before *aliyah* from Romania was permitted, we would never have gotten into such an argument . . . If the Jews of Russia were allowed to leave, Kaplan would not wrangle over population make-up, cost and so forth . . . The situation in Romania may soon be the same as in Russia." [42]

Surprisingly, Ben-Gurion was among those who felt Israel should not pay the higher price demanded by the Romanians. He was certain that they intended to halt emigration anyway, and that the monetary issue was only a camouflage. Nonetheless, he proposed the appointment of committee to study all aspects of *aliyah* from Romania, including a demographic profile of the *olim,* their age, working ability, marital status, etc. Ben-Gurion was particularly concerned about health. The spread of contagious diseases around this time had sparked panic in the Israeli public. Ben-Gurion was very much influenced by Dr. Haim Sheba, his appointee for the directorship of the Ministry of Health, who repeatedly warned him that Israel was being reckless in admitting *olim* without screening or supervision.

As the government and the Jewish Agency grappled with these questions, immigrants continued to stream into Israel from Poland. The exodus of Romanian Jewry was in full swing, and pressure began to mount from other countries, too. Just then, an astonishing development took place in Iraq.

Immigration from Iraq: Operation Ezra and Nehemiah

The bill to legalize Jewish emigration presented to the Iraqi parliament by Salah Jaber, the minister of the interior, in early March 1950 struck the Jewish community of Iraq like a thunderbolt. The Jews could hardly contain their excitement.

Of all the Arab countries, Iraq was the most belligerent toward Israel and the only one that had refused to sign a cease-fire agreement after the War of Independence. Thus, the sudden move to allow the Jews to leave was suspect to many eyes. As Shlomo Hillel, then a Mosad operative in Iraq, wrote years later: "At the time, we did not know if it was a conspiracy, or a show of goodwill, or if they wanted to arrest Jews who declared their intention to emigrate." [43]

In Israel, too, there was much bewilderment and speculation about possible motives. One was that Iraq had been unable to suppress illegal emigration. Thousands of Jewish families had secretly crossed the border to Iran and the number continued to grow throughout 1949. Between October 1949 and February 1950, thousands of Iraqi Jews reached Israel in this manner.[44] Among those who escaped were wealthy citizens who managed to take their property with them. It was presumed that the Iraqi government was interested in legalizing Jewish emigration so that it could exercise greater control. The poor relations between Iraq and Iran, which took a turn for the worse in wake of the border crossings, were also thought to weigh heavily on the Iraqi government. Another theory was that Iraq had doubts about the loyalty of its Jews. Many supported the Zionist movement, and the Iraqis saw them as sowing opposition to the government. Moreover, many young Jews were active in the Communist underground. Among the motives attributed to Iraq were economic advantage, foreign-policy considerations, bowing to international pressure, and even a plot to flood Israel with tens of thousands of destitute Jews in order to hasten its economic collapse.[45]

The Jewish community itself was perplexed. Applying for emigration required automatic renunciation of Iraqi citizenship, and the exit routes were far from clear. Iraq was surrounded on all sides by Arab nations hostile to Israel. Iran, also a Muslim country, might well refuse to allow the passage of Jews through its territory. Just a few months earlier, the Iranian authorities had ordered all Iraqi Jews to leave Iran within three weeks. The Jews of Iraq were afraid that, if they gave up their citizenship and found no way to leave the country, they would become defenseless nonentities victimized by the government and the local populace.

It was difficult to predict the number of immigrants, and the Israelis were at a loss how to prepare for their arrival and absorption. Activists of Mossad le-Aliyah Bet in Iraq, who had done so much to encourage the pioneering underground and organize clandestine immigration, found themselves in a dilemma. The Iraqi government was pressing for the Jews to leave hastily, whereas the Mossad preferred to delay registration of the *olim* until travel arrangements had been made.[46]

Various alternatives were weighed in choosing an exit route. Traveling by railway to Turkey was one possibility, but the train passed through Syrian territory, which was problematic. Other options were buses through Jordan, or leaving via Basra or Abadan and continuing on through the Persian Gulf and the Suez Canal to Eilat. In the eyes of the Iraqi authorities, crossing the border to Iran was the best choice. However, the Iranians were loath to allow large groups of Jewish refugees to use their country as a transit point. They were also worried about the reaction of Muslim fundamentalists. Israeli emissaries feared that Iran might seal its borders while Iraqi Jews were still in the country. Mossad le-Aliyah Bet reported from Iran that the Joint Distribution Committee refused to enlarge its transit camp in Teheran until there was a definite route for the Jewish exodus from Iraq.

Another problem was saving Jewish property in Iraq, valued at approximately LP60 million. One suggestion was to establish a commercial enterprise in the guise of an international Iraqi-Turkish-American corporation that would liquidate and transfer assets. As this and other schemes were discussed, the Jews of Iraq hesitated to make plans and the emigration rate slowed. In February 1950, 1,030 persons left the country via Iran, whereas only 110 expressed an interest in doing so during the first week of March. Mossad le-Aliyah Bet reported that organized illegal emigration had also stopped and that Iraqi Jews were waiting to see how matters developed.[47]

The climate in Iraq did not allow them to remain idle for long. The Mossad told of political turmoil, diplomatic resignations, and demonstrations in the streets. The Iraqi newspaper *Istiqlal* called for the suspension of *aliyah* and a freeze on Jewish assets. Rioting broke out in a market selling Jewish merchandise, and real estate in Iraq dropped to 10 percent of its worth, scaring off potential buyers.[48] As tension mounted, conflicts were reported between Jews and Arabs in Basra and elsewhere. There were rumors that the Iraqi government planned to freeze property holdings and tighten customs at the border to prevent illegal crossings and smuggling of capital. The Jews of northern Iraq were forbidden to travel to the center or southward. At the news of massacres in Kurdistan, many Iraqi Jews took to their heels and fled to Teheran, where the synagogues were teeming with refugees. On 18 March 1950 the transit camp in Teheran was occupied by more than 1,400 Iraqi Jews, and hundreds more found shelter in private homes and hotels. The Iranian authorities, apprehensive about Muslim fundamentalists, ordered that the refugees be evacuated to a camp outside the capital.

While this was taking place, meetings were being held in Israel to estimate the number of Jews leaving Iraq and the rate at which they could be expected to arrive. According to the data in the hands of *aliyah* officials, the Iraqi Jewish community totaled 100,000–138,000 in Baghdad, 20,000 in Basra and the South, and 18,000 in the northern towns of Mossul and Kirkuk. About 10 percent were wealthy and most of the others were middle-class. All feared for their property, and only 150 registered for *aliyah* in the month after the passage of a law freezing Jewish assets. Nevertheless, contacts to procure the release of Iraqi Jewry continued.

Ben-Gurion insisted on a widespread campaign to register Iraqi Jews even before a settlement was reached on the matter of property. He argued that the Iraqis might have second thoughts and revoke their decision to free the Jews. In view of the wavering of the community, Ben-Gurion proposed that the young people and those without property be brought to Israel first. The Mossad in Iraq began to prod the Jews into preparing for departure.

The mood in Iraq changed swiftly. On 9 April 1950 a bomb was thrown into a Jewish café in Baghdad, injuring several patrons. Jews were assaulted and harassed in neighborhoods throughout the city. All at once, the number of applicants for *aliyah* surged. By mid-April, 23,372 Jews had signed up in Baghdad,

An immigrant from Kurdistan with her baby son, upon their arrival at the Lod Airport.
Photograph by Teddy Brauner

15,000 in Basra and environs, and 1,000 in the North—a total of 40,000 persons. To accelerate their departure, it was decided to organize an airlift. In early May, after feverish negotiations with airlines and government officials, an Iraqi company was commissioned to fly the *olim* to Cyprus and from there to Israel. Landing in Cyprus required the consent of the British, who governed the island; following contacts with London, permission was given.[49] On 21 May 1950 the first group of Iraqi immigrants reached Lod, marking the start of Operation Ezra and Nehemiah. At a press conference in Paris, the representative of the Joint Distribution Committee, Joseph Schwartz, called it the most massive airlift in history.

The number of Jews preparing to leave Iraq was estimated at between 60,000 and 100,000.[50] Once again, the debate over absorption reared its head. The newspapers covering the arrival of the first planes also ran stories about a polio epidemic that seemed to be spreading in the country. A headline in *Yediot Aharonot* read "The Shavuot holiday—under the shadow of polio."[51] All kindergarten and school parties were canceled, and some children reportedly died of the disease. It was rumored that an outbreak had begun in the immigrant camps.[52] Public attention was thus drawn to conditions in these camps and the immigrants who continued to pour in. The Jewish Agency called for strict medical screening of all the *olim*, including Iraqi Jews. This fact enraged the emissaries in Iraq; they claimed that Israel had promised to admit all members of the Iraqi Jewish community without exception. Eliezer Kaplan was one of the leading advocates of quotas and medical supervision, but even he agreed that no restrictions whatsoever should be imposed on immigration from Iraq.

In June 1950 the number of arrivals was still small—2,000 at most. After the decision to fly the immigrants to Israel, the volume was expected to increase. In July the response was somewhat greater—3,500—and in August it reached 2,500, as well as several thousand more who made their way via Teheran. From the onset of legal emigration, a total of 10,000 Jews had left Iraq. The figures began to pick up toward the end of the summer. The Iraqi government was pressing for the Jews to depart more quickly, and the authorities in Israel were asked to make the necessary arrangements. At the same time, the Romanians stepped up their demands, placing Israel in a position where it hardly knew where to direct its energies. Both the government and the Jewish Agency were inclined to give priority to immigration from Iraq on the assumption that those who remained in Iraq were in greater danger.

As the Iraqi government's March 1951 deadline approached, the Jews made a final dash to leave. On 10 March the Iraqi parliament in Baghdad passed a law freezing the assets of Jews who had renounced their Iraqi citizenship, of whom there were 103,866 at the time. The tension in the Jewish community rose to new heights. The law encompassed all Jewish property, including shop merchandise and bank accounts. The government also ordered the dismissal of bank clerks and other employees who had applied for *aliyah*. The atmosphere described by the Mossad was ominous: "After the passage of the law, banks closed and Jewish proprietors were forbidden to open their shops. The police seized any Jew walking in the street with a suitcase or package . . . The law hurts tens of thousands of Jews who have not yet liquidated their businesses. Great sums of money have been frozen in the banks. Jewish bank holdings in Iraq were valued at over one million dinars."[53]

Thereafter, the situation of the Jews deteriorated rapidly. The Mossad filed this report:

> Following the closure of all the shops by the police, the Jews have been forced to
> buy food, including meat, from Arab shops. The police have raided goldsmith

shops and homes where goods or gold might be found. Today, all cars belonging to Jews were confiscated. Many Jews whose ticket money was deposited in the bank or left with moneychangers, are now penniless. Families have been found who do not have enough money to survive. These Jews are knocking on the camp gates, pleading to be taken to Israel without charge. Such a crisis has never been known here. The police displays its barbarity with every arrest or search . . . These days are being treated by the Arab public and the press as a great national holiday.[54]

There was no more time for delays, either by the Jewish Agency or by Iraqi Jews trying to salvage their property. The Jewish Agency resolved to bring over as many immigrants as possible within the allotted period. A hurried, large-scale undertaking was all the more difficult in view of the announcement from Romania that the SS *Transylvania* would be doubling the number of trips to Israel as of 1 April. It would sail four times a month, carrying 2,000 passengers each time, i.e. a monthly total of 8,000 immigrants. Josephthal, who had visions of the utter collapse of the absorption network, protested. If the rate from Iraq was 25,000 a month, he said, the number of Romanian immigrants must be halved. Even then, the figures were twice as high as the original plan. Eshkol and Kaplan agreed with Josephthal, in spite of Sharett's warnings that any modification might lead to a complete halt in emigration from Romania.[55] In April 1951 the mass exodus of Iraqi Jews reached a peak of nearly 22,000 persons, bearing in mind that Israel's immigration total for that month was 30,000 from all countries. Efforts were under way to persuade the Iraqi leadership to stretch the deadline, but rumors circulated that the date would not be extended beyond the end of May. Some of the remaining Jews panicked and fled the country illegally, registering for *aliyah* in Iran.[56] In May, 18,000 Iraqi Jews reached Israel. That month, a synagogue was bombed; fortunately, no one was hurt. A notice in the newspapers designated 18 July 1951 as the last date for Jewish emigration from Iraq. The Mossad implored the authorities to get all the planes ready for the final airlift. Of the 20,000 applicants for *aliyah,* 15,000 left in June and the remainder in the weeks that followed. By the end of June, a total of 103,000 Iraqi Jews had departed for Israel. During the period from January to July 1951, the total of immigration from all countries was 128,000, of which two-thirds was from Iraq.

None of the features of this wave of *aliyah* were determined in advance. Permission to emigrate was achieved through the labor of dozens Jewish Agency and government emissaries who begged and bribed the leadership of various countries to let their Jews go. The response, which was far beyond expectations, and the coincidental timing, which led to a mass exodus from several countries simultaneously, placed Israel's policymakers and executive agencies in an unenviable position. They were forced to choose between overloading the absorption network and risking its total collapse, or obstructing the free flow of immigration. Amid conflicting pressures, the government and the Jewish Agency were called upon to reach a decision without delay. A further dilemma was whether to give preference to those countries where the Jews or the future of *aliyah* were in the greatest jeopardy, or to impose restrictions equally on immigration from all countries. The Arab and Communist regimes set a deadline for Jewish emigration, and slowing the pace was certain to pass sentence on some who desired to leave. One option remained: to cope with the absorption problems at home as well as one could—a mission that seemed virtually impossible considering the lack of basic resources and the financial crisis which plagued the country. The manner in which the immigration enterprise progressed was thus determined, not by a coherent policy, but by constraints from within and without. This left the field wide open to the activists, who proceeded as they saw fit, often in contradiction to the decisions of the Israeli authorities.

A Nation of Camps

For many, the epoch of the great homecoming was a bitter joke. The masses of immigrants were taken to camps where tens of thousands were crowded together in makeshift housing. These camps and the *ma'abarot* that came after them were seen as a symbol of Israel's failed immigration policy. Newspapers in Israel and abroad wrote of a nation of camps, bringing back memories of the DP camps in Europe. A journalist wrote to Ben-Gurion: "From a historical standpoint, the camps in Israel must be one of the most ironic failures in the world. Jews running camps for Jews. And it seems that they have learned nothing from their own tragedy." [57] The flood of immigration, which commenced in the summer of 1948 and continued with even greater force in 1949 and 1950, was channeled into transit camps at the country's gateways. These camps were established by the Jewish Agency as a stopgap until permanent housing could be found for the newcomers. At first, the absorption authorities used converted British army camps. When these were full, additional camps were built using whatever materials were available. The *olim* were quartered in wooden and tin shacks, tents, and canvas-walled huts. The population of these camps grew steadily; by the end of 1949, it was close to one hundred thousand. The amount of time spent there also lengthened to several months. The hardship was great. As 1949 drew to a close, Israel's absorption network was on the verge of collapse.

Immigrant Hostels

Before the founding of the State of Israel, no infrastructure existed for the absorption of large numbers of immigrants, and there was no time to address the problem after the outbreak of the War of Independence. Most of the *olim* who came in the Mandatory period, including the large waves of immigration in the 1920s and 1930s (the Fourth and Fifth Aliyah), were absorbed directly into the *Yishuv*. Some were assisted in finding housing and work by the movements to which they belonged. The majority, however, relied on family and friends or managed on their own. Those with money or a needed occupation obviously integrated with greater speed and ease. For others the process was more arduous, but the Jewish Agency handled only a small proportion of them.

During the prestate years, there was little public housing for *olim*. In the 1940s, when shiploads of penniless Holocaust survivors began to arrive, primitive hostels were set up to accommodate them. It was discovered that many of the newcomers required medical attention in addition to employment and housing assistance. In 1946, 1947, and especially 1948, more hostels were opened to meet the growing demand. By the time Israel declared independence, twelve such institutions were in operation.[58] These were run by the Jewish Agency's Absorption Division, which had offices in Jerusalem, Tel Aviv, and Haifa. From early 1948 until the establishment of the state, sixteen thousand immigrants reached Israel's shores, most of whom stayed at these hostels for a few days until they were assigned permanent housing.[59] In May 1948 there were nearly seven thousand persons in residence.[60]

After the establishment of the state, the absorption of new immigrants became increasingly difficult. The housing shortage was already evident during the Mandate, but now overcrowding was so severe that many *olim* remained homeless.

Immigrant Camps

Israel's immigrant camp period, which lasted from the establishment of the state until the end of 1949, may be divided into three stages: the first and least troublesome, from May 1948 to August 1948; the second, from September 1948 to March 1949, characterized by population growth and a progressively longer stay; and the third, from April 1949 until the year's end, when conditions turned catastrophic.

Throughout this period, the immigrants found themselves entangled in a web of problems and contradictions from which they were unable to emerge without assistance. No less devastating than the physical hardships they were forced to endure was the sense of dependence and humiliation. Absorption officials stood helpless before the mountain of problems piling up. The manner in which the *olim* responded and tried to fight the obstacles in their path contributed to their eventual place in Israeli society.

May–August 1948

The major problem confronting the Israeli absorption network was the shortage of housing. The country's few immigrant hostels filled up quickly, and newcomers were sent to British army camps, some purchased from the Mandatory authorities and others abandoned when the British departed. These camps were hardly suitable for immigrant absorption. On leaving, the soldiers had vandalized whatever they could. Furniture, windows, and doors had been smashed, and the buildings themselves were damaged.[61] Because of the pressure of immigration and the lack of resources, only the most essential repairs were made.

When a cease-fire was declared in July 1948, a huge tide of immigrants swept into the country—more than seventeen thousand all at once, including ten thousand women, children, and elderly released from detention in Cyprus. Two camps were set up in Pardess Hannah, each one capable of handling 3,000 persons. Another camp in Binyamina could absorb sixteen hundred, and the Agrobank camp near Hadera could take fifteen hundred. Many of the younger immigrants joined the army as soon as they arrived; others found a niche in the towns and cities. In the sphere of employment, this wave of *aliyah* was also fortunate: most army-age men had been drafted and jobs were readily available on the civilian market. The majority of *olim* during this period were employable adults.[62] They had relatively little trouble finding lodgings, either through relatives or on their own. Those who had been trained as pioneers in their home countries settled on kibbutzim, and others took up residence in Arab neighborhoods abandoned during the war. At the time, the length of stay at immigrant camps was short—only a few days—and the high turnover enabled the absorption of large numbers of people. But as *aliyah* increased in volume, the situation became more difficult. Available housing ran out, a change took place in the immigrants' family makeup, and the economy deteriorated. As a result, the immigrants were forced to remain in camps for longer intervals.[63]

September 1948–March 1949

The Zionist Actions Committee's resolution to reorganize the immigration and absorption network of the Jewish Agency went into effect in September 1948. The Kelitah Department was separated from the Aliyah Department and began to make arrangements for absorbing large groups of immigrants from different countries, most arriving by sea and a small number by air.[64] This period can be subdivided as follows:

• (a) September–December 1948: The number of immigrants doubled, reaching a total of seventy thousand within the span of four months. The time spent at immigrant camps was still relatively brief. The government had called for the neighborhoods and villages abandoned by the Arabs to be repopulated by Jews, and most of the *olim* of 1948 were referred to these areas.[65] The Kelitah Department, which had control of all the buildings, shops, and factories, set about repairing and adapting them for the use of *olim* with the help of the Jewish Agency's Technical Department. The Central Housing Committee operated by the Kelitah Department sent immigrants to former Arab neighborhoods throughout the country: first to Jaffa, lower Haifa, and parts of Safed and Tiberias; then to Ramleh, Lod, and the surrounding villages; and later, following the conquest of the South, to Beersheba, Migdal Gad, and other areas.

Because of the rush of immigration toward the end of 1948, the stopover at the camps became longer than it had been previously, but still no more than three or four weeks. Only twenty-eight thousand of the one hundred thousand immigrants who passed through were still there at the year's end. Bearing in mind that most of these people had emerged not long ago from concentration and DP camps in Europe, great efforts were made to keep their stay in camps as short as possible. Many families from eastern countries were prepared to accept dilapidated housing rather than remain in the camps. Thus candidates were found to populate neglected neighborhoods in Jaffa, Lod, Haifa, and on the outskirts of Tel Aviv. The winter of 1948–49 was a particularly harsh one. The rainstorms and fierce winds caused landslides around the country, resulting in the loss of lives and property. Once again, attention was drawn to the plight of the immigrants. The newspapers were full of articles on the subject, and discussion panels were organized to involve the public in immigrant absorption.

At the beginning of 1949, when nearly all the vacant buildings had been occupied, the housing crisis deepened. Levi Eshkol, head of the Jewish Agency's Settlement Department, tried to promote a major waterworks program and other schemes dependent on the referral of *olim* to agriculture. A few months before he had recommended the establishment of encampments near veteran farm settlements, enabling interested immigrants to be trained as farmers.[66] This was an early version of the transit or work camp advocated by Eshkol, an idea which was adopted the following year and which produced the *ma'abara* in its first configuration. At this stage, no one imagined that the *ma'abara* would develop as it did and become such a central feature in the absorption process. Eshkol also envisaged the founding of new centers populated by a suitable number of *olim* who would be taught farm skills by instructors from the older settlements, with the aim of turning these centers into a permanent home for the *olim*.[67] This was the principle of the *moshav olim,* which soon became part of the Israeli landscape.

• (b) January–March 1949: Throngs of immigrants continued to arrive, filling the camps far beyond capacity. More camps were urgently needed. These were built with the utmost haste in the realization that controlling *aliyah* was not to be. The flow, as we have said, was largely dictated by unforeseen developments that made advance preparation impossible.

On 18 January 1949 the British colonial authorities suddenly unlocked the gates of the refugee camps on Cyprus, setting free ten thousand Jews who had been anxiously waiting to immigrate. *Aliyah* also continued from other countries, bringing one thousand newcomers a day. In its report to the 23rd Zionist Congress, the Kelitah Department wrote: "This was the beginning of the liquidation of the Bulgarian and Yugoslavian diasporas. Day in and day out, ships docked in Haifa, bringing entire communities ashore. Everyone came—old and young, sound and infirm. Not only those in good health and fit for work were brought over, but also [the inmates of] hospitals, old-age homes and mental institutions. Everything was dismantled and shipped to Israel."[68]

New camps opened and the older ones became more and more cramped. In March the number of *olim* exceeded one thousand a day. The roads from Haifa were clogged with vehicles coming from all over the country to transport newcomers to the immigrant camps.[69]

In spite of the obstacles, 190,000 Jews made their way to Israel between May 1948 and the end of March 1949; 45,000 of them (less than one-quarter of the total) remained in immigrant camps. Many of the others settled in Arab neighborhoods and villages that had been deserted during the war. From September 1948 until April 1949, the Kelitah Department set up sixteen camps and its employee roster grew to 1,560 persons, in addition to medical and social staff.

Camp Life

The immigrant camps were located in the center of the country, which invariably affected the subsequent stages of absorption. They were mainly clustered in three areas. The largest cluster, in Pardess Hannah, was made up of four camps with a population of 15,000. Next came Be'er Yaakov with three camps and a population of 10,000, and then three more near Hadera (Agrobank, Neve Haim, and Brandeis) with a population of 6,500. Sizeable camps also operated in the Haifa suburbs, Atlit, Netanya, Binyamina, Ra'anana, Beit Lid, and Rehovot.[70] In all, there were twenty-three immigrant camps in March 1949, not including Sha'ar ha-Aliyah, a reception center established later that month and already holding 4,000 *olim* in April.

Living standards deteriorated by the month. Although new camps were opened, the authorities could not keep up with the demand. Tents and huts were added as needed, using every inch of space.[71] The length of time spent at the camps also increased, from an average of four to six weeks at the end of 1948 to twelve weeks and more in April 1949. In order to facilitate the preparation and serving of meals, keep the food fresher, and cut labor costs, the Kelitah Department built large dining halls in each camp that could accommodate hundreds of diners at once. In Pardess Hannah, a giant kitchen was set up to feed 25,000 *olim* a day. The immigrants were dissatisfied with this arrangement. Outbursts of anger and protest were caused by food that was not to the immigrants' liking. Many refused to eat in the communal dining hall, preferring the privacy of their tents. The result was chaos, which the camp directors were helpless to control.

The suffering was worst in the winter. Living in tents and exposed to driving wind and rain, the immigrants were constantly ill; their misery was compounded by the shortage of medical staff. As time passed, they began to vent their rage through noisy protests, hunger strikes, and demonstrations outside the Jewish Agency offices.

Sha'ar ha-Aliyah

In an effort to make absorption procedures more efficient and take some of the pressure off the camps, a plan was devised (in January 1949) to screen the immigrants for health problems as soon as they landed in Israel. Straight off the boat, all the newcomers would be taken to a reception center in groups of four thousand to five thousand. There they would undergo registration and medical examinations and would be directed onward—the sick to hospitals and the sound to immigrant camps or other housing.

New immigrants and their belongings waiting for the first arrangements after arriving at the Sha'ar ha-Aliyah camp, near Haifa. *Photograph by Zoltan Kluger*

The site chosen was a former British army camp dating from World War II on the southern outskirts of Haifa. The reception center, known as Sha'ar ha-Aliyah (Gateway to Aliyah), could accommodate three thousand persons (four thousand under less favorable conditions). The absorption authorities prepared tents in case the number of arrivals was higher. Sha'ar ha-Aliyah opened its gates on 14 March and immediately received a shipload of immigrants. This was a peak month for *aliyah,* with more than one thousand newcomers landing daily. The scene at Sha'ar ha-Aliyah was described as follows: "The *olim* scurried from place to place, hopping from one line to the next, from the medical screening board to Kupat Holim and on to the baggage warehouse." [72]

The underlying idea seemed logical enough. The absorption authorities had visions of *olim* stopping at Sha'ar ha-Aliyah for two or three days, undergoing checkups, and being sent on. Then, supposedly, another group would be brought in and the cycle would begin over again. However, the gap between theory and reality was wide. Due to the lack of available housing and the serious overcrowding in the immigrant camps, the *olim* stayed at Sha'ar ha-Aliyah far longer than anticipated and new contingents arrived daily. Sometimes thou-

Newly arrived immigrants line up for lunch at the dining hall of the Sha'ar ha-Aliyah camp, near Haifa. *Photograph by Teddy Brauner*

sands descended on the camp in a single day. On 11 April the director of Sha'ar ha-Aliyah wrote in his diary:

> Four ships came in today and all 5,340 passengers were sent to Sha'ar ha-Aliyah. The first 300, who sailed with the SS *Eilat* from Italy, arrived at noon. At the same time, the area began to fill with trucks and automobiles spouting people and baggage. Kalman informed me by telephone that these were the 3,850 passengers of the SS *Bulgaria* . . . Towards evening, another 350 *olim* arrived from North Africa . . . In the midst of all the noise and bedlam, 878 *olim* from France came knocking. A mad day. We have never had one like it. A record for *aliyah*. What if this tempo continues? . . . All of them have to be fed; all have to be put up in cabins and tents; all need blankets and bedding. Everything must be on file. How can one work under such pressure? All day long, the lines stretched over kilometers.[73]

The following week Israel had to cope with another 9,307 immigrants. Gone were the dreams of a quick, orderly absorption. Thousands of families huddled together at Sha'ar ha-Aliyah for weeks and months with nowhere to go. The congestion was such that it was impossible to maintain basic hygiene. According to the testimony of the camp director, the place swarmed with mosquitoes, flies, mice, and rats. The cesspools of the toilets and showers overflowed, and the dining hall was thick with grime.[74] Thus, instead of easing the suffering of the immigrants and streamlining their absorption, Sha'ar ha-Aliyah exacerbated the problem:

> The *olim* were locked behind barbed wire with armed policemen on guard. At times, overcrowding in the wooden shacks and stone barracks left behind by the British army reached the point of cruelty. Three times a day they stood in long lines just to receive their food rations. The queues for health and customs services trailed on for kilometers. The *olim* often waited hours for a turn in the showers . . . The water supply was not always sufficient. There were frequent power shortages, and at night, the camp was enveloped in darkness.[75]

Among the newcomers were hundreds of children who had lost their parents in the Holocaust. They arrived exhausted and frightened, and many of them were ill. But circumstances at Sha'ar ha-Aliyah were such that little could be done to relieve their discomfort.

April–October 1949

When the introduction of a reception center failed to improve matters, the authorities concluded that only a cutback would solve the problem. Beginning in April it seemed that immigration had indeed begun to slow down and a steady drop was noted in new arrivals. Perhaps the calls to stem the flow had finally made an impact on the emissaries, or maybe the immigrants were responding to rumors of economic recession in Israel. In any case, the lull lasted only a few months. In the summer the tide of immigration resumed as Jews were airlifted from Yemen. Conditions in the camps grew worse, and the chronic housing shortage kept people there for increasingly long periods. Even the hasty establishment of more camps could not satisfy the tremendous need.

Tempering the enthusiastic press coverage of the exotic *aliyah* from Yemen were the Kelitah Department's reports of life-threatening tropical diseases and children suffering from severe malnutrition.[76] As the Yemenites flooded the country, the department rushed to establish special camps for them. Facilities for 5,000 were built in Pardessyah near Beit Lid, and another site was opened in Rosh Ha'ayin. By October the population of camps reached 92,500 immigrants, with 2,000 more Yemenite *olim* waiting to be flown in from Aden. Then came

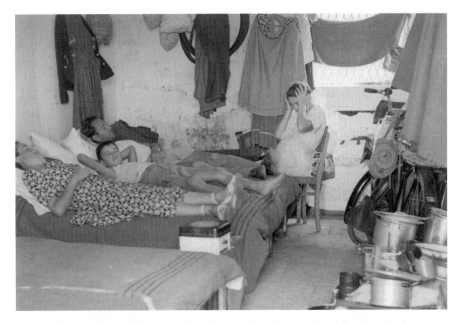

An immigrant family rests in the corner of their hut at the Sha'ar ha-Aliyah camp, near Haifa. *Photograph by Zoltan Kluger*

the unexpected announcement of the Polish government. The absorption authorities were overwhelmed. By their own admission they were able to move out of the camps only one-third of the number of immigrants coming in.[77] There was no doubt that emergency measures were needed.

Work Camps

In October 1949 the Kelitah Department decided to turn its absorption facilities into work camps. Practically speaking, this meant closing the kitchens and making the immigrants responsible for their own livelihood. They could live in the camps until they found substitute housing, and only the sick and disabled who were unable to work would receive food.

The first steps in implementing this decision were taken in November. The kitchen in Kiryat Shmuel, which fed 1,000 persons, ceased to operate, and other camps followed suit.[78] By the end of the month, the Jewish Agency claimed the number of immigrants in its camps was down by 5,400. In fact, the population remained the same; the Jewish Agency was reporting only those who required food and services, and this population dwindled as the public kitchens closed.

The immigrants from Poland who arrived in November were sent to a new camp, Mahaneh Yisrael, and the Yemenite Jews of Operation Magic Carpet went to Ein Shemer—another new facility. In December thousands more came to Israel, but the Jewish Agency widened the circle of camps without meal programs. The number of dependents thus dropped to 78,000.

The next step was to transfer all the sick, disabled, and elderly who could not support themselves or their families to special camps offering a full range of services, including food. Some of the former camps were shut down and others were reorganized.

The term "work camp" was ironic because no jobs were offered to the immigrants who continued to live there. These camps did not solve the problem of housing or employment, nor they did open the door to new opportunities. All in all, the immigrants fared no better than before. These camps were essentially created to reduce the huge deficit of the absorption network: by eliminating the food budget, an enormous sum of money was saved. Outwardly, the Jewish Agency spoke of social and educational goals such as expunging idleness and encouraging a more constructive way of life. Working would bring about a material improvement of the immigrants' lot and lessen the emotional distress connected with accepting charity. However, it was no secret that the job market was in a slump. The immigrants sat idle through no fault of their own, and the work camps provided no solution. In a familiar scenario, each body tried to thrust responsibility for immigrant absorption on someone else. The Jewish Agency attempted to unload the burden on the government, the municipalities, the labor collectives, etc. The older settlements demanded that the Jewish Agency cover their expenses in this sector, but the Jewish Agency itself was floundering and determined to narrow its deficit. From all sides, the influx of immigration was blamed for plunging the country into crisis. The absorption authorities struggled desperately to stay afloat, but the deluge of immigrants and the resources to absorb them were beyond their control. The financial deadlock worsened and posed a threat to the entire system.

CHAPTER THREE

Financial Crisis and Policy Implications

THE MOST PRESSING PROBLEM facing the absorption network was shortage of money. The Jewish Agency was in serious debt, government coffers were empty, and no alternative sources of capital were available. This was the greatest obstacle to the continuation of immigration; as a result, the future of the entire enterprise hung in the balance. Much of the friction and debate over Israel's immigration policy was triggered by the acute financial situation.

The economic troubles of the Jewish community had begun before Israel's independence. The UN partition plan of November 1947 had called for two states within the borders of Palestine, one Jewish and the other Arab, which were supposed to cooperate economically and use a common currency. The fierce opposition of the Arabs to such a scheme and the conflict with the British during the weeks before the termination of the Mandate led to mounting tension that also affected the economy. The British declaration in February 1948 that Palestine was excluded from the sterling bloc was part of a deliberate policy to create chaos and leave the Yishuv in a state of disarray. The handing over of public utilities such as postal services, telephones, ports, and railways to Jewish authorities was not executed in an orderly fashion. The transfer was to be done in stages in keeping with the pace of British withdrawal, but no timetable was provided and the Yishuv was unable to prepare ahead of time for the supply of vital services. The biggest threat to economic stability, however, was the introduction of a new currency.

For the exchange system to run smoothly and efficiently, it was imperative that the public put its trust in the new currency; otherwise, the whole system could go awry and produce a state of economic anarchy. With proper financial legislation, problems were avoidable. However, it was wartime and Israel's leaders had not a moment to spare for even the most burning economic matters. On 16 August 1948, the Anglo-Palestine Bank was charged with issuing the new currency. Later the Bank of Israel took over its duties, which included minting notes and coins and determining the exchange rate of the Israeli pound. Only after the second cease-fire did the government have time to formalize its arrangements with the Anglo-Palestine Bank.[1]

The Israeli public showed trust in the new currency, but the war effort strained the economy to the breaking point. The government had no choice but to print money, a measure that threatened the country with spiraling inflation. Nor did the problems end there. Foreign currency needed to purchase weapons and military equipment, finance *aliyah,* and pay for wheat, fuel, and raw materials was always in short supply. The reserves dropped so low that the government feared being unable to meet its financial obligations and losing credibility in the eyes of countries with whom it did business. One of these countries was Czechoslovakia, a major arms supplier during the critical days of the War of Independence. Israel owed Czechoslovakia millions of pounds, and only days before the debt came due the treasury ran dry. Moreover, the war was not over yet, one-sixth of the population had been drafted, thousands of *olim* were arriving each day, and tens of thousands more were anticipated.

Throughout the summer and fall of 1948, the government wrestled with its financial woes and the situation appeared hopeless. Two potential sources of foreign currency were overseas loans and Jewish fund-raising, but neither was guaranteed. Obtaining loans in Europe was problematic because these countries were themselves in the middle of post-war financial recovery. Israel thus looked toward the United States, where a presidential campaign was going on, in the hope that the Jewish lobby would be able to extract promises of a substantial loan. The United Jewish Appeal in America was another source of funding. However, the organization had been hurt by internal disagreements in the summer of 1948, and its fund-raising efforts had suffered. For Eliezer Kaplan, the United Jewish Appeal represented Israel's last hope, but the government could only sit by and wait.

United Jewish Appeal in Conflict

The confrontation in the United Jewish Appeal pitted Abba Hillel Silver and his trusted friend, Emanuel Neumann, against Henry Montor, who enjoyed the backing of the non-Zionist organizations, which were prepared to collaborate, mainly in the sphere of *aliyah.* The confrontation developed into a battle over status and power that was deepened by bitter personal rivalry.

Abba Hillel Silver, a Reform rabbi and brilliant orator, had been a leading figure in the American Zionist movement since the 1920s and 1930s. A firm believer in political activism, he persuaded the American Jewish Conference, the first representative body of all American Jewry since World War I, to come out on behalf of a Jewish commonwealth in Palestine in 1943, at a time when many American Jewish organizations were not openly Zionist. As president of the Zionist Organization of America (1945–48), he struggled to win American support for a Jewish national home, and when the issue was brought before the United Nations in November 1947 he served as spokesman of the Jewish Agency. After Israel's independence, he became chairman of the American Section of the Jewish Agency, while Emanuel Neumann took over the presidency of the Zionist Organization of America.[2]

Heading the opposition camp was Henry Montor, general director of the United Palestine Appeal, who enjoyed the support of Henry Morgenthau Jr., secretary of the United States Treasury from 1934 to 1945. Morgenthau was a non-Zionist who developed an interest in Israel and tried to assist the country financially. The conflict between Silver and Montor was over control of the monies raised by the United Jewish Appeal,[3] although disagreements of this sort had been plaguing the organization for years.[4] Silver insisted on making all decisions regarding allocation of funding; Montor argued that some of the donors did not identify with the Zionist Organization and would object to having part of their money spent on its operations in the United States. He maintained that such contributions should be transferred directly to the Jewish Agency in Israel, and this body would decide on their distribution. There was also opposition to Silver's reorganization proposals for the United Jewish Appeal (two-thirds of the executive would be representatives of Keren ha-Yesod and the Jewish National Fund, with the remaining third, non-Zionists). Montor resigned in protest, an action that seriously impaired the success of subsequent fund-raising drives. In many respects this conflict echoed the political rivalry between General Zionists and the Labor movement in Israel as they fought for positions in the Zionist executive. The Israeli government and the Zionist executive were disturbed by the quarreling in America. Kaplan and David Ben-Gurion, together with the bulk of the Zionist executive, were inclined to agree with Montor and Morgenthau. However, they could not impose their opinion on Silver. It was an American affair, Silver said, and Israel had no right to intervene. As the battles in the Negev raged, Ben-Gurion found time to meet with Morgenthau, who was visiting Israel, and asked him to mobilize more funds. Morgenthau responded that he was interested in helping the government but that "the three rabbis [Rabbi Stephen Wise, Rabbi Silver, and Rabbi Israel Goldstein] are a hindrance." He claimed that, of the 25,000 donors who supplied 90 percent of the contributions, perhaps 3,000 were Zionists.[5]

Morgenthau admitted that, while he did not call himself a Zionist, Israel's achievements and victories had strengthened the status of Jews in America, and he was therefore prepared to raise funds to bolster the army and *aliyah*. Above all, he wished to eradicate the DP camps, which he claimed were fodder for America's anti-Semites. Morgenthau made it clear that, if United Jewish Appeal funding was used for any purpose other than defense and immigration, his support would be withdrawn. There were many who wanted to see him appointed chairman of the United Jewish Appeal, but Morgenthau refused unless all the money collected by the organization was sent straight to the Jewish Agency without the intervention of the Zionist Organization of America. Silver saw this as a grievous blow to his authority.

Ben-Gurion's clash with the American Zionists, who hungered for an active part in the Israeli government, also crept into the present conflict. Ben-Gurion held that "a state is a sovereign entity which cannot be limited by any outside force." [6] He also bore a grudge against Silver for demanding that certain departments of the Jewish Agency be moved to the United States. [7] The leaders of the Zionist Organization of America, whose political role had diminished after Israel's independence, felt that they should at least have control over the manner in which contributions were spent; this would allow them some measure of influence in Israel. But Ben-Gurion refused to let this happen. His position in the United Jewish Appeal controversy was thus shaped by his attitude toward the American Zionists in general and his interest in strengthening the bond between non-Zionists and the settlement enterprise. [8]

The leaders of the non-Zionist organizations, wealthy capitalists with great influence in American government circles, worried that their identification with Israel would affect their status and undermine their credibility as loyal citizens of the United States. Ben-Gurion hoped that through Morgenthau he could draw them closer to the Jewish state. The two men met repeatedly, even during the fierce battle for Jerusalem, as Ben-Gurion tried to impress upon Morgenthau the importance of increasing financial support and preserving the unity of American Jewry.

Morgenthau's idea of establishing another fund-raising organization was not welcomed by Ben-Gurion. As Ben-Gurion explained, Zionism had previously relied on European Jewry, which no longer existed. The future of the Jews was now dependent on two groups—the Jewish communities of Israel and America. In his diary he wrote, "The establishment of the state and the victory of the Israeli army have unified American Jewry. The damage, internal and external, will be very great if they separate now." [9]

But the infighting in the United Jewish Appeal persisted and its revenues dropped. The Jewish Agency could not meet its obligations in the spheres of immigration and absorption. As the deficit increased, the inhabitants of the immigrant camps were denied even the most basic services. The United Jewish Appeal dispute and its implications for the absorption network in Israel were frequently mentioned at meetings of the Zionist executive and the Israeli government.[10] The dearth of funding affected the stand taken by these bodies on the continuation of *aliyah* and was cited by those who called for restrictions. In February 1949 members of the Zionist executive flew to New York in the hope of settling the disagreement among the directors of the United Jewish Appeal. At the end of a stormy debate, the vote was to allow Montor and Morgenthau to continue their activity. Silver resigned in protest from the chairmanship of the American Section of the Jewish Agency and Neumann from the United Jewish Appeal executive.[11]

Budgetary Deficits Versus Mass Immigration

As the volume of *aliyah* mounted, the financial distress of the Jewish Agency mounted, too. The Jewish Agency budget proposal for October 1948-September 1949 was based on an approximate income of IL 32 million from Keren ha-Yesod, the Jewish National Fund, various fund-raising drives, and loans. Its actual expenditure from October through March was close to IL 15 million, whereas the incoming sums during this period reached only IL 10 million. The largest budgetary allocation—IL 5 million—was to the Kelitah Department for the upkeep of the immigrant camps. In fact, 96 percent of Jewish Agency spending was on immigration and absorption. Reporting to the Zionist Actions Committee, the Jewish Agency's Finance Department emphasized that the outlay for *aliyah* had grown to the point where it was out of control. The needs of the departments were so urgent that they could not be ignored, regardless of whether the Jewish Agency had enough revenue.[12]

At the end of its first fiscal year (March 1949), the deficit of the Jewish Agency was more than IL 16 million, with expenditures exceeding revenue by 40 percent.[13] The sums owed to banks steadily swelled. In reality, the problem was much worse. The Kelitah Department was forced to operate on an empty budget, constantly searching for sources of temporary funding such as loans to be paid off with the money it hoped to receive. Food suppliers threatened to stop deliveries to the camp kitchens, which fed tens of thousands of immigrants. Costs grew higher as these suppliers, who worked on credit, raised their prices yet delivered low-grade merchandise.

A certain amount of responsibility for the maze of fiscal problems facing the Jewish Agency was attributable to the persons in charge of its financial operation. When duties were divided between the government and the Jewish Agency in August 1948, the ministers serving on the executive were asked to step down, thereby divesting this body of much of its power. Eliezer Kaplan, the Jewish Agency treasurer, was a strong figure who had dealt with finances for years and was highly influential in the Jewish Agency and the United Jewish Appeal. His appointment as minister of finance increased his authority all the more. Like the other cabinet members, he resigned as treasurer of the Jewish Agency in September, and it was thought that Levi Eshkol, an expert in financial management and a man of action, would take his place. However, Ben-Gurion preferred to appoint Eshkol as head of the Settlement Department, a department he considered central to the *aliyah* enterprise. The finance portfolio was then claimed by the General Zionists, who elected Israel Goldstein, a member of the Jewish Agency Executive in America.

Goldstein was not able to cope with the Jewish Agency's severe financial problems. Government and bank loans were obtained, but the Agency could not pay them back. As budgetary demands grew, The Jewish Agency only sank deeper in debt. Goldstein returned to the United States in August 1949 after serving one year as treasurer. His successor was Yitzhak Gruenbaum, a forceful man unafraid of controversy. Nevertheless, he, too, stayed on for only a short time. His proposals for slashing the deficit aroused fierce opposition in the Zionist executive and, in a moment of passion, he resigned. Although he lacked the qualifications, Berl Locker, chairman of the executive, took over temporarily until a suitable candidate could be found.[14] Meanwhile, the deficit continued to grow.

Negotiations with the Joint Distribution Committee

One proposal for extricating the Jewish Agency from its financial straits was to join forces with the Joint Distribution Committee. In view of the Agency's strained relations with non-Zionist organizations in the United States, many were understandably suspicious of such an arrangement. The plan was to ask the Joint Distribution Committee to finance the care of the sick and elderly. The very idea set off a loud debate in the Jewish Agency and government circles.

Even Berl Locker, who was in charge of the negotiations, was uncomfortable about bringing in the Joint Distribution Committee; his concern was that it would attempt to intervene in the absorption process. As a countermeasure, it was proposed that the JDC operate in partnership with the government and the Jewish Agency rather than independently. The JDC would cover half the expenses, although it would be represented on the boards of the institutions in the same one-third ratio as the Jewish Agency and the government, to insure that it did not work at cross-purposes with the government. Finance Minister Kaplan felt that such a partnership would impose a financial burden on the government; Ben-Gurion was not enthusiastic either. On the other hand, Shlomo Z. Shragai applauded a sharing of high treatment costs that would otherwise fall entirely on the government's shoulders. Another suggestion was JDC participation in the funding of camps for Yemenite immigrants in Israel rather than in Aden, but the idea was abandoned because it was feared that the organization would then claim entitlement to a larger cut from the United Jewish Appeal and try to meddle in absorption affairs. Nevertheless the negotiations with the JDC continued, and an agreement was reached whereby it assumed responsibility for handicapped, sick, and elderly immigrants. The outcome was the establishment of a network of institutions known as Malben.

In November 1949 this gargantuan financial task was placed on the shoulders of Levi Eshkol, who was appointed treasurer of the Jewish Agency in addition to his directorship of the Settlement Department. The wisdom of this decision was to become obvious within a short time.

Eshkol as Jewish Agency Treasurer

Eshkol swiftly alerted Israel's leaders, particularly Ben-Gurion and Kaplan, to the impending bankruptcy of the Jewish Agency and warned of the economic and political turmoil that would accompany the collapse of the absorption system. In response to Eshkol's demand for immediate coverage of the Jewish Agency's deficits and payment of all sums promised by the government, the Knesset Finance Committee commenced feverish deliberations. Eshkol also petitioned the government for additional grants and loans. The Finance Committee, chaired by David Zvi Pinkas, agreed to approve such loans on condition that the Jewish Agency produced guarantees, stayed within the planned budget, and repaid its debts on schedule.

To meet these conditions, the Jewish Agency Executive felt it had no choice but to impose limits on immigration; it established a maximum quota of 150,000 *olim* a year. The matter was kept secret for a while, but it eventually appeared in the newspapers. Despite the criticism heaped upon the Jewish Agency in wake of this decision, Eshkol stood firm. He emphasized that three factors had been taken into account when drawing up the Agency's budget: the enforcement of immigration quotas, government construction of 50,000 housing units, and state funding of vital services such as medical care. If all three materialized according to plan, the number of immigrants in the camps—more than 90,000 in October 1949—would drop by half and significantly reduce the expenditure in this sector. To trim spending further, all residents of immigrant camps who held outside jobs would be expected to support their families and, whenever possible, camp residents would share in cleaning and kitchen duties.

Meanwhile, the budget was exceeded over and over again as plans to limit immigration came up against reality. In spite of endless talks at the Jewish Agency and the Knesset during the peak period of *aliyah* from Yemen and Poland, nobody was prepared to staunch the flow lest emigration from these countries be halted indefinitely.

The financial situation was further complicated by political considerations. Kaplan, a Mapai leader and ally of Ben-Gurion and Eshkol, could not deviate from the budget without the consent of the Knesset Finance Committee. This committee was composed of representatives of the various political parties and operated on a coalition basis. Its chairman, Pinkas, a feisty Mizrachi activist, was not prepared to serve as a rubber stamp for Kaplan, particularly while Mizrachi and Mapai were locked in battle over the issue of education in the immigrant camps.

The Jewish Agency began to search for other ways of covering its debts. Reparations from Germany were then under discussion, but obtaining money in this way would clearly take time.[15] At a joint meeting of the government and the Jewish Agency, Eshkol came up with an unconventional solution: a massive fund-raising campaign in the United States within the framework of the Israel independence loan, which had been inaugurated to raise capital for arms. Ben-Gurion refused to give up this loan; he agreed to a drive for absorption funds toward the end of the year after the arms campaign was over. Eshkol was visibly disappointed. Nevertheless, Ben-Gurion was willing to consider other proposals put forward by Eshkol. As the mediator between the Jewish Agency and the government, Kaplan suggested that they meet in a restricted forum—just Ben-Gurion, Eshkol and himself—to work out some way of channeling state funds into absorption; they were unsuccessful.

In spite of the pressure exerted by Ben-Gurion and Eshkol, Kaplan was unable to divert money from the national budget. Pinkas, as head of the Knesset Finance Committee, would not give his approval and demanded that a proper forum be set up to examine the absorption problem in depth. Pinkas was a spokesman for the religious sector in the debate over education in the immigrant camps. Israel's religious public accused Mapai and its representatives in the Kelitah Department of imposing their secular beliefs on observant *olim*, especially the Yemenite Jews. Pinkas maintained that, rather than giving more money to the Jewish Agency, the government should handle immigrant absorption itself. He demanded the evacuation of *olim* from camps run by the Jewish Agency. Yohanan Bader, a Herut representative on the Finance Committee, also supported such a move.

To Eshkol's dismay, the Finance Committee approved only a loan to the Jewish Agency, and the sum did not begin to cover its enormous deficit. Eshkol called upon the government to convert this money into a grant, but it was feared that such a demand might rekindle the debate in the Knesset and cause further delays. Having no alternative, Eshkol accepted the offer of a loan and the Jewish Agency remained over its head in debt.

Austerity

The public was largely unaware of the seriousness of the economic situation. In 1949–51 the economy operated from hand to mouth. Reserves of food, fuel, and foreign currency were down to zero. After the formation of the government in March 1949, it was decided to introduce austerity rationing (*Tzena*), allowing for an equitable distribution of the country's meager food supplies to all citizens, including new immigrants. To prevent further price rises and inflation after the cost of basic commodities rose 30 percent in 1948, strict price controls were imposed. A separate government office, the Ministry of Supply and Rationing, was established for this purpose. At its head was Dov Joseph, who, as military governor during the siege of Jerusalem in the War of Independence, had organized food and water supplies to the city's inhabitants. In 1949 only foodstuffs were rationed; by July 1950 rationing was extended to clothing and shoes, which were distributed according to a point system.

Israel's program of austerity could not succeed without a tight rein on currency, exchange rates, and the price of raw materials. Such controls were justified on the basis of the country's commitment to mass *aliyah*. In 1949 a large majority of the population complied with the austerity regulations. But in 1950, as supervision became stricter, a black market emerged that threatened to upset the cart.[16] A parliamentary body was appointed to investigate the black-market phenomenon, and Ben-Gurion tried to rally public opinion against it. If Israel was to uphold its policy of mass immigration, he said, austerity had to be accepted. Nevertheless, the public became increasingly dissatisfied with the government's economic policy in general and its program of austerity in particular.

Budget talks in August and September 1950 also touched upon the volume of *aliyah*. Eshkol cautioned once again that only predetermined immigration quotas would enable Israel to stay within its budget. These were the days of *aliyah* from Romania and Poland, and exodus from Iraq loomed on the horizon. The very mention of restricting immigration from any of these countries drew showers of protest. The Jewish Agency and the government were thus dragged into a maze of inner conflict; the cost of transporting these immigrants was beyond Israel's means, but no one dared to draw limits. Kaplan predicted that, unless immigration was scaled down, the entire economy would collapse. Foreign currency reserves were so low that the government could not release shipments of sugar and cotton that had arrived at Haifa port.

An Economic Conference

Ben-Gurion sent an urgent cable to Israel's ambassador in Washington, D.C., Abba Eban: "The wheat and grain situation is desperate. At the end of February, there will be no bread. By the end of January (1951) there will be no food supply for the chicken coops. We require an immediate shipment of at least 50 thousand tons of wheat." [17]

Even so, Ben-Gurion was reluctant to place any limits on the number of immigrants. His solution was to build up a larger pool of resources by inviting 1,000 philanthropists from the United States and other Western countries to an economic conference that would include a tour of the immigrant camps and *ma'abarot*. Ben-Gurion's economic advisers were skeptical, but arrangements for the conference were begun.

In August 1950 the prime minister asked members of the American section of the Jewish Agency and the United Jewish Appeal to come to Israel to discuss the launching of a special immigration and absorption loan of IL 1 billion. The money would be obtained from four sources: (1) increased activity of the United Jewish Appeal; (2) the sale of Israel bonds in the United States; (3) aid from the American government; and (4) private investors. The idea of loans from individual Jews in the United States through the issue of redeemable Israel bonds was a new one. In addition, efforts were made to attract capitalists and business owners to invest in Israel and develop local industry. Ben-Gurion urged his guests to pressure the American government into granting Israel a sizeable loan, which was expected to motivate wealthy American Jews to contribute as well. [18]

Kaplan, who was familiar with the world of American finance and a veteran in the race to negotiate loans and extend payment schedules, had his doubts. He maintained that bankers in the United States, afraid of another world war, were refusing to extend credit and sought the explicit consent of the American government before granting loans. Even if Ben-Gurion's prayers were answered and a major loan was approved, it would be a long time in coming. Meanwhile, tens of thousands of immigrants would come to Israel on the strength of some future infusion of capital while the country's coffers were bare.

With the United States gearing up for nationwide elections in November 1950, Ben-Gurion calculated that there was no better time to seek a loan. He planned for the American fund-raisers to convene in Israel within a month. However, the difficulty of assembling a group of businessmen on short notice soon became clear. Reluctant to postpone the conference, which had been scheduled for early September, Ben-Gurion agreed to a smaller forum. The heads of all the major American Jewish organizations attended, alongside the Jewish Agency Executive, Knesset members, officials of the Jewish National Fund, and representatives of the Anglo-Palestine Bank.[19] Ben-Gurion hung high hopes on this conference; he looked forward to a great improvement in absorption that would also boost *aliyah*. In fact, the conference had an impact on other spheres as well, the most important of which was foreign policy. Until that time, Israel had tried to maintain a position of neutrality in the cold war between the East and West. Turning to the United States for assistance in the midst of the Korean crisis meant that Israel had joined the Western bloc for all intents and purposes. It was thus conceivable that emigration from Eastern Europe might be halted.

In May 1951 Ben-Gurion flew to the United States to inaugurate the Israel bonds campaign. Over the next few weeks, he traveled the length and breadth of the country and was enthusiastically received by the Jewish public. He returned to Israel with the promise of a loan and assurance that the battle for economic and military aid waged in Washington by Abba Eban and Teddy Kollek would not be ignored; the request also included weaponry. These efforts were crowned with success. In October 1951 Israel received its first round of economic aid from the United States: $64 million, $50 million of which were slated for absorption.

However, the need was so great that these sums barely made an impression and the search for additional sources of funding continued.

German Reparations

The financial crisis was a factor in one of the most dramatic decisions of the government under the leadership of David Ben-Gurion: the appeal to the Allied occupation powers for restitution from Germany. World War II was still raging when Ben-Gurion expressed concern over the vast amount of Jewish property lost to the Nazis. This topic had been raised by the Jewish Agency and Jewish organizations in the United States on many occasions.[20] Ben-Gurion firmly believed that this claim should not be written off and that Germany must not be allowed to profit from its crimes, maintaining that compensation for stolen property was the elementary right of the victims and their heirs and that Israel was the legal recipient of funds that would assist in the rehabilitation of Holocaust survivors. Mass immigration was so important to Ben-Gurion that even accepting aid from Germany was justifiable in his eyes.

Israel thus addressed a claim to the four Allied powers demanding the restoration of property and monetary compensation from Germany. These actions were carried out secretly because the Israeli public was sensitive about formal relations with Germany when the atrocities of the Nazis were still so fresh in mind. On 12 March 1951 the Foreign Ministry presented a document drafted by Leo Cohen, a Hebrew University professor and adviser to the ministry, and David Horowitz, director-general of the Ministry of Finance and later governor of the Bank of Israel. Cohen summarized the historical background and tragic events upon which Israel based its claim, while Horowitz, who had participated in the debates on this subject throughout the 1940s, prepared the financial calculations. Israel had taken in one-half million Jews who had suffered at the hands of the Nazis and lost all their worldly possessions. According to Horowitz's estimate, resettling these immigrants and helping them to rebuild their lives would require an overall expenditure of $1.5 billion.[21]

Direct contacts between Israel and Germany took place over the following weeks, and meetings were held with Chancellor Konrad Adenauer. On 27 September 1951 Adenauer announced in the Bundestag that Germany was willing to negotiate with representatives of the Jewish people and the State of Israel to compensate the victims of the Nazis for the damage done to them. The Bonn regime accepted the claim submitted by the Israeli government as a basis for dialogue and offered to pay in goods that would further the country's development.[22]

When the issue of negotiations with Bonn came before the Knesset on 7 January 1952, it became apparent that large segments of the public were deeply opposed. Ben-Gurion's request that the government be empowered to bargain directly with Germany triggered an emotional outcry and a series of violent demonstrations outside the Knesset that culminated in stone-throwing. After a heated debate that was repeatedly disrupted, sixty-one Knesset members voted in favor of negotiations and fifty voted against. The opposition crossed party bounds, including members of Herut, Mapam, the General Zionists, and the religious parties.[23]

Giora Josephthal, director of the Jewish Agency's Kelitah Department, was asked to serve as one of Israel's chief negotiators. This task, which required a large amount of traveling, preoccupied him throughout 1952. In his absence, his duties in the Kelitah Department were fulfilled by David Tene. One point that deserves to be made is that the reparations agreement between Israel and Germany provided for the staggering of payments over many years. While this agreement certainly held great promise for the future, economic relief was not immediate. Germany undertook to deliver a total of DM3 billion in goods; by the end of 1965, Israel had received $850 million worth of shipments.

. . .

The settlement of masses of immigrants in Israel required vast financial resources and the economic crisis threatened to bring it to a halt. Israel's prime minister was determined to keep the immigrants coming, and this fact was reflected in the country's economic policies. A strict austerity program was inaugurated in the domestic sphere, and strenuous efforts were made to mobilize foreign currency through fund-raising as well as loans and grants from American Jewry and the United States government. Paradoxically, the very actions meant to stimulate large-scale immigration could also cut off the flow from Eastern Europe. The appeal for restitution and indemnification from Germany exposed a sensitive nerve in Israeli society and ignited a major controversy. As time passed, the payment of reparations was blamed for creating differences between *olim.* Thus, none of the solutions adopted by the government solved the problem in its entirety, and in fact new problems were spawned.

Demands to Scale Down Immigration

The ambivalence toward mass immigration, already present from the earliest days of the Zionist movement, took a new turn once the State of Israel was born and dreams became the stuff of reality. The call to limit immigration was already sounded in the first few weeks, albeit in the privacy of Jewish Agency Executive meetings so as not to arouse public opinion. Even when many people became critical of the work of the immigration authorities, the topic was not broached openly. The vital need for mass immigration was a myth that could not be challenged. There were some among the Jewish Agency Executive and the Knesset who agreed with the Zionist leaders of old about the undesirability of uncontrolled *aliyah.* However, they refrained from using the word "selection," which brought back bitter memories of the Holocaust; they preferred less-charged terms, such as "regulation."

Reading the minutes of these early meetings, it is surprising to discover how often the immigration authorities, and especially the Jewish Agency Executive, voted to restrict immigration. All deliberations and decisions in this sphere were strictly confidential, and any rumors were swiftly denied. These decisions were not made public. The question of immigration quotas came up at nearly every meeting, and a formal decision was reached at least once a year and sometimes more. Unexpected developments and conflicting interests among the concerned parties explain why the issue was put to the vote time and again and why the decision was never acted upon.

During the fall of 1948, as the stream of immigrants swelled to nearly 1,000 a day, panic began to set in. Israel Goldstein, the Jewish Agency treasurer, sought limits on immigration from countries where Jews were not in danger. Zvi Herman, head of the Kelitah Department, reported in a tone of impending catastrophe, "There is no housing, no place in the camps, no blankets, no iron for beds."[24] The implications seemed obvious, but not to Herman's partner, Yehuda Braginsky, who opposed any attempt to curb immigration.[25] This was only the beginning of a battle that was to escalate steadily over the coming months.

The debate over *aliyah* had clear political overtones: The chief denigrators of the current policy were affiliated with Mapam. Braginsky, for instance, supported large-scale immigration but relentlessly attacked the government over its mishandling of absorption, as did other members of the opposition. The political wrangling intensified, along with the ferocity of the dispute over immigration. As the country bent under the weight of its problems, more and more people—not only from the opposition—came to share the view that a pause in immigration was imperative.

The approach of winter added to the misery in the immigrant camps, and unemployment soared. The job-seekers were joined by large numbers of soldiers who had been discharged after the War of Independence. As word of the absorption difficulties in Israel reached potential *olim,* some of them decided to postpone their plans or change their destination. Moshe Shapira related that many Jews interned in DP camps in Germany were reluctant to register for *aliyah* upon hearing of the housing shortage. But despite all these obstacles, immigrants from Europe and other countries continued to pour into Israel without hiatus.

Whenever the subject of immigration was raised in the Knesset and the Jewish Agency, as it often was, tempers flared. Kaplan and Shapira flung accusations at the government; Josephthal, Herman, and others had harsh words for the Jewish Agency Executive. Many believed that the current pattern of immigration was illogical and should be halted immediately. The Aliyah Department was charged with deliberately concealing its plans and ignoring the decisions of the Jewish Agency Executive on such matters as the pace and volume of *aliyah* and the introduction of selective criteria based on health, age, and so on.

The absorption authorities protested loudest of all. They were strangled by the sparsest of budgets, whereas the immigration authorities enjoyed the largesse of the Joint Distribution Committee. This money covered most of the expenditures connected with organizing the *olim,* holding them in transit camps, and transporting them to Israel. The JDC, as noted, was not bound by the decisions of the government and the Jewish Agency. Moreover, it was suspected of making a particular effort to send the sick, disabled, and elderly to Israel so as to free itself of the burden of supporting them overseas. The Aliyah Department was accused of conspiring with the JDC to increase the rate and magnitude of *aliyah* in defiance of all orders. It was claimed that, together, they found ways of evading the registration and screening procedures carried out in the countries of origin under the supervision of Ministry of Health physicians. Caring for the aged, the handicapped, and other dependents was an exceedingly complex and costly undertaking for the absorption network, requiring special housing and employment solutions.

When the Jewish Agency closed its camps in Israel, the first to be evacuated were families that were capable of sustaining themselves. This left thousands of dependent *olim* and their households. The heavy strain thus imposed made it difficult to improve living conditions in the camps, and many new arrivals in need of temporary shelter were turned way. As immigration increased the number of dependents rose. This became such a problem that it overshadowed many other issues, taking the forefront whenever restrictions on immigration were discussed. The result was a profound change in Israel's approach to immigration.

The Human Component

When Israel's leaders spoke of the problematic "human component" of immigration during this period, the reference was to Holocaust survivors as well as Jews from Islamic countries. This term, generally negative in connotation, revolved around the makeup of the immigrants as a group, that is, the relatively small number of employable adults as opposed to the large number of children, elderly, sick, and incapacitated.

Israel's absorption officials found a serious cause for alarm in the reports from the camps and abandoned neighborhoods taken over by *olim*. As Shapira, the minister of immigration, noted, "From a human standpoint, aliyah is moving from bad to worse. Large families with small children may be good from one perspective, but from the perspective of absorption, it is very difficult. More welfare cases, a multitude of handicapped and sick." Shapira was not in favor of cutting back the number of immigrants but in being more selective:

On the one hand, we must promote large-scale immigration; on the other, we must have some kind of regulation, a system which will not allow anyone who so desires to load Jews on a flimsy boat and transport them to Israel, even if they are 80 years old. This is not an immigration system; it is a system which will lead us to catastrophe. If people who have just come ashore find themselves without a bed or a mattress or a blanket, imagine the impression that will be made upon them of their first welcome to the camps. I know that when we talk about regulation, it may mean fewer immigrants. But I also say that the coming years will determine the fate of aliyah, that is, if we have the sense to populate not only the corridor between Haifa, Acre and Tel Aviv, but also to settle hundreds of thousands of Jews in the Negev and the Galilee. If not—we shall find ourselves in a very grave situation . . . I, too, support large-scale aliyah, but it depends on what kind of aliyah, how we direct it and the choices we make.[26]

The "human component" of the immigrant masses was already on the agenda in the days of the Provisional Council of State. At that time, council members accused those in charge of absorption of being oblivious to any needs beyond basic survival. In the opinion of Zerah Warhaftig, a member of the Aliyah Committee, "not only are we not marching forward, but we are marching towards catastrophe." In January 1949 Shapira pointed a finger toward Ben-Gurion: "I have the feeling that it is not the Jewish Agency which determines the dimensions of aliyah and certainly not the government. Someone else, higher than high is doing this and having people sent without checking them properly, without exercising proper supervision. This must change, but I do not see how it can at the moment."

Neither was there any change after the elections, when Mapai formed Israel's largest party and Ben-Gurion, "higher than high," was asked to put together a cabinet and lead the nation.

Public Opinion

The shift in public opinion was gradual. At the beginning of 1949, the newspapers reported with great emotion the opening of the gates of Cyprus and the release of the "ransomed prisoners." But as time passed a note of criticism crept into these reports—at first barely detectable and later, not disguised at all. Describing the exodus from Bulgaria, the papers noted that the whole community arrived: not only those who were fit for work but also hospital patients, old people from nursing homes, and the mentally ill.

In March 1949, when the rate of immigration reached a thousand and more per day, the press openly depicted the distress of the newcomers and criticized the mass-immigration policy of the Jewish Agency. "The *olim* are in despair," announced *Yediot Aharonot*.[27] Another paper, *Ha-Mashkif*, published an article by Meir Grossman, a Revisionist on the Zionist Executive, who declared,

Since the establishment of the Jewish state, over 160,000 *olim* have been brought to this country without any consideration of where they would live and what would become of them . . . Despite the fact that Israel's immigrant camps now hold 40,000 persons, and despite the shortage of housing and money, immigration is on the rise . . . It would be criminal negligence to watch these developments with equanimity and make no attempt to bring them under control with forceful and decisive action. Rather than a blessing, aliyah may, God forbid, bring a curse . . . Aliyah must not be turned into a risky adventure.[28]

Grossman believed that only young pioneers or persons of means should be admitted, an idea that amounted to selective immigration. The minister of immigration, who had foreseen the crisis building up in the absorption sector, told the Provisional Council, "I have no doubt that we are approaching very hard times. We shall require a tremendous investment of spirit to introduce law and order in immigration." Harsh criticism also appeared in other newspapers.[29]

Attacks on the Jewish Agency and the government intensified as the tide of immigration continued. The Jewish Agency was blamed for the failures in absorption, while the government was blamed for shirking its responsibility in this sphere and passing it on to the Jewish Agency. Newspapers of every hue drew attention to the problems of the immigrants, claiming that the mishandling of absorption threatened the entire social system. *Ha-Aretz* wrote: "The question is not whether we have succeeded in absorption; we have already failed . . . If the term "immigrant absorption" means that every *oleh* will have a roof over his head, even of the most modest kind, without having to wait very long, and will be able to integrate in the national economy, even if he lives in poverty and earns a minimum wage—then it is obvious that we have flunked the test. With every ship of immigrants, the gap between need and ability grows wider."[30]

Ha-Mishmar listed the weak points in the handling of the immigrants.[31] The papers overflowed with stories about life in the camps, hunger strikes and demonstrations held to protest the lack of jobs and housing.[32] A. Gelblum, a reporter for *Ha-Aretz,* even masqueraded as a new immigrant and took up residence in one of the camps, communicating a series of lengthy articles about the conditions and local lifestyle.[33]

The newspapers also published shocking revelations about the number of sick and handicapped who were planning to immigrate from Germany and other countries. They described the squalid existence in the camps and the poor sanitary facilities. A camp of 4,000 residents, for example, was equipped with only fifty toilets.[34] Nearly every day there were reports of demonstrations outside the government offices in Tel-Aviv and the Jewish Agency. The immigrants even threatened to storm the Knesset. The residents of the camp in Netanya declared a hunger strike and riots broke out. The journalists wrote of "a wave of bitterness sweeping over the camp." The *olim* complained of unbearable living conditions, long months of idleness, tasteless food, and utter lack of hygiene. The Netanya immigrant camp was designed to hold 1,100 persons, but there were now 3,200 people, of whom 1,800 slept in tents.[35] *Ha-Aretz* covered a demonstration of 200 unemployed workers from Ramleh who claimed to represent 800 jobless immigrants. Among their gripes were the frequent power shortages that disrupted work in the town's factories. The demonstrators marched from the government headquarters in Tel-Aviv toward the Jewish Agency on Nahalat Binyamin Street, demanding the repair of 400 rooms that had been promised to them. From there, they marched to the Agricultural Center, calling for more families to be given land for farming and poultry-raising. Another demonstration was held by handicapped immigrants, and a particularly violent one consisted of *olim* from Tel-Hanan who gathered at the Jewish Agency offices in Haifa and tried to break in by force. The police were summoned and made arrests.[36]

A survey conducted by a government polling institute in August 1949 discovered a dramatic shift in public opinion over the course of the year: 82 percent now supported controlled immigration, while only 18 percent favored free and unrestricted entry for any Jew who desired to live in Israel.

A Call for Limitations

At the end of its first year of statehood, Israel seemed to be on the edge of an abyss. The economy was collapsing, much of the population was jobless, and the cold winter had set in. The immigrant camps were bursting, yet newcomers continued to flood the country. The Jewish Agency Executive insisted that immigration must be controlled. To make this point, radical measures were proposed such as keeping new arrivals aboard ship for several days and not permitting them to disembark.

The executive was particularly upset over the poor health of the newcomers. Herman was scandalized by the blunders he discerned in absorption; Josephthal warned of the peril to the country at large: "The government must know that 47 persons [in one hall] in the camps is a keg of dynamite that endangers the entire nation." He could enumerate many reasons for the overcrowding, but had no remedies to offer: "In the realm of housing we have failed for a thousand reasons, among them a shortage of funding, manual labor and construction materials, and the dictatorship of the major contractors."[37]

In the thunderous Knesset debate that followed the first government's inauguration, the government through its policies was accused of aggravating the economic hardship and the distress of the immigrants. Over the coming months, as many more arrived and the period spent in immigrant camps lengthened, criticism grew sharper. Public construction could not keep pace with the rate of immigration and unemployment was rampant. It was argued that a slowdown in immigration would give the country time to deal with the absorption of those already in Israel and enable it to plan for the future.

In view of the volatile situation in the camps and the barrage of criticism from all sides, the Zionist executive and the government took a series of steps. One was the establishment of a Joint Absorption Committee.[38] Unhappy with the immigration program drawn up by Raphael, which called for the *aliyah* of 172,000 persons between April and December, the Zionist executive resolved to limit the number to 150,000 and to introduce strict medical screening. These orders directly affected immigration from two sources: the camps in Germany, Austria, and Italy, where the percentage of sick and disabled was very high; and the Jewish communities of North Africa, whose "human component" was seen by the Zionist executive and others as "extremely inferior from an absorption standpoint."[39]

Taking Sides

Raphael remained staunchly opposed to any restrictions on immigration. He claimed that the news had been taken badly in the camps in Germany, where arrangements had already been made for larger quotas. Urgent telegrams arrived from the Zionist Federation of Holocaust Survivors voicing fierce objection to such a move. Imposing limits on *aliyah* from Germany was liable to push these Jews into emigrating elsewhere, and it was no secret that thousands of them possessed visas for the United States and Canada.[40] Josephthal agreed that a scale of urgency ought to be applied to immigration from various countries, but certainly not out of fear that someone might flee to America. He argued that a person who was not sincere in the desire to immigrate and did so unwillingly "will be an affliction, because we shall turn him into one here."[41]

Mossad le-Aliyah Bet worked together with Raphael to accelerate *aliyah* and block the restrictions. Upon receiving instructions from Israel to refrain from sending ships for a month, the Mossad replied, "This order cannot be complied with. We can understand the request for a slowdown and have begun to make the necessary arrangements. However, an immediate halt is out of the question, as is a cutback to the minimum."[42]

On another occasion, the Mossad did not even protest; it simply announced the launching of such and such ships with a certain number of passengers. As its activists explained, "From time to time, we must take into account certain phenomena in the Diaspora which in our estimation will have an impact for generations, in addition to immediate concerns which cannot be turned off on demand."[43]

Aliyah emissaries in Germany were insistent that 8,000 Jews interned in the American zone be allowed to immigrate, even though the Jewish Agency had established a ceiling of 3,000. The already-tense atmosphere in Germany turned to panic when the Americans announced that the DP camps would be closed and the Joint Distribution Committee decided to withdraw as well. A number of emissaries flew to Israel to explain their position, and Raphael reported the pressure being brought upon him by the Federation of Holocaust Survivors in Munich. As letters of distress continued to arrive from different countries, Raphael called to reopen the debate on the subject of quotas. He did the same when negotiations commenced with the Imam of Yemen and when news reach Israel of the deteriorating plight of the Jews of Egypt.[44] More than a thousand members of the Jewish community were incarcerated and thousands of clerks and public servants were dismissed from their jobs. Jewish businesses were threatened, and Jewish-owned factories and workshops were forbidden to operate. Many Egyptian Jews did not wait for the local *aliyah* emissaries to arrange their departure; they fled to Italy and France and appealed to the emissaries in those countries to help them reach Israel. Israel was bombarded by emotional pleas to let these people in. The Mossad worked tirelessly to annul the restrictions on immigration, urging the Jewish Agency Executive to personally visit the countries in question and to order an immediate supplement in the number of *olim*.[45]

The Joint Distribution Committee also contributed to the undermining of Israel's immigration policy. It turned down the Zionist executive's proposal to detain *olim* until places were vacated in the immigration camps, and it announced that it could no longer maintain them in European transit camps because it had run out of funding. All the while, the number of arrivals continued to exceed the monthly quotas and it became apparent that nothing much could be done to enforce the decisions of the Jewish Agency in this realm.[46] The cost of organizing and transporting the immigrants was borne by the JDC, and increasing the budget for travel expenses was a logical step because it saved money that would otherwise be spent on transit camps. The Jewish Agency was powerless to alter the situation.

Fully aware of the sensitivity of this issue for the Zionist executive, the Mossad and the emissaries leaked word to the press of the draconian restrictions on immigration. Although the newspapers had been critical of the absorption process, they were quite ready to attack Raphael for ordering Israel's emissaries to staunch the flow. Raphael, who had conspired with his colleagues on the executive to keep this decision secret, rushed to deny the allegations: "Due to unforeseeable circumstances, the departure of several convoys of *olim* from Europe has been detained. During the first ten days of this month, there have been no deviations from the immigration plan for 1949 determined by the Jewish Agency Executive and endorsed by the Zionist Actions Committee at its last session. Immigration is continuing from all countries where such a possibility exists. The rumors that immigration from North Africa has been halted are completely baseless."[47]

Dobkin, an executive member who was in England at the time and not hemmed in by Israeli public opinion, spoke more openly: "Due to absorption problems and border closures in the countries of Eastern Europe, it is no longer possible for immigration to continue at the current rate of 20,000 to 25,000 persons a month. Inconceivable sums of money would be needed to overcome the difficulties."

As in other spheres, party politics could not be separated from the debate over immigration. Most Mossad operatives were affiliated with Mapam, which opposed cuts in immigration. Hence their surprise to hear that Braginsky, head of the Aliyah Department and a member of Mapam, was among those battling for restrictions. Mossad activists in Paris informed Braginsky of the rumor and Mapai was implicated. Representatives of Ha-Poel ha-Mizrachi, Mapai, and Mapam working for the immigration and absorption authorities flung similar accusations at one another.[48]

The Jewish Agency Executive may have been intent on limiting immigration but it did not succeed, chiefly because of Ben-Gurion. The prime minister admitted from the Knesset podium that the absorption network was in serious trouble. While he could not ignore the "bitter truth" and recognized that "over 53,000 *olim* still reside in appallingly overcrowded immigrant camps . . . in inhumane conditions," he did not see curbing immigration as the solution. However grave the problems were, it was his conviction that "we have no moral right to tailor the dimensions of *aliyah* to economic needs, real or imagined."[49] Ben-Gurion continued to stand by this belief throughout 1949, rebuffing any attempts to hold back *aliyah* or impose restrictions. He liked to compare the economic and social undertaking required for nation-building to Israel's physical battle for independence:

> The military effort was made, not in keeping with our financial and economic ability, but with the enormity of the danger. The rate of aliyah is no less vital and momentous than physical defense. No one knows what the day shall bring, not in the countries of exodus and not in our region. The first law of survival tells us that we must ingather the exiles with the utmost speed, losing no opportunity.

This was the purpose for which the state was established and it is only this which will guarantee its existence. The desperate struggle imposed upon us last year to defend ourselves from Arab aggression is the same struggle we must wage now to absorb immigration.[50]

Tens of thousands of immigrants thus continued to reach Israel's shores, far in excess of any quota, under the inspiration and orders of David Ben-Gurion. This fact did not eliminate additional rounds of debate each time a tidal wave of immigration swept in without warning—from Yemen, Poland, Romania, and Iraq.

The major reason for instituting immigration quotas was the grievous lack of funding for absorption. Pressure on the Jewish Agency treasury mounted, especially after hopes were dashed for a greater fund-raising total from the United States. Nevertheless, Raphael clung to the belief that restrictions on *aliyah,* particularly from Yemen, could not be implemented. "The Yemenites are wandering in the streets and the desert," he said. Ben-Gurion shared these sentiments, noting in his diary, "I have decided to wire the Joint to send more planes and bring the Yemenites over faster. Will also request more ambulances."[51]

At a special meeting to examine funding options for Yemenite immigration, Ben-Gurion ridiculed Yitzhak Gruenbaum's fears that 20,000–25,000 *olim* might come instead of 15,000. He exclaimed, "The Yemenite Diaspora must be liquidated as soon as possible. Children are dying like flies. We must save them. It is true that mortality is high here, too, but the care is more efficient and more devoted. No economic question or financial difficulty should create a delay."[52]

In making these remarks, Ben-Gurion was not out of touch with reality, as had been claimed by some of his detractors. The remarks were jotted down in his notebook alongside a report from David Horowitz, director-general of the Ministry of Finance, about the shortage of foreign currency for food, fodder, raw materials, and military supplies. Only days earlier, the government secretary had informed him that the roads could not be paved because the country had no gravel, cement, or steamrollers. Pipes were also in short supply.[53] Even Josephthal's regular updates on the state of affairs in the camps did not change Ben-Gurion's mind.

Jewish Agency Decisions

At the end of 1949, those in the Jewish Agency who favored restrictions were chiefly concerned with barring entry to the sick and disabled. Berl Locker, replacing the treasurer who had resigned, made it clear that reducing the number of arrivals by at least 10,000–12,000 a month was absolutely imperative "if we do not wish to break our necks." This step had to be taken "even if 10,000 [*olim*] had to sit in Marseilles to wait their turn." Furthermore, if it became necessary to arrange the hasty passage of Yemenite Jewry, *aliyah* from other countries would be pared down accordingly.[54] Raphael reminded his colleagues that the Polish government had agreed to release Jews only if they gave up their citizenship and left the country within two months. In his assessment, Israel could expect 5,000 Polish Jews over the next three months. Another 2,500 were already on their way from Cyrenaica, Hungary had also promised to let out 3,000 Jews over a period of two months, and immigration from other countries was brisk.

In order to appease the Jewish Agency Executive, Raphael said he would try to regulate *aliyah* from Yemen somewhat so that arrivals in October would not exceed 10,000. The same number would be admitted over November and December, bringing the immigration total from Yemen for 1949 to 20,000. The executive was skeptical: The Joint Distribution Committee was responsible for the airlift and tended to increase the number of flights as the camp in Aden became crowded. In principle, Dobkin objected to granting priority to immigration from Yemen: "You are smothering aliyah from other countries. By next year, I fear there will be no *olim*." Herman felt that immigration should be brought to a full stop for a certain period of time: "There are no camps, nowhere to put them . . . I will be forced to give orders to leave [them] at the airport in Lod." Eshkol declared that allowing the monthly quota to go beyond 10,000 would be a crime: "We shall fail so dismally that later there will be no *aliyah* at all." [55] Under pressure, Raphael instructed his personnel in Europe to keep the total from each country below 10,000 over the next three months. In the event that this "lethal cutback" was disregarded and the *olim* could not be stopped in their home countries, some would be held over in Marseilles and Italy.[56]

In fact, disregarding the restrictions became almost routine. Aliyah Department employees and Mossad operatives in Europe would write or cable Raphael that it was impossible to abide by the decrees. *Aliyah* organizers in Tripoli begged for a two-month postponement because many of the Jews had liquidated their property and were "sitting on their bags, ready to sail." Tension also mounted in Germany. In Egypt, the Jews were advised to travel to Rhodes or Cyprus on their own and then to pressure the Israeli government to let them in. Raphael's idea of detaining *olim* in Marseilles and Italy was rejected because the Joint Distribution Committee refused to increase the capacity of its camps.[57]

The Mossad informed Raphael that it could not accept such restrictions and threatened to leave the stage unless its opinions were respected. Writing to his colleagues in Israel, the Mossad director in Paris was blunt: "The realization has come to me that the continued activity of the Mossad, whose strength lies in dynamism and promoting aliyah, has been stripped of purpose . . . There are some jobs which can be performed by the Mossad only in its traditional format . . . only under conditions in which there are no drastic limits on aliyah, when its freedom to work is respected and the atmosphere is supportive. . . . [Otherwise the Mossad] will turn the work over to some clerical office." [58]

At this point, Nahum Goldmann joined the fray. He sent a cable from New York warning the government not to let the United States find out about the restrictions on *aliyah*. Publicity was sure to do harm and would take its toll on fund-raising, which lay emphasis on Israel's massive absorption needs. [59] Word from Yemen about the spread of typhus raised the specter of border closures and danger to the Jewish community. This development prompted Raphael to push for an increment of at least 5,000 *olim* above the current three-month quota. [60] Meanwhile, in October more than 19,000 immigrants arrived and it was doubtful that the number could be reduced to 12,000 over the coming months as had been decided.

Members of the Knesset spoke out about the critical situation and the impotence of the Jewish Agency. It was felt that the government should also be involved in what was happening in the camps; they were not the territory of the Jewish Agency alone. Hillel Kook (Herut) looked forward to the end of this monopoly over immigrant absorption. Harking back to Ben-Gurion's remarks, Rabbi Kalman Kahana (United Religious Front) maintained that absorption was a national affair, analogous to war, and that taking it out of the hands of the Jewish Agency in no way diminished the responsibility or obligations of the Jewish people in this sphere. [61]

Planning and Regulation

In 1949 the tidal wave reached a peak: 240,000 immigrants sought refuge in the State of Israel. Between 15 May 1948 and the end of 1949, the number of arrivals exceeded 340,000. With a natural increase of approximately 25,000, the Jewish population now stood at around one million, of which one-third were new immigrants. [62] The problems confronting the country were of such magnitude that the government was forced to rethink its policies and restrict the flow of immigration.

As the newspapers grew louder in their criticism of the absorption network, attention was drawn to the need for planning and regulation in the sphere of *aliyah*. It was evident that immigration had to be controlled in either quantity or quality—or both. The Jewish Agency decision to establish "work camps" in late 1949 did little to improve its budgetary deficit. Although the government initiated road-building and afforestation projects to provide jobs for the immigrants, this was not an adequate solution.[63] The newspapers did not remain silent. "Ninety thousand immigrants in the camps! One hundred thousand by next month!" ran the headlines of *Ma'ariv*.[64] Many believed the whole system was in need of change: "The camps are no good for those who live there. People decline in the abnormality of camp life. In Germany and Cyprus, the people had hope—hope for the Jewish state. There can be no hope in the camps here unless something is done immediately."[65]

Ben-Gurion, as we have seen, was able to ward off the pressures. At the opening of the Second Session of the Knesset, he delivered a lengthy speech on the subject of immigration: "We have opposed and will continue to oppose any curbs on immigration . . . and even if we need to exert ourselves mightily to keep up with the rapid pace . . . we shall not falter."[66] He then presented a list of long-range programs to alleviate Israel's problems in the spheres of employment, housing, etc., although he recognized that immediate action was necessary, too.

The Jewish Agency Executive held another meeting, attended by its overseas members, to discuss Israel's shortcomings in the handling of immigration. The American contingent supported a drastic cutback in 1950, which it claimed was for the immigrants' own good. Nearly 5,000 *olim* (5 percent) had returned to their home countries between April and September 1949, and the stories they spread about Israel were extremely harmful. Many Mahal volunteers had likewise left the country after trying unsuccessfully to settle down there. Nevertheless, when the *New York Times* broke the news of Israel's immigration restrictions, the response was one of rage. Jewish Agency officials in the United States worried about the negative effect on fund-raising for Israel, which was already in difficulty.[67]

As a last resort, when *aliyah* continued unremittingly, the Jewish Agency Executive ordered a further cut in the Kelitah Department budget. The department heads angrily protested. Quoting Golda Meir, the minister of labor, Herman exclaimed: "She said that we are cruel, that we are anti-Semites, that we treat Jews in a manner that Gentiles would never dare." The plight of the immigrants, he said, was steadily worsening: "At one time, an immigrant leaving the camp was given an initial grant so he could buy a kerosene burner and a dish. Today they do not give even that. It is no secret that there have been cases of real hunger."[68]

The Jewish Agency was not intimidated by the protests; it insisted that the restrictions must be enforced. Raphael was ordered to draw up a monthly list indicating how many *olim* were planning to immigrate from each country. Early in 1950, the policy began to take effect. From January, a sharp drop was registered in the number of *olim*, and only 8,000 arrived in April. This decrease was not entirely deliberate. Many potential immigrants in Western Europe and North

Africa were discouraged by the tales of woe emanating from Israel. Nevertheless, it seemed that the dark clouds were lifting. The Kelitah Department believed that, if the Ministry of Labor fulfilled its promise to accelerate housing construction, the crisis would be over. But reality did not converge with these hopes. Stormy weather kept the builders at home, and the desired number of immigrants could not be evacuated from the camps. The greatest turning point of all was the unexpected wave of immigration from Iraq and Romania.

When it became clear that *aliyah* from these countries could not be restricted in any way, the Jewish Agency and the government had to reassess their policy once more. Iraq had expressed its intentions very vaguely and was liable to change its mind; it was feared that the Romanian authorities might do the same. All the while, immigration from Yemen, Poland, and other countries continued in spurts, creating a serious dilemma for Israel's policymakers.

The Coordinating Committee

When the Zionist Actions Committee convened in April 1950, one of its decisions was to create a bureaucratic coordinating committee allowing the government and the Jewish Agency to engage in joint planning and budget preparation. The distribution of portfolios was to be agreed upon by both parties.[69] In May the committee was approved by the Ministerial Committee and the chairman of the Jewish Agency Executive.

The new body's task was to collaborate on matters of immigration, absorption, immigrant housing, settlement, and development. It would also draw up budgets for these purposes and decide on the delegation of duties between the government and the Jewish Agency.[70] The Coordinating Committee met every two weeks and sometimes more often under the leadership of David Ben-Gurion. It was staffed by eight persons—four government ministers (the prime minister, minister of finance, minister of labor, and minister of immigration) and four Jewish Agency Executive members (chairman, treasurer, the head of Aliyah Department, and a Kelitah Department representative). A delegate of the Jewish National Fund was also present at its meetings.[71] In light of his disagreements with Mapam, Ben-Gurion decided not to ask Braginsky, who shared the directorship of the Kelitah Department with Herman, to join the committee. Mapam, which was constantly criticizing the government for its handling of immigration and absorption, was infuriated by this move. It encouraged party members all over the world to send telegrams of protest, but to no avail.[72] The Jewish Agency was represented on the Coordinating Committee by Locker, Eshkol, Raphael, and Herman. Giora Josephthal, director of the Kelitah Department and a highly respected figure, was invited to participate in staff meetings. Ben-Gurion tended to pay greater heed to his remarks than to those of many others.

With the establishment of the Coordinating Committee, the Jewish Agency hoped to reach forthright decisions in the matter of *aliyah*. The Kelitah Department, the Jewish Agency treasurer, and the minister of finance supported immigration restrictions in keeping with the availability of financial resources; they called for mandatory quotas. Shapira, the minister of immigration, also took this side. To insure the Aliyah Department's compliance, a subcommittee (composed of Shapira, Raphael, Josephthal, and Herman) was appointed to investigate the situation in various countries and determine a specific quota for each one. The makeup of this committee seemed to guarantee that the quotas would be strict and, on the whole, this was true. However, as conditions worsened in certain regions, even those who advocated restrictions were persuaded to endorse a larger number than they originally figured upon.

The subcommittee's task was to submit recommendations which would then be approved by the Coordinating Committee. Finding himself in a minority on the subcommittee, Raphael preferred to see the quota debate revert to the Coordinating Committee. Gearing up for a direct conflict with those who favored rigid quotas, Raphael lay out precise figures, reports, and telegrams he had received from Aliyah Department emissaries and Mossad le-Aliyah Bet in order to demonstrate the perversity of turning away *olim* from Islamic countries and Eastern Europe. He advised the Coordinating Committee to determine the scope of *aliyah* on the basis of this data. In this way, the committee became a platform for constant bickering over immigration quotas. Most of its deliberations in the summer of 1950 revolved around immigration from Iraq and Romania. Moshe Sharett also urged the committee to speed up the *aliyah* of 3,000 Kurdish Jews who had reached Teheran and were languishing there in great distress: "Many children are dying and the entire scene . . . is horrifying . . . My demand to increase the monthly quota is dedicated to these forsaken brothers of ours and the quick termination of their terrible suffering . . . They uprooted themselves from their homes and embarked on this journey after hearing on 'Kol Yisrael' that Israel had opened its gates to any Jew desiring to become part of the homeland."[73]

In the midst of these deliberations, immigration from Central and Western Europe—Germany, Austria, Belgium, and France—took a sudden leap.[74] Raphael claimed that Israel could not meet even a third of the urgent demand from these countries. Evidently the escalation of the fighting in Korea and the fear of another world war triggered a sense of impending doom that also affected the Jews. Many of those living in Europe now decided that the time had come to move to Israel. Kaplan was against increasing the tempo in their case. "When things were good, they sat and had no desire to immigrate," he said. As always, Raphael did not give up easily: "In America and Poland, people sat, too, and no one punished them." Golda Meir argued that restricting immigration from any country was unthinkable. This set off another round of debate between the Jewish Agency and the government. Kaplan was furious with those who called for unhampered immigration, especially Raphael and Meir. He made his position clear: "There is no way that we can go on without a correlation between means and absorption needs. You can say: adjust absorption to the means or the means to absorption, but this gap cannot continue." [75]

International politics actually motivated Golda Meir and Ben-Gurion to persist in their support of unabated *aliyah*. America's painful defeat by the Koreans in July 1950 set everyone on edge. "Now we are able to bring Jews here," said Meir, "but who knows what will happen if disaster strikes again in the wake of a new war?" Nevertheless, she concurred with Kaplan about the need to guarantee the immigrants a basic income. Ben-Gurion took the opportunity to restate his beliefs on the subject of immigration: "We must bring over Jews from Eastern Europe while they are still allowed to leave, as well as all the Jews from Arab lands, Turkey and Persia, and the surviving remnant from Austria and Germany."

He emphasized the importance of allowing immigration to flow freely even from countries where the Jews faced no immediate danger, such as Turkey, but "this must be done in time, before the next world war and before an economic crisis begins in America." [76]

Controversy over Quotas

The debate over immigration quotas was not one of principle; it was a response to pressure. Toward the end of 1950 and throughout 1951, the absorption network found it increasingly difficult to cope. From all over the world there came desperate pleas not to obstruct the flow of immigration. During this period Jews began to arrive from Iraq and Romania. At a meeting of the Coordinating Committee, Foreign Minister Moshe Sharett entreated his colleagues to lift all restrictions on *aliyah* from Iraq. In addition to 36,000 already in Israel, there were 90,000 Iraqi Jews waiting to leave and May had been set as the deadline. Sharett cautioned, "For the first time in the history of the State of Israel we are in danger of losing Jews who will no longer be able to immigrate."

Ben-Gurion of course agreed with him: "We have no choice. Time is running out . . . I do not think that our economic or political situation will be fundamentally changed by the addition of 23,000 Jews [beyond the existing quota] over the coming months. On the other hand, circumstances in this country may greatly change if we do not bring these Jews over." He mocked those who cited economic factors as a pretext for limited immigration: "There is an historical irony here. England and the United States, who were so hostile to mass immigration when the state was first established, are now imploring Israel to make haste and get the Jews out of Iraq. This is in their political interest. Failure to respond to these pressures may ruin our chances for a large grant from the United States government. And then, of course, there is the moral consideration: If we do not rescue Iraqi Jewry, how will we face America and its Jews?"

For Ben-Gurion, there was only one conclusion: "We must insure that anyone who signs up to immigrate is allowed to do so." He was prepared, when the Iraq affair was over, to consider a more comprehensive *aliyah* effort in countries where the Jews were less threatened, such as Egypt, Turkey, and North Africa. Raphael quickly added that cutbacks were unacceptable "wherever people's bags were packed."[77]

Alarmed by the calls to step up immigration, the Kelitah Department announced that no more immigrants could be accommodated in the camps due to budgetary constraints. The United States had promised a large loan for the purchase of tents, but all transactions had been frozen due to the Korean War.

When word reached the Iraqi Jewish community that Israel was also considering limits on *aliyah* from Iraq, people there were shocked. Operatives of Mossad le-Aliyah Bet inundated the Aliyah Department with letters telling of the Iraqi authorities' insistence on accelerating customs inspection and issuing 400–500 travel documents a day. The citizenship of anyone registering for *aliyah* was automatically revoked, and the Iraqi prime minister threatened to halt the airlift if the pace was not quick enough. The emissaries described angry outbursts among those waiting to leave, clashes with Arab rioters in Basra and elsewhere, and police brutality as Jews were chased from outlying villages to Baghdad, where they took refuge in the synagogues. Several children and adults had died, and a typhus epidemic was feared.[78] Raphael circulated these reports and demanded an increase in the quota for October to December 1950, which had been set at 10,000.

With the approach of winter, the Jewish Agency began looking into the purchase of tents and cabins for the immigrant camps. The Coordinating Committee advised the Kelitah Department to provide canvas huts rather than tents on the basis that they were more weatherproof. An argument then ensued over who would provide the extra money. Kaplan maintained that Israel lacked the foreign currency for this transaction and that it would be a long while before the shipment arrived. At this point, a new idea was suggested: tin shacks instead of canvas or wooden huts. Levi Eshkol claimed responsibility for this "invention." The Settlement Department had the required amount of tin and was prepared to hand it over to the Ministry of Labor for the construction of housing, thereby saving time and money. The young children would still be accommodated in wooden huts, as planned.

An increase in the number of *olim* from Iraq made a larger budget necessary. Space had to be found for them in the camps and additional *ma'abarot* needed to be built. Eshkol again appealed to Raphael to pare down immigration from Romania so that more Jews could be brought from Iraq and Poland. "Let there be a serious, well-calculated attempt to explain to these goyim [the Romanians] that during the coming months . . . the number of *olim* will be 5,000 and not 7,500," he said. Meanwhile, housing could be constructed and land found for new *ma'abarot*.

Despite the overtures of the emissaries in Iraq, Jewish Agency officials made a serious effort to enforce the quotas. Only 3,500 Iraqi Jews immigrated in August, and a similar figure was expected for September. Again the offices of the Jewish Agency were flooded with letters of protest: "The situation in the main synagogue . . . where the travelers are assembled and prepared for departure, has become chaotic beyond description . . . They are strewn everywhere in an appalling state . . . At first they use up the money somehow secured to pay for the flight, then they become a burden to the community. Nearly fifty babies have died."

Salah Jaber, Iraq's minister of the interior, informed the Near East travel company that he was dissatisfied with the rate at which the Jews were leaving. Moshe Sharett had voiced concern over the instability of the Iraqi regime and his forecast proved correct. In September the government collapsed and Nuri Said came to power.[79] Mossad activists in Iraq raced to move the *aliyah* enterprise forward. Said had warned the Jewish community of Baghdad to make haste; otherwise, he would take the Jews to the border himself. In October it was rumored that the government planned to fly the Jews to Amman; from there, they would be taken across the border to Israel. By this time more than 83,000 members of the community had reportedly lost their Iraqi citizenship.[80]

In the face of all this pressure, the Jewish Agency in Israel refused to cancel its immigration quotas and took pains to insure that deviation from the original plan remained minimal. Even in mid-January 1951, when a bomb was thrown at the synagogue in Baghdad where Jews registered for *aliyah* resulting in the loss of life and dozens of wounded, no significant rise was detectable in the number of *olim* from Iraq.[81] The Joint Distribution Committee complained that the Iraqi Jewish community was sending hundreds of blind people to Israel and it would refuse to handle them. At the same time, the emissaries in Iraq kept pleading with Israel to open its gates to more *olim* whose lives were at risk.[82]

At the meetings of the Coordinating Committee, Eshkol was mortified that his colleagues could still call for an intensification of *aliyah*. Such a step would be catastrophic and would bring Israel back to where it had been before, he said. The dearth of housing and employment ruled out any deviation from the established quotas. In principle, Golda Meir was in favor of free immigration, but as superintendent of the *ma'abarot* she was very much aware of the problems. All the grandiose schemes for development, which were expected to employ large numbers of *olim,* had failed to materialize, and the sums that were channeled into government-sponsored projects were astronomical but insufficient. Hopes that the immigrants could earn a living from agriculture alone had been dashed; outside jobs were necessary to supplement their income. The greatest problem of all—housing—was compounded by the shortage of building supplies. Josephthal's recommendation was to cut back *aliyah* from other countries, detain some groups in Marseilles, and set aside an emergency budget for absorbing Iraqi Jewry. If the lack of housing persisted, the Jewish Agency would have to build out of any material that was available—even mats.

Ben-Gurion once again emerged the victor. He was not impressed by the arguments of his opponents and as chairman his summary of the meeting was as follows: "We all agree that it is incumbent upon us to bring [to Israel] all the Jews of Iraq for as long as we are allowed to." He shrugged off the comments of Eshkol, Josephthal, and Golda Meir with a mixture of playfulness and seriousness, suggesting that Israel manufacture houses out of clay "like the Arabs, who build villages without cement and without foreign currency, using only materials available locally." The Coordinating Committee voted to endorse full-scale *aliyah* from Iraq on the condition that the flow from other countries be drastically contained. The subcommittee that was formed to handle the matter (Raphael, Herman, Josephthal, and Shapira) was no more successful in controlling immigration than had been the previous one.[83]

The Law of Return—1950

On 27 June 1950, at the height of the controversy over immigration restrictions, a new bill was brought before the Knesset: the Law of Return, which was described as the "bill of rights of the Jewish people." As the Knesset debated this proposal, the broad consensus that existed on the subject of the ingathering of the exiles was highlighted once again. Speeches from both sides of the political spectrum left no doubt about the basic conviction that Israel had been established for the sake of Jews the world over and that it was the natural right of every Jew to settle there at any time he so desired.[84] In this respect, the Law of Return differed from immigration laws enacted in other countries. The latter dealt primarily with quotas and various restrictions upon the immigrant until receiving citizenship, a process which sometimes took years. The Law of Return, by contrast, automatically awarded citizenship to any Jew who expressed a desire to settle in the Jewish state. Ben-Gurion explained the underlying principle: "The State is not conferring upon Diaspora Jews the right of return. That right preceded the State of Israel and enabled it to be built. This right originates in the historical bond between Jewish people and its homeland, which has never been severed." [85]

The Law of Return was passed on 5 July 1950 after three readings. [86] The right of return, which Ben-Gurion spoke of as applying to all Jews, was also the core of remarks by Knesset member Israel Bar-Yehuda, who later became minister of the interior. [87] Bar-Yehuda maintained that "immigration to Eretz Yisrael, to the State of Israel, is a natural right that no one can give or take away." [88]

These talks were all on the theoretical plane. They dealt with the entitlement of every Jew to immigrate—not the actions taken by the state and the Jewish Agency to organize *aliyah* from various countries, which became a source of controversy. It should be added, however, that there were three cases in which the minister of the interior was not obligated to grant an immigrant's visa: if the applicant "(a) is engaged in an activity directed against the Jewish people; or (b) is likely to endanger public health or the security of the State; or (c) is a person with a criminal past, likely to endanger public welfare." In these exceptional cases one could hear echoes of the debates over demographic makeup that left their mark on the Immigration Ministry back in 1948.

The task of regulating mass immigration gave rise to perplexing problems that put Israel's policymakers to the test time after time. The Jewish Agency Executive voted to introduce restrictions at the end of 1948, in May 1949, in October 1949, in 1950, and again in early 1951. The need to vote so many times shows that the decision was never implemented; it was disregarded repeatedly by *aliyah* activists who had different ideas about what needed to be done. Raphael measured the achievements of his department by its success in mobilizing large-scale immigration; the Mossad, too, saw its mission as the encouragement of *aliyah* all over the globe. The Joint Distribution Committee, which financed the upkeep and transportation of the immigrants, was not bound by the decisions of the Jewish Agency and, like the Mossad, could ignore them. Raphael, as a member of the Jewish Agency Executive, was not in the same position. However, he had his own ways of circumventing Jewish Agency directives and increasing *aliyah*.

He publicized urgent telegrams from *shelihim* and community officials depicting the dangers confronting the Jews and their great torment. Some of these telegrams were commissioned by Raphael himself as a pressure tactic. The Mossad advised *olim* to set out on the first leg of their journey in order to create hard facts; the Jewish Agency dared not leave them stranded. This was the case with thousands of Egyptian Jews who left for Italy and with other *olim* who reached Marseilles.

Let us not forget that all deliberations on this subject were veiled in secrecy. The Jewish Agency leadership was loath to appear publicly as blocking immigration—the lifeblood of the young nation. *Aliyah* was one of the banners waved during the 1948 elections, and the Jewish Agency did, after all, represent political parties. In 1949, when the critical situation in the camps was reported in the newspapers, the Jewish Agency still took precautions to keep the public in the dark with regard to its decisions on immigration. During this period Israeli society was largely unaware of the immigrants' plight. Only when people began to hear of the medical neglect and high incidence of infectious diseases did they change their minds about mass immigration. In the years to come health considerations were to play a dominant role in shaping both public opinion and national policy.

It is also noteworthy that views on this subject cut across political lines. Every party and movement had its own supporters and opponents of mass immigration. Shapira discerned an interesting phenomenon: "There seems to be an inverse ratio between the number [of *olim*] and the responsibility of the speaker. The smaller the responsibility, the larger the numbers; the greater the responsibility, the smaller the numbers." [89] This was also an allusion to the opposition, but the major schism was between *aliyah* activists, who defended unfettered immigration, and absorption workers, who sought to introduce controls.

The endeavors of the Jewish Agency to collaborate with the government and draw up joint recommendations on the subject of immigration quotas did not succeed. The work of the committees became a wrestling match between those who were for and those who were against. The key to a binding decision was in the hands of David Ben-Gurion. As long as he continued to defend mass immigration, there was no way of enforcing decisions to limit it. Nevertheless, he was not insensitive to the urgent problems and tried to create a formal body to devise solutions. He originally favored a format similar to the committee that planned mass immigration during World War II (1943–45). [90] He wanted a small team of economists and national-planning experts to deal comprehensively with all aspects of absorption. However, pressed by the Jewish Agency for immediate action, he founded the Coordinating Committee, whose members were carefully selected to insure efficiency and conformity with his own ideas. The Coordinating Committee played an instrumental role in elucidating various aspects of immigration policy, but it was unable to curb immigration. Because of the unexpected exodus of Jews from Yemen, Iraq, and Romania, none of the committee's recommendations on the subject were implemented.

The disagreement over the quantitative and qualitative aspects of *aliyah* became more and more fierce. Finally, at the end of 1951, it was decided to introduce restrictions, but these differed from any that had been recommended previously. This change was partly due to altered circumstances, but it was also very much a product of the shift in Ben-Gurion's thinking.

CHAPTER FOUR

From Immigrant Camps to Ma'abarot

Housing, Employment, and Health

ISRAEL INVESTED an enormous amount of imagination, emotion, and money to move the Great Aliyah from dream to reality, all of which made the painful inadequacy of the absorption network even more glaring. The question is, why were such great difficulties in absorption allowed to develop in the first place?

While Israel's leaders marveled at the "ingathering of the exiles" materializing before their eyes, they were not blind to the obstacles that lay ahead; they saw a certain amount of difficulty as an inevitable and normal part of the country's transition to statehood. Yet no one anticipated that the problems would be so severe or that the climb to overcome them would be so steep.

The most pressing task was to find temporary shelter for tens of thousands of homeless people, for whom camps seemed to present the best solution. Transit camps were first proposed during the prestate period.[1] At that time Ben-Gurion sat with a team of experts who envisaged way stations where masses of immigrants could be registered and classified. After a period of vocational training, they would be referred to permanent housing and jobs. The newcomers were to stay at these facilities for only a few weeks. It never occurred to the creators of the immigrant camps or *ma'abarot* that people might languish there for years.

As far as Ben-Gurion was concerned, there could be no higher national priority than *aliyah*. Without it, he said, Israel's survival was at best tenuous.[2] His goal was to bring in 1.5 million *olim* over the next decade, raising the Jewish population in Israel to two million. He counted on the arrival of 150,000 immigrants a year.

But on the eve of Israel's founding, the Jewish Agency planned for the absorption of 150,000 *olim* over a period of two years. It was assumed that half the newcomers would spend a month at immigrant hostels, after which they would either move to kibbutzim, *moshavim* and Youth Aliyah institutions, or join their relatives. The other half of the *olim* would be sponsored by the Jewish Agency until housing could be found for them in urban centers.[3]

There was an enormous gap between the forecasts and reality. No one imagined camps populated by 100,000 immigrants at one time, some of whom were forced to remain there for six months and more as the crush of new arrivals continued unabated.[4] The camps themselves were built hastily using the shoddiest of materials; the most urgent task was to provide the immigrants with a roof over their heads. Then there was the problem of finding them jobs. There was no question the only way to alleviate the immigrants' suffering and to lighten the financial burden on the Jewish Agency was by thinning out the camp population.

Yet another hurdle was medical care. *Aliyah* emissaries were aware that a large number of Holocaust survivors were sick or handicapped, and the same was true for immigrants from Arab countries. No precise figures were available, but it was clear that the local medical establishment, with its limited resources, could not stand alone. The future of these immigrants and the continuation of *aliyah* was thus dependent upon the performance of the absorption network.

Solutions to the Housing Shortage

A major effort was made to overcome the housing problem, but the path seemed forever strewn with obstacles. The various bodies involved—the Jewish Agency, the government, and public housing companies—failed to synchronize their activities so that the work was not carried out systematically. A vicious cycle was created, whereby the greater the pressure, the more the authorities resorted to hasty and provisional solutions, which would be replaced later by solutions that were just as impermanent. The problem was not so much that the absorption authorities were shortsighted as that objective circumstances kept changing.

Immigrant housing was originally in the hands of the Aliyah Department's Housing Division, but this task was clearly more than it could handle. The Ministry of Labor, which was responsible for public building, seemed a better fit for the job. In September 1948 the ministry established a National Housing Department to take charge of development on a nationwide scale. A committee was appointed to examine all aspects of the construction industry (materials, hauling, building techniques, hiring contractors and builders, etc.) and to draw up a two-year building plan accordingly.[5] Experts were brought in to study 150 experimental housing projects in different parts of the country to find the model best suited to Israel's climate and budgetary constraints. However, the very thoroughness of the committee led to its downfall. Meticulous research of every component was extremely time-consuming, whereas the tens of thousands of immigrants waiting in the camps required an immediate solution. The work of the committee was thus suspended.

One-quarter million immigrants were expected during 1949. The supply of housing in abandoned Arab villages was running out quickly, and it was imperative to build thousands of new units without delay. As a result, all the building contractors in the country, both public and private, were brought together under a single roof to undertake the gargantuan task of constructing immigrant housing.

For this purpose "Amidar" was founded in 1948 with a basic capital of IL 5 million. Shares were held by the government, the Jewish Agency, the Jewish National Fund, and various building firms. It was managed by representatives of all the shareholding institutions as well as a five-member board. In addition to the capital invested by the partners, it hoped to mobilize funding by floating IL 500,000 in bonds on the international market.

Upon its establishment, Amidar drew up plans for the construction of low-cost housing on a massive scale. The first stage called for sixteen thousand units in or around urban centers.[6] Sites were chosen with an eye to saving time and money, which meant building where infrastructure already existed. Developing new towns in far-flung locations called for a much greater investment. Another consideration was the proximity of jobs. Work began on thousands of housing units made of wood or concrete blocks, averaging twenty-six square meters per unit. Amidar did its best, but on its own it could not keep pace with the demand.[7]

Temporary Encampments

The Kelitah Department, confronted daily by mobs of protesting immigrants, decided to take some steps on its own. It imported 6,000 cabins from Sweden, setting up a series of temporary encampments on the outskirts of cities, large *moshavim* and kibbutzim, on the assumption that the immigrants would find work nearby. The housing was cheap and quick to assemble, and it eased the pressure in the camps to a certain extent. The Ministry of Labor planners, however, objected strongly. They feared that these temporary neighborhoods would become permanent fixtures and turn into slums, which would perpetuate the immigrants' misery.

Regional planning efforts did not progress much in 1949. The government was still working on its national development policy and a map of new settlements was on the drafting table. Amidar's projects fell far short of answering the tremendous need. By springtime, the Kelitah Department decided on the con-

struction of thirty tent cities for thirty thousand to forty thousand immigrants
who would be evacuated from the camps. Part of the reason for this decision was
financial; once these people were out of the camps the Jewish Agency would no
longer need to support them. Tent cities were built in the vicinity of Tel-Aviv,
Petah Tikva, and other places. The construction of permanent housing was
turned over to the Ministry of Labor, now headed by Golda Meir, who had been
summoned in March 1949 from Moscow, where she served as Israel's diplomatic
representative.

Government Housing Programs

In May 1949 the minister of labor announced that 30,000 housing units would
be built by the end of the year. She added that eight neighborhoods, consisting
of 2,250 units each, could be readied for occupation within a few weeks. Much
of the construction work would be done by the future residents as part of a dual
housing and employment project. But for a whole host of reasons this project
was not implemented.[8]

First of all, many sites slated for public building were owned by private individuals and as such were not open to expropriation. In some cases, land purchased by the Jewish National Fund had been promised to parties who put up
resistance. Abandoned Arab property and tracts of Arab land in Jewish territory
were also a source of conflict, pitting local development authorities against the
government.

The selection of sites was further impeded by the absence of national and regional development programs. The immigrants themselves were anxious to live
in the center of the country near large towns where job opportunities were more
plentiful. Thus the Ministry of Labor devoted most of its attention to this region. However, vacant land was difficult to obtain in the center of the country, a
fact that greatly slowed the building process. Delays were also caused by the
shortage of engineers and other professionals. Most of the immigrants hired to
work in construction were unskilled, and it took time to train them. Construction materials were hard to find and had to be imported. As always, money was a
problem and Israel's foreign currency reserves were low.

The first stage of the Labor Ministry's program, calling for 10,000 housing
units, encountered serious resistance in the Knesset. The main objection was the
concentration of building sites along the coast. Ninety percent of Israel's Jewish
population lived in the strip between Rehovot and Acre, and it was felt that further development in this region ran counter to the government's policy of population dispersal.[9] The ministry also came under fire for its slow pace and low

building standards. Having been criticized for its reliance on wooden huts, the ministry decided to build more extensively in concrete and to improve the quality of housing. Dwellings larger than the standard 26 square meters were designed for families with many children.

Amidar was slated to execute most of the work but failed to live up to expectations. Rather than functioning as a trailblazer in remote corners of the country, it gave priority to low-cost housing projects in prime locations. Amidar's chief contribution thus lay in building up the periphery of existing settlements, mainly along the coast and in the center of the country. toward the end of 1949 the company suffered a serious financial setback; the partners reneged on their commitments, and plans to mobilize overseas capital dissolved. Within a year the partnership broke up, leaving only the government and the Jewish Agency. Amidar continued to operate, albeit on a smaller scale, but it was no longer Israel's "national" housing company; it was a company like any other. [10]

A Race Against Time

With building running so far behind schedule, the Ministry of Labor decided to coordinate all aspects of public housing itself. The ministry's Housing Division was charged with planning, commissioning, and supervising the construction of immigrant housing all over the country in accordance with the government's policy of population dispersal. The duties of this division were broad. They included scouting out appropriate tracts of land; drawing up architectural plans; determining size, construction materials, and techniques; connecting the buildings to the water supply; and other development work. Preparations commenced for the implementation of the government housing program for 1950, calling for the construction of forty thousand units. However, the program remained mostly on paper. Stormy weather kept construction workers away during the early months of the year, and only twenty-eight thousand units were built in all, through the combined efforts of the government, Jewish Agency, and Amidar.

Because of the needed haste, the housing was constructed on the outskirts of existing settlements without planned sites and without topographic surveys or planning. Consequently, the builders confronted one problem after another, and troubles continued even after the tenants moved in. In Herzliya, a row of houses was built on a slope at the edge of a precipice. After the first rains, several homes had to be bulldozed before they collapsed. In other areas roofs blew off and walls cracked. [11]

In effect, the Housing Division lay the groundwork for the settlement map of the new state. It was invested with so much power that it operated virtually autonomously and was the decisive factor in many aspects of planning and development. This division continued to grow and eventually became a separate ministry—the Ministry of Housing.

Meanwhile, the absorption authorities searched anxiously for emergency housing solutions. In October 1949 the construction of transit and work camps provided some relief, but not enough to keep pace with the rate of immigration. By the end of 1950 nearly 100,000 immigrants were living in camps and *ma'abarot,* and the number rose to 250,000 in 1951. The task of moving these people into permanent housing continued for years. Consequently, the *ma'abara* became one of the stock features of the Israeli landscape during the country's formative years.

Employment Problems

One of the most serious problems in the immigrant camps was the lack of employment. The majority of immigrants were utterly destitute upon arrival; they had neither money nor property. Jews leaving Eastern Europe were forbidden to remove any capital, and other countries permitted only paltry sums. Immigrants from Arab countries were forced to leave their possessions behind or sell them for a fraction of their worth. If any money remained, it generally was used up on the long journey to Israel. Those few people who managed to bring their assets with them were able to secure housing and support their families until they found employment, but the overwhelming majority were penniless and totally dependent upon the Jewish Agency and the government.

The immigrants who arrived in 1948 were usually able to find jobs, replacing Israelis who had been drafted. However, the winter of 1949 was a harsh one and marked the onset of growing unemployment. In the early months the immigrants were employed in such seasonal jobs as fruit-picking in nearby agricultural settlements, but this source dried up when the season was over. In addition, some forty thousand soldiers had been demobilized since the beginning of the year and required job placement, among them new immigrants and volunteers who had served with *Mahal* and *Gahal.* The Ministry of Defense ordered employment bureaus to give preference to former soldiers, further increasing joblessness in the immigrant sector.

So that employment could be provided for the tens of thousands who joined the workforce every month, the problem needed to be addressed on a national level. There was a need for careful regional and local planning along with a massive injection of capital and intensive training. The time factor was especially critical. Unfortunately, the physical planning, which was meant to encourage population dispersal, did not coincide with socioeconomic planning. Housing for immigrants was put up hastily without a comprehensive development scheme, and most of the camps and temporary shelters were located in the center of the country. Such a large workforce in one area naturally created pockets of unemployment. Moreover, many of the immigrants lacked the type of vocational skills required in Israel, and thousands were categorized as "hard core" (most problematic) on account of their age, medical condition, or other factors.

Public Works, Small Farms, and Kiosks

Projects sponsored and financed by the government to provide jobs for the immigrant population were generally connected with building or agriculture. Such public works as paving roads and digging canals were problematic because the immigrants were unaccustomed to physical labor; their level of productivity was low and they found it hard to adjust to the new tasks. The same held true for work in the construction industry. There were also objective difficulties involved, such as shortages of equipment (tractors, cement mixers, etc.), raw materials (asphalt, lumber, steel, etc.), and skilled manpower (engineers, foremen, etc.). A quarry near Haifa, for example, could not be operated for lack of machinery. Water was always in short supply because the plumbing infrastructure was old and inadequate.

Many immigrants were hired on a seasonal basis by local farmers. In winter they picked citrus fruit and in summer they harvested grapes and olives. However, these jobs were not a steady source of livelihood. It was thought that those immigrants who were sent to abandoned Arab villages could run auxiliary farms to supplement their income. But drawbacks of this plan included an insufficiency of water, the fact that instructors had to be brought in, and the need for money to reclaim the land and purchase farm implements. Furthermore, agriculture required a constant input of labor; as part-time employment, farms were far from ideal. All this affected the motivation of the immigrants, which was not particularly high from the outset. Considering the relatively large investment in resources and manpower, there was a question whether starting up such farms was worthwhile at all. The majority of immigrants were not inclined to take the risk and much preferred an ordinary full-time job. Unsuccessful attempts to establish farms in the Ramleh and Lod regions were seen as proof that the scheme was not a feasible one.

Finding suitable employment and housing was even more daunting for those immigrants who had health problems. They could not do the type of strenuous labor required in government-initiated projects, and opportunities for less-demanding jobs, such as peddling, were mainly in the center of the country. Complaining to the Coordinating Committee about the overly large ratio of elderly immigrants, Josephthal said, "Such a disproportion is unhealthy even in our country, which is accustomed to the abnormal. We are now planning to build 1,500 kiosks and 600 shops [for the elderly]. Every local council is up in arms against us."[12]

Immigrants in the Workforce

Comparing the Great Aliyah to immigration during the British Mandate, which was also quite substantial in relation to the resident population, we find that, within the span of thirty years (1919–48), the Jewish community increased eleven-fold, from 56,000 to 650,000 souls.[13] These earlier newcomers, however, did not require a lengthy stay at transit camps. The reason for this seems to have been demographic. *Aliyah* was more selective at that time, as reflected in the age of the immigrants. Until the end of the Mandate, the proportion of children under the age of fourteen was 17.6 percent and, among the *ma'apilim* who arrived during World War II, only 6 percent. The proportion of old people was also low, accounting for 5–6 percent of the *olim* and 2–3 percent of the *ma'apilim*. Most of the prestate immigrants were of working age—between fifteen and fifty-nine years old; 77 percent of the *olim* and 90 percent of the *ma'apilim* were in this category.

Family status was another factor; there was a high percentage of bachelors among the *olim* of the Mandatory period. Sixty-seven percent of all adult males who immigrated to Palestine in 1919–23 were unmarried, as were 66 percent of the *ma'apilim*. Only in the 1930s, when more families began to immigrate, did the proportion of bachelors drop.[14]

Age distribution during the Great Aliyah was entirely different from the previous generations. The number of children and elderly was high, and the number of working adults was low. Family status differed, too. Bachelors now accounted for only 35 percent of the *olim*. There were more married couples and families were generally larger, especially among those from the Asian countries. As a result, the ratio of breadwinners and dependents changed.[15] Moreover, whereas 43 percent of those who immigrated during the Mandate came without their families, after the establishment of the state this was true of only 22 percent.

There is no question that variables such as age, family status, and health had a pivotal impact on the absorption process. During the Mandate, fewer than 30 percent of the *olim* in the fifteen to fifty-nine age bracket were financially dependent; after statehood, the number was almost twice as high—56 percent.[16] Those who arrived during the Mandatory period found their niche with greater ease; they were young, robust, and unmarried, and they quickly joined the workforce. Immigrants with large families had more difficulty finding jobs and housing. Their problems were compounded by the economic crisis that struck during the early years of independence and hampered preparations for the great waves of *aliyah.*

Immigrant absorption was likewise affected by competition between veteran settlers and newcomers and by the interest of certain institutions in protecting their past achievements. The workers' councils were afraid that cheap, unorganized labor by thousands of immigrants would undermine their struggle for fair wages and workers' rights. Political interests were at stake, too. Hence, radical measures were taken to keep the immigrants from penetrating the job market.

The absorption authorities were aware of all these difficulties, but they were powerless to help. Most distressing was the sense that solving the immigrants' problems would take time and money—both of which they did not have. The deliberations of the Jewish Agency Executive point up the frustrating position in which the absorption network found itself.

Health Problems

The health of the immigrants was a particularly sore point; it figured prominently in every discussion of immigration policy and was behind much of the criticism levelled at those responsible for organizing *aliyah.* Later it would cause a shift in the public attitude toward immigrants and immigration as a whole.

As tens of thousands of immigrants crowded into squalid immigrant camps, it was impossible to ignore the vast numbers of sick and handicapped, elderly persons and babies. Most of the medical problems had started while the immigrants were still in their home countries, but some fell ill or took a turn for the worse en route to Israel. Under the conditions in the camps, diseases spread and the health of those who were most susceptible deteriorated rapidly.

Health problems weighed heavily on immigration and absorption from the start. As soon as Israel declared its independence, Moshe Shapira, who was concurrently minister of immigration and head of the Jewish Agency Aliyah Department, drew attention to the medical profile of the immigrants. Doctors working at the DP camps in Germany, Austria, and Italy reported that at least 10 percent of the inmates required treatment. There were crippled people and some suffering from tuberculosis and other contagious diseases. Youth Aliyah officials spoke of 5,000 orphaned children in Germany, Holland, and Belgium who had survived the Holocaust after being hidden by Christian families; many of these were frail and in need of medical attention.[17]

In December 1948 the Zionist executive approved a plan to screen *aliyah* candidates in Europe for health problems. Before receiving a visa, all candidates would be examined by a team of doctors under joint government and Jewish Agency supervision. This team would be responsible for drawing up a list of illnesses that would disqualify a person for *aliyah*. The executive also voted to bar the entry of handicapped persons.[18]

Overseas Medical Treatment

According to the health reports submitted to the Zionist executive, there were thousands of invalids in the DP camps in Germany and widespread illness among the North African Jews, many of whom tried to conceal the fact that they suffered from chronic or infectious diseases. Raphael proposed the transfer of these people to a special camp in Marseilles, where they would receive medical treatment.[19]

Marseilles : The medical delegation sent to Marseilles by the Aliyah Department was totally disoriented: "The human component of people from North Africa was unfamiliar both to the Israeli emissaries and to the physicians who were specialists in the problems of European immigrants. The mentality, intelligence, and customs were different. The basic rules of hygiene were completely unknown. The diseases were different."[20]

The doctors arrived with no knowledge of North African Jewry or their medical complaints and were shocked by what they saw. They were quick to adopt negative stereotypes, especially with regard to North African culture and mannerisms. Above all, they were horrified by the number of persons in need of treatment. In 1948 a total of three hundred immigrants, most of them European, were detained in Marseilles for medical reasons. In 1949, when the majority of immigrants hailed from North Africa, more than five thousand of the twenty-five thousand people who were examined required long periods of hospitalization in intensive care. Close to 70 percent were suffering from trachoma, a contagious eye disease. Skin diseases and tuberculosis also were prevalent.

The medical delegation recommended calling in OSE, a relief organization that had administered aid to survivors in post-war Europe.[21] The workload was so heavy that at least two hundred doctors and medical technicians were needed. In 1949 more than two thousand *olim* were admitted to French hospitals, and the same number were treated at Mount Scopus, a hospital operated jointly by OSE and Israeli doctors.

Immigrants in need of medical attention continued to pour into Marseilles at such a pace that French hospitals refused to admit any more for lack of beds. The OSE and Israeli delegations were also working at full capacity and were unable to add beds, laboratories, or surgical wards. It was decided to shorten the course of treatment and to transfer patients to Israel before they had completely recovered. This change imposed an additional burden on Israeli medical institutions and infuriated the Jewish Agency, which insisted on keeping persons with contagious diseases out of the country.[22]

Aden and Cyprus: Back in 1945 a group of four thousand Yemenite Jews on their way to Palestine had been stopped by the British and forced to remain in Aden for several years. At the end of 1947, they were sent to "Geula," a transit camp where they were joined by others seeking to immigrate. By September 1948 more than five thousand persons were living in the camp in cramped and unhygienic conditions that bred germs and disease.[23] The results of blood tests were alarming. More than 80 percent of the immigrants were found to be carriers of various strains of malaria. The Jewish Agency Executive brought this fact to the attention of the government, but it was decided that all the Yemenites would be airlifted to Israel, including those with communicable diseases.

The detention camps in Cyprus were full of frail Holocaust survivors whose health was made worse by substandard housing and malnutrition. The mothers were so weak that they could barely feed their infants, who were disease-prone and suffered from many complications due to the lack of medical attention.

Sickness and Epidemics in Israel

Few of the decisions to impose medical selection were implemented. In those countries where the Jews had to be evacuated without delay, entire communities were brought over regardless of health. Sometimes the local authorities would not permit examinations, as was the case in the Communist countries, and at times the sick and disabled could not be left behind because no one remained to care for them. When the Jews of Bulgaria left en masse in late 1948 and early 1949, an entire ship was filled with residents of an old-age home. There were communities that sent their invalids to Israel, while the healthy stayed home or moved to other countries.

Caring for these people in Israel imposed a heavy burden, especially when hospitalization was required. Israeli hospitals could not accommodate even half of those who needed their services. As the immigrants kept coming and the percentage of seriously ill continued to grow, the situation in the camps went from bad to worse.

Tuberculosis, which was considered incurable at the time, was widespread among Holocaust survivors and immigrants from Asian countries. The Ministry of Health reported 1,760 active cases among the 200,000 immigrants who reached Israel during its first year of statehood. Many of these lived at large in the immigrant camps for lack of hospital beds. Another 3,000 were diagnosed with suspected tuberculosis. As many as 1,500 mental patients walked around untreated, posing a danger to themselves and others, because there were no facilities for them.[24] In addition, the camps were full of crippled people, blind people, and retarded children, adding to the sense of despair.[25]

From time to time, epidemics flared up in the camps and spread like wildfire due to the overcrowding and weakened condition of the immigrants. A meningitis epidemic struck during the summer of 1948, killing children and babies. On its heels came a polio epidemic. The camp directors were ordered to pay greater attention to hygiene and sanitation, but there was little they could do.

Zvi Herman of the Zionist executive pronounced the situation in the Israeli camps worse than that in the camps in Germany. He was appalled at the large number of diseased and handicapped immigrants who had arrived recently. Even those who supported nonselective *aliyah* were shocked by the magnitude of the problem. Josephthal, head of the Kelitah Department, described the immigrant camps as a keg of dynamite:

> Those of us who work in absorption on a daily basis are on the brink of nervous collapse . . . With 50 men, women and children sleeping together in one hall, no wonder the atmosphere is impossible. These are degrading conditions that must not be allowed to continue. Every kind of social crime is committed in the camps with the exception of murder: prostitution, thievery, violence, dishonesty. Upon arrival, the better elements quickly sink into depression, to the point where they no longer have the strength to do anything but weep quietly.[26]

Shortage of Doctors and Nurses

The shortage of doctors, especially pediatricians, put a serious strain on the health-care system in the camps. Plans to employ some seventy immigrant doctors were impeded by their unfamiliarity with local conditions. The Ministry of Health arranged for them to work alongside experienced doctors but the immigrants did not trust them.

The shortage of nurses was graver still. In 1948 there were reportedly two thousand nurses in the country, but most of them had left the profession. It was particularly difficult to find nurses willing to work in the immigrant camps, in health education, preventive care, and nursing duty in the infirmaries. Very few responded to an appeal in which nurses were asked to come of their own free will; as a result, emergency measures were declared. In July 1949 a mobilization order was issued requiring all nurses to report for work in the camps. However, the majority ignored the order, and those who did appear brought proof that they could not serve. Of the 300 summoned in Tel-Aviv, only 120 showed up and 99 percent asked for a release. Among their excuses were family responsibilities, transportation difficulties, unwillingness to do night or Sabbath shifts, and low pay. Equally unsuccessful were a live-in arrangement for young nurses and an accelerated nursing course for girls. The young women had trouble adjusting to life in the camps. Aside from their social isolation, they slept in tents or shacks without hot water and the work was both mentally and physically exhausting. The few who consented did not stay on long. The shortage of nursing staff and the frequent turnover took a severe toll on the quality of health care in the camps. On the outside, the situation was not much better. The opening of a hospital in Jaffa was delayed because "not a single nurse could be found to assist the doctor in the maternity ward in the event of an operation." [27]

Infant Mortality

When the public became aware of the high infant mortality rates in the camps in July-August 1949, there was a great uproar in the Knesset and news media. During the British Mandate, the Yishuv had made considerable progress in this sphere, achieving one of the lowest rates of infant mortality in the world: twenty-nine deaths per thousand. In the wake of the Great Aliyah, the figure rose to fifty-two per thousand.[28] This did not reflect the rate in the immigrant camps, which was much higher than for the general population.

There were a number of reasons for this depressing state of affairs. First of all, the mothers were themselves in poor health. Many were concentration camp survivors suffering from malnutrition and other physical disorders. Morbidity was also high among women from Islamic countries. The hardships of the journey and the primitive living conditions in the camps caused a further deterioration in their health, which adversely affected their offspring.

The shortage of hospital facilities was another critical factor. Yisrael Rokah, a cabinet minister and mayor of Tel-Aviv, bemoaned the fact that every night dozens of children from the immigrant camp in Be'er Yaakov were turned away by Tel-Aviv's municipal hospital because it was full and the doctors could not accept a larger patient load. In the camps in Ra'anana, he said, two hundred out of three hundred children had dysentery, but only twenty were in the camp's prim-

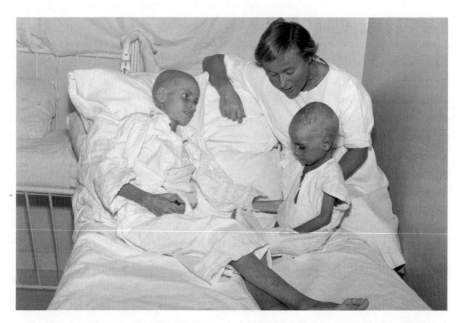

Malka and Hannah from Yemen adjusting to the miracle of seeing for the first time after eye surgery at the Haifa Government Hospital, Haifa. *Photograph by Teddy Brauner*

itive infirmary.[29] The hospitals admitted only the severest cases, and deaths were on the rise. To add insult to injury, a rumor had begun to circulate among the immigrants that most of those who were hospitalized did not survive. As a result, many parents—Holocaust survivors, in particular—avoided hospitals and tried to care for their children on their own. Sometimes they sold their valuables to hire a private doctor. Parents were afraid to leave their children in the camp infirmaries, which had been set up with seven hundred beds. In the words of one eyewitness,

> The basic problem with isolation rooms [in the camps] was not treating the small children but winning the parents' trust . . . We were strangers in their eyes and they did not trust us; their past experience had taught them that even Jews were not to be trusted . . . The fear gleamed in their eyes. When a sick child or infant was finally given over to us the scenes were heartrending. The parents were overwrought, as if they were parting from their child forever. This conduct was trying and painful, but understandable. After all, the sick infant or child was the core of their "new life," of all their hopes and dreams for rebuilding their shat-

tered family. Most of these children were the product of second marriages or born after the first offspring were lost in the Holocaust.[30]

During the summer of 1949 many children in the camps came down with an intestinal disorder accompanied by vomiting and diarrhea. Hospitalization and intravenous treatment were necessary to prevent dehydration, but bed space and medical equipment were lacking; as a result, as many as 50 percent of the ill children died.[31]

Missing Children

With so many children ailing and in need of emergency care, tragic errors sometimes occurred. In the summer of 1949, Operation Magic Carpet brought over masses of Yemenite Jews, a large proportion of whom were sick and broken from their travels and confinement in Aden. Infants were starving, and some one-year-olds weighed no more than eight to ten pounds. Diseases and epidemics encountered in Israel struck them harder than anyone else, pushing the mortality rate ever higher and creating a painful problem: missing children. Dr. Sheba, then chief medical officer of the IDF, testified about that summer:

> Since a hospital was needed for the immigrants of Operation Magic Carpet, Ben-Gurion was consulted, as he was on every issue, and we were instructed to open three buildings (of the army hospital) for the children. The problem at the time was the death of children from typhoid fever, malaria, and infectious diseases; from the age of one, they were being cut down like flies. Within 24 hours, in Passover 1949, we opened a pediatric ward at the army hospital. For lack of cribs, an ordinary bed was used for every three infants, with cardboard dividers between them. Sometimes the children died, and their parents, who had meanwhile been moved from Rosh Ha'ayin to some other camp, were not located. As they saw it, the child had "disappeared."[32]

The camp directors also told of "lost" children. Great efforts were made to unravel the mystery of their disappearance, in some cases successfully and in others not, taking a tragic toll on the families' peace of mind.[33] Finding clues was rendered all the more difficult by the outbreak of a fire in the health-service archives, which destroyed most of the relevant documents. Some families have refused to give up hope and continue to seek their loved ones to this day.

Media Response

When the DP camps in Germany were evacuated in the spring of 1949, the Aliyah Department wrestled with the difficult question of whether to permit the immigration of sick immigrants. On the list of visa seekers were 1,160 tuberculosis patients, 440 chronically ill people, 200 mental patients, and 600 invalids. Together with their families, this group numbered close to 6,000 persons. Once the camps were closed and most of the Jews had left, it was unthinkable "to abandon these unfortunates and leave them to their own devices or the mercy of the non-Jews." With great reluctance, however, the department decided against handling these applications for the time being.[34]

The Israeli newspapers were quick to report the fact that many candidates for *aliyah* were disease-ridden and disabled; they warned of harm to the country and to the immigrants themselves, who were destined to "a debilitating existence that would ruin their health, corrupt their morals and undermine their emotional stability."[35] As stories about the health crisis in the camps proliferated, public anxiety increased. The minister of the interior was criticized for allowing business licenses to be granted without health checks: "Sick persons, even some with skin diseases, have opened food and greengrocer shops, thereby contributing to the spread of infection."[36]

At the end of 1949, the press maintained that immigrants accounted for close to fifty thousand welfare cases, among them sick, handicapped, and elderly persons in need of attention. Ironically, blame for the failure of the health-care system fell on Moshe Shapira, who had tried to alert the government to this eventuality before the onset of *aliyah* in 1948. Shapira cited various objective reasons for the current state of affairs. The skeletal hospital network was a legacy of the Mandate, and the chronic shortage of equipment and staff was a matter of money. Then, of course, there was Israel's mass immigration policy: "We have brought over immigrants and disabled in numbers that no normal country, even one with enormous resources, would agree to handle. We have admitted crippled, emotionally disturbed and lung-diseased partisans from Europe in astonishing numbers. The aged, too, have been conveyed in multitudes."[37]

Dr. Meir, director-general of the Ministry of Health, acknowledged that the camps were a breeding ground for disease. His picture of the future was hardly optimistic: "If we get through this summer without a serious medical emergency in the absorption camps, it will be the greatest miracle since the founding of the state."[38] However, there was to be no miracle. Early in 1950 a polio epidemic erupted in Rosh Ha'ayin and soon reached epidemic proportions; the entire country was affected. The press spotlighted the horrific conditions in the camps and *ma'abarot,* triggering widespread panic. The public accused the Jewish Agency and the Ministry of Health of playing with the health of its citizens, and the immigrants were portrayed as harbingers of impending disaster.

Inadequate Hospital Facilities

When the British withdrew from Palestine, the country's hospitals were in shambles. As soon as the War of Independence began, beds were needed for thousands of wounded. Dr. Sheba, chief medical officer of the Israeli Defense Forces (IDF), ordered hospitals to be set up in abandoned British army barracks. The situation worsened at the start of 1949, when the Knesset passed the Disability Law requiring the state to treat and rehabilitate injured soldiers. More than twelve hundred persons had been disabled in the fighting, some of them severely.[39] The country's maternity hospitals were also overflowing, and many women had to give birth in the camps and *ma'abarot.* The high percentage of infant mortality and spread of communicable disease forced the Ministry of Health into action. Despite the overcrowding, even more beds were added to the existing hospital facilities, and a search was made for new buildings. The ministry negotiated at length with the Catholic and Scottish churches for permission to use the French convent in the Talbiyeh section of Jerusalem and the French and Scottish hospitals in Jaffa. The Acre fortress was converted into a mental hospital with four hundred beds. Even so, the country was still short thousands of beds.

At the first session of the Knesset in 1949, one member after another raised the subject of hospitalization. The minister of health pointed out that hospital beds throughout the country numbered twenty-five hundred at most, whereas the demand was twice as high. Two deathly ill patients were fighting for every bed, he said. Aside from five thousand beds for ordinary cases, thousands of places were needed for immigrants with tuberculosis, mental illness, chronic conditions, and communicable diseases.[40]

When it became public knowledge that many of those on their way to Israel were ill, attempts were made to prevent their coming. After the Polish government agreed to grant passports to all Jews who wished to emigrate but would not allow any kind of selection, the Ministry of Health considered holding the sick for medical treatment in Vienna or Italy. However, that summer the Joint Distribution Committee was phasing out its work with Holocaust survivors in Europe and refused to take on such a project. The Jewish Agency tried to convince the JDC and the International Relief Organization to continue their sponsorship of the survivors after they reached Israel. Eventually, the JDC agreed to assume responsibility for five thousand sick and dysfunctional persons from the camps in Germany and to establish rehabilitation centers for them in Israel. Co-operation between the Jewish Agency and the JDC gradually broadened to in-clude immigrants from other countries, and the JDC inaugurated a network of welfare institutions known as Malben.

Immigrant Health Services

During the early days of the state, the duties of certain authorities overlapped. This situation was both cumbersome and a waste of time and money. In the sphere of health, for example, there were at least ten different bodies that tended to compete with one another—if not openly then in a roundabout manner. At times the rivalry was personal or politically motivated. The Ministry of Health, the Jewish Agency, the Hadassah medical organization, the IDF medical corps, the municipalities, the national sick funds (Clalit, Leumit, Amamit, Maccabi), private hospitals, and Malben were all involved in the Israeli health-care system. The outcome was an ongoing battle over budgets and areas of jurisdiction.

The Immigrant Health Service was set up by the Jewish Agency at the end of World War II (December 1944) to provide medical care for survivors of the concentration camps. Before the establishment of the state, this service was run by Hadassah. In October 1946 this organization assumed responsibility for health care at immigrant hostels and transit camps. Medical supervision and budgets were the joint province of the Aliyah Department and Hadassah.[41] After independence, when immigration intensified and the *olim* were detained in camps for long periods, a debate arose as to who would organize and finance medical treatment. Once Hadassah ceased to perform this task, Josephthal of the Jewish Agency Kelitah Department proposed that the IDF step in, but this idea was not well received.[42] The government and the Jewish Agency thus de-cided to operate a health service together. The Ministry of Health assembled a staff of doctors and nurses, both veteran Israelis and new immigrants, and opened clinics and sick rooms in the camps. However, the problem of financing was the source of much conflict. The ministry claimed that the Jewish Agency had promised to foot the bills while it provided the administrative mechanism. The Jewish Agency denied this. Finally, at the end of 1948, an agreement was reached to divide expenses between them but the Jewish Agency failed to pay its full share.

The third partner, Hadassah, which had covered half the immigrant health budget before the founding of the state, reduced its participation to IL 120,000 a year, which accounted for only 16 percent of the budget. The reason given was a drop in fund-raising revenues in the United States. The Ministry of Health implored the Hadassah women in Israel and America to enlarge their contribution, but to no avail. Another battle was waged between Kupat Holim Clalit (which was affiliated with the Histadrut) and the other health funds. According to the agreement worked out by the Jewish Agency on the eve of Israel's independence, Kupat Holim Clalit was to perform an initial checkup on each *oleh,* who was then entitled to register with any fund he chose. The government promised to cover insurance premiums for the first three months.[43]

Medicine and Politics

The political parties took advantage of the health issue to build up their membership in the immigrant sector. Competition among the sick funds assumed political overtones that reverberated from the Knesset podium and in the daily press. The Kelitah Department was accused of favoritism toward Kupat Holim Clalit. The other sick funds claimed that it received a larger share of the budget and enjoyed greater exposure among the immigrants, in disregard of the March 1948 agreement. Kupat Holim Clalit was the only fund represented in the immigrant camps. After being examined by Kupat Holim Clalit doctors, it was customary for the *olim* to be directed to the Histadrut office, where they received a temporary membership card and automatically became members of this organization and Kupat Holim Clalit, without being given information about any other fund. The Kelitah Department did not respond to these charges. Josephthal maintained that Kupat Holim Clalit was the only sick fund with clinics all over the country and that the immigrants chose it because their final destination was unknown. However, this did not silence the protests; the other sick funds continued to contest the Labor Party's hold over the medical establishment.

Sometimes the public-health controversy overstepped party politics and touched upon the national agenda. A conflict erupted between Dr. Chaim Sheba, chief medical officer of the IDF and a Labor loyalist, who favored the inauguration of a national health system in Israel, and Dr. Soroka, chairman of Kupat Holim Clalit, who wanted to see his institution remain independent and fought to broaden its powers and budgetary framework.[44] The leaders of Mapai and the Histadrut supported Siroka; they also believed that nationalizing the health system would weaken Kupat Holim Clalit and topple the Histadrut.

In 1949 health became a major stumbling block in the absorption process. The prime minister was inundated with gloomy reports about immigrant health and there were clear signs of a reversal in public opinion. At first the Yishuv wholeheartedly supported mass immigration, but as time wore on people became less certain about nonselective immigration and eventually voiced outright opposition. A public opinion poll on the subject found that 82 percent of Israelis favored restrictions on immigration.[45]

Misery in the *Ma'abarot*

In the camps, some form of control had existed as far as health matters were concerned. This was no longer the case when the *olim* were scattered in dozens of *ma'abarot* all over the country. Entire communities were transplanted together with their old and sick, adding to the buildup of overcrowding and misery. A physician working in the *ma'abara* in Kfar-Ono wrote:

> I found . . . a little girl with diphtheria who had been sick in her tent for three days. She had a bad throat and high fever. Over a period of six days, her mother had taken her to the hospital six times. She received ambulatory care in the hospital and from myself, but she was not hospitalized . . . We must point out the many risks in this case . . . walking, traveling on a public bus, exhausting the child . . . by moving about with such a dangerous disease, endangering the public in the *ma'abara*...[and] the passengers on the bus.[46]

Scores of persons with suspected typhus and other diseases were referred to hospitals and sent home again. Dr. Sheba, who became director-general of the Health Ministry, proposed that the army supervise health care in new *ma'abarot* for a period of six to eight weeks, after which the civilian health authorities and Kupat Holim Clalit would take over. This proposal was turned down. In light of the severe shortage of medical personnel, the government made one year of service in the *ma'abarot* and immigrant neighborhoods a requirement for all doctors after their graduation from medical school. The Ministry of Labor was responsible for organizing this program, but again, it was not successful.

Transportation was another problem. There were medical emergencies in which getting the patient to a hospital was a matter of life or death. Hundreds of babies were born in tents because women could not reach the hospital in time. Some women refused to give birth in a hospital altogether, particularly the Yemenite women, who were not accustomed to doing so. Others were interested in receiving the grant of IL 15, which was paid for home births to cover the family's expenses. This sum, equivalent to twelve days of work, was a substantial incentive for delivering at home. Within the span of one week, ten babies were born in the tents of Rosh Ha'ayin.[47]

In one painful episode, a large group of invalids was transferred to Israel by the International Relief Organization (IRO), which was closing its doors in Germany. The IRO demanded that Israel take responsibility for the four thousand persons in its care, of whom twelve hundred were disabled. It announced that any not admitted would be placed in German institutions and the matter would be publicized worldwide. Israel received the sum of $3 million to pay for their care.

The Jewish Agency was beside itself. "How can we tell these Jews to stay in Germany?" asked Raphael. "Even without the IRO, we would be morally obligated to bring them over." However, the health-care establishment was not in a position to handle them. Dr. Sheba wanted them taken to hospitals and Malben institutions the moment they arrived. The municipal and welfare authorities protested that others had been waiting for months and that the newcomers must wait their turn. Sheba insisted that the immigrants be given priority. The Coordinating Committee was called upon to settle the matter. The agreement with the IRO was that at least one thousand sick and handicapped would be admitted, but once their families joined them the number was closer to three thousand.

Again, the possibility of treating the sick in Europe was discussed. Dozens of Polish immigrants already had been sent to Italy for medical care, and *olim* from North Africa and Egypt had been detained in Marseilles in spite of the high cost of treatment and the heavy burden of maintaining the sick along with family members from whom they could not be separated. Raphael reported that 80 percent of the North African children were suffering from a contagious skin disease, which had spread to French youngsters in the vicinity of Marseilles. Curing the disease took nearly six weeks, and it had become necessary to employ a staff of kindergarten and primary school teachers to keep the children occupied.[48]

Bilharzia was another serious affliction. This parasitic disease, communicated by drinking from contaminated water sources, affected as many as 30,000 immigrants and was especially prevalent among the Yemenites. Dr. Sheba warned that, unless steps were taken to eradicate the disease, it would spread beyond the *ma'abarot* and affect the veteran population as well. Nearly eight hundred cases of typhoid fever were diagnosed every month, and more than sixty thousand persons suffered from trachoma. Sheba continued to feel that the army should be brought in to improve sanitary conditions in the *ma'abarot*, regulate the supply of soap and water, and vaccinate the population against typhus and other diseases.

In addition, health problems made it more difficult for many of the *olim* to earn their livelihood. Those unable to support their families became dependent on welfare. The handicapped had special housing and job requirements, and income supplements were usually necessary. There were large numbers of the elderly who were bedridden or in need of ongoing treatment, as well as widows with small children. The welfare cases ran into tens of thousands.

It was the health crisis that raised public consciousness with regard to immigration. Communicable diseases and epidemics that began in the immigrant camps spread rapidly to older population centers. *Olim* and veteran Israelis met face to face in the hospitals. Disconcerted by the severe medical problems they encountered and the deteriorating health situation in the *ma'abarot*, the Israelis broke their silence. They lashed out fiercely at the Jewish Agency and the government, and a growing segment of the population clamored for tighter immigration laws that took health into account.

Transition to *Ma'abarot*

Hoisting the *olim* out of the morass of the immigrant camps called for a scheme that was bold and unconventional. The creators of the *ma'abara* sincerely believed that they had devised a plan that would rescue the *olim* from their misery and move them one step closer to Israeli society.

In 1949 the Jewish Agency decided to abolish the immigrant camps, which had become long-term lodging for tens of thousands rather than the way stations they were originally intended to be. They were not designed to accommodate people for lengthy periods of time, and their operation consumed a sizeable chunk of the Jewish Agency budget. The plan was to phase out the camps one step at a time. Some would be turned into "work camps." The immigrants would continue to live there as before, but the communal kitchens would be closed and the residents would go out to work for a living. Those who could not do so (the elderly, sick, disabled, widows with small children, etc.) would be moved to other camps where a full range of services was available.

Because of the chronic shortage of permanent housing, the Jewish Agency established "transit camps" to enable people to leave the immigrants camps. These were the seeds of the *ma'abarot*, although they were not referred to as such until the spring of 1950. It was decided that *olim* from Sha'ar ha-Aliyah would go straight to the new camps. They would live in makeshift housing until their permanent accommodations were ready, and they would support their own families.

Those who had hoped in the beginning of 1950 that the crisis was beginning to lift were soon disappointed. Housing for the immigrants was not completed at the promised rate and they could not move out of the camps. Work at the construction sites was further hampered by inclement weather, and the scheme to transfer the *olim* to "work camps" was thus abandoned.

Children at the Pardes Hanna Ma'abara. *Photograph by Teddy Brauner*

A Step Toward Absorption

In March 1950, in the wake of the unexpected exodus from Iraq and the constant strain on the Jewish Agency budget, treasurer Levi Eshkol came up with a "revolutionary proposal" for the Agency Executive:

> I propose that we dismantle the immigrant camps and put up immigrant housing throughout the length and breadth of the country, beside every settlement from Dan to Nir-Am that has some foothold in the economy. We will establish sixty neighborhoods for up to 1,000 persons. The *olim* will be employed in afforestation, fruit-tree planting, reclamation, terracing and landscape clearing. In this manner, the *olim* will be dispersed all over the country and a wide sector of the population will shoulder the burden of their care.[49]

The chief purpose of the *ma'abara* was to provide the immigrants with a source of income, freeing them from dependence on the Jewish Agency. Eshkol's idea was to employ the residents in afforestation and land-reclamation projects initiated by the Jewish National Fund. The Kelitah Department would finance housing construction and the supply of drinking water, while the Settlement

Department organized the work and acted as overseer. During the spring of 1950, Eshkol traveled all over the country choosing suitable locations. He hoped to create a workforce for the labor villages of the future, "people who already know how to wield a hoe and pruning hook." Meanwhile, the inhabitants would be able to work in nearby settlements.

Eshkol meant well; he sought to move the immigrants out of the camps to a life of independence. He had no idea of either the numerous obstacles that lay in his path or the fierce opposition he would encounter from those he had envisaged as patrons—the local authorities. His motivation was clear and simple: to liberate the Kelitah Department from the oppressive financial burden of the immigrant camps.

Obstacles Encountered

The 1950–51 absorption budget worked out by the Jewish Agency treasurer and the Kelitah Department was based on strict monthly quotas for the number of incoming and outgoing *olim*. The plan was to evacuate 150,000 *olim* from the camps by the end of the year. There were three placement options: permanent housing, agriculture, or *ma'abarot*. By March 1951 the population of the immigrant camps was to be no more than 50,000.

As head of the Settlement Department, Levi Eshkol was also responsible for new agricultural settlements, kibbutzim, and *moshavim*. In this sector, the immigrants had two tracks open to them: settling on a *moshav olim,* modeled after the existing *moshavim,* or joining a labor village, where residents had outside jobs and operated small home farms to supplement their income.

However, the pressures were mounting and winter was on the way. The Kelitah Department was thus more interested in programs that could be implemented within a short span of time, and *ma'abarot* seemed the perfect solution. There were several different kinds. One type was situated on the edge or inside existing settlements and would be ready to absorb 3,000 families by early summer; the immigrants living there were expected to find jobs in the vicinity. Ten *ma'abarot* were planned in development areas as the core for new settlements. These were to be located in the Negev, Galilee, and Jerusalem corridor, with the residents employed in public works. A total of 300 families would be referred to each. Another type were "JNF *ma'abarot,*" for whom afforestation and land-reclamation projects would provide the economic base. There were also plans to turn certain immigrant camps into *ma'abarot* and then build permanent neighborhoods on the site.

Tents and Cabins

While grandiose schemes were being spun by the Israeli leadership, the Kelitah Department was busy with mundane matters such as purchasing tents. Without tents, no *ma'abarot* could be set up or immigrants moved out of the camps. The Jewish Agency Executive approved the acquisition of fifty thousand tents and the months of May and June 1950 were spent looking for a supplier. A search for good-quality, low-cost merchandise was launched in the United States, Europe, and even Japan. The Allied forces had large stocks of military tents left over from the war, and Israel was anxious to gain hold of them as soon as possible. Negotiations were carried out with the United States, France, and Hungary, and an order was placed for 20,000 tents.

At the end of June, Josephthal announced that the first shipment of five thousand tents would arrive in late July. Golda Meir returned from the United States with the news that the American army had another fifteen thousand tents to sell. However, the cost was nearly $1 million, which was more than the Jewish Agency could afford. No progress was made on the *ma'abarot* throughout the month of July while workers waited for the tents. The Jewish Agency received word of thousands of tents left over from the war in Japan and Iraq, but shipping from Japan was slow and the Jewish merchant handling the negotiations in Iraq refused to allow the merchandise to be examined. Israel managed to purchase several thousand tents from Belgium.

The American army had large quantities of tents for sale, but it demanded immediate cash payment and delivery costs were high. In addition, the Americans preferred to deal with agents. A direct sale would have brought the price down by one-third but meant forgoing quality control. Estimating that nearly half the tents were defective, the Jewish Agency agreed to work through an agent. The drawback was that Israel was in a great hurry. The agents took advantage of that fact, gouging prices and imposing conditions that were unacceptable to the Jewish Agency.

While negotiations were going on, it was discovered that the American army had a stock of high-quality tents that were sold for military purposes to allies and friendly countries. The IDF had purchased similar tents in the past, but when Israel needed them for the *ma'abarot* it was told that they were sold for civilian use only to countries on a certain federal list—upon which the State of Israel did not appear. At this point, the diplomatic corps sprang into action. The Israeli consulate in Washington was ordered to contact the State Department and request that Israel be added to the list of those eligible for U.S. Army surplus. The intervention of Moshe Sharett, Israel's foreign minister, was sought to accelerate the process.

Meanwhile, precious time was lost. With the approach of winter, the need for tents became critical. The Kelitah Department estimated that 70,000 immigrants would be living in tents that winter. The year before scores of tents had collapsed in the storms, and the Jewish Agency workers were anxious to reinforce as many tents as possible with a double layer of material. Minister of Labor Golda Meir, who was placed in charge of *ma'abarot* affairs, examined such possibilities as moving families from the immigrant camps to *ma'abarot* together with their tents. This was ruled out when it was discovered that the tents had been coated with tar for waterproofing purposes. During the summer the tar had dried out and hardened, so that handling it would make the material crumble. Moreover, in the camps the immigrants slept two to three families to a tent; in the *ma'abarot* each family was given a tent of its own as a step toward autonomy. Finally, the tents in the camps were needed to accommodate the fresh surge of immigration from Iraq and Romania in the summer of 1950.

One of the lessons of the previous winter was the importance of equipping each *ma'abara* with a few dozen cabins, in which the health clinics and child-care centers would be housed; in case of emergency, violent storm or freezing temperatures, the young, sick, and elderly could sleep there. Patients could be isolated and food stored in case the roads became impassable. People could be evacuated quickly if their tents collapsed.

However, the acquisition of cabins was even more difficult than that of tents. Large quantities were hard to find and the price was steep. The Jewish Agency tried to order them from several countries but the shortage of foreign exchange imposed limitations on how many it could buy. The *ma'abarot* project thus got off to a limping start. With tents and cabins in short supply, all the plans went awry and there was little hope for improvement as the tide of immigrants continued to swell.

Theory and Practice

As in other administrative matters during the Great Aliyah, a certain redundancy was evident in the handling of the *ma'abarot*. The Jewish Agency on the one hand, and the government and local authorities on the other, tended to operate separately. The immigrant camps were run solely by the Jewish Agency, which built and maintained them, made decisions, and supervised all educational, health, and welfare services brought in from outside. The *ma'abarot* were established to move the immigrants out of the camps and relieve the Jewish Agency of their care. In the *ma'abara,* the *oleh* would become a citizen like any other and receive services directly from local councils and the government. The early *ma'abarot* were appendages to existing towns and villages; only a few were planned in advance as autonomous neighborhoods.

From the start, the *ma'abarot* program ran into difficulty. The original inclination was to build *ma'abarot* in areas slated for permanent settlement. However, regional development plans were not ready in 1950, and there was much work to be done. Data still had to be collected, sites earmarked for housing, industry, and factories on the basis of topographical, climatic, and other factors, and development costs assessed. Meanwhile, conditions in the camps reached the point that the Kelitah Department could not wait for the planning results. *Ma'abarot* were put up without consulting the planning and development authorities and sometimes in disregard of their objections.[50]

As mentioned, one of the chief reasons for establishing *ma'abarot* was lack of money. The Jewish Agency demanded that the government finance their construction and the cost of moving the immigrants into them. The Ministry of Labor was supposed to be an active partner; it had promised to clear and drain the land, lay water and sewage pipes, and build access roads and housing. The ministry was also responsible for initiating public works to provide employment. Golda Meir was asked to oversee all government activities in the *ma'abarot* and coordinate them with the Jewish Agency Executive.

Although Josephthal of the Jewish Agency and Golda Meir of the Ministry of Labor belonged to the same political camp—Mapai—and shared similar views on absorption policy, the cooperation between the two left much to be desired. If the *ma'abarot* were to be established in a systematic manner, the various departments had to join forces and carefully follow the blueprints, step by step. However, the Kelitah Department, deeply pressured and frantic over circumstances that were beyond its control, failed to meet critical deadlines and acted without conferring with the Ministry of Labor.

With tens of thousands of immigrants crowded into the camps in the summer of 1950 spreading disease and suffering untold hardships, the Kelitah Department decided there was no time to waste; the *ma'abarot* had to be readied before winter. Officials of the Jewish Agency spent the next few months hunting for sites and supervising building activities in a race with the clock.

Building and Populating *Ma'abarot*

In choosing *ma'abara* sites, the overriding concerns of the Jewish Agency were time and money. It was interested in building quickly at the lowest possible cost. A further consideration was the wealth of job opportunities. The driving spirit and organizer of these activities was Giora Josephthal of the Kelitah Department, who worked with the assistance of Levi Eshkol and Golda Meir. Ben-Gurion was openly supportive.

The Kelitah Department's policy was to attach *ma'abarot* to existing towns and villages. This was the principle followed when determining the location of the first forty-two *ma'abarot,* erected on the outskirts of settlements including Tiberias, Afula, Nahariya, Zikhron Ya'akov, Binyamina, Hadera, Netanya, Kfar Saba, Bnei Brak, Bat Yam, and Rehovot.

Priority went to fertile agricultural regions where the immigrants could work as farm hands. Projects organized by the Ministry of Labor and JNF afforestation programs were other possible sources of employment.[51] Industry was practically nonexistent or in the early stages of development and could not be relied upon to employ immigrants on a large scale. The *ma'abarot* generally consisted of rows upon rows of tents. Structures that were more solid were only built in colder areas, such as in the Galilean hills.

The Kelitah Department soon realized that purchasing tents and cabins was a complicated, expensive, and extended process. The brisk pace it had planned for the establishment of *ma'abarot* was unrealistic. The Korean War, which erupted in the summer of 1950, impeded efforts to mobilize loans and made it doubtful that the *ma'abarot* would be ready by winter. The Kelitah Department thus insisted on strict compliance with immigration quotas, making it clear that any immigrants beyond the quota would not have tents.

When the building of the *ma'abarot* commenced in May 1950, 100,000 persons were living in immigrant camps, many for half a year and more. In deciding which *olim* to move to a *ma'abara,* the Kelitah Department chose those who were young and capable of supporting their families. The welfare cases (elderly, infirm, handicapped, and widows with small children), who at the end of July numbered 30,000, remained in the camps.

When the time came for them to leave, the immigrants balked. They resisted being taken to some faraway place where jobs were hard to find. At one point, Josephthal even considered police intervention to remove them.[52] Some were waiting for employment and housing opportunities to materialize in one of the large towns. Many insisted on remaining close to the center of the country, especially near Tel-Aviv.

Problems sprang up not only in vacating the camp residents but also in convincing to stay those who had been placed in *ma'abarot* directly upon arrival. Many of the Iraqi Jews brought to Israel in Operation Ezra and Nehemiah were taken to *ma'abarot,* but they soon found other quarters. Jewish Agency officials reported that some ran off to Jaffa. Many Iraqi youngsters went to kibbutzim,

Tin huts of a *ma'abara* in front of Tiberias on the Sea of Galilee.

but most of them stayed there only until they could find an acquaintance in town.[53] The social process in the *ma'abarot* was the same as in the immigrant camps: those with gumption got out as soon as they could, while the vulnerable and weak were left behind.

Some immigrants lingered in the camps to save money. In theory, the employed were required to pay for food and services. The salaries of immigrants who found jobs through the employment bureau were sent to the camp administration, and these sums were automatically deducted. However, many camp residents did not register with the employment bureau. At Mahaneh Yisrael, only 40 percent of the workers went through official channels. The Polish Jews in particular were suspected of obtaining jobs on the private market and concealing their income in order to avoid paying for their upkeep.

In certain cases, entire immigrant camps were reorganized as *ma'abarot.* The immigrants were not asked to move, but they had to support themselves and services were no longer provided free of charge. This changeover caused more problems than anyone had anticipated. The camps were located in the center of the country, where unemployment was rampant. The concentration of such a large pool of manpower in a single district severely strained the job market. When politics was added to the brew, the atmosphere became positively volatile.

The immigrants' bid to break into the job market sparked an uproar in May

The shopping center at Beit Lid immigrants' camp. *Photograph by Teddy Brauner*

1950. Thousands were hired as fruit-pickers and seasonal laborers without going through the employment bureau. It was feared that flooding the market with cheap labor—the immigrants received approximately half the going wage—would lead to anarchy. Employment officials charged that the immigrants were upsetting the wage scale and undermining their system of distributing jobs fairly on the basis of time waited, seniority, and so on.

It was hard to keep political interests at bay. As long as Lishkat ha-Ta'asuka, the employment bureau, enjoyed a monopoly over the job market, it was also in a position to politically influence the workers. This was especially true for the immigrants, for whom finding a job was crucial. Employment bureaus were first established in the 1920s by the workers' movements, mainly to prevent exploitation by farmers and fruit-growers. Because most of the employers belonged to centrist parties, an ongoing political battle developed between them and the employment bureaus. The tension mounted as the country geared up for local elections in 1950.

That summer the Kelitah Department arranged for twelve thousand families to be moved to *ma'abarot*. Another eight thousand families were to join them by the end of January 1951. Josephthal believed that, if immigration did not exceed the forecasts, the population of the Jewish Agency-sponsored camps could be reduced by fifty thousand by the end of September. By preserving a balance between incoming and outgoing residents, he hoped that they could manage through the winter.

In late summer, however, the velocity of immigration increased as Jews began to arrive from Romania and Iraq. The number of immigrants was twice as high as anticipated, disrupting the Kelitah Department's plans.[54] Angry protests to the government and *aliyah* authorities were of no avail. Eshkol presented an ultimatum: the Agency would freeze its handling of the immigrants unless the quotas were followed.

To expedite the changeover to *ma'abarot,* the minister of labor pushed for the quick preparation of new sites, to which the immigrants would be sent upon arrival. The Jewish Agency took the view that all those transferred to work camps and *ma'abarot* were "settled" as far as work was concerned; they were on their way to self-sufficiency.[55] For this reason, the Kelitah Department preferred to build near urban centers. Josephthal hoped to direct at least one-third of the immigrants to such places on the assumption that jobs were more plentiful there. On the other hand, the Ministry of Labor busied itself preparing immigrant housing in development areas in order to implement the government's policy of population dispersal. The sequence of events was as follows: Most of the immigrants who arrived during the first two years of statehood went to live in abandoned Arab villages and provisional housing put up for them outside cities and *moshavim.* From the summer of 1950 on, the newcomers were sent primarily to *ma'abarot.* These were initially clustered in the center of the country and were later scattered throughout the country in regions earmarked for permanent settlement.[56]

Contrary to plan, the *ma'abarot* were not temporary way stations. People continued to live in them for years, and they left an indelible stamp on the permanent settlements that were built up around them.

Ma'abarot in the Eyes of Planning Experts

The *ma'abarot,* built hastily without consulting planning experts, were a disaster from the start. They were poorly built and were situated on land that was topographically unsuitable. They were overcrowded and lacked basic infrastructure such as sewage, water supply, electricity, and telephone lines. The Planning Authority had been uncomfortable with the very idea of establishing *ma'abarot,* and it was not happy about the way they were constructed. It was hoped that they would soon be dismantled and the immigrants resettled permanently in those parts of the country officially slated for development. For this reason, Israel's planning experts did not make any special effort to improve conditions in the *ma'abarot;* they believed that investing money in them would only perpetuate their existence. When the *ma'abarot* were first built, the planners did not actually protest; they did not see the early *ma'abarot* as threatening their blueprints for national development in any way. On the contrary, the *ma'abarot* seemed to offer breathing space. The planning and housing authorities would be able to draw up long-range plans thoughtfully rather than rushing headlong into the construction of permanent settlements.

The Kelitah Department was guided by similar considerations when deciding on standards for *ma'abara* housing. The tents and tin shanties were placed on bare ground without flooring. In the face of complaints, Josephthal replied, "We are not installing floors, not only because of the shortage of cement, but for budgetary reasons . . . I do not think it worthwhile spending these sums on shanties that will be standing for no more than a few months. Floors for the tents are even costlier. The authorities cannot afford to lay out hundreds of thousands of pounds for a few months." [57]

In the estimate of the Kelitah Department, converting *ma'abarot* into permanent neighborhoods was a more expensive proposition than constructing durable homes in another location. The *ma'abarot* were thus perceived as a brief, transitional arrangement that did not justify a major investment of resources.

Similarities and Differences

The absorption authorities were aware of the suffering in the *ma'abarot,* but they saw it as part of the process. They were convinced that, aside from slashing the Jewish Agency deficit, the move to *ma'abarot* would benefit the immigrants by accelerating their economic and social integration. This was not to be. The immigrants were no better off than they had been before, and in some respects their situation worsened. Physically, there was little difference between the *ma'abarot* and the immigrant camps. Like the camps, the *ma'abarot* were teeming and slum-like, with endless rows of flimsy housing.

On an organizational and administrative level, the difference between the camps and *ma'abarot* also appeared to be insignificant. However, moving to a *ma'abara* did represent a turning point for an immigrant, especially from an emotional and social standpoint. As time passed a web of bad feeling grew up between the immigrants and the absorption authorities and between the local government and old-timers. As a result, the *ma'abara* came to symbolize the failure of immigrant absorption in the early days of the state. The bitterness was to remain in the hearts of *ma'abara* dwellers for a long time.

Although the immigrants had not fared well in the camps, in a certain respect they were more at ease there than in the *ma'abarot*. Both the immigrants and their hosts perceived the immigrant camps, unpleasant as they might be, as a transitional stage and an inevitable part of life in those days. What is more, the organizational framework of the camps gave the immigrants the feeling that someone—the Jewish Agency—was there to take care of all their needs. The knowledge that the camps were a passing episode offered some consolation on the rocky path to absorption, and this was the message conveyed throughout the process, from the moment of contact with *aliyah* emissaries abroad. There was a sense of homecoming, even if home was but a tent or shack. The *olim* were not like ordinary emigrants who made their own decisions and had to fend for themselves and their families. Upon arrival in Israel, the patronage of the absorption authorities gave them a measure of self-confidence, a sense that someone was in control of their destiny.

There was also a difference in the relationship of the immigrants with the surrounding community. So long as they were in the immigrant camps, they were virtually isolated from the rest of Israeli society. The camps were remote from population centers and were fenced in. One needed a permit from the camp administration to enter or leave. The *ma'abarot*, on the other hand, were meant to facilitate integration and enhance social interaction, to bring the immigrants into direct contact with the veteran community in the spheres of employment, health services, education, etc. Reality proved otherwise. The immigrants, who were supposedly striking out on their own, found themselves reliant upon the old-timers and their institutions at every step of the way.

The *ma'abarot* program did not proceed smoothly. It was difficult to find sites, to convince the immigrants to move in, and to manage them on a daily basis. More complications arose when the second stage of the program was implemented in 1951. The *ma'abarot* were conceived in distress and built on improvised solutions. In the end, they became a trap.

As the *ma'abarot* dwellers dealt with the government, the local authorities, and their neighbors, a traumatic conflict developed that was to sour the relationship between immigrants and Israeli society for many years to come.

CHAPTER FIVE

The Conflict over Education

THE POLITICAL BATTLES waged before Israel's independence continued with renewed vigor after the declaration of statehood. The policy of granting immediate citizenship to every *oleh* turned the immigrant public into an electoral force of considerable weight. By the beginning of 1950 immigrants accounted for one-third of the population. Such a demographic configuration constituted both a boon and a threat to the various political parties. Consequently, the political parties immersed themselves in community work and made an effort to become involved in every facet of immigrant absorption.

Few of the immigrants were politically affiliated upon their arrival. Seizing upon their unfamiliarity with Israeli politics and their dependence on the government, the parties fought tooth and nail to win their souls. They knew that those who greeted the newcomers and assisted them on the path to economic and social integration had a golden opportunity to shape their political behavior. The parties thus scrambled to gain a foothold in bureaucratic mechanisms that dealt with immigration and absorption. This led to constant bickering within the Jewish Agency, among the ministries, and between the government and the Kelitah Department. The political parties tried to slip as many of their own people into these mechanisms as they could. As the absorption process and the stay in temporary camps lengthened, the officials became increasingly powerful. In 1949–52, the Jewish Agency Kelitah Department had a staff of three thousand people working around the clock to provide vital services. With the immigrants so utterly reliant upon them, these officials were also in a position to wield considerable political influence.

During the early years of the state, Mapai was particularly successful in winning the immigrant vote; the election results for the first and second Knesset made this clear. However, the ruling party's organizational achievements and control over the absorption network were no guarantee of long-term political dominance. Israel's politicians were cognizant of the fact that, once the immigrants became less dependent upon the authorities and more aware of what was going on around them, political victory would be determined by social factors. The stage was thus set for a battle that accentuated ideology and tended to highlight differences, thus increasing tension and discord. The confrontation over the education of immigrant children was a case in point.

Education as a Political Tool

The political contest over education, which was already in full swing before Israel's independence, may be traced back to the earliest days of the Zionist movement. As Jewish settlers came to Palestine, they brought with them many ideologies that pushed and pulled in opposite directions, vying for power and influence. Every movement hoped to leave a mark on the social and political character of the nascent Jewish state.

Studies on the history of the Yishuv have emphasized the role of ideology in shaping the Israeli political system. Some scholars insist that Israel's leaders were driven by ideology and were consciously bent on creating a country that conformed with their notions of social reform. Others feel that political and organizational interests overshadowed ideology.[1] Whatever their stance on this question, all agree that the educational network that developed at this time was a dominant factor in determining the face of Israeli society. As a growing number of immigrants poured into the country, the competition between the political camps assumed a fiercer mien and education became a major bone of contention.

Trends or Uniform Education

The controversy over the education of immigrant children was fueled by the structure of the existing school system. Schools in the Yishuv were divided into "trends," each one of which was closely linked with ideological and political organizations.[2] The affiliation went beyond ideology. Most of these institutions were built and run by parties and were employed as instruments of political socialization. The school system was based on the principle of "self-determination," which allowed parents to choose the educational trend most attuned to their social and political beliefs.

Schools belonging to a certain trend set educational goals that reflected the values and ideals of its founders. *Ha-Zerem ha-Klali* (The General Trend) (1913) lay the groundwork for Jewish national education, followed by Mizrachi (1920) and Labor (1926). The trend system was officially endorsed at the Zionist Congress in 1929. Mizrachi and Labor schools were clearly sponsored by political parties, but the connection between the General Trend and the General Zionists

Prime Minister David Ben-Gurion visits the school at Farradiya Ma'abara.
Photograph by David Eldan

was less straightforward. Educators of this trend favored an apolitical stance, allowing them to pursue the goal of strengthening national unity and creating a new Jewish culture. The ideological principles of the General Trend were an outgrowth of the liberal nationalism of nineteenth-century Europe. These principles could be summed up as maintaining loyalty to the national Zionist mission, becoming part of the progressive pedagogic world, and preserving the independence and spiritual-educational identity of the Jewish school.

Zerem ha-Mizrachi, the Mizrachi schools, tried to inculcate the values of the religious-Zionist movement, which aspired to build a new society in Israel combining modernity and democracy with Jewish tradition, religious observance, and Torah study.

Zerem ha-Ovdim (The Labor Trend) saw its mission as the national-social renaissance of the Jewish people. Sponsored by the Labor movement, it upheld Zionist-socialist views and looked forward to a Zionist revolution in all spheres of life: social, cultural, economic, and political. The role model in Labor schools was the *halutz,* the pioneer who practiced Zionism by creating a new man, the antithesis of the Diaspora Jew in appearance, values, and lifestyle. The casting off of Diaspora mentality, so central to labor ideology, was accompanied by the rejection of religious tradition, which was scorned as a vestige of the Diaspora.

The Orthodox Agudat Israel clung to old-style Jewish learning and continued to run traditional "Heder" and "Yeshiva" institutions. In the prestate years, the schools of Agudat Israel remained outside the national system. However, the Compulsory Education Law of 1949 accepted them as a separate trend—*Ha Zerem ha Atzma'i,* under the category of "non-official recognized schools." [3]

The bulk of the immigrants who came in the early days of the state were unfamiliar with the structure of the educational system and the ideologies represented by the different trends. Also, because the immigrants were not politically affiliated, the principle of "self-determination" was meaningless to them. Ideology and politics thus played an intrinsic part in the debate over trends versus unification.

Before the establishment of the state, the General Trend, the only one not sponsored by a particular party, was in favor of depoliticized education that would promote national unity. After independence, the heads of this trend urged the government to adopt their approach and introduce uniform schooling for all immigrant children. However, it was feared that the Labor movement, with its enormous political influence and hegemony in immigrant absorption, would exploit its position to seize control of the educational network. Indeed, the figures show a steady decline in the percentage of pupils in the General Trend; whereas nearly half the student population was enrolled in this trend in 1948, the number dropped to 27 percent by 1953, compared with 43 percent in the Labor Trend and 19 percent in Mizrachi (both of which had enjoyed 25 percent enrollment in 1948).

Party interests weighed heavily in the educational debate. For the religious sector and the Labor camp, schools constituted a major source of power and influence. The General Zionists and Herut, however, did not operate schools of their own. The centrist parties were anxious to abolish educational trends to put a stop to separatism and political schism.

The religious camp supported the creation of trends as the sole means of assuring their children an Orthodox education. Freedom to choose their own curriculum and employ pedagogic supervisors who identified with religious values and conducted a traditional lifestyle were issues that could not be compromised. This meant keeping religious education under the wing of the religious parties. It was felt that only they could protect the religious schools from harm. The leaders of this camp rejected the call for uniform education and insisted that religious schooling for the children of observant immigrants was an elementary right, linked to freedom of conscience.

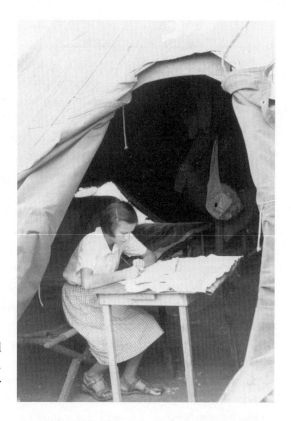

Doing homework at Beit Lid
immigrants' camp.
Photograph by Teddy Brauner

The labor movement was divided over the question of uniform education. Mapam was a staunch supporter of the Labor Trend and refused to consider a nondenominational school system. The leadership contended that ideological education was vital for the strength and continued existence of the movement. Political motives were also involved, such as preserving the organizational status quo and uniqueness of the labor movement. Mapam feared that a generalized framework would blur ideological distinctions and diminish party support.[4] There were conflicting opinions in Mapai. Some members were strongly opposed to abolishing the Labor trend for reasons similar to those of Mapam, but others, most prominently David Ben-Gurion, embraced the idea of one form of schooling for all.[5] After independence Ben-Gurion spoke excitedly about the prospect of state education and felt the time had come to relinquish the particularist tendencies that had been carried over from the prestate period. He argued, as he had in connection with the disbanding of the Palmah, that sovereignty required transferring as many functions as possible to the government and its agencies, the most important of which was supervision of the educational network.

Ideological arguments aside, the debate over the Labor Trend signified a sharpening of the conflict between Mapai and Mapam. The dissolution of the Palmah (summer of 1948), the exclusion of Mapam from the government (winter of 1949), and Mapam's move toward the left, which became more entrenched in 1950 with the outbreak of the Korean War and the escalation of tension between East and West—all these, compounded by the education issue, led to a growing rift between Mapai and Mapam and the eventual split of the kibbutz movement.

The education controversy, which contained all the elements of the ideological and political dispute between the parties, became a precipitating factor in the government crises of 1950 and 1951.

Educational Anarchy

With the educational system in a state of disarray and a public debate going on over government-sponsored schooling, a tug-of-war erupted over education in the immigrant camps. During British rule, the establishment of schools was in the hands of the local authorities, subject to the approval of Va'ad ha-Leumi's Education Department. The local authorities dealt with the physical aspects (construction, maintenance, secretarial services, and janitorial services), while pedagogic supervision, teaching methods, and subject matter were determined independently. Each trend had its own educational goals and curricula and operated its own teacher-training programs. After independence, the school system remained much the same. The Provisional Council, which ran the country from the proclamation of statehood until the convening of the government in March 1949, did not appoint an education minister. When Zalman Shazar became the minister of education and culture in the new government, no major structural changes were made in the system. Education and cultural affairs were dealt with in two separate wings. The Education Division, directed by Dr. Baruch Ben-Yehuda, a leading figure in the General Trend, operated as before, with the chief inspectors of each trend continuing to perform their duties under its auspices. The Culture Division consisted of three departments: the Department of Adult Education, the Department of Literature and Art, and the Department of Hebrew Language Instruction and Cultural Absorption.

The status of the Cultural Absorption Department was not clear. It began by organizing cultural activities and Hebrew language classes for the older immigrant population. Later, however, it added educational programs for immigrant children without seeking authorization for this kind of work from any official

body. The Jewish Agency Kelitah Department, which was charged with providing the immigrants with vital services (food, housing, etc.), was not involved in
education. Neither the Education Department of Va'ad ha-Leumi nor the Ministry of Education and Culture in its early days saw it as their duty to open
schools for the immigrants living in camps, abandoned Arab villages, or neighborhoods outside the jurisdiction of the local authorities. The confusion in this
sphere was described by Baruch Ben-Yehuda: "Immigrants arrived but we were
not approached in an official capacity by the Jewish Agency or any other body
regarding the schooling of immigrant children. Although we had no budget for
it, we could not bear to watch children roaming the streets of Jaffa without
learning."[6]

The Education Division tried to comply with requests to establish schools in
immigrant neighborhoods, but nothing was done in the immigrant camps.
When the Cultural Absorption Department stepped in to fill the void, the Education Division welcomed the initiative: "When we began to open schools in
abandoned villages, the needs were so great that we were glad for the time given
us by [the Cultural Absorption Department] to attend to other matters."[7]

The activity of the Cultural Absorption Department was not perceived as en-
croaching upon the duties of the Education Division: "The Jewish Agency regarded the camps as an extension of the Diaspora; a person's aliyah to Eretz Israel
began from the day he left the camp."[8]

This view was relatively widespread. During the first months after the proclamation of independence, the camps were thought of as reception centers
through which the immigrants would pass briefly before moving to permanent
lodgings. Hence the lack of attention to schooling. The issue came to the fore
only when *aliyah* increased in volume and the newcomers were detained for
months at a time. In addition, the demographic profile of the immigrants
changed in 1949. From May 1948 until the year's end, close to one hundred
thousand persons arrived, mostly Holocaust survivors. The number of children
in Nazi Europe was very small; many infants had been killed and pregnancies
terminated. Children between the ages of five and nine years accounted for only
4 percent of the European immigrant population, compared with 12 percent
among the Asians and North Africans.[9] In 1949-fifty *aliyah* from Arab countries
accelerated, bringing in a large proportion of children. By early 1950 the immigrant camps were holding ninety thousand persons, 40 percent of them youngsters below the age of seventeen. The stay at the camps also lengthened
considerably; in March 1950 immigrants lingered there an average of six
months.[10]

Immigrant children at *ma'abara* at Rehovot. *Photograph by Moshe Pridan*

Tug-of-War

The origins and cultural backgrounds of the immigrants affected the intensity of the battle over schooling as well as the particular trends involved. In the prestate years, the contest was mainly between the Labor Trend and the General Trend. But as immigration swelled, tension mounted between the Labor Trend and Mizrachi. The first wave of immigration in 1948 consisted primarily of survivors. These came from communist regimes in Eastern Europe (Poland, Czechoslovakia, and Romania) and the Balkans (Bulgaria), and most of them were nonreligious. Of the Jews who began to pour in from Arab lands in 1949, the overwhelming majority came from traditional homes. The Orthodox were adamant that the state owed their children a religious education. The pressure was especially strong in the case of the Yemenites, who were known for their religious piety. The proponents of uniform schooling countered that the myriad cultural traditions of the immigrants were proof that a common, unifying educational base was needed; trends would only increase the separatism. Both sides tended to paint their position in an ideological light and generally hid their political motives. In practice, the conflict pitted the Labor movement against the religious parties. Because of internal disputes in the centrist camp, Labor did not anticipate serious opposition from this corner. However, the religious camp bitterly fought all attempts to abolish its autonomous educational track and diminish its political influence. Supporters of uniform education were anxious to avoid a head-on confrontation with this sector. They did so by introducing their programs through the back door, as it were, exploiting the void in the immigrant camps.

Cultural Absorption Department

As we have said, the Cultural Absorption Department took charge of schooling in the immigrant camps, there being no other group in the government or Jewish Agency to handle this matter. The department was run by Nahum Levin and enjoyed the support of the Jewish Agency Kelitah Department and the minister of education.[11] It was allowed to operate at its own discretion, and it even received funding to expand its activity among the immigrants.[12] The fact that Levin and the top officials of the Ministry of Education were on the same ideological and political wavelength presumably had much to do with this fact.[13] In terms of contents and goals, the work of the Cultural Absorption Department harmonized with the uniform education policy of the Ministry of Education. Its strategy, too, conformed with the ministry's idea of exposing the immigrants to socialization as early as possible and at a time when they were still open to influence: "The cultural activity in the state and sponsored by the state must contribute seriously to the task of cultural absorption, exerting maximum influence on a spiritual task that has no parallel in history—the process of transforming fragments of a people into a cohesive nation."[14]

The Cultural Absorption Department began with Hebrew language classes and informal educational activities such as organized trips, youth groups, and culture clubs, but it soon branched out. In early 1949 it established classroom facilities known as "child centers" in the immigrant camps. Within a short time it was catering to a large population of immigrants, adults as well as children, throughout the country. By the beginning of 1950 cultural centers were operating in twenty-two immigrant neighborhoods, twenty-four immigrant camps, and five transit camps. *Ulpanim* (centers for intensive study of Hrebrew language) were opened for the study of Hebrew; *Prozdor,* a vowelled newspaper, was published weekly; and youth activities were offered, featuring Hebrew classes, parties, and trips.[15]

Controversy over the work of the Cultural Absorption Department erupted in connection with the organization of children's classes, especially after the Orthodox population of the camps began to grow. The department refused to offer any form of religious education. "It is our duty as well as that of the state to insure that the exiles do not remain in exile; they must be transformed into loyal partners in the mighty Israeli revolution," exclaimed Levin.[16] As he saw it, this was the same revolution attempted by the Zionist socialist pioneers, whose values formed the ideological basis of the Labor Trend.

As the true nature of the Cultural Absorption Department's work dawned upon the religious camp, it girded up for battle. Its complaints went largely unheeded until the end of 1949, when the matter finally reached the Knesset. Mizrachi delegate David Zvi Pinkas took advantage of this forum to accuse Levin and his associates of "cultural and religious murder."[17] He demanded that the trend system of education be instituted in the camps and called for an end to the monopoly of the Cultural Absorption Department. "Are the camps not part of the State of Israel?" he asked. "Who gave the Minister of Education the right to entrust the education of tens of thousands of children to a man who is busy destroying the Jewish religion, cutting off sidelocks, exerting financial pressure, and employing threats to withhold jobs and housing?"[18]

This outburst was the culmination of a quiet struggle that had been going on for months.[19] Mizrachi and Agudat Israel eventually despaired of achieving their aim in a peaceful manner and chose to publicly attack the Cultural Absorption Department, an act that was accompanied by wide media coverage. Their cause was strengthened by the protests of religious Jews in Europe and the United States, who staged mass demonstrations in the streets of New York and other cities. Unless their demands were met, Mizrachi and Agudat Israel leaders threatened to sabotage fund-raising efforts in the United States.[20]

The religious sector sought an immediate termination of the current system of education in the camps and the inauguration of trends, which would allow parents to educate their children as they saw fit. It also demanded the appointment of a parliamentary committee to more thoroughly study the matter of education in the immigrant camps.

Committee of Inquiry

On 17 January 1950, in the wake of the serious charges against the Cultural Absorption Committee and the political parties that stood behind it, the government appointed a committee of inquiry,[21] known as the Frumkin Committee for its chairman, Judge Gad Frumkin. This committee was asked to concentrate on three issues: (a) the accusations regarding religious coercion in the camps; (b) the media tirades and those responsible for them; and (c) the sources of propaganda in the Diaspora. Emphasis was placed on the political overtones of the controversy. The government assumed that merely appointing a committee would calm the atmosphere and enable a compromise to be reached. However, the outcome was very different. The committee met thirty-three times over many weeks and heard 101 witnesses, among them ministers, Knesset members, public figures, and a substantial number of camp workers and residents. Their testimony revealed the bitter truth—that *olim* were being educated in a manner that contradicted their beliefs.

When the committee's findings were published five months later, on 9 May 1950, many of the harsh accusations against the Cultural Absorption Department were proven true.[22] The conclusions reached by the committee left no doubt as to the nature of the conflict in the immigrant camps. Orthodox witnesses who had appeared before the committee testified that the Mapai leadership had devised a deliberate scheme to impose its principles on religious immigrants. The committee rejected this claim; it firmly denied that any religious coercion had been intended on the government's part. Most of its criticism was reserved for the Cultural Absorption Department for "failing to adapt itself to the needs of a basically religious population." Although the department was found guilty on most counts, the committee did find something to say in its defense: "None of this was done in a calculated battle against religion as a goal in and of itself, but in order to foster the desired acculturation process."[23]

The emphasis in the testimony and deliberations was on the "cultural war" occurring between the religious camp and its opponents. Nevertheless, the committee determined that neither side could be declared free of political motives: "On the one hand, there was a desire to prepare the *oleh* and young people for joining the Histadrut rather than the religious parties. On the other hand, while the excited response of the religious circles was honest and for the sake of Heaven, here, too, the wish to bolster the religious parties and weaken the hold of other parties was not absent."[24]

Operating in a volatile atmosphere, the committee did its best to remain objective and present the facts in an unbiased manner. It was extremely cautious in its conclusions and phrased them in a way that could not be interpreted as a definite confirmation of guilt. In consequence, the committee was taken to task by both sides. The religious maintained that the committee had watered down the charges and detracted from their severity; the Labor movement insisted that the committee's methods of investigation had distorted the facts. In the Knesset tempers flared and members of the committee were subjected to verbal abuse.[25]

The committee presented its report to the government, which officially accepted its conclusions.[26] However, the tone of the report and its implication of the government "as the bearer of collective responsibility for all affairs of the state" angered many Labor Party representatives. Ben-Gurion, too, questioned the methods of the committee and felt that it had "overstepped its bounds." He disagreed with the idea that the education of religious immigrants must be in the hands of observant Jews and was incensed by the committee's contention regarding political motives. He even considered appealing against the findings of the committee and consulted with the government legal advisor about such a step. However, Ben-Gurion eventually changed his mind so as not to aggravate the dispute with the religious.[27] In the wake of the inquiry, the director of the Cultural Absorption Department and two of his associates were dismissed.

The Battle Continues

While the committee of inquiry gathered data, the conflict over education continued. On the one hand, the religious parties pushed for trends in the immigrant camps; on the other, they worried that the Histadrut would open schools or classes sponsored by Ha-Oved ha-Dati, the religious workers' faction of the Histradrut.

Ha-Oved ha-Dati had established schools for its members in several towns before the founding of the state. When the flow of Orthodox *olim* increased, the Labor Trend decided to run schools of this type under its own auspices—Ha-Oved ha-Dati (the Religious Worker). Before long the number of institutions had multiplied dozens of times over. In 1951, fifty-three such schools were operating with a student population of 4,300 and a teaching staff of two hundred. The religious parties accused Mapai of developing this track with the sole purpose of competing with them, and they maintained that in many cases the children were being offered secular education in disguise.[28]

In two immigrant camps, Ein-Shemer and Beit Lid, where the majority of the inhabitants were Yemenites, the controversy over education even led to blows. According to the minister of police, the first incident took place at Ein Shemer on 14 February 1950. Two yeshiva students who appeared at the camp were detained by the administration for allegedly refusing to identify themselves. A crowd of close to one thousand immigrants gathered, attacking the camp director and policemen, and freeing the yeshiva students. The director and five policemen sustained injuries in the fray, and property was damaged. On 17 February rioting also broke out in Beit Lid. These episodes sharpened the tension between the religious parties and the Labor movement and set off an exchange of fiery rhetoric in the Knesset. In view of the fierce determination of the religious camp and Mapai's desire to avoid another flare-up, a compromise was reached whereby the Yemenites would be given religious schooling and a dual educational track would be introduced in other camps. However, this arrangement proved unsatisfactory and the conflict soon resurfaced.

In 1951 a ministerial committee determined that only religious schools under the supervision of religious inspectors would be opened in Yemenite *ma'abarot*. Other *ma'abarot* would offer three types of schooling: a religious school sponsored by Mizrachi and Agudat Israel, a General Trend school, and a Labor Trend school. Even then, affairs did not proceed smoothly. There were questions about whether "labor villages" should be considered equal to *ma'abarot* and about whether certain *ma'abarot* were indeed Yemenite. Meanwhile, each trend did its best to create facts. Ha-Oved ha-Dati schools, which were not under the form of supervision specified by the ministerial committee, were opened in Yemenite *ma'abarot* and residents of other immigrant settlements complained that they were not receiving the services they had been promised.

Government Crises

With the approach of local elections in the autumn of 1950, tension between the religious parties and Labor mounted. When Ben-Gurion presented a plan to reshuffle his cabinet in October, the Religious Front joined the opposition, leading to the resignation of the prime minister. Two weeks later, the religious parties recanted in the wake of promises that a ministerial committee would investigate their demands and that no change would be made in the status quo until the committee's conclusions were finalized. The fall of the government was thus averted, but the education crisis continued. Bringing in soldiers to teach immigrant children, as part of the *ma'abarot* campaign launched in the winter of 1951, was strongly opposed by the Religious Front, which saw this as a violation of its agreement with Mapai.

At the Knesset debate on 5 February 1951 addressing education in the immigrant camps and *ma'abarot*, emotions ran high. The General Zionists and Herut proposed abolishing trends in favor of a unified curriculum throughout the country, and this idea was clearly in line with Ben-Gurion's own thinking: "I would not be divulging a secret if I said that in my view, the trend system is a poor one. Thirty years ago, when it first came into being, I believed . . . it would be the root of much bitterness." Ben-Gurion was "not convinced that only parents have the right to educate. Even now I do not agree that the state has no say . . . and that parents alone can do as they please." [29] This position angered the religious parties and led them to vote against the government. Instead, a proposal of the General Zionists was adopted giving the government one month to draft a law on the depoliticization of the school system. To appease the religious, the General Zionists appended a clause offering parents the choice between state nonreligious and state religious education. As far as Ben-Gurion was concerned, the actions of the religious parties were tantamount to a motion of no confidence. He promptly submitted his resignation and announced the dispersal of the Knesset. Elections for a new government were scheduled for 30 July 1951.

The State Education Law

Economic affairs and "austerity" were the driving issues behind the elections for the Second Knesset. This time around, the General Zionists succeeded in tripling their power and the religious lost some of theirs. For the religious parties, the actions of Mapai served as an omen of what could be expected if they remained outside the government. As soon as the Knesset was dissolved, Mapai ministers began to flood the Knesset with proposals dealing with the military conscription of girls, equal rights for women, and so on. In their desire to join the coalition, the religious parties thus agreed to support the State Education Law. However, these parties, especially Agudat Israel, pushed for the law to be put on hold for two years and for the status quo to be retained in the interim. During this period, the government would work out the organizational structure and means of implementing state education.[30] The proponents of a nationalized school system now saw their way clear to a full execution of their ideas.

Yet the battle over education, particularly education among the immigrants, was far from over. The religious enjoyed even less clout in Israel's fourth government, approved by the Knesset on 23 December 1952. This government included the General Zionists but not Agudat Israel. In educational matters, however, the religious parties did not loosen their grip. On 1 January 1953, a ministerial committee was appointed by the government to finalize the State Education Law; a religious education division, ultimately run by Mizrachi, was set up at the Ministry of Education and Culture. This division operated autonomously as far as curricula, teaching, and pedagogic inspection were concerned, and had a separate administrative mechanism; it was like a ministry within a ministry. Agudat Israel continued to maintain its own school system, *Hinukh Atzma'i* (independent education), outside the jurisdiction of the Ministry of Education.

Colleagues of Ben-Gurion who objected to abolishing the trends noted that the system was essentially unchanged apart from the closure of the Labor Trend. The Religious Trend operated as before, while state education was merely a continuation of the General Trend. The State Education Law became effective all over the country, including immigrant camps and *ma'abarot,* in 1954. The shift was particularly traumatic for many Labor Party activists, who felt that abolishing the Labor Trend was a major factor in weakening the party and tipping the country's political scales. The schools of the kibbutz movement did not introduce any changes and continued to preserve a Labor orientation.

The schools became a battlefield because they stood for different ideologies and were perceived as valuable tools in the political socialization of the immigrant population. The political parties were the main combatants but, in truth, the issues ran much deeper than politics. The religious public, in particular, was shaken to the core. Moshe Unna, a Knesset member affiliated with the religious kibbutz movement, accused the secular parties and especially Mapai of insensitivity and intolerance: "One has the feeling that, in this sensitive issue, anti-religionists are prepared to employ any means, even the most reprehensible. . . . The secular community has never experienced a shock as deep as that of the religious public in the wake of the scandal over religious schooling in the immigrant camps."[31]

The whole episode proved extremely trying for the religious immigrants, whose protests over physical hardship in the camps could not compare with their outspokenness in the matter of schooling. The Yemenite Jews explained, "At first we were like blind men; we did not ask and no one asked us. Now the brain is confused." In their bitterness and indignation, they expressed regret over having come to Israel at all: "All the time we were in Yemen, we never desecrated the Sabbath and no Arab government official would approach us on the Sabbath or holidays. . . . It seems that we would be better off returning to Yemen, where we could observe the laws of the Torah, great or small."[32] Observant *olim* from other countries were equally distraught. These outbursts reflected a grave rift between the immigrants and Mapai, which was to have political implications for many years to come.

Immigrants and Municipal Government

Throughout the Great Aliyah period political tension ran high, in view of the great electoral potential of the immigrants. The race to win their souls reached a peak when voting time drew near, such as before the Knesset elections in January 1949. In these elections, Mapai emerged victorious with forty-six mandates and took the United Religious Front, with sixteen mandates, as its coalition partner.

With the approach of municipal elections, originally scheduled for June 1949, the immigrants were again targeted. However, the election date kept being changed as the government haggled over the provisions of the proposed Municipal Election Law. The General Zionists, who had dominated the larger municipalities and local councils since Mandatory times, were among the leaders of the debate. They sought to turn local government into a bastion of political influence on a par with the national institutions, where the workers' movement, Tenu'at ha-Poalim, was entrenched.[33] The religious parties, notwithstanding their membership in the coalition, perceived the General Zionists as allies in their battle against Tenu'at ha-Poalim.

It should be noted that municipal elections had last been held in 1935, and the status of local councils under Israeli rule was as yet undefined. The contest was extremely fierce, made even more so by the enormous growth of the Yishuv. Before an election could be called, laws had to be passed to establish voting procedures, delegate powers and duties, and clarify the relationship between local and central government. For this reason, the municipal campaign actually began in the Knesset.[34]

During the Mandate period, municipal election procedures had been governed by two laws: the Municipal Corporations Ordinance of 1934 and the Local Council Ordinance of 1941, both of which granted broad powers to the British High Commissioner. There was also a problem of uniformity: different authorities had their own election procedures. It was thus imperative to revise the legislation and exercise greater control over polling for municipal office. A bill on this matter presented to the Knesset set off a heated debate that began in the summer of 1949 and continued through 1950.

Voting Rights

At the end of 1949, Interior Minister Moshe Shapira proposed the amendment of the Municipal Corporations Ordinance. There were thirteen municipalities, forty-nine local councils, and thirteen regional councils operating in Israel, all of them elected under Mandatory law; another seven regional councils were in the process of formation. As many as 250 settlements came under their purview.[35] The Municipal Corporations Ordinance enfranchised men above the age of twenty-five who paid at least 500 mils a year in property taxes or 1 Lira a year in municipal taxes. The very same law that denied laborers and persons with low incomes the right to vote granted the franchise to nonresidents who paid city taxes.[36]

Shapira's bill drew to the fore such issues as voting age, minimum residence requirements, and the introduction of same-day elections all over the country. During the course of the discussion, two camps emerged: the General Zionists and Progressives, backed by the religious parties, and Mapai and Mapam. The General Zionist camp was in favor of enacting twenty years as the minimum age to vote and twenty-four years as the minimum for candidates. At least one year of residence would be required, and elections would be held for a person rather than a party, with separate dates for each locality. The opposing camp wanted the voting age lowered to eighteen, a minimum of six-months' residence, and same-day elections. The Herut Party vacillated between the two camps; it supported eighteen as the voting age and a twelve-month residency requirement.

The Immigrants as Voters

In the background loomed the question of voting rights for immigrants. From the establishment of the state until the end of 1950, more than 500,000 immigrants had been absorbed, 330,000 of them adults above the age of eighteen. Deducting a certain percentage who were disqualified by law, there were still close to a quarter of million eligible voters in the immigrant community.[37] Obviously, this was not a figure to be scoffed at. Positions on the amendment to the law were thus determined by each party's attitude toward the immigrants as an electoral body. Mapai, which was interested in as many immigrants as possible taking part in municipal elections, wanted the residency requirement lowered. The General Zionists, on the other hand, were anxious to retain their power and perceived the *olim* as a threat. This party enjoyed very little foothold in the absorption network and had no influence over the immigrants. It favored raising the minimum voting age and instituting a residency requirement of at least one year. Joseph Sapir, a Knesset member and mayor of Petah Tikva, was appalled at the idea of allowing newcomers to decide how the government should be run: "If Israeli residents cannot learn the issues within a few months . . . [how can we expect this of] new arrivals from other countries who speak different languages and understand no Hebrew. During their first six months, they do not even know what is going on. It is quite likely that a substantial number of *olim* within the purview of a certain local authority will vote there, determining the character and leadership of the place, after which the whole group will be moved elsewhere."[38]

At the time, there had been talk of merging the *ma'abarot* with neighboring settlements for purposes of local government. Because the *ma'abarot* were perceived as temporary and their residents were expected to relocate, it was argued that they had no right being invited to the polls to determine the future of the district. Naturally, it was the General Zionists who had most to lose from a large immigrant population being appended to districts under their control. In Petah Tikva, in particular, that possibility was very real. In the summer of 1949 the Rosh Ha'ayin camp, inhabited by 12,000 immigrants, was slated for conversion into a *ma'abara*. Joseph Sapir worried that it would be appended to Petah Tikva, in keeping with precedents set in other parts of the country. He demanded that voting rights be limited to taxpayers and property-owners, as was done during the Mandate.[39]

Candidates Versus Parties

Another issue that occupied the Knesset was the structure of the electoral system: Should the entire public go the polls on the same day, or should each municipality and local council set its own election date and voting procedures? Zerah Warhaftig (Religious Front) sided with the General Zionists in their objection to simultaneous elections. He was concerned about a clash between parliamentary and municipal affairs: "The parties' local and regional interests are not necessarily identical."[40] Knesset members Joseph Sapir (mayor of Petah Tikva) and Israel Rokah (mayor of Tel-Aviv) tried to convince their colleagues to support personal elections for mayor and local councillors, as had been the case in Mandatory times.[41]

Mapai dismissed the arguments of the General Zionists. Assuming that the national elections were properly organized and the maximum number of immigrants went to the polls, Mapai hoped to do as well locally as in the Knesset. Herut agreed with the General Zionists on most issues, but not with regard to elections. Lacking a foothold in the municipalities, Herut's only card was in the national arena; it preferred to steer the election campaign toward general topics and matters of national concern, such as the severe economic crisis, the austerity policy, the shortage of basic foodstuffs, and the outbreak of polio in the summer of 1950. Sowing dissatisfaction among the *olim* was yet another way to break the government's hold on a local level.

The bill formulated by Mapai enfranchised persons older than eighteen years living in the district for at least six months. It called for uniform, same-day elections for all local authorities, based on party lists rather than individual candidates. This proposal was approved by majority vote.[42]

In spite of the fact that all their proposals were turned down, the General Zionists did exceptionally well in the local elections on 14 November 1950, winning 24.5 percent of the vote as opposed to 5.8 percent (seven mandates) in the Knesset. Mapai received only 27.3 percent compared with 38.2 percent (forty-six mandates) in the Knesset. These election results exacerbated the political strife, with the immigrants having the misfortune of being caught in the middle.

The new law stated that local elections would be held in three years and, the next time around, in four years. However, the elections scheduled for 1953 were put off for another two years after an agreement between Mapai and the General Zionists, who had meanwhile joined the coalition.

The municipal election debate triggered an emotional response because it reflected attitudes toward the immigrants and was a determining factor in the relationship between local and national government. It raised questions about the centralization of local politics, that is, whether the national leadership of a political party should dictate policy on the local level or municipalities should be granted their freedom. Mapai adopted the former approach, which was to have a lasting impact on relations between the center and the periphery.

Political Rivalry in the *Ma'abarot*

The power struggle that began before the Knesset elections continued long after the campaign was over and a coalition government had been formed. Tremendous tension existed, not only between the coalition and opposition parties, but also within the coalition itself, between the National Religious Front and Mapai. One of the glaring issues, as we have seen, concerned schooling in the immigrant camps, for which no satisfactory answer was found. The 1950 municipal elections, with the focus on immigrants, fanned the flames; further damage was done by the alignment of the religious parties with Mapai's opponents. Toward the end of 1950 a political crisis erupted over the state of the economy. The General Zionists, together with Mapam, spearheaded an attack on the government's economic policies. They were joined by the Religious Front, which was already furious over the government's handling of immigrant education. Challenged on these two issues, Ben-Gurion submitted his resignation for the second time and called for new elections.[43] During the period between the dispersal of the Knesset (February 1951) and election day (30 July 1951), the parties competed furiously for supporters, especially among the immigrants.

Because the immigrants were enfranchised soon after their arrival, the political parties lost no time in pursuing them. The immigrants constituted an enormous electoral potential; during the period between the First and Second Knesset elections, 570,000 immigrants reached Israel, nearly half of whom were eligible to vote.[44] Of the 925,000 persons on the voting register for the Second Knesset, as many as 370,000 (40 percent) were new immigrants who had come after the establishment of the state.

Just as the political parties could benefit from this situation, they could also lose. The election results were thus anticipated with much apprehension. Some felt there should be restrictions on voting rights for immigrants; Mapai was for enfranchising the entire immigrant population.

As in the municipal election campaign, some of the considerations had more to do with politics than with ideology. Those parties who expected the support of immigrants were anxious to enfranchise as many as possible; those who feared that the immigrants would vote against them tried to limit their participation. Mapai was confident that it would receive a large number of immigrant votes and wanted the electoral circle widened. Mapai's opponents accused it of pressuring the immigrants and offering them enticements in return for their vote. As far as the opponents were concerned, the fewer immigrants at the polls the better.

Electioneering in the *Ma'abarot*

The political parties directed their energies toward the *ma'abarot,* home to tens of thousands of potential voters. The special circumstances in the *ma'abarot* and the great dependence of the immigrants upon government institutions made them more open to persuasion than was any other group. The 1951 parliamentary elections law addressed the problem of electioneering in the *ma'abarot* by declaring *ma'abara* directors and their employees inadmissible as candidates unless they left their jobs.[45] However, such regulations did not stop the parties from campaigning wildly to win the allegiance of *ma'abara* dwellers using whatever tactics they could. Charges of corruption, psychological pressure, misleading propaganda, and acts of violence filled the newspapers and resounded in the Knesset as each party tried to undermine the credibility of the other.[46]

Party activists were not the sole actors on this stage. Government and Jewish Agency officials played a role, too. In those days, government ministries were not apolitical national institutions. With the whole country run by parties, the ministries were perceived not so much as executive tools for carrying out government policy as the ministers' private domain. When the institutions of government were first inaugurated, ministry heads manned their offices with party associates, turning government bureaucracy into a nest of political support. In effect, the structure and scope of duties of each ministry was more a matter of manipulative skill than political clout. A party's strength was determined by its acceptance into the government coalition, that is, by its bargaining ability rather than its electoral achievements. In this manner, small parties in the coalition had more power than larger parties who remained in the opposition. Certain parties were even prepared to compromise their basic beliefs in order to join the government. They tried to justify their actions by accumulating electoral strength, thereby sharpening the competition and introducing greater militancy in the battle for the immigrant vote.

In the early years of the state, some government ministries assumed responsibilities that went beyond those actually imposed upon them. For example, at the urging of David Ben-Gurion the Ministry of Defense became involved in the socialization of immigrants. Other ministries failed to gain control over institutions that were really within their purview. The Ministry of Health had no say in the administration of Kupat Holim Clalit, which provided health insurance and medical care to most of the population; the Immigration Ministry did not decide the future of immigration and absorption. Both ministries were headed by Moshe Shapira (Ha-Poel ha-Mizrachi). However, when Shapira served as minister of the interior he was able to gain a measure of influence over the immigrants.

The Interior Ministry Versus the Jewish Agency

In early summer 1950, while the first *ma'abarot* were being established, the financially strapped Kelitah Department tried to shed responsibility for many of the services it had organized for the immigrants. The director, Giora Josephthal, urged the Interior Ministry to assign municipal affairs in the *ma'abarot* to nearby local councils. Toward this end, the Kelitah Department provided the ministry with the location of existing *ma'abarot* and a list of settlements beside which *ma'abarot* would soon be built. In this way, the *ma'abarot* could be incorporated in advance in the ministry's plans for local government.[47]

Since his appointment as head of the Interior Ministry's Immigrant Settlement Department in late 1949, Dov Rosen of Ha-Poel ha-Mizrachi had worked tirelessly to develop his ministry's sway in the immigrant community. His initial efforts were in immigrant neighborhoods and repopulated Arab villages. When he heard about the Kelitah Department's request, he lost no time drawing the attention of his superiors to the significance of this development. He was prepared to take the administration of the *ma'abarot* into his own hands, asking the minister of the interior to approve a budget that would be channeled through his department.[48] Rosen was convinced that the Immigrant Settlement Department could play an important role in enhancing Ha-Poel ha-Mizrachi's image among the immigrants. Rosen's colleagues in fact recognized the golden opportunity that was within their grasp. The Interior Ministry submitted a request to the treasury for a special allocation, taking pains from then on to strengthen its foothold in the *ma'abarot*. Delegates of Ha-Poel ha-Mizrachi on a joint committee of the ministry and the Jewish Agency demanded that at least 25 percent of the workers sent into the *ma'abarot* be members of their party.[49] Rosen also met with officials of the

Ministry of Religious Affairs to draw up plans for religious services in the *ma'abarot*.

As local elections approached and the education battle between Mapai and the religious parties moved into full swing, the Interior Ministry stepped up its activity among the immigrants and became increasingly eager to see the Kelitah Department leave the *ma'abarot* altogether. At this point, Mapai woke up to Rosen's intentions and realized that yielding full responsibility to the ministry was not so wise after all.

The *ma'abara* directors made many crucial decisions: how long the immigrants stayed, when and where they received permanent housing, and the services to which they were entitled. By 1950 there were more than three thousand officials working in immigrant camps and *ma'abarot,* and the number continued to grow.

In the summer of 1950, a few months after the first *ma'abarot* were established, the Interior Ministry informed the Kelitah Department that it would assume responsibility for "municipal services . . . the organization of public life . . . and the inclusion [of residents] in a legal municipal framework after their move to permanent housing." The Jewish Agency would remain in charge of the water supply, basic sanitation, and home repairs, but would no longer operate an administrative network in the *ma'abarot.* To accomplish the above, the ministry requested office space at each site and access to statistical material compiled by the Jewish Agency.[50]

The Kelitah Department insisted that the bulk of its staff continue to work in the *ma'abarot.* In answer to the ministry's query about the duties of its "caregivers," the department explained that they welcomed new arrivals, provided them with cash and basic necessities, registered them for permanent housing, and obtained the required documents. They also looked after the disabled, opened stores in the *ma'abarot,* helped the immigrants find jobs, and offered guidance on all subjects. The great power enjoyed by the *ma'abara* director was another source of concern. The Interior Ministry demanded that the Jewish Agency give up this post. Its refusal to do so signified the beginning of an ongoing feud over control of the *ma'abarot.*[51]

The Kelitah Department argued that *ma'abara* affairs could not be handed over to the local authorities while the population of the *ma'abarot* was growing so wildly. A conflict of interests was envisaged between the authorities and immigrant absorption needs. Kelitah officials also maintained that the newcomers required special attention to help them settle in, which would not be provided by the local authorities. The status of the Jewish Agency, they said, was basically that of a "proprietor." Because it had been trusted with the upkeep of buildings and public property, its workers had to be physically present.[52]

The Interior Ministry was not prepared to change its mind about the local authorities annexing the *ma'abarot* in their district and taking charge of all municipal services. It accepted the proprietorship arrangement, on condition that the Kelitah Department relinquish management of the *ma'abarot* and withdraw all its employees with the exception of one or two maintenance and cleaning supervisors. The ministry was set on integrating the *olim* in a municipal framework "in which they would cease to be thought of as immigrants in transit and [be] treated as full-fledged citizens." [53]

The Kelitah Department saw all this as an attempt to win control over the *olim*. Nevertheless, Josephthal made it clear that he did not object to the Interior Ministry taking over such "technical services" as lighting, water supply, and sanitation.[54] Ministry officials assured him that their sole interest was to end the absorption process as quickly as possible and move the immigrants to permanent surroundings where they would become an integral part of the population. The Interior Ministry, they said, was motivated only by the desire "to transform the *ma'abarot,* immigrant housing projects and work camps into an organic part of the local administration or municipalities in their own right." [55]

This declaration was problematic, in that the Interior Ministry had not coordinated its position in advance with the local authorities. Such a plan was found unacceptable, mainly for budgetary reasons, prompting local leaders to declare war on both the Interior Ministry and the Jewish Agency. The Interior Ministry tried to foist responsibility on the Jewish Agency; their objections stemmed from the fact that the Jewish Agency had not consulted with local authorities before determining *ma'abara* sites and preparing blueprints. But when the ministry itself faced opposition to its annexation proposal, it ignored the cries of the local authorities and forced them to comply by passing a law in this regard. It was stipulated that immigrants living temporarily in *ma'abarot* would be considered citizens of the district in which the *ma'abara* was located and were entitled to all municipal services available to other residents. The ministry further ordered the Jewish Agency to close its offices in the *ma'abarot* by 1 January 1951, leaving one official "to fulfil the Jewish Agency's obligations toward the *olim* and perform all the duties of a proprietor, including sewer-cleaning." [56]

Second Knesset Elections

As long as Mapai and the religious parties were coalition partners, they tried to contain conflict between them. Once the government fell, however, the dam burst. The Interior Ministry continued to ignore the protests of the Jewish Agency and the local authorities, and as parliamentary elections neared, the tension escalated. The quarter of a million *ma'abara* and camp dwellers were hungrily eyed by all the parties. In spite of the fact that everyone was vying for their votes, the immigrants had little control over their own destiny. A committee appointed to study the *ma'abara* problem described the damage caused by the intrusion of politics into the lives of the immigrants:

> Rival parties competed over the immigrants' love . . . Goods and services were distributed free of charge . . . Freedom from the obligations of citizenship kept them strangers in their new homeland. They were treated as children and therefore they responded as children. They accepted government services as their due, angrily demanded more, and made no effort to better their situation . . . The Jewish Agency complained about the Interior Ministry's practice of sending "secretaries" into the *ma'abarot*. . . . These secretaries carried out the functions of municipal government until a local council could be established. . . . The Interior Ministry, on the other hand, complained that the *ma'abara* directors would not allocate space to the secretaries, keeping them from fulfilling their duties. . . . This is yet another example of the institutional contest to gain the immigrants' allegiance. . . . The multiplicity of authorities boosted the ego of the *ma'abara* dwellers and lured them into playing one authority against another in order to win benefits.[57]

In the preelection period, the political parties agreed to divide up the *ma'abarot* as follows: For each sixteen *ma'abarot,* Mapai would command seven; Mapam, five; Ha-Poel ha-Mizrachi, two; and Ha-Oved ha-Tzioni, two. The religious parties were dissatisfied with such a small share, and the whole arrangement was fiercely criticized in the press: "The *ma'abarot* became ghettos. They were guarded by sentries and the party emissaries did all they could to make the immigrants feel helpless without their patronage."[58] The election campaign itself was tense. The parties employed aggressive tactics and lay great emphasis on *olim* and *aliyah*. It was clear that the immigrant vote constituted the great unknown in Israeli politics.

Although most of the barbs in the election campaign were aimed at the government, Mapai emerged with forty-five mandates, only one short of the previous elections. The religious no longer ran as a single bloc; four separate parties were listed and they won a total of fifteen mandates, again a drop of one mandate.[59] Most astonishing was the success of the General Zionists, who managed to triple their power. Mapam went down from nineteen mandates to fifteen, and Herut from fourteen to eight, a record low for this party.

On 11 September 1951, the president empowered Ben-Gurion to form a new government. Ben-Gurion surprised the country by putting together a cabinet that was almost identical to the outgoing one. In spite of their meteoric success, the General Zionists were not asked to join, although Ben-Gurion thought of them as a possible alternative should negotiations with the religious parties fail. The latter were anxious not to be excluded from the government lest antireligious laws be passed that would cloud their achievements until then.[60] This fear was not without grounds. Soon after the resignation of the government, Knesset members from Mapai had presented bills on the conscription of women and women's rights that took advantage of a secular majority strengthened by the votes of Mapam and the General Zionists.

In wake of the numerous disputes of the previous year, Ben-Gurion's talks with the religious parties were tinged with bitterness. Eventually they did join the coalition, but they wrangled with Mapai over religious and educational issues until the very last moment, just before the presentation of the new government on 7 October 1951.[61]

The election results showed that the Interior Ministry's efforts to break the Kelitah Department's hold over the immigrants were unsuccessful. Mapai's strength did not diminish and the religious camp made no gains. Transferring control of the *ma'abarot* to the local authorities failed to prevent the upward climb of the General Zionists, who dominated the cities and municipalities where 20 percent of the immigrant population lived. The religious parties tried their best to build up influence in the immigrant sector, but there was no competing with Mapai, which controlled the ministries of finance, housing, and labor in addition to the Jewish Agency Kelitah Department. The General Zionists won the votes of many old-timers—mainly because of the economic crisis, the expansion of the austerity program, and the virulent campaign against Mapai, for which the religious were in no small measure responsible. Recognizing the enormous electoral potential of the immigrants, the General Zionists inundated them with propaganda, both oral and written (they published material in eight different languages). In consequence, they rose to a position of power second only to Mapai and presented a coalition alternative to the religious parties, for whom this constituted a mighty blow.

In spite of predictions that the government would never last a year, it completed a full four-year term, weathering several crises. The accords reached in the spheres of religion and education were to have important implications for the social development of the country over the coming years.

CHAPTER SIX

Confronting the Old-Timers

THE *MA'ABAROT* were born at a critical juncture in Israel's history, as the state faced the daunting task of finding shelter for multitudes of homeless immigrants. From the summer of 1950, wherever a vacant plot of land could be found tens of thousands of makeshift dwellings were erected, utilizing whatever materials came to hand. The second stage of the *ma'abara* program, started in 1951, was supposed to be more organized and to follow a detailed national blueprint. These planned *ma'abarot* were to be the core of permanent settlements. Once again, intentions and reality failed to coincide. After the immigrants moved to *ma'abarot* they were no longer protégés of the Jewish Agency, but neither did they become masters of their own destiny. Other governing bodies appeared on the scene, each with its own ideas about how the *ma'abarot* should be run.

Planning the *Ma'abarot*

Two bodies were formally in charge of the *ma'abarot:* the Government-Jewish Agency Coordinating Committee and the Higher Planning Council. The Coordinating Committee, headed by David Ben-Gurion, was expressly formed to develop *aliyah* and absorption programs in partnership with the Higher Planning Council. Members of the Coordinating Committee saw themselves first and foremost as policymakers; their job was to establish priorities on the basis of statistics compiled on both sides of the ocean and to issue orders and directives. Members of the committee had been carefully chosen by Ben-Gurion to insure that its decisions would have force in the Knesset and the Jewish Agency. In practice, the committee spent most of its time addressing urgent fundamental issues and had no leisure to deal with the nitty-gritty of *ma'abara* management. Meeting only once in two weeks, the committee was unable to keep close tabs on day-to-day affairs and found itself constantly at odds with the Higher Planning Council.

The Higher Planning Council had been charged with drawing up a map of *ma'abarot* that would serve as a core for permanent settlement. Seven government ministries were represented on the council, in addition to the Jewish National Fund and the Jewish Agency. The Interior Ministry representative held the position of chairman. With so many members, there was always disagreement. It was difficult to attain a consensus even on basic principles. Some planners favored a network of urban and semiurban centers of varying sizes; others envisaged a few large settlements. Among the supporters of the first approach was the Settlement Reform Committee, a group that actively lobbied for population dispersal in 1948–51—the policy eventually adopted by the government. Much of the committee's influence lay in its membership. One member, for example, was Zvi Berenson, director-general of the Ministry of Labor and Housing, for whom the views of the committee were close to heart.[1]

Differences of opinion in the Higher Planning Council delayed the building of *ma'abarot* in Hadera-Caesarea, Kiryat Shmona, Beit Sheaan, etc. Plans for Carmel City (on the slopes of the southern Carmel), Zippori, Morsas, and Nebi Rubin remained on paper. As the bickering persisted, the Jewish Agency called for the establishment of a subcommittee made up of its own officials and representatives of the ministries of labor and defense who would scout out locations for *ma'abarot* and work to accelerate the building process. Construction on location was carried out by the Kelitah Department, which found the tempo of the Higher Planning Council much too slow. The planners insisted on adhering to professional guidelines, but the main considerations of the Kelitah Department were time and money. Work was often done without consulting the planners or their decisions were ignored.[2] In effect, the Jewish Agency Kelitah Department built the *ma'abarot* more or less at its own discretion, while the voice of the two official bodies remained unheeded.

Building the *Ma'abarot*

The Immigrant Camp Department was one of eight subdepartments affiliated with the Jewish Agency Kelitah Department. The maintenance crews of this department had repaired tents and other structures in the immigrant camps; now they were called upon to build the *ma'abarot*. Because private contractors were reluctant to undertake low-paying construction jobs in outlying locations, especially when the work had to be completed quickly, the Immigrant Camp Division opened special workshops of its own where hundreds of carpenters assembled prefabricated housing around the clock.[3]

The *ma'abarot* were constructed in such haste that national planning was all but ignored. During the first stage the majority of *ma'abarot* were built near cities in the center of the country, or around large settlements and *moshavot* in the agricultural sector. Apart from saving time and money on infrastructure, the idea was to be close to sources of employment.[4] Kelitah Department officials attested to the fact that the cheapest makeshift housing was used, primarily tents and canvas siding attached to wooden poles.[5]

Even the second, better-planned stage bore little resemblance to the official blueprints. The great wave of immigration in early 1951, which reached a peak between March and July, brought nearly one hundred thousand persons into the country within four months, the majority from Iraq. Under the circumstances there was nothing to do but improvise. As Giora Josephthal quipped to a group of planners, "Once we sent *olim* to places with a city and jobs; later we sent them to places even without jobs. As the scope of aliyah has increased, we have built *ma'abarot* in places where a future city is planned . . . Now we are prepared to build where a future city is no more than a dream . . . Tell me what sites you dream of and I'll put up *ma'abarot* there without a moment's delay."[6]

Another decision made by the Kelitah Department was the type of housing built. Wooden cabins were generally used for kindergartens, nurseries, infirmaries, mother and baby clinics, offices, etc. But they were expensive and took too long to assemble to be used as dwellings. The choice was thus between tents, canvas huts, or tin shanties, which were much cheaper and easier to put up. In Israel's climate, each had their advantages and disadvantages. Canvas huts were more comfortable in hot weather; tin shanties were more rainproof but were sweltering in summer. Hence, tin shanties were chosen for the Galilee and Jerusalem hills, where the summers were cooler; while canvas huts were used for the center, coastal plain, and South, where winters were milder. When the supply of tin shanties and canvas huts ran out, the alternative was to pitch tents.

After the dwellings were up, there was still work to do. The immigrants needed guidance as they settled into their new homes. The Jewish Agency appointed a director for each *ma'abara* and a maintenance crew to carry out repairs, install water piping, etc. The Jewish Agency also coordinated a variety of vital services. However, the authority of the *ma'abara* director was not clearly defined. This oversight led to continuous conflict between the government ministries, municipal authorities, and voluntary organizations that maintained a presence in the *ma'abarot*.

Local Authorities

The immigrants sent to *ma'abarot* were supposed to be on an equal footing with their neighbors. It was assumed that each *ma'abara* would be under the jurisdiction of the nearest municipality and that *ma'abara* residents would enjoy the same services as everyone else; this was not so. The municipalities had been absorbing immigrants at a dizzying pace since the establishment of the state, and their deficits were enormous. Most of the newcomers lacked steady employment and could not pay their taxes. At the same time, they required more social services than did the old-timers. The municipal authorities were financially overburdened even before the *ma'abarot* came along. Now they found it difficult to fulfill their elementary duties, let alone provide the *ma'abarot* with special services.

These special services included lighting, sanitation, road construction, and more. In older settlements, the municipality financed lighting and sanitation in the public domain. In the *ma'abara*, the public domain extended to showers and toilets, which were shared by a large number of families. When the *ma'abarot* were first built, the Jewish Agency was in charge of utilities; it installed water pipes and electricity, sent in repair workers, and supervised sanitation. After the *ma'abarot* were annexed to local municipalities, the Jewish Agency claimed it could no longer be responsible for such maintenance, citing lack of money and manpower.

Another complicating factor was the transient nature of life in the *ma'abarot*. The size and population were changing all the time. A certain portion of the residents stayed on for long periods, but others came and went. Under such conditions, the local authorities found it difficult to plan and organize services. Many municipalities were reluctant to comply with the Interior Ministry's orders regarding *ma'abara* annexation; they preferred to see the Jewish Agency retain its managerial position.

Government Ministries

Because of the unusual circumstances prevalent in the *ma'abarot*, its residents required more services than did ordinary citizens. Living in a temporary environment as they were, many immigrants had trouble finding steady jobs and became dependent on handouts. In fact, it was unclear who was responsible for providing them with services. In the immigrant camps, all services had been channeled through the Kelitah Department; in the *ma'abara*, they were offered directly— by government ministries, local authorities, settlement bodies, health funds, women's organizations, political parties, immigrant associations, the army, etc.[7]

In many spheres the state took responsibility. The Ministry of Labor's employment and housing divisions helped the immigrants to find work and built permanent housing for them. The Ministry of Welfare provided social services, shared the cost of running day-care centers and family clinics, instructed women in home economics and nutrition, and arranged transportation for those in need of medical care. The Ministry of Education supervised nurseries, kindergartens, and primary schools; organized evening and Hebrew language classes; set up social clubs; and distributed milk and school lunches. The Ministry of Health carried out sanitary inspections, organized preventative care, ran mother and child clinics, and taught hygiene in schools. The Interior Ministry supervised the work of the municipalities but reserved certain powers for itself, such as determining how much of the municipal budget would be devoted to services in the *ma'abarot.* The Postal Ministry, the Ministry of Transport, and the Ministry of Commerce and Industry also provided a range of services.

Volunteering in the *Ma'abarot*

The Jewish Agency and the government did not operate in the *ma'abarot* in a vacuum. Women's organizations brought in volunteers to instruct young mothers, care for babies and children, and participate in health and educational activities. These organizations also launched special drives to collect warm clothing and to place *ma'abara* children with Israeli families during the winter. Immigrant associations, youth movements, and settlement societies also found a niche in the *ma'abarot,* playing an important role in making them more habitable.

Duplication of Services

In many respects, this multiplicity of custodians was cumbersome and wasteful. The same services might be rendered by two or three different bodies without any coordination or partnership between them. Choosing *ma'abara* sites, for example, was done by the Government Planning Department, the Higher Planning Council, the Kelitah Department, the IDF, local municipalities, the Jewish National Fund, and other groups. Water supply was in the hands of the Kelitah Department, which installed the pipes; local authorities, which turned the water on; and Mekorot, which controlled the water at the source. Housing construction was the responsibility of the Ministry of Labor, the Jewish Agency Technical Department, and Amidar. Tin shanties and wooden cabins were put up by the Ministry of Labor; tents and canvas huts, by the Jewish Agency. Maintenance was supervised by the Kelitah Department, while the municipalities were in charge of lighting, water, sanitation, and waste removal.

Health care was the prerogative of the Ministry of Health, Kupat Holim Clalit, Hadassah, and Malben, although the municipalities ran the clinics. The Ministry of Transport, the Ministry of Welfare, and Magen David Adom all transported the sick. Advice on child-care was given by the Ministry of Welfare, Kupat Holim Clalit, Hadassah, various women's organizations, and the Ministry of Education's Nutritional Guidance Department. Social clubs and evening classes were organized by no less than six different bodies.

In none of these spheres was there a coordinator to oversee joint endeavors or prevent redundancy. This problem was compounded by the self-interest and political motives of some of the institutions, which further impeded the smooth operation of services. The immigrants thus found themselves in a dense bureaucratic web, trapped by political forces competing for control of the *ma'abara*.

Opposition of the Old-Timers

The old-timers viewed the clustering of the immigrants in their vicinity with fear and trepidation. As long as the newcomers remained in the camps, being fed and clothed by the Jewish Agency, the local population knew little of their suffering or the problems connected with absorption. However, when immigrant housing projects began to be built on the outskirts of the cities and *moshavot* in 1950, and even more so when *ma'abarot* were erected within their municipal boundaries, the veteran communities raised an outcry about the burden suddenly thrust upon them.

As we have said, most of the *ma'abarot* were put up hurriedly in the summer of 1950, without adequate preparation or coordination with the local authorities and at times clearly against their wishes. The constraints of this unplanned stage cast a dark shadow on the entire *ma'abara* enterprise and caused veteran Israelis to be reluctant about cooperating with the Jewish Agency in the years to come. The insistence of absorption authorities that nearby settlements provide the immigrants with services was viewed as a serious financial imposition. Their municipal budgets were generally limited, if not in deficit, and there was no question that having to care for the *ma'abarot* greatly increased their expenses.

The local authorities did not disguise their opposition. Some settlements organized public committees to stop the building of *ma'abarot* in their midst, and they deliberately obstructed Jewish Agency efforts to locate suitable tracts of land. The mayor of Ra'anana, for example, was one of those singled out by the Kelitah Department for his lack of cooperation: "We have not received any assistance from the local council in connection with the establishment of a *ma'abara*. For months we have been asking you for a tract of land. Instead we have had all sorts of proposals, some of them about land that has been allocated already, and of course your offer of the dump is out of the question. Also, we have had no help from you in planning the water supply." [8] Strong municipalities such as Ramat-Gan and Tel-Aviv were able to pressure the Jewish Agency into canceling plans for *ma'abarot* in their environs or limiting their size. As soon as a settlement found out that a *ma'abara* was to be built nearby, it leaped into action and tried to block the scheme or have it postponed.[9] Quite a few settlements accused *ma'abara* dwellers of stealing from their fields and orchards and ruining their livelihood. As Josephthal ruefully noted, "The settlements, be it Kibbutz Merhavya, Ramat Yohanan or the Farmers' Association, do not want a *ma'abara* in their neighborhood . . . On the other hand, establishing *ma'abarot* too far from the settlements is not good from a social standpoint. The problem is that when a piece of land is secured after so much running around, we put the maximum number of buildings on it.[10]

In the face of violent opposition, the Jewish Agency was forced to alter plans, sometimes to the point of absurdity. Large *ma'abarot* were built on the outskirts of small towns unable to absorb the newcomers. Many went up on land that was topographically unsuitable or a long way from the nearest settlement. The *ma'abara* outside Karkur was three kilometers from town and situated on heavy topsoil; the Kfar Saba *ma'abara* was also three kilometers away, in an old, neglected orchard. Others were located in low-lying areas that flooded in the winter and turned into marshy swamps, or on windblown slopes where it was hard to keep the tents tethered to the ground. In areas in which most of the land was privately owned, such as Rehovot and Petah Tikva, the *ma'abarot* were also a considerable distance from town.[11]

Even when the Kelitah Department clung tenaciously to its original plans, *ma'abara* development sometimes came to a standstill because the local authorities balked at assuming responsibility for such essential services as water supply, waste removal, and road-building. Often the reason was financial rather than sheer defiance. Meanwhile, the idea of small-scale *ma'abarot* of two hundred to three hundred families had turned into a much larger proposition. In Holon, Tiberias, and Pardess Hana, for example, the number of *ma'abara* dwellers equaled or exceeded the municipal population. In other cases, two or three times as many people could be found in the *ma'abara* as in the settlements nearby. The local authorities, with all good will, could not meet the needs of a population that size. Needless to say, the standard of living in the *ma'abarot* suffered. Without increasing their physical boundaries, more and more immigrants were squeezed in—with chaotic results.

As immigration swelled, the Kelitah Department continued to build *ma'abarot* throughout the country. During the winter and spring of 1951, the exodus from Iraq reached a peak. As many as 1,000 Iraqi Jews arrived each day, in addition to *aliyah* from other countries. They were brought over in such haste that there was no time for transit camps; nearly 80 percent of Iraqi immigrants went straight from the airport to *ma'abarot*. The number of *ma'abarot* rose steadily. In early April 1951 there were sixty-five *ma'abarot* with a total population of 70,000; in July—eighty-five, with a population of 138,000; and in September—eighty-seven, with a population of 170,000.[12]

Objections to Expansion

Although new *ma'abarot* were cropping up everywhere, the demand showed no signs of abating. The Kelitah Department felt it had no alternative but to multiply the number of *olim* in existing facilities. This was a major factor in the breakdown of relations between veteran settlements and the Jewish Agency. The Kelitah Department was aware of the municipalities' objections but chose to proceed behind the backs of the local authorities. The Amishav *ma'abara* near Petah Tikva was supposed to absorb five hundred families in February 1951. Twice as many people were brought in within a two-month span, and another five hundred arrived several months later. The same scenario was reenacted in dozens of *ma'abarot* throughout the country.

Even those settlements that had consented, willingly or under duress, to having a *ma'abara* in their neighborhood were furious that the Jewish Agency had failed to consult with them or take into consideration their finances and size.[13] Some settlements simply voiced their dissatisfaction; others took action. Municipal clerks were instructed not to register additional families or refer them to the employment bureau. The Jewish Agency, however, was not deterred. Plans for Halssa, an Arab village near the Rosh Pina-Metulla road, were practically reversed. The original scheme called for an agricultural colony in the village, taking advantage of the arable land, and an immigrant housing project on a nearby slope. Nearly eight hundred *olim* were sent to Halssa in 1948. By 1950 the population had risen to five thousand and the foundations had been laid for the town of Kiryat Shmona.[14]

This was not the only instance of a *ma'abara* being built on land designated for other purposes. The Arab villages of Saqiya and Kafr 'Ana near Ramat-Gan had been totally destroyed during the War of Independence, but no housing development had been planned for this region. National policy at the time was to avoid concentration of population in the center of the country and to exploit arable soil for intensive agriculture. However, the need for immigrant housing was so great that *ma'abarot* were established here, too. Within a short time, Saqiya, Hiriya, and Kafr 'Ana were overflowing and additional *ma'abarot* were built beside them. Close to 2,700 families (approximately 13,000 persons) found shelter there. Another 1,000 families were sent to a *ma'abara* in the Holon area, which had not been planned in advance.

One reason for the opposition to *ma'abarot* was the fear of job competition. Even immigrants who had barely settled down were concerned about the arrival of new families. The residents of Lod and Ramle were unhappy about the establishment of nearby agricultural colonies lest the farmers seek employment in their towns. When the Jewish Agency arranged for the transfer of more families to existing *moshavim,* the core group worried that the market for hired laborers would be flooded.

The Kelitah Department was thus caught between absorbing a growing tide of immigrants and overcoming the wall of opposition to the *ma'abarot.* Josephthal used every resource at his disposal, including his personal and political connections, to build additional *ma'abarot* and expand those already standing. Appealing to local and regional councils headed by members of Mapai, he was able to establish the country's largest immigrant housing projects. A *ma'abara* originally designed for 1,000 families was put up outside Tiberias (prestate population: 5,800); others were built on the outskirts of Hadera, Afula, Kfar Saba, Ness Ziona, Beer Sheva, and elsewhere. As long as Joseph Sapir, a General Zionist, was mayor of Petah Tikva, the town refused to have anything to do with *ma'abarot.* When Sapir was replaced in November 1950 by Mapai leader Pinhas Rashish, Petah Tikva agreed to cooperate and take the neighboring immigrant settlements under its wing. Ha-Poel ha-Mizrachi mayors were also encouraged to annex *ma'abarot.* Kfar Hassidim took on a nearby *ma'abara* after it had been promised to Ha-Poel ha-Mizrachi.[15]

Apparently, Mapai mayors who allowed *ma'abarot* to be put up in their vicinity were told that substantial funding would be made available to cover their expenses. The municipalities were funded by the Interior Ministry. The Ministry of Labor, however, was in charge of employment and housing, and it could channel monies for these purposes into settlements that absorbed immigrants. Because of lack of coordination, however, few of the promises to these mayors were kept, bringing some towns to the brink of bankruptcy.

The inefficiency of the government created frustration and despair even in towns with a sincere desire to help their immigrant neighbors. The level of anxiety increased even more when the army pulled its soldiers out of the *ma'abarot* at the end of the winter, leaving the local authorities to take over their duties.[16]

Broken Promises

The Interior Ministry's efforts to wean the immigrants from dependence on the Jewish Agency could not succeed without the cooperation of the local authorities. To soften their opposition, the ministry promised that municipalities would be reimbursed for services to the *ma'abarot*. In reality these sums never arrived in full or were paid late—and only after considerable begging and pleading on the part of the local authorities.

The Interior Ministry received dozens of complaints about the enormous expense of keeping the *ma'abarot* clean, the water running, and the children in school. The local authorities threatened to shut down services or disconnect the water supply unless the ministry stood by its obligations. The ministry argued that the government could not be expected to finance all utilities, and it recommended taxation as an alternative: "Immigrants come under the same law as other citizens and should be incorporated in the body of taxpayers; aside from the financial value, taxes are an important educational tool." [17] However, preaching and offering advice on how to turn the immigrants into good citizens did not fill municipal coffers. In fact, collecting taxes from the immigrants was virtually impossible because so many of them were unemployed and likely to move.

Then came the Interior Ministry announcement that it would pay for no more than half the expenses incurred by the local authorities, with the intention of cutting down further at some future date. The small towns, forced to maintain an immigrant population that was several times larger than their own, felt bitterly deceived. They vented their anger on both the Jewish Agency, which had built the *ma'abarot*, and on the Interior Ministry, which had led them to believe they would be compensated for their trouble.

The Interior Ministry clung to its line that municipal activities should be financed through taxation. It was even suggested that the local authorities should demand property taxes from the Jewish Agency on the grounds that it was proprietor of the *ma'abarot*. Josephthal found the idea ridiculous. The *ma'abarot* were not property but "social institutions." The ministry proposed that the Jewish Agency make no housing referrals unless the immigrant could produce a document showing he had paid his taxes. The municipalities dismissed all these proposals as totally unrealistic. Some swore that they would never use their authority to file claims against jobless immigrants living in miserable shanties.[18] Others warned that they would withhold services or cut off the water supply, but none of these threats seem to have had any effect.

The local authorities thus found themselves continuously clashing with the Jewish Agency and the Interior Ministry, and it was the immigrants who were caught in the middle. The municipalities also accused other government ministries—welfare, education, health, and others—of reneging on their promises of assistance. The educational problems in the *ma'abarot* were especially severe. Without buildings, equipment, or teachers, the school system could barely operate, and hundreds of children were forced to sit idle. Building and maintaining schools was a municipal task, but the local councils simply did not have the money to do all that was needed.[19]

The Ministry of Welfare was criticized for shirking its responsibility toward the numerous welfare cases in the *ma'abarot*. As a result, their care fell on the municipalities, too. Even those settlements that had demonstrated good will and were prepared to devote themselves to immigrant absorption were outspoken in their condemnation of the government on this score. Ultimately, it was the residents of the small towns, most of them working-class people with low incomes, who had to shoulder the burden. It was a task that weighed heavily upon them and generated a tremendous amount of tension between the old-timers and newcomers.

Physical Isolation

Most of the *ma'abarot* were built several kilometers away from existing settlements, even if they belonged to the same municipality. Buses rarely stopped nearby, and the immigrants were forced to walk long distances from the main road. For the handicapped, this situation meant total isolation from the outside world. In stormy weather the entire population was cut off. There were no paved access roads and the dirt tracks leading to the *ma'abarot* turned into huge mud puddles that even cars could not cross. Such was the situation in Kfar Saba, Rehovot, Hadera, Petah Tikva, and dozens of other *ma'abarot*. In consequence, the winter also brought with it shortages of food and other basic supplies.

The lack of transportation was a problem for *ma'abara* workers, too. Doctors, nurses, teachers, and social workers were often late or did not arrive at all. The difficulty was especially great in those *ma'abarot* located far from population centers. The Ministry of Welfare complained that its workers in the Negev and the Jerusalem Corridor could not keep to their schedules. Social workers, it should be remembered, were often the only link between the *ma'abara* dwellers and the outside world: "If a baby is ill, the counselor rushes with it to the hospital because the new immigrants do not know where to go or how to make themselves understood. There is neither transportation nor telephone, and hence no contact with any other settlement." [20]

The Health Ministry reported that its physicians could not reach the *ma'abarot*. Weeks went by between doctors' visits to those in the southern Negev. Most *ma'abarot* had no telephone lines and could not summon emergency assistance. The citrus workers' council wrote to say that the *wadi* outside a certain *ma'abara* had filled with water during the rains and even an ambulance could not approach. A woman who had just given birth was forced to wade through the *wadi* on her return home from the hospital.[21]

A large percentage of *ma'abarot* were not connected to the electricity grid; it was pitch black at night and the only illumination came from gas lamps inside the tents. Under the circumstances, it was impossible to keep up social contacts outside the *ma'abara* or hold cultural events such as film showings and lectures on a regular basis. The Interior Ministry lamented, "There is no organized cultural or social life. On the other hand, there is plenty of drinking, brawling, gambling and, according to some, prostitution." [22] The plight of immigrants living in *ma'abarot* far from the center was even worse. Without access to public transportation, the sense of isolation and alienation was great indeed.

Water Shortages and Poor Sanitation

Rainfall was sparse in 1951, causing a drought that was acutely felt by summer. According to a report from the Migdal-Ashkelon *ma'abara,* which was inhabited by more than three thousand persons, water was piped in for only two hours a day and the quantity was far from sufficient. The residents had no choice but to haul water from town, 3.5 kilometers away. Dozens of other *ma'abarot* were in similar predicaments. [23]

The majority of *ma'abarot* had no plumbing because pipes were in short supply and there was no foreign currency to buy them. Taps were also hard to come by. A single tap was installed every 250 meters and served a large number of families. *Ma'abarot* in agricultural regions had water for only a few hours a day. The intermittent and inadequate supply in the hot summer months caused intense discomfort and endless quarreling among the *ma'abara* dwellers.

Sanitary facilities that were hastily and improperly built soon became health hazards. When the *ma'abarot* were planned, it was decided that one communal outhouse containing five showers and five toilets was sufficient for every 100 families. In reality, the number of persons using these facilities was many times higher. Because of the chronic water shortage and the absence of proper drainage, the facilities were dirty and foul-smelling. On many occasions, the Ministry of Health called attention to the gross lack of hygiene in the *ma'abarot.* The ministry recognized the objective difficulties, but felt that the human component was also to blame. It claimed that neither the municipalities nor the *ma'abara* inhabitants were doing enough to maintain proper standards of cleanliness. This set off a spate of name-calling, as each authority accused the other of incompetence and of perpetuating conditions that would lead to the spread of epidemics. [24]

Enforced Idleness

The work programs initiated by the government, primarily in afforestation, road-building, agriculture, and construction, could not provide jobs for all the immigrants. One of the most distressing features of life in the *ma'abara* was unemployment, which threatened to keep the immigrants endlessly tied to the apron strings of the bureaucrats—the *ma'abara* directors, employment bureaus, etc. The diversity of the population in terms of culture, education, and vocational training increased the sense of bitterness, especially among those who saw themselves as having come from a higher socioeconomic class. A large percentage of *olim* from Iraq were seasoned professionals and businessmen. They were reluctant to accept the low-paying jobs they were offered and were unaccustomed to manual labor, which they considered undignified and a blow to their pride. The Iraqi immigrants dispatched hundreds of letters to the Jewish Agency, Knesset members, and the prime minister in this regard. There were vast differences in education and living standards between those who came from cities (mainly Baghdad and Basra) and those who came from small towns and villages, not to mention from other countries, such as Yemen and Persia. These factors led to growing polarization in the *ma'abarot* and to adjustment problems, particularly in the sphere of employment.[25]

One of the municipalities' chief arguments against having *ma'abarot* in their midst was the inadequate supply of jobs. In July 1950 Josephthal received a letter of protest from Karkur, whose population had doubled: "Moving 250 immigrant families to a colony which has only 250 established older families is bound to lead to disaster . . . Public works and jobs available on the local market will yield no more than two to three days of work per week for 100 new families."[26] The Ministry of Labor's commitment to initiate more public works could not solve the problem, which was aggravated with each wave of immigration.

Crowds of unemployed immigrants demonstrating in front of the Jewish Agency and municipal offices became a daily affair, culminating at times in violence. The Kfar Saba council demanded that Josephthal stop sending immigrants to the *ma'abara,* which was now populated by 1,000 families and 190 bachelors, hundreds of them out of work. When Josephthal did not respond, a letter was sent announcing the council's decision to bar newcomers because of the employment situation.[27] The Rosh Ha'ayin employment bureau was praised for finding work for 1,400 breadwinners in the quarries, agriculture, and construction, although 500 persons still remained jobless. In most cases the immigrants were hired on a part-time basis, two to three days a week at best. Day and night, long lines could be seen outside the employment bureau. The search for work thus became an integral part of *ma'abara* culture.

Unemployment worsened in the spring of 1951. The Ministry of Labor explained that a shortage of raw materials was holding back industrial development: "Several factories established . . . at our urging in new areas, cannot be completed for lack of construction supplies."[28] Government road-building and housing projects were hampered by a shortage of cement and asphalt. The drought altered plans to hire large numbers of immigrants as farm laborers. Close to 12,000 fruit-pickers joined the ranks of the unemployed as the season ended. Forecasts for the summer were gloomy.

The poor health of the elderly and many of the immigrants from Poland, Romania, Iraq, and other nations placed a heavy strain on the municipalities. The percentage of widows among immigrants from Arab countries was exceptionally high. In February 1951 the Jewish Agency counted 600 widows with children among the 38,000 Iraqi immigrants living in *ma'abarot*. The local authorities were furious at the Jewish Agency for dropping so many "invalids, widows, old people and other social cases" in their lap.[29] To create jobs for them that were not physically taxing, the authorities began to dispense shop and vending-stall licenses, to the point where the townscape was literally studded with kiosks. The towns' demands to be allowed some say in selecting the immigrants transferred to their region were ignored by the Kelitah Department. Those in the center of the country were forced to accept a particularly large number of welfare cases because it was assumed that suitable jobs were in greater supply there.

Municipalities Caught in a Web

The local councils decried the irresponsibility of the government, which had plunged them so deeply into debt. Those that had complied with the government's call and extended themselves to help the *ma'abarot* felt especially taken in. Rather than treating the council heads as partners in the sphere of immigrant absorption, the ministries were seen as harboring insensitive and insulting attitudes:

> Subjectively, all of us feel that we are performing the function of government. But when we meet with the central government, we feel that we are a superfluous limb of no consequence. Our opinion is ignored . . . In the ball game being played out between the institutions of the government and the Jewish Agency, the local authorities have no one to pass the ball to . . . The crux of the problem is not lack of resources, but our disconnection from the central government.[30]

Tens of thousands of immigrants thus sat in *ma'abarot* all over the country with very little prospect of full-time employment. This situation was compounded by the water and power shortages, scarcity of raw materials, and lack of vocational training facilities. Government-sponsored work programs could not satisfy the demand. The outcome was social unrest in the *ma'abarot* that ticked away like a time bomb, affecting the work of the authorities and casting a shadow over relations between the *olim* and the old-timers.

Relations with the Kibbutzim

The planners of the *ma'abara* hoped that kibbutzim and *moshavim* would be among the veteran settlements to come to the immigrants' aid. When Levi Eshkol unveiled his *ma'abara* program, he spoke of *ma'abarot* "resting on settlements from Dan to Nir Am." By mentioning the names of kibbutzim, he meant not only the geographical distance but also a form of relationship. Israel's leaders, key figures in the Labor movement, looked forward to the kibbutz movement playing an active part in immigrant absorption. Meanwhile, however, the kibbutzim had plunged into a deep crisis of their own and were preoccupied with saving themselves.

On the eve of independence, the Israeli kibbutz movement had boasted 159 collective settlements with a population of 45,000—25,000 of them adults. Now the kibbutzim found themselves on the verge of financial and social collapse, and their organizational leadership was entirely engrossed in seeking a cure. On the face of it, the prospects for economic revival were good. Large stretches of agricultural land had come into Israel's possession since the war, and much of it had been given to the kibbutzim. However, the increase in land did not coincide with a growth in membership.[31] The pioneer movements in Europe had been annihilated during the Holocaust, and many of the graduates of the Palestine youth organizations had chosen to put their ideals into practice by joining a national institution such as the IDF rather than a kibbutz. The new immigrants found kibbutz life strange and unfamiliar. Hence the movement was left with nowhere to turn for new members.

The recurrent debate over the role of the kibbutz in immigrant absorption, which began soon after the founding of the state, soured relations between the kibbutz movement and the national leadership. The latter accused the kibbutzim of disregarding the crying needs of immigration. On the other hand, those who did employ immigrants as outside labor were censured by the heads of the kibbutz movement. This created an uncomfortable reserve between the kibbutz and its immigrant workers. In cases where a kibbutz deliberately avoided hiring immigrants who lived nearby, the relationship was even more complex.

In 1951, just as the *ma'abarot* were being established, internal conflict in the Kibbutz Hameuhad movement caused a split.[32] Beset by their own problems, the kibbutzim lacked the strength and fortitude to initiate programs that could change the face of immigrant absorption. Many did make a genuine effort to help; they participated in the clothing and shelter campaigns and took thousands of *ma'abara* children into their homes—three times as many as did any other sector.[33] These acts, however, were one-sided; reciprocal social relations were not fostered. The organizational structure of the kibbutz movement, with its autarkic, countrywide marketing and supply networks, and separate educational and communal facilities, minimized direct contact with the immigrants and set up a barrier they found hard to cross. When immigrants worked in local or regional kibbutz factories, the employer-employee relationship that developed tended to highlight the distance between them and increase their sense of alienation.

Relations between the kibbutz and the immigrants were also affected by local politics. During the election campaigns in late 1950 and the summer of 1951, the kibbutzim went into the *ma'abarot* to recruit support for their parties. Their political rivals struck back with mudslinging and verbal abuse, which succeeded in changing the immigrants' view of the kibbutz and planting in them deep seeds of resentment. Even the efforts by the kibbutzim to render assistance were turned against them; it was claimed that they were only acting in their own self-interest. All this added to the existing mistrust. The patronizing attitude of the kibbutzim toward the "Diaspora mentality" of the immigrants and their cultural and social traditions served to poison the atmosphere further and intensify the hostile feelings. In short, the kibbutz movement, which had been a trailblazer during the prestate period, was not able to find a niche for the Great Aliyah.

Another type of workers' settlement, the *moshav ovdim,* responded differently. When the State of Israel was proclaimed, there were seventy-three *moshavei ovdim* in the country with a total population of sixteen thousand. The *moshav* movement surprised absorption officials with its willingness to cooperate and help the newcomers acclimate. Between 1949 and 1951, the Jewish Agency Settlement Department established dozens of new *moshavim* throughout the country, and the *moshav* movement of Mapai and the *moshav* federations of Ha-Poel ha-Mizrachi offered to train the settlers. Individual *moshav* members volunteered their services in nearby *ma'abarot.* The federations, however, concentrated on the *moshavei olim,* (*moshavim* whose settlers were new immigrants) and were able to leave a tangible mark.[34]

The *ma'abarot* and workers' settlements also had contact with one another in the regional councils. The relationship was similar to that which evolved in other frameworks, with politics usually assuming a dominant role.

Relations with the Regional Councils

The regional councils performed municipal tasks that could not be done by individual settlements. They built roads and sewer systems, ran schools, and organized cultural activities for a whole bloc of settlements. These councils were located in rural areas and served either a group of kibbutzim, a group of *moshavim,* or a combination of the two. They differed from municipalities and local councils both in organizational structure and in certain fundamental respects.[35]

Regional councils had been formed in Mandatory times for such purposes as security, official representation, operation of schools, road-building, and sanitation. Sometimes economic enterprises such as waterworks, trucking companies, and so on were established under these auspices, especially where there were clusters of kibbutzim.

Because of the diversity of settlements in a single region, organization on a regional basis had been problematic from the start. Such factors as population makeup, financial status, and the age of settlements could vary widely. Resistance to regional councils increased after the establishment of the state, even among those settlements that formed a homogeneous bloc such as the kibbutzim of the Jordan Valley. There were disagreements over boundary lines, municipal responsibilities, and issues connected with the fact that cooperative and other settlements were massed together. All this was compounded by the tension between local and central government. Relations between the regional councils and the *ma'abarot* were uneasy for many of the same reasons.

After independence, Israel's national planners carved out twenty-four administrative districts, "complete units that are socially and economically balanced, and promote interaction between the agricultural hinterland and urban centers."[36] This approach was different from the previous one, which had created a strict separation between urban and rural settlements. The goal here was to bring together diverse settlement types in the same region under a common local government. The break with tradition was so great that engaging the settlements' cooperation proved difficult. Rural settlements feared that the authorities would meddle in their internal affairs or force municipal duties upon them against their will.

The "Local Municipalities Ordinance—Jordan Valley Regional Council, 1949" represented a compromise. It defined the legal and organizational status of Israel's first regional council, and it recognized the authority of the settlement committees, enabling additional councils to be established. However, the division of tasks between the regional councils and the settlement committees was not spelled out clearly enough, leading to endless conflict and confusion. The law was equally vague on the status of the *ma'abarot* and the degree to which the regional councils were responsible for them.

Attitudes toward the establishment of a *ma'abara* were influenced by a number of factors: the various settlement types represented in the regional council, their political leanings and social character, and the neighborly relations between them. If settlements were already quarreling over land and boundary lines, a request to set aside tracts for immigrant housing or *ma'abarot* was likely to be met with even greater hostility. Grievances within the community also affected receptivity to newcomers, and there was little the Interior Ministry could do to change this situation.

In one instance, the Interior Ministry took steps to establish a regional council incorporating eight settlements in the southern Sharon: three *moshavei olim,* two communal villages, and three *moshavot.* The population of the nearby immigrant housing projects and *ma'abarot* was several times higher than that of all these settlements combined. The local residents opposed a regional council on principle because they did not want to assume responsibility for the immigrants. The Interior Ministry refused to give in, calling countless meetings with the residents over the next two years.[37] Those who supported the idea of a regional council focused on the advantages of a larger development budget; they envisaged the construction of roads, the improvement of water and sewage systems, and the inauguration of community schools. Opponents argued that the settlements would lose their individuality, chunks of land would be confiscated, and the region would be engulfed by immigrants. Taking on the *ma'abarot,* they maintained, was simply more than they could handle.[38]

Regional councils that agreed to take *ma'abarot* under their wing soon joined the local councils clamoring for the Interior Ministry and other government agencies to fulfill their obligations. The problem was most serious in regions where the immigrants outnumbered other residents. The population of the Sulam Tzor regional council, for example, grew from seventeen hundred to seven thousand within the span of two years.[39] Out of eleven settlements, only three belonged to old-timers; all the rest were newly established. There were two young kibbutzim, two *moshavei olim,* and four labor villages. Sulam Tzor was willing to assume responsibility for all the immigrants, but only on condition that its expenses were paid. These included guarding the fields against thieves and marauders, which was one of the official duties of regional councils in frontier areas. The Arabs had been crossing the border more frequently of late to plunder and terrorize the population, and a number of serious incidents in May-June 1951 had led to a deterioration of security on the Syrian front. Another request was that the Interior Ministry pressure the Ministry of Welfare into keeping its promise to fund welfare and child-care services in the *ma'abarot*.[40]

Both regional and local councils wrestled with the problems of immigrant employment and schooling. The Emek Hefer regional council, with a population base of sixteen hundred, became responsible for five *moshavei olim* and two *ma'abarot* inhabited by nearly four thousand immigrants from Yemen, Romania, and Iraq. The council did its best to help the new farmers, but the government had not provided them with basic agricultural implements or with an adequate water supply. A vegetable garden was planted in the Kakun *ma'abara,* but it could not survive without water. According to the council's report to the Interior Ministry, a cooperative for roof tiles had been established in the *ma'abara* and a cooperative bakery was being planned.[41] These and other enterprises were dependent upon financial aid from the government, but in fact the ministries' coffers were dry.

The Histadrut urged regional councils affiliated with the Labor movement to initiate cultural and educational activities in the *ma'abarot.* When the Hof Ashkelon regional council was approached, it claimed that Hebrew classes, cultural events, and parties could not be organized without a proper budget. This council proposed the establishment of a regional culture committee and an immigrant welfare program offering nutritional guidance, clothing, and emotional support, but again, it would do nothing without funding.[42]

Regional councils handling a homogeneous population or settlements belonging to a single movement were generally better organized and more active than the others. This was particularly true if the councils in question received support and financing from the parties in power. The Interior Ministry actively encouraged regional councils to annex neighboring *ma'abarot* but was not always forthcoming with assistance once they did—especially if there was any suspicion that their activities might benefit the ministry's political adversaries, as in the case of the Upper Galilee regional council. This council had complied with the request of the Kelitah Department to assist the Rosh Pina and Halssa *ma'abarot* in administration, schooling, and employment, but the Interior Ministry took a negative view of this intervention. It insisted on annexing the Rosh Pina *ma'abara* to Rosh Pina in spite of the local council's objections, and it removed the Halssa *ma'abara* from the jurisdiction of the regional council. A ministry overseer was appointed instead.

Municipal Status

The local authorities in Israel were pulled in two directions. On the one hand, they were committed to the promises made to their electorate; on the other hand, they were bound legally and financially to the central government. The local authorities did not operate in a vacuum; their strength depended on resources, and the central government controlled the purse strings. The powers of the local authorities were also delegated by the central government.

As the immigrant population swelled, the local councils could barely take a step without government assistance, which, of course, further undermined their power and independence. The councils found themselves torn between obligations to their voters and their own platforms, and the responsibility of caring for *ma'abarot* dwellers—who had not even elected them. This dilemma was felt more intensely in the regional councils. Whereas municipal and local officials were elected directly by the residents, the regional council was made up of settlement committee delegates, one per settlement. Each settlement elected a committee, which, in turn, sent a representative to the regional council. This layering had both legal and practical implications. From a legal standpoint, both the regional council and the settlement committee were "local authorities." They controlled the same geographical area without a clear division of authority.[43] In practice, tasks were divided according to the balance of power at the time. The outcome was chronic tension between the regional council and the individual settlements it comprised; the addition of the *ma'abarot* only made matters worse. The *ma'abarot* were not part of a specific settlement, nor were they represented by an elected committee as were other settlements. In the absence of direct elections for the regional council, the *ma'abarot* had no delegate on the council executive.

When the idea of electing *ma'abara* committees arose, one of the questions was whether this body would have the same clout as did other settlement committees. There were several problems involved. First of all, *ma'abara* dwellers were considered temporary residents, some of whom were expected to move to other parts of the country. Without a stable population, it was difficult to map out a clear electoral public. Second, the fight between the Kelitah Department and the Interior Ministry over control of the *ma'abarot* kept an agreeable arrangement for choosing a committee from being worked out.

The older settlements were concerned about the growing number of immigrants. If they received equal representation in the regional council, the balance of power was likely to change. For rural settlements matters became more complex after the passage of the "Local Municipalities Ordinance—Jordan Valley

Regional Council, 1949." This ordinance specified that a settlement's cooperative affairs committee would also serve as its local committee and that elections
would be general, proportional, and conducted by secret ballot. All residents
aged eighteen years and older were eligible to vote, no matter which settlement
they lived in.[44] Old-timers, especially in the farming sector, worried that the immigrants who joined the regional council would have the same decision-making
power as they did. This possibility, as we have said, was one of the reasons why
some regional councils objected to *ma'abarot* in the first place.

The ordinance raised immediate questions about budget planning and taxation. The unclear division of responsibilities between the local committee and
the regional council in these two spheres provided fertile ground for dispute. It
also affected the debate over municipal status for the *ma'abarot* and opened
doors for the political parties vying to control them.

Ma'abara Committees

The Interior Ministry was anxious to sever the bonds between the Jewish Agency
and the *ma'abarot*, which it planned to accomplish by either attaching them to
municipalities or granting them independence. It was the ministry that determined which settlements would be annexed and which would become local
councils in their own right. In the latter case, a committee was needed to represent the residents and take charge of the council. The Interior Ministry and the
Jewish Agency did not see eye to eye on this matter.

Local committees had been operating in most of the resettled Arab villages
and in a number of *ma'abarot* since 1950, prior to the Interior Ministry's involvement. The ministry now refused to recognize these committees on the
grounds that the Histadrut was behind their election and manipulated them to
serve its own ends. Calling the Knesset Interior Affairs Committee into action,
the Interior Ministry won a mandate to confer municipal status on the *ma'abarot*
and to ready them for democratic elections.[45]

The ministry thus set about organizing local committees in immigrant settlements that did not fall within municipal boundaries. Labor villages, "agricultural *ma'abarot*," and *moshavei olim* in the same geographical area were brought
together under joint frameworks that resembled regional councils. The Interior
Ministry also established two councils in the Jerusalem Corridor and the
coastal plain consisting of eighteen immigrant settlements accountable to the
ministry. By the middle of 1951, twenty-one immigrant settlements had been
annexed to nearby local authorities. The municipal status of another sixty remained undefined.

After the change in status these settlements were expected to proceed with elections. It was on this score that controversy erupted. The municipal office of the Histadrut wanted to see the same political balance in the elections committee as in the local committees. The Interior Ministry objected because these committees had been organized by the Histadrut without government supervision. Again the Interior Affairs Committee was called upon to make the final decision:

> In immigrant settlements where elections have already been held . . . election planning will be carried out by a committee appointed by the Minister of the Interior in keeping with the municipal elections code. In immigrant settlements which have not held elections, planning will be in the hands of an oversight committee or officials delegated by the Minister of the Interior, with the provision that wherever an oversight committee is requested or feasible, such a committee will be in charge of election planning.[46]

The Interior Ministry exerted great pressure on the Kelitah Department to submit to its demands. It announced that elections in the *ma'abarot* would be held under its surveillance and, "in order to educate the committees in proper municipal procedure, the ministry will appoint, prior to the elections and in a public announcement, committee secretaries who are experts in administrative and organizational work."[47] These secretaries—ministry functionaries—remained in office without a time limit and basically replaced the directors of the Kelitah Department. This was a substitute for transforming the *ma'abara* into an independent municipal body governed by self-elected officials.

The Jewish Agency was interested in activating the old *ma'abara* committees. Even when a *ma'abara* was annexed to a local council, a neighborhood committee was needed to represent the residents' interests. Many of the nearby settlements preferred to see the *ma'abarot* fending for themselves and welcomed the establishment of committees that would help to organize daily affairs, collect taxes, and involve the immigrants in local government. The Interior Ministry, which spoke so much about self-elected committees as a means of developing the immigrants' sense of citizenship and belonging, came out against this proposal. The minister objected to committees in *ma'abarot* that were affiliated with a local council on the assumption that the local council would influence them politically.[48]

As a rule the ministry preferred to grant these settlements independent municipal status, allowing the ministry it to remain in direct control, rather than annex them to local authorities that were the province of the Labor Party. In early 1952 the Interior Ministry's Immigrant Settlement Department listed 270 settlements populated by three hundred thousand immigrants as being under its jurisdiction;

only 60 percent had been annexed. The rest were supervised by the ministry, which declared its foremost aim as "the provision of vital services, the establishment of an administrative apparatus, and the organization of a local committee to represent the residents before the government and the public."⁴⁹ The ministry, however, seemed to be in no haste. Its appointees continued to run the *ma'abarot* as before.

Observing the lethargy of the Interior Ministry in this regard, the Kelitah Department decided to take steps of its own to organize an election campaign. The ministry was predictably piqued. It dismissed the Kelitah Department's claim that residents' committees were imperative for the smooth operation of the *ma'abarot* and argued that associations of this sort would only hinder the establishment of formal committees. Accused of stalling, the ministry cited organizational difficulties: "As long as there is instability in the *ma'abarot* and the population turnover is very high, there is no practical way of preparing a voters' list and holding elections according to law."⁵⁰

The clash between the Interior Ministry and the Kelitah Department continued throughout 1952. The ministry demanded that the Jewish Agency close its offices in the *ma'abarot,* while the Jewish Agency insisted that the ministry keep its word and confer municipal status on the *ma'abarot,* either as part of an existing authority or as municipalities in their own right.

The interministerial committee assigned to study *ma'abara* affairs in 1954 found that 98 out of 129 *ma'abarot* were affiliated with local councils. Of the remaining 31, 17 had their own committees. In theory, the majority of the *ma'abarot* were part of a municipal complex, but this idea had little bearing on everyday life.⁵¹ Even when the Interior Ministry approved the establishment of a *ma'abara* council, its powers were severely limited and the bulk of its decisions required government endorsement. In regional councils, the *ma'abara* did not enjoy the same representation as did other settlements—even when the number of inhabitants was greater than all the other citizens combined. It was argued that *ma'abara* dwellers were temporary residents and that there was no assurance that, when permanent housing was built, it would be populated by these same people.⁵²

Because of the heterogeneous population makeup, *ma'abara* residents tended to group themselves by country of origin and to elect committees on this basis. Sometimes differences of opinion led to the establishment of two separate committees from the same country. In the Hadera *ma'abara,* the Iraqi and Syrian Jews each had their own committees and competed with one another for the residents' support.⁵³

From the start, the *ma'abarot* were like an unwanted stepchild. The local authorities, already in debt, felt the noose tighten as *ma'abarot* sprouted around them—islands of poverty and social despair. Many blamed the immigrants themselves. By dodging their civic duties and evading taxes, they brought alienation upon themselves. The Interior Ministry claimed that the misguided absorption policies of the Jewish Agency were to blame, and that only a reformation of these policies could better the plight of the immigrants and change the attitude toward them:

> One of the goals we must keep up front is how to make the *ma'abara* dweller aware that he is no longer an immigrant but a free citizen of the State of Israel, his own country. And what is the difference between an immigrant and a citizen? An immigrant says: Give me, give me, while the citizen is asked to give of himself . . . If an immigrant is under the care of the Kelitah Department, it means he has not yet been absorbed . . . If he is dealt with by the local authorities, he slowly begins to feel like everyone else.[54]

In reality, the immigrants remained stigmatized even after their settlements were declared independent municipal entities. Only when newcomers were directly absorbed into an older settlement did the distinctions gradually fade away. For the majority of the immigrants this was but a distant dream.

Immigrant Absorption and the IDF

Ben-Gurion never lost the hope of involving the community in immigrant absorption, but he believed that national institutions, among them the Israel Defense Forces, should bear primary responsibility. For Ben-Gurion, the IDF was more than a military machine; he saw it as an effective tool for promoting education and culture. He used the term "security" in a broad sense, maintaining that national unity, social values, and cultural standards were no less crucial for the future of the country than was military might. For many reasons he sought to transform the IDF into Israel's main channel of immigrant absorption. In the first place, Ben-Gurion's control over the army, structurally and operationally, made it a convenient framework for carrying out his plans. Second, politics did not get in the way; in the army, Ben-Gurion had no opposition to contend with. Third, the army was by nature diversified; it consisted of many different branches and brought together large numbers of people from all sectors of the population.

The IDF Myth in Israeli Society

In democratic countries, especially those recently moving from foreign dominion to independence, military involvement in civilian affairs would seem to touch on a sensitive nerve. The military-civilian relationship has been studied by social scientists in various parts of the world, but little attention has been paid to this subject in Israel.[55] One explanation may lie in the unique approach to the army among Israeli citizens. The IDF was idolized and was the source of great national pride. For Israelis, the army's influence in the social sphere was considered both legitimate and a national mission. Its centrality was recognized by all sectors of the public in view of the fact that defending the country was tantamount to preserving the existence of the Jewish people.[56] The fact that Israel has been in a state of war since inception has also contributed to its preoccupation with the military; security and security-related matters were never far from the headlines.

The IDF did not achieve this central role in the public mind without assistance. Ben-Gurion deliberately built up its image and prestige, hailing the IDF as a direct descendant of the Jewish armies of old, the "issue of ancient military stock." In his version of history, "the Jewish people's first war came immediately after the exodus from Egypt, under . . . Joshua Bin-Nun. This war was waged in Refidim, where the Israel Defense Forces fought its last battle . . . at the end of 1948."[57] Ben-Gurion perpetuated the IDF myth as a way of bringing the nation together and creating national consensus. Here was a body that was free of the defects plaguing so many other sectors of society, a marvelous task force that would protect the physical existence of the Jewish people in its homeland and, at the same time, function as a powerful educational tool. For Ben-Gurion, the IDF was a new creation that came into being with the state; it was not an extension of the Haganah.[58] It pursued one goal embraced by all and was unencumbered by party interests—unlike the military organizations of the prestate years, which Ben-Gurion fought so hard to disband. Ben-Gurion's control over the IDF was uncontested; the top brass were among his loyal supporters.[59] He was convinced that with their help he could meet the social challenges that faced the Jewish people.

The public was not insensitive to the implications of opening up the civilian sphere to the military, but there was a certain wariness of tarnishing the IDF's reputation. Although Ben-Gurion was careful to establish limits, he was convinced that the current state of emergency legitimized asking the army to perform duties that were not strictly military. With the establishment of a Jewish state and the victory over the Arabs, the Jews had taken two major steps toward their goal of national renascence. The third step was to build a new society through the absorption of mass immigration. In this sphere, too, Ben-Gurion had carved out a central role for the IDF.[60]

Defining a state of emergency was problematic, both constitutionally and otherwise. Ben-Gurion thus clung to the more general term "security." He evoked this notion constantly, speaking about the security aspect of domains entirely outside the military, such as immigrant absorption, education, agricultural settlement, and the advancement of science and technology. In Ben-Gurion's eyes, secure borders were not enough:

> Unless we become a united people and conquer the wilderness—we will have no security . . . Our security problem differs from that of other nations of the world, not only in that we are few against many, but because we do not constitute a people and do not have a land. A population which does not understand each other's language and is not immersed in the culture and lore of land will not be able to confront its enemies and oppressors in times of need. Only by raising ethical and intellectual levels to the maximum, will our army have fulfilled its duty of making this country secure.[61]

The IDF was envisaged as an important partner in the Zionist pioneering effort, borne chiefly by voluntary organizations—especially the kibbutzim—in the days of the British Mandate. Ben-Gurion hoped that the IDF, aside from having responsibility for Israel's defense, could further national goals in the realm of settlement, realizing that "settlement of the type that reinforces security will not be achieved without a great upswing in pioneering." [62] Army service was thought to be a valuable tool in the education of young people and the molding of Israeli society:

> The army will have failed to accomplish its mission . . . if military service is not oriented toward raising the physical, cultural and moral standards of young people. Neither our security needs nor those of our nation will be met unless the army becomes an academy for fighting-pioneering youth . . . The army can and must be a consolidating and inspiring force in shaping the new visage of our people and blending it into the new culture and society emerging in the State of Israel.[63]

The 1949 National Security Service Law enumerated the social goals of the IDF as follows: "Educating the soldier-settler . . . fostering pioneering values and loyal citizenship . . . encouraging the organization of core groups for pioneer settlement . . . instilling a Jewish, Zionist, pioneer-oriented education, nurturing a native Israeli lifestyle to uplift the soldier spiritually and culturally." [64]

Aside from these goals, which applied to all conscripts, the IDF was to place special emphasis on immigrant absorption. It would be a melting pot where young people from all parts of the Diaspora would converge and strike roots in their new homeland. New immigrants, in particular, would be encouraged to join pioneer settlements. In Ben-Gurion's words, the army was to be a "pioneering, educating force, a builder of nations and a redeemer of the wilderness." It was planned from the outset as an open, impartial framework. The Compulsory Service Law insured that all sectors of the Jewish population would be called up for military duty, and soldiers would move up the ranks in keeping with objective criteria. To promote integration, basic-training units would be heterogeneous, bringing together the educated and uneducated, persons from different social backgrounds, immigrants and native Israelis. This situation would create an opportunity for direct, informal contact between sectors of the population that would not normally meet in civilian life.

IDF Aid to the *Ma'abarot*

In November 1950, as the Kelitah Department bowed under the burden of caring for 130,000 homeless immigrants packed into primitive camps and *ma'abarot,* the IDF was approached for assistance. Giora Josephthal feared that the coming rains would turn the camps into muddy swamps and that the mishaps of the previous winter—collapsed buildings, flooding, and epidemics—might repeat themselves. It occurred to him that the army could be mobilized in the case of emergency, and he appealed to Ben-Gurion in this regard. He asked that army vehicles stand ready to transport food and that a fleet of ambulances be made available to administer first aid and handle the evacuation of patients and children.

The previous summer, Dr. Sheba of the Health Ministry, formerly chief medical officer of the IDF, had urged Ben-Gurion to allow army health personnel into the *ma'abarot* in view of the high incidence of polio and other diseases. The flow of nonselective immigration from Romania and Iraq further increased his concern. He and Josephthal thus requested that Ben-Gurion draw up a plan to utilize the IDF in the *ma'abarot.* As Coordinating Committee chairman, the prime minister was well informed about the state of affairs in the *ma'abarot;* as minister of defense, he had the power to call the army into action.

In general the presence of the IDF in the *ma'abarot* was welcomed. Officials of the Kelitah Department and the Immigrant Health Service, who had failed in their efforts to cope with the problems of the previous winter, were nothing short of enthusiastic. The local authorities were also pleased. The average citizen,

214 I *Immigrants in Turmoil*

however, did not seem to care one way or the other; *ma'abara* affairs were still far from the public mind.

Operation *Ma'abara*

In early November 1950 Ben-Gurion asked the IDF chief of staff to examine possibilities for service in the *ma'abarot*. Mordechai Makleff, the assistant chief of staff, appointed a committee to gather data, recommend specific *ma'abarot*, and suggest appropriate spheres of activity. The committee members visited *ma'abarot* and workers' villages and met with representatives of the Kelitah and Settlement Departments, the Ministry of Health, Kupat Holim Clalit, the Histadrut, and agricultural authorities.

The committee's impression of the *ma'abarot* was a painful one. They returned with tales of severe overcrowding, barefoot women dressed in rags, half-naked children, erratic delivery of supplies, and a virtual absence of vegetables and milk products. In an indirect manner, the immigrants themselves were criticized: "The head of the household is the main eater, and we suspect that the children do not receive adequate nourishment. In some places, the problem has been solved by establishing a child-care center where food is distributed." [65]

The committee concluded that the IDF must take action immediately rather than wait for a state of emergency "since the prevailing situation is already an emergency." The chief of staff ordered the committee to draw up a list of the *ma'abarot* that were most in need based on distance from the center of the country, disciplinary problems, and so on.

The army became involved in the *ma'abarot* at the request of the Kelitah Department, but it did not accept the department's approach. Rather than preparing for the mass evacuation of children and adults in the event of flooding, the IDF preferred to eliminate that need by repairing roads, finding vehicles suitable for transporting food and emergency supplies, making arrangements for medical care, and establishing day-care centers staffed by soldier-counselors. In principle, it was decided not to evacuate the immigrants at all or, in the worst case, just the children. The idea was for life to continue as usual, even during the winter. [66]

The Jewish Agency Settlement Department, which had thirty-two immigrant settlements to care for, anxiously awaited the army's help in paving access roads and delivering food to settlements cut off during inclement weather. One of the most important contributions of the IDF was the building of an emergency supply warehouse that could store food for an entire month. Tin-sided storerooms were also put up outside the kitchens to insure that undernourished children were fed as needed and would be able to withstand the rigors of the coming winter. Raanan Weitz, Eshkol's deputy in the Settlement Department, appointed two persons to handle contacts with the IDF and instructed department employees all over the country to work closely with army personnel.[67]

The IDF did not establish a separate framework to aid the *ma'abarot;* each command set aside some of its troops for this purpose. The chief of staff reported that his senior commanders responded willingly, as did the navy, the air force, and the superintendent of police. Operation *Ma'abara* was officially launched on 17 November 1950: "We have been called upon to prove once again that the battles may be over but our work is not done. We shall not hesitate to participate in that pioneering endeavor of the highest order . . . immigrant absorption. We must also prove to the *olim,* accustomed as they are to seeing the army in their land of birth as an enemy and an oppressor, that the army of the State of Israel can be their champion and defender."

The participation of the IDF in educational and cultural programs was wholly in line with Ben-Gurion's views. In order to allay fears that the military was overstepping its bounds, the chief of staff issued a public statement accentuating the significance of the operation for Israel's defense: "The *ma'abarot* have an important role to play in safeguarding the nation's borders. If we do not turn every *ma'abara* into a commanding ground and all *ma'abara* dwellers into persons who are capable and willing to defend themselves, we shall have no security."[68] This same argument was used in the Knesset.

The Kelitah Department was impressed with the IDF's ability to organize quickly and pursue the mission at hand in true military style. It gladly accepted the army's presence and made an effort to obey orders. The IDF took over such matters as sanitation, preventive medicine, health care, and maintenance of child-care institutions. In addition, it worked to winterize the *ma'abarot* by repairing roads, building drainage systems, buttressing cabins and tents, laying pathways, improving plumbing and water supply, putting away emergency food supplies, and preparing for the evacuation of children should it be necessary. Special camps were set up to take in children from various *ma'abarot.* The largest, able to accommodate one thousand youngsters, was established near the air force base in Tel-Nof. Smaller camps were organized in Jerusalem and elsewhere. The IDF also distributed winter clothing, both army surplus and garments donated through civilian drives. Operation *Ma'abara* was to end on 1 April 1951.[69]

The IDF medical corps encountered a high incidence of disease in the *ma'abarot,* with many children suffering from tuberculosis, trachoma, ringworm, tropical sores, etc. It was decided to isolate these children in camps to facilitate intensive treatment, lab tests, radiation therapy, and so on. Another goal was to provide proper nourishment in order to build up the youngsters' resistance. Within the *ma'abarot,* the IDF established separate children's camps. The buildings in these camps were more weatherproof and a close watch was kept on the children's health. Meals were provided, because the level of nutrition among the kindergarten and school-age children was pronounced very poor and it was found that parents were not feeding them properly.[70]

At first the parents objected to being parted from their sick children, but eventually they gave their consent. Because the children stayed in these separate facilities all year round, the IDF became responsible for their education. This situation developed into an ongoing source of conflict and discord.

The Religious Camp Versus the IDF

Once again, the *ma'abarot* became a battleground. The religious parties in the government coalition demanded that their representatives take part in administering the *ma'abarot.* From the outset, different parties had been granted control of the *ma'abarot,* much in the manner of feudal estates. By June 1950, for example, ten of the forty-seven first-stage *ma'abarot* were designated as the "province" of the religious. Several more *ma'abarot* put up that summer and the following winter were divided among Agudat Yisrael, Ha-Poel ha-Mizrachi, and Poalei Agudat Yisrael.

Throughout 1950 the immigrants were swept up in one battle after another. It began with the feud over education in the immigrant camps, which led to the fall of the government in October, and continued with the local-authority dispute. In consequence, the appearance of any new element triggered immediate suspicion. It was soon apparent that even the IDF was not immune. The religious leadership swiftly cabled Ben-Gurion to warn against "any attempt, direct or indirect, to undermine the religious faith of those who are loyal to the Torah."[71] Complaints were soon being lodged about the mistreatment of religious immigrants. Journalists and religious party activists charged that the army was interfering in their spiritual life and educational choices. Binyamin Mintz, one of the heads of Poalei Agudat Israel, protested that an army officer had called a meeting to preach about the economic folly of raising families without birth control and that an army doctor had recommended shaving off the immigrants' sidelocks to improve their hygiene.[72] The religious parties suspected the IDF of being an arm of Mapai, intent on harassing the religiously observant. Some army personnel who belonged to the Labor movement did try, consciously or not, to influence the behavior of the immigrants. The Actions Committee of Ha-Poel ha-Mizrachi submitted a formal complaint to Ben-Gurion about the "unauthorized involvement of the army in educational and cultural affairs."[73] In this way, the conflict between the IDF and the religious population of the *ma'abarot* steadily gathered momentum.

Anxious to avoid a confrontation, the government appointed a ministerial committee to investigate charges of coercion in the educational frameworks run by the IDF. This committee, which began its work on 14 December 1950, determined that the minister of education and culture would henceforth be responsible for education in the children's camps. It was further decided, under pressure from the religious parties, that the children's camp near Ekron, established and funded by the Ministry of Welfare, would be religious in character. Only Orthodox counselors would be hired, and any secular staff members or soldiers who worked there would refrain from intervening in matters of lifestyle.[74]

Sometimes a crisis could not be warded off. During a visit to the Kessalon *ma'abara*, founded by the Jewish Agency Settlement Department, the minister of welfare, Rabbi Yitzhak Meir Levine (Agudat Israel), was approached by residents who claimed that they had been prevented from opening a religious school for their children. Rabbi Levine informed the prime minister and apparently encouraged them to write letters to the chief rabbis and various cabinet ministers. The Kessalon residents charged that "soldiers took our sons and daughters, even the married ones, forcing them to join the Gadna (youth corps) against our will and leading them into bad ways . . . The counselors and soldiers, both male and female, desecrate the Sabbath. They make us angry, smoking and committing all sorts of Sabbath violations . . . We demand a religious school where our sons can study the laws of Moses and we can restore our fallen glory."[75]

Similar complaints about the army emerged from other *ma'abarot*. These complaints, too, reached the highest echelons and set off rounds of political debate. The controversy in the Jisr *ma'abara* nearly brought down the government.

Committee of Inquiry in Jisr

In the Jisr *ma'abara*, the province of Agudat Yisrael, a counselor and several residents accused the army of offending religious sensibilities by spouting antireligious propaganda, desecrating the Sabbath, and threatening to cut off sidelocks and beards as a means of treating lice. Welfare Minister Levine demanded an investigation, and he was asked to join forces with the minister of labor, Golda Meir, to pursue the matter further. Together they visited the *ma'abara* to question the chief IDF officer, counselors, and residents. The controversy revolved around the authority of the IDF commander and the procedures followed for medical examinations.[76]

The Yemenite Jews who inhabited this *ma'abara* maintained that it was against their custom and code of modesty for women to be examined by male doctors and medics. They claimed that the army staff treated them in an undignified manner and made a deliberate effort to poke fun at their lifestyle and religious beliefs. The IDF commander was criticized for lecturing about birth control, which contradicted religious tradition. In the wake of their visit, Levine and Meir presented the following recommendations:

> The chief of staff must make the soldiers in these camps aware of the background of the Jews of Yemen and their sensitivity in matters of religion and modesty. They must be forbidden to enter into any religious discussions or to attempt to influence the religious beliefs of the residents, adults or children, in any way. In all instances of body disinfection, strict orders should be given that women and girls be handled solely by female medics, soldiers and civilians. Medical examinations of women should preferably be performed by female doctors. If this is not possible, a female medic or soldier should be present to assist the doctor.[77]

However, these recommendations failed to alleviate the tension, and the hostility between *ma'abara* workers and soldiers continued.

Operation *Ma'abara* II

In late March 1951, as Operation *Ma'abara* was about to end, the Kelitah Department as well as various local authorities and *ma'abara* directors urged the IDF to continue. The army leadership agreed; many of the newer *ma'abarot* were situated on the frontier and constituted "an important contribution to spatial defense." From the IDF's perspective, aid to the *ma'abarot* was a "defense mission of the highest order." In April 1951 the IDF decided to devote special attention to fortifying immigrant settlements on the country's borders. In addition to dispatching female soldiers to work with the children and army doctors to supervise health care, troops would be sent in to perform military exercises and train the immigrants. In July a committee was appointed to organize the second stage of Operation *Ma'abara*.[78]

All this coincided with the government crisis over immigrant education and the Second Knesset election campaign launched in July 1951. As matters stood, the opposition parties, and especially the religious parties, were extremely wary of the plans for a new Operation *Ma'abara*. They knew that the immigrants tended to associate the army with the current government, and they feared that Mapai would exploit the prestige of the IDF for its own political gain.

In midsummer Josephthal presented the IDF with a list of twenty-four *ma'abarot* that were suffering from one or more of the following problems: (a) faulty water supply, (b) poor sanitation, (c) delay in establishing medical and child-care institutions, and (d) community infighting and lack of discipline. It was emphasized that this last category applied to all the *ma'abarot* on the list.[79] The IDF's chief task was thus to create a sense of community and introduce some orderliness into the immigrants' lives. The work would be done by regular troops and reserve soldiers, and throughout the operation the *ma'abarot* would be under the administrative control of the IDF.[80]

To accomplish its aims, the IDF planned a massive information campaign among the immigrants. By exposing the immigrants to models of good citizenship and social behavior, instilling in them a love of the land, and familiarizing them with the country's fundamental problems, it was hoped to bring them together as a group and facilitate their absorption.[81] This presentation of goals and objectives was welcomed by Ben-Gurion, Josephthal, and others, who believed that one of the major cures for the ills of the *ma'abara* lay in education. Among the activities planned by the IDF were publishing a daily newspaper in vowelled Hebrew; opening Hebrew language classes for adults; screening a film once a week; and bringing in civilian lecturers to speak about flora and fauna, Jewish history, and contemporary affairs. The religious camp, suspicious of the social and cultural programs drawn up by the IDF, raised an outcry against giving the army free rein in the *ma'abarot*.

The second stage of Operation *Ma'abara* was scheduled to begin on 10 August 1951 and to last for three months. However, with the election campaign that summer generating so much political heat, it was decided to wait until 10 November to begin. The program was to encompass twenty-four *ma'abarot* recommended by the Kelitah Department as well as eight immigrant settlements under the aegis of the Settlement Department, for a total of fifteen thousand families. Colonel Yitzhak Rabin, head of the IDF Operations Unit, was placed at the helm. He outlined his mission as follows:

a. Educating the *ma'abara* inhabitants in the spirit of nationalism and Zionism.

b. Raising morale, organizing, and introducing discipline and internal unity in the *ma'abarot*.

c. Helping the *ma'abarot* to get through the winter season.[82]

The work was distributed among various IDF commands. Among the duties were setting up a framework for twelve hundred school-age children, establishing a medical screening camp, and organizing treatment centers for children with ringworm and other ailments. The IDF had been in the *ma'abarot* for only a few days when a great storm erupted, causing extensive damage. The soldiers proved to be the mainstay of the rescue effort. They evacuated inhabitants from areas that had been flooded, propped up tents and canvas huts, carried out repairs, and dug drainage ditches. IDF personnel stationed in *ma'abarot* throughout the country submitted detailed reports on the damage sustained and the action taken. The IDF chief of staff, Yigael Yadin, urged the minister of defense to declare a state of emergency until all tents were replaced with cabins, at least in those *ma'abarot* that were most prone to disaster. Hundreds of families were taken to public shelters where the army distributed food, clothing, and blankets, and where the children and sick were cared for. The children's camps were expanded and more staff members were brought in. This relief work went on for several weeks. However, Operation *Ma'abara* was scheduled to end on 31 March 1952, leaving little time to pursue other items on the agenda.

The IDF's performance that winter was recognized as indispensable and worthy of the highest praise. Nevertheless, it was barred from entering the schools and putting its educational programs into practice by the objections of certain sectors of the population, particularly the religious. The IDF's work in the children's camps was limited to serving meals and providing medical care. Most of the youngsters sent to these camps were from religious homes. During a campaign the previous year to find temporary shelter for *ma'abara* children, it had been difficult to find host families for the religious children. Rather than sending them to kibbutzim or nonobservant families, they were taken to camps staffed by the army chaplaincy.[83]

Migrating to another country and joining a new society is normally a shocking experience, but when expectations and reality are very different, the shock is that much greater. Unlike migrants headed for other countries, *olim* did not have the perception that they were going to a strange place. *Aliyah* conjured up images of a joyful return to one's beloved homeland. Exaggerated expectations were also implanted by Jewish Agency and government emissaries who dealt with the immigrants before their journey. As a result of the controversy over the establishment of the *ma'abarot,* which pitted the local authorities, the Jewish Agency, and the government ministries against one another, and the disagreement over who would finance immigrant services, the *ma'abarot* came to be seen as an extraterritorial entity that had no connection with the old-timers. The harsh living conditions in the *ma'abarot,* the shortage of jobs, the dependence on government institutions, the feeling of being caught between political rivals and discriminated against for cultural and ethnic reasons—all these factors added to the immigrants' sense of alienation and helplessness. More than they were hurt by the rigors of *ma'abara* life, they were wounded by the condescending attitude and apathy of the veteran Israelis. These feelings stayed with the immigrants even after they left the *ma'abara*. After the immigrants were sent to remote parts of the country where they suffered physical isolation and economic hardship, the rift widened to the point where the immigrant community became synonymous with the "other" Israel.

CHAPTER SEVEN

Changes in Immigration
and Absorption Policy

ONE COULD HARDLY IMAGINE a more symbolic stage setting for the demise of the *ma'abarot* than the raging storms of 1951. Rising flood waters, tents lashed by the wind, tarpaulin twisted in the mud, immigrants fleeing in panic—these were the final scenes of a period that had been ushered in with such hope.

In 1951 Israel's absorption network tottered on the brink of collapse. Every solution it improvised seemed to breed a new slew of problems. Closure of the immigrant camps and *ma'abarot* and the provision of permanent housing, roundly agreed to be the best course of action, were impossible without a slow-down or temporary freeze on immigration. A majority of government and Jewish Agency officials now shared the belief that Israel's problems could not be overcome without a change in immigration and absorption policy. Closing down the camps and regulating the flow of *aliyah* became all the more urgent as the mood in the *ma'abarot* turned rebellious.

The absorption network found itself lacking 250,000 permanent housing units as winter approached. Some sixty thousand families—20 percent of the population—were living in temporary shelters: thirty thousand in tents and canvas huts, ten thousand in tin shanties, and ten thousand in wooden cabins. The tent dwellers, who numbered close to seventy thousand persons, were worst off. Tents had not held up well during the rains, and the Kelitah Department planned to move at least thirteen thousand families into cabins or canvas-sided huts, which were sturdier. These plans, however, were thwarted by budgetary constraints, the scarcity of construction supplies, international shipping delays that worsened when the seamen went on strike, and a deliberate work slowdown initiated by the building contractors who had not been paid.

At a meeting of the Jewish Agency Executive, Giora Josephthal warned that heavy rains before the end of November would produce utter and uncontrollable chaos in the *ma'abarot*.[1] In the middle of his remarks, Josephthal was called away to the telephone. He returned with upsetting news:

> I have just received word from Tel Aviv that the *olim* have forceably taken over the roofless cabins in the Petah Tikva *ma'abara;* they have chased the builders away and are doing the roofing themselves. The administrative offices have been occupied. The offices and cabins of longstanding residents in Hirya have been taken over and the clerical staff has fled. The warehouses are being plundered. The offices in Kfar Ono have been occupied and the grocery store is being looted. The clerical staff has fled. The police have gone out to all these places in the company of our officials. Similar reports have been coming in from Holon and elsewhere.[2]

This first wave of insurrection just before winter was a dramatic omen of things to come. As the Jewish Agency floundered financially, the Kelitah Department had no way of repaying the millions of pounds it owed. Contractors cut off credit lines and deadlines could not be met. On the assumption that a shipment of cabins would be arriving from overseas, the Kelitah Department decided not to spend money on extra tent siding, although many of the tents had already gone through a winter so that exposure to the elements had greatly weakened the fabric. Moreover, because of the shortage of used army-issue tents on the world market and the forbidding cost of new ones, the department had not replenished its dwindling supply.

The *ma'abara* residents seethed over the delay in providing them with weatherproof housing, and the Jewish Agency feared that a wave of uprisings was imminent. Meanwhile, precautionary measures were taken. Infants and children were evacuated before the rains began and emergency crews were organized to handle flooding and structural damage. None of this was done a moment too soon. During the second half of December 1951, fierce storms hit the country damaging twenty-three *ma'abarot* and nearly leveling nine of them. Tents collapsed by the hundreds, wooden cabins blew away, and walls toppled. In Nahariya 350 families were evacuated when the Ga'aton riverbed overflowed, flooding the entire *ma'abara*. Canvas huts were pulled out by the stakes. Over the weekend of 21 December, after a week of torrential rain, 2,750 residents were rescued from the flooded Amishav *ma'abara*.

The same scenes were repeated in Netanya, the Galilee, Kfar Saba, Hirya, Holon, and elsewhere. Hundreds of concerned citizens joined forces with the army and police in rescue missions all over the country. The soldiers were partic-

Rain seepage in a tent at Rosh Ha'Ayin camp. The immigrants had to place large boulders on the ground to help bypass the mud. *Photograph by Teddy Brauner*

ularly singled out for their bravery in Kfar Saba, where they "crossed a deep, turbulent wadi and formed a bridge with their own bodies in order to rescue the women and children."[3] Emergency shelters were organized in schools, kindergartens, and synagogues in the nearby towns. During the next few days the immigrants began to demonstrate en masse. As Josephthal noted in his diary:

> Panic was widespread, especially where people had been living in tents for two or three winters, as in Rishon Lezion. This *ma'abara* held a demonstration of 300 outside the Jewish Agency building in Tel Aviv. There was a great uproar . . . they could tolerate no more. There have been five demonstrations at the Jewish Agency . . . The Rehovot *ma'abara* is in a state of panic due to the extensive flooding there . . . I was physically attacked in Rehovot . . . The Holon *ma'abara* suffered major damage. In less than two hours, 60 canvas huts—about ten percent of the *ma'abara*—were destroyed. Some *ma'abarot* have been cut off. Our sole link with Ahisemekh near Ramleh is a tiny boat, which was used last night to evacuate two women in labor.[4]

Abandoning the *Ma'abarot*

Realizing that shouting and demonstrations were ineffective and having lost their faith in the absorption authorities, the immigrants resolved to take charge of their own destiny. Families began to pack up their meager belongings and leave the *ma'abarot* in search of a better life. This was not a new phenomenon, but the numbers were much greater than before.

The immigrants were anxious to leave the *ma'abarot* for a variety of reasons. Many had been placed in parts of the country in which they had no desire to live and in total disregard of the ratio between employment opportunities and job seekers. Adjustment to their new homes was made more difficult by the trying physical conditions and the sense of isolation. For the majority, moving out of the *ma'abara* and becoming part of the Yishuv was but a dream. Some families asked to be transferred to another *ma'abara* where they had friends or relations, or which seemed to be more conveniently located. *Ma'abarot* in the center of the country were in demand because the immigrants believed that jobs were in greater supply there.

The severe overcrowding and constant tension created fertile ground for disagreement and quarreling among *ma'abara* dwellers. Some of the immigrants belonged to clans that had been feuding for years, long before their arrival in Israel. Much of the friction between the Iraqi immigrants, for example, was a carryover from the old country. A violent argument in the Kfar Saba *ma'abara* culminated in murder; in Tiberias, there was an attempted murder.[5]

While the number of transfer requests was small, the *ma'abara* directors tried their best to accommodate the *olim,* dealing with each case individually. But doing so was no longer possible in the summer of 1951, as the applications began to pour in. Many *olim* did not wait for permission. They moved their families to other *ma'abarot* or towns, squatting in any abandoned tents or buildings they could find. Before long, hundreds of immigrant families were wandering the length and breadth of the country. As the election campaign gathered momentum, the political parties began to woo the immigrants with false hopes. Josephthal recalled this period as one in which "we created havoc in the immigrant settlements and *ma'abarot* by making baseless promises and buying votes in a most degrading manner. The parties and movements competed with one another, each pledging better conditions than the next."[6]

Large groups of Yemenite Jews abandoned the outlying *ma'abarot* to which they had been sent, migrating toward the center of the country. The local councils took a negative view of this phenomenon; they responded to it by refusing to register the squatters as local residents and withholding services and food vouchers. When informed by officials that the buildings they had occupied were hazardous and unfit for human habitation, the immigrants countered that they preferred death to returning to the *ma'abara*.[7] By October 1951 entire settlements had been emptied of their inhabitants.

Inundated with newspaper reports of the roaming immigrant population, rowdy demonstrations outside local government offices, and the plight of families forced to sleep in dilapidated buildings or out in the open, the public could not fail to be aroused. Complaints reached the Jewish Agency, which issued a statement that it had no intention of bowing to pressure. It refused to approve transfers of *olim* who had left their *ma'abarot* without authorization.[8] The public was called upon to cooperate with the Jewish Agency in order to halt this trend. Within the span of one month, it claimed, more than two thousand families had asked to be relocated near the large cities, principally Tel Aviv. Permission had been granted to only one hundred of them, for reasons of unemployment or social maladjustment. Dozens of housing units now stood empty in *ma'abarot* throughout the country while the *olim* trespassed on property that did not belong to them.

When in November the exodus of *ma'abara* dwellers turned from a trickle into an unchecked flow, an iron-fist policy was adopted by the Jewish Agency and the Ministry of the Interior. Housing rights, employment, and vital services were denied any immigrant who left his *ma'abara*, work camp, or *moshav olim* to seek his fortune in the center of the country.[9]

Attempts to Restrain the Immigrants

The Jewish Agency and the government found the migration of immigrants distressing and perceived it as the beginning of a rebellion. Food vouchers, which entitled the immigrants to basic supplies, were not issued to those who had left the *ma'abarot* as a tactic to keep them where they were. The Jewish Agency asked the Interior Ministry not to approve a change of residence for immigrants without consulting with the Jewish Agency.[10] At the same time, Josephthal appealed to Golda Meir, the minister of labor, for her assistance.

For Josephthal, the massive desertion of the *ma'abarot* threatened to undermine the government's policy of population dispersal and encouragement of rural settlement. He attributed the phenomenon to the immigrants' desire to avoid physical labor and engage in commercial pursuits, along with their belief that more job opportunities awaited them in the cities. Josephthal maintained that immigrants had been leaving *ma'abarot* and development towns at the rate of one thousand families each month since August 1950. This figure had grown even higher since mid-1951. During the second half of 1951, as many as three thousand families had illegally occupied tents in the Tel Aviv region; when the authorities offered canvas huts or cabins to replace these tents, they attempted to improve their lot by "terrorizing the *ma'abara* director and demonstrating at the Jewish Agency offices." [11]

The national institutions were also concerned about newspaper reports that two-thirds of the country's factory workers had left their posts. Josephthal reached the decision that "educational tactics" alone—persuasion and reasoning with the immigrants—would not stop the wave of desertions. He thus proposed that the immigrants be confined to the settlements to which they originally had been sent. Josephthal envisaged a legal authority that would determine the placement of *olim* as soon as they reached the country. This authority also would be responsible for transfer approvals, distribution of food vouchers, and job referrals. Such a body would be composed of representatives of the Ministry of Labor and the Jewish Agency Kelitah Department, and officials from various parts of the country. [12] In Josephthal's opinion, keeping the immigrants at their jobs would help to minimize the number of families on the move.

But legislation in this sphere was problematic, so the minister of the interior asked the government legal adviser to investigate this issue. He urged the country "to shoulder the burden to solve this problem of reining in the mobility of the immigrants." [13] After several weeks, the Interior Ministry submitted a proposal drafted in conjunction with the legal advisor, according to which persons "who move from place to place will be asked by the registry clerk to bring written proof of his having moved to a new place. In the case of transferring from one *ma'abara* to another, proof will be brought from the director of the *ma'abara* to which he has moved." [14] The Interior Ministry was aware of the burden this would impose on Israeli citizens—including veteran residents who changed their place of residence—but cracking down on the immigrant migration phenomenon was considered more important.

The wording of this order was so general that it was difficult to enforce; in fact, things proceeded as before. A person who changed his address could inform the registry clerk, and his statement was sufficient for a permit to be given. On the basis of this permit, citizens were entitled to request food vouchers in their new place of residence, so that nothing was achieved with regard to keeping the *olim* stationary.

In its efforts to prevent or at least reduce the amount of movement, the Jewish Agency sometimes called in the police. Mainly, however, it appealed to the local authorities. The district officers of the Interior Ministry were told to be particularly strict in the matter of immigrants moving from one *ma'abara* to another. The immigrants, however, found plenty of ways of getting around these orders, and the desertions continued throughout 1952. Only the drastic drop in *aliyah* eased the problem somewhat.

Further proof of the immigrants' refusal to accept authority was the operation of a black market in the *ma'abarot*. These activities were pursued in a totally undisguised manner and on a large scale; efforts of the government and the *ma'abara* directors to put a stop to this phenomenon were unsuccessful. *Ma'abara* dwellers sold their subsidized food rations at great profit in the neighboring towns. Aside from the fact that this was illegal, the health and welfare authorities complained of the harm to the children of the *ma'abara,* who were suffering from malnutrition. The phenomenon was so widespread, however, that little could be done.

It seems that all the warnings of those who opposed mass immigration were coming true. The economy was unstable, the health system was collapsing, the demand of vital services could not be met, and, above all, the immigrants were rebelling. All this seemed more than the young State of Israel could bear. Calls to limit immigration began to resound once more.

Reassigning the Absorption Portfolio

The question of mass immigration was addressed on a number of occasions during the summer of 1951, in anticipation of the upcoming Zionist Congress in Jerusalem. As various bodies fought with one another over status and power, and political and personal rivalry came into play, the functioning of the Jewish Agency's immigration and absorption departments became the butt of criticism. More and more voices began calling for absorption to be removed from Jewish Agency hands and transferred to the government. Some members of the Jewish Agency Executive felt the same way, among them Zvi Herman, the head of the Kelitah Department. He argued that the government was in any case financing the absorption budget and should take full responsibility in this sphere. Eliezer Dobkin supported this move. He felt that the source of all the tension between the Jewish Agency and the government stemmed from the fact that the Jewish Agency had taken on more than it could handle. Rather than always being the "beggar at the door," he believed that the Jewish Agency should give up absorption and concentrate on youth *aliyah* and settlement.[15] Most of the other executive members did not agree; they feared that reassigning the portfolio would be the first step in dismantling the Jewish Agency as a whole. They claimed that, if the chief problem was monetary, the Jewish Agency should be awarded a larger budget.

Braginsky, with whom Herman shared the directorship of the Kelitah Department, was among the main detractors of the idea of giving up absorption. He explained that, practically speaking, separating immigration and absorption would create problems and harm the system as a whole.

During the course of these discussions, the traditional political beliefs of various party representatives were evident. Braginsky and Zerubavel belonged to Mapam, which was in the Opposition. They fought tooth and nail to retain their power in the Jewish Agency. Most of the Mapai supporters on the Jewish Agency Executive were in favor of transferring authority to the government, where their party reigned. The religious, although they also belonged to the government, were anxious to retain their status in the immigration network and feared that transferring authority to the government would harm them. Raphael wanted Mossad le-Aliyah, which was on the decline, to become part of his department, but he operated behind the scenes to avoid stirring up opposition.[16]

The 23rd Zionist Congress, which met in Jerusalem (14–30 August 1951), was the first such congress to be held in the Jewish state. After many hours of debate, it ended without bringing new tidings or initiating any dramatic change in immigration and absorption policy. No unified stand was reached on controversial matters and the future of Mossad le-Aliyah was basically left up to the Jewish Agency Executive. The political wrangling over this body eventually led to its demise. Under pressure from Sharett and Raphael, Ben-Gurion agreed to close it down and transfer its duties to the Kelitah Department (March 1952). Mossad le-Aliyah had long been a source of controversy. Now its activities in North Africa were limited to clandestine operations under the directorship of Isser Harel.[17]

Even after the congress, the tempest did not die down. Rumors circulated that the government was interested in taking over absorption and possibly immigration as well. It was said that the Foreign Ministry had plans to establish a body to replace Mossad le-Aliyah, which would handle illegal immigration and operate under the auspices of Reuven Shiloah's department, already in charge of Egypt, Syria, and Eastern Europe. Raphael was worried that the Foreign Ministry would gain control of North Africa, Iran, and Turkey, and diminish the importance of the Aliyah Department. He thus engaged in all kinds of manipulations to eliminate outside interference and keep others from usurping his department's authority.[18]

Council for Aliyah Affairs

One of the resolutions of the 23rd Zionist Congress was to establish a Council for Aliyah Affairs as an advisory body to the Jewish Agency Aliyah Department, but its starting date was postponed month after month because of arguments over staffing and duties. In mid-1952 Raphael took concrete steps to make this council a reality in the hope of gaining control over it.[19]

From the outset the Council for Aliyah Affairs was basically powerless; it had little influence over the Jewish Agency Executive and the Coordinating Committee, which were manned by senior Agency officials and top government officials. Raphael looked for ways to use the council to promote his own aims. He proposed, for example, that the head of the Aliyah Department be in charge of convening and chairing council meetings. In spite of an aura of self-importance, the Council for Aliyah Affairs failed to bring about any change in immigration policy. It turned out to be no more than a debating club for low-ranking officials; the final say was in the hands of the Coordinating Committee.

Closing the *Ma'abarot*

The construction of *ma'abarot* commenced in mid-1950 and continued until the end of 1951. Together with immigrant housing projects and transit camps, they provided accommodation for 257,000 immigrants. Before winter, the government planned to replace the tents in the *ma'abarot* with cabins. When these plans were delayed, pandemonium occurred. The *ma'abarot* became fertile ground for epidemics, residents began to flee en masse, and violent demonstrations were frequent. The large concentration of elderly and sick was especially problematic.

During the three years of the Great Aliyah, the composition of the immigrant population underwent a major metamorphosis. In 1948, 86 percent of the newcomers hailed from Europe and only 14 percent from Asia and Africa. In 1949 and 1950 the proportions shifted to half and half; by 1951 they shifted to 28 percent from Europe, 60 percent from Asia, and 12 percent from Africa. After the closure of the Communist bloc and the subsequent decline in *aliyah* from these countries, Iraqi Jews began to account for more than half of the total immigration. Owing to their hasty departure and short travel time, the majority of *olim* from Iraq were sent to *ma'abarot* as soon as they arrived. In 1951 people began to move out of the *ma'abarot*, either on their own or at the urging of the Jewish Agency. Of those who lingered, 80 percent were from Asia and North Africa; European Jews, primarily Romanians, made up the remaining 20 percent. The first to leave were young people and skilled professionals who found jobs in the cities. A survey carried out in nine *ma'abarot* in 1954 found that those who stayed put were large families and older people; only 27 percent were younger than thirty-five years old. Another 14 percent were widows with small children. Most of the lingering *ma'abara* dwellers held part-time or temporary employment; 6 percent were sales clerks or peddlers. As many as 30 percent were unemployed or on welfare.[20] Moving out of the *ma'abara* meant purchasing an apartment and meeting regular mortgage payments, which was simply beyond their means.

One-quarter of a million people—one-sixth of Israel's Jewish population—were still living in *ma'abarot* and immigrant camps in mid-1952. For 61,500 families, flimsy huts and tents remained the sole accommodation. Back in 1951 the prime minister had promised that tents would be replaced with sturdier dwellings; shipping delays, coupled with a new tide of immigration from Iraq, kept this plan from being carried out on schedule. During the summer of 1952 the Ministry of Labor began to draw up blueprints for each *ma'abara,* setting aside land for the construction of wooden cabins—but an appropriate site was not always available. In those *ma'abarot* slated for permanent settlement, it was decided that cabins would be kept to a minimum to avoid overcrowding.[21] The undertaking as a whole met with considerable resistance. Some of the immigrants refused to move into new quarters, either because they were already accustomed to their surroundings or because they were afraid they might lose their welfare subsidies. Many felt as if they were being evicted and would not cooperate until the local authorities took drastic action, such as tearing down the old housing.[22] At the large Rehovot *ma'abara,* inhabitants fought over the cabins and staged rowdy strikes and demonstrations. When it was found that there were not enough cabins to house all those evacuated from their tents and that one hundred families would be moved elsewhere, the protests grew louder still.

Toward the end of 1952 the Ministerial Committee for Budgetary Affairs was asked to evaluate a Ministry of Labor plan for closing the *ma'abarot* over a period of two years. Between 1953 and 1955, *ma'abara* dwellers would be resettled in agricultural communities, development towns, or urban centers. Priority would go to agricultural communities in light of the employment possibilities they offered. In the end, only 10 percent of the immigrants were in fact referred to agriculture.[23] The Jewish Agency Executive decided that settlement was more appropriate for immigrants below the age of thirty-five; older people were sent to development towns and cities. Prospective settlers were taken under the wing of the Jewish Agency Settlement Department, which found places for them with the help of the *moshav* movement. The Ministry of Labor's Housing Division was given the responsibility of building houses for the immigrants in development towns.

In early 1953 there were 157,000 persons living in *ma'abarot.* These figures dropped to 108,000 in early 1954, and by year's end to 88,000. Even though

1953–54 was a slow year for immigration, it was still impossible to close the *ma'abarot* altogether.

By this time, the immigration authorities had learned their lesson. When the next wave of *aliyah* commenced in 1954, immigrants were given permanent housing as soon as they arrived, without recourse to provisional solutions. Nevertheless, the *ma'abarot* remained an ugly blot on the Israeli landscape and eliminating them was an ordeal that continued for years to come. The *ma'abara* period, ushered in with such fanfare, thus faded out in bitter silence. It was in the *ma'abara* that one-quarter of a million newcomers began the slow process of absorption and received their first glimpse of Israeli society. In fact, because of rapid population turnover, the number of immigrants who spent time in the *ma'abarot* was actually much higher. Some stayed only a short time—weeks or months; others remained there for years. For all the immigrants it was an extremely trying chapter in their lives, one which would stay firmly etched in their memories. The very mention of the word *"ma'abara"* in Israel today conjures up images of a botched job.

Selective Immigration

Absorption officials blamed the terrible conditions in the camps and *ma'abarot* on the government's sanction of unrestricted mass immigration. The issue of selectivity came up again as the architects of Israel's immigration and absorption policy sat together to reassess the situation in the fall of 1951. In October, Yitzhak Raphael predicted the arrival of 120,000 *olim* in the coming year: 11,000 from Eastern Europe (at least one-third from Romania); 30,000 from North Africa, a large contingent from Iran, Egypt, Syria, and India; and a small number from America and elsewhere.[24] Romania, Libya, and Iran warranted special attention: Romania seemed about to close its doors, demanding advance payment for the use of its passenger ship, the SS *Transylvania,* and threatening to stop granting exit permits.[25] The political situation in Iran was tense and a halt on emigration seemed likely there, too. *Aliyah* emissaries in Libya felt that all prospective immigrants should be evacuated before the country declared independence at the end of 1951.

Handling a great throng of immigrants was further complicated by the lack of control over the health and age of the people brought in. The tide of immigration that commenced after Israel's independence had just begun to wane when the Jewries of Romania, Iran, and Libya were declared endangered.[26] Entire communities had to be liquidated with the utmost haste, regardless of their numbers or suitability for *aliyah.* The Romanian government had made it clear that the Jews could leave on condition that Israel accepted them all, without selection. In Libya and Iran it was also imperative to rescue as many Jews as possible before the gates clanged shut. In consequence, a large percentage of the immigrants who reached Israel in the summer and fall of 1951 were sick, disabled, or elderly.

Adverse Selection

Between October 1950 and September 1951, 50,000 immigrants from Romania arrived in Israel. When these numbers began to taper off toward the end of the year, it was rumored that the Romanian Jews were now postponing their *aliyah,* having heard of the difficulties of life in the *ma'abara.* Raphael insisted that many of Romania's 200,000 Jews were still lining up to leave, but even he admitted that, where health and age were concerned, the recent arrivals from this country left much to be desired. The younger people were indeed putting off their departure, and only the old and sick continued to stream in.[27]

A similar situation existed in Libya. After the UN decision to create an independent state in Libya in January 1952, the Jewish Agency drew up plans to resettle the entire Jewish community in Israel. The 4,000 Jews of Cyrenaica and about a thousand villagers and mountain Jews were assembled in Tripoli and transported to Israel. A small number found to be suffering from communicable diseases, particularly eye infections and ringworm, were held back for medical treatment sponsored by the JDC or OSE. Some 5,000 Libyan Jews left for Israel in 1951. Of the 5,000 who remained in Libya, nearly half were wealthy property-owners who had no desire to emigrate. The candidates for *aliyah* were mainly elderly, sick, and disabled, who came to Israel with their families. Of the 746 passengers who disembarked in Haifa in October 1951, the majority fell into this category. The Israeli public was outraged, and stories filled the daily newspapers about the rich Libyan Jews who stayed home and palmed off their crippled neighbors on Israel.

As the political tension in Iran worsened, Israel worked feverishly to expedite *aliyah* from this country. The efforts of the *aliyah* officials continued even after diplomatic relations with Israel were severed. Here again, financially established families tended to put off their departure. In 1951, 13,500 Iranian Jews crossed the border to Turkey and boarded ships to Haifa. Because there was no systematic medical screening of these immigrants, a large percentage were ill or handicapped.

Throughout 1951 absorption officials, and especially those in charge of health, carped and complained. This was not nonselective immigration, they

234 I Immigrants in Turmoil

protested. It was selectivity in reverse. From all corners came the cry that the profile of these immigrants was not representative of the communities from which they hailed. There was clearly a tendency for the educated, wealthy, or professionally trained to stay put or to emigrate to more desirable countries; the weak and needy were shipped to Israel. It was not uncommon for families to send only their physically or mentally handicapped members. This is not to say that there were no solid, educated families, ardent Zionists or young pioneers among those who made *aliyah,* but they were certainly in the minority.

From the outset of the Great Aliyah, Israelis were frustrated and disappointed over the fact that only a handful of Jews from established Jewish communities in the free world chose to join them, and that most of the immigrants from countries with Jewish communities in distress came from the indigent lower classes. This trend apparently intensified in 1951, as discouraging stories about life in Israel circulated in North Africa, Romania, Iran, and elsewhere. Even Raphael, one of the leading proponents of nonselective immigration, admitted that nearly 80 percent of the immigrants who reached Israel in 1951 were from distressed countries and had not undergone medical screening.[28]

Caring for the old and sick placed a great burden on the absorption network, and even the loudest opponents of restricted immigration were loathe to support "adverse" selection. The debate thus shifted to the need for some kind of control over the body of immigrants reaching Israel. While such proposals were not new, it appears that Israel was now determined to put them into practice.

Selection Criteria

The first step was to draw up a list of objective criteria for the selection of *aliyah* candidates and to establish guidelines for their use, taking into account the political situation in the country of origin and other factors. The principle of nonselective immigration from countries of distress had not been abandoned, but the definition of the term "distress" came under debate in 1952. There was a question about whether or not Morocco and Tunisia should be included in this category, and whether selective criteria could be applied there.

The Jewish Agency Executive convened in November 1952 for a series of urgent talks on the subject of selection criteria. The four-man committee charged with drawing up the *aliyah* program for the coming year was evenly balanced on this issue.[29] In all previous debates, Ben-Gurion had been a loyal advocate of nonrestrictive immigration and had successfully vetoed attempts to impose limits. Because only a shift in Ben-Gurion's position could tilt the scale, the two sides engaged in a fierce tug-of-war to win his support.[30]

Ben-Gurion's Position on Selective Immigration

Ben-Gurion remained true to his conviction that *aliyah* was crucial—as much for the immigrants themselves as for the Jewish state. He opposed those who called for restrictions on immigration, arguing that it was wrong to allow temporary problems such as budgetary constraints or the economy to dictate Israel's immigration policy. In May 1951 he flew to the United States to launch the Israel bonds drive. Crossing the country from east to west, he enjoyed wide public support and set American capitalists digging into their pockets. The success of the drive exceeded all expectations. Considerable progress was also made in the German reparation talks. All of this increased the likelihood of an upswing in Israel's economic development.

Toward the end of 1951 even Ben-Gurion's confidence in the principle of unrestricted mass immigration seems to have taken a blow. He was nevertheless determined that financial matters should not become an obstacle to *aliyah* and Kelitah. He believed that the problems of housing and employment could be solved and that, even if many of the immigrants were unschooled, they could be educated and taught a trade in Israel. At the same time, he was concerned about the newcomers' poor state of health; a large proportion were seriously handicapped or suffering from chronic illnesses. A deluge of thousands of disabled immigrants in need of special services was a genuine threat to the economy. The social absorption of these immigrants was as much of a problem as absorbing them physically. Together with their families, their number ran into tens of thousands. While Ben-Gurion had taken into account the possibility that many of the *olim* would be old, sick, or disabled—the inevitable outcome of mass immigration and the liquidation of overseas communities—the data showing an increase in adverse selection caused him to have second thoughts.

In October 1951 after lengthy negotiations, a new government was formed. This time the coalition was a narrow one: Mapai's only partners were the religious parties.[31] The cabinet was reshuffled in January 1952. Kaplan resigned from the Ministry of Finance and was appointed deputy prime minister and minister without portfolio. Levi Eshkol took his place as minister of finance and turned over his post as treasurer of the Jewish Agency to Giora Josephthal, who continued to direct the Kelitah Department. At the 23rd Zionist Congress in August 1951, Josephthal had been elected to the Zionist executive, automatically making him a member of the Jewish Agency Executive. As Josephthal's power in the immigration and absorption network increased, so did his influence over Ben-Gurion.

Decisions to Restrict *Aliyah*

Israel's immigration policy took a sharp turn in November 1951. After long discussions, the Jewish Agency Executive and the Coordinating Committee reached a decision to introduce restrictions on *aliyah* from those countries whose Jewish communities faced no immediate danger. At a meeting of the executive on 18 November, it was agreed that immigrants from those countries would be required to meet strict health and employment criteria.[32] Eighty percent of these immigrants would be Youth Aliyah protégés, members of pioneer groups, skilled workers younger than thirty-five years, and families headed by a breadwinner younger than thirty-five. With the exception of skilled workers and those who could afford housing, immigrants would sign a paper committing themselves to two years of agricultural work. Visas would only be issued after a thorough medical examination supervised by an Israeli doctor.[33]

In order to satisfy Ben-Gurion and secure his blessing, a special clause was added to exempt "rescue missions" from the above restrictions. In the cases of North Africa and Romania, the quotas established in the 1952 immigration program could be exceeded on condition that the Jewish Agency Executive and Coordinating Committee gave their approval. A special effort would be made to eliminate "adverse" selection from Romania. It was emphasized, however, that emergency operations were not subject to the same rules and would be decided upon separately by the Executive and the Coordinating Committee. In this context, the Executive instructed the Aliyah Department to accelerate *aliyah* from Egypt and Syria.[34]

These decisions were approved by the Coordinating Committee on 27 November 1951. However, the debate was not yet over; it continued with intensity as the countries affected complained that the restrictions were too severe. In February 1952, the Jewish Agency agreed to raise the maximum age for breadwinners from thirty-five to forty years and, with Dr. Sheba's approval, 200 sick children were treated by the Ministry of Health at a Kelitah Department camp in Israel.[35]

Immigration Declines

From November 1951, the number of immigrants from North Africa and Europe declined steeply. Several factors worked together to create a slowdown: the discouraging reports from Israel, the new selection procedures, and political developments in the immigrants' home countries. The Romanians stopped issuing exit permits, and the flow from other countries in Eastern Europe, primarily Bulgaria and Hungary, slowed to a trickle.[36] The total immigration for 1952 came to 23,375 people, compared with the Aliyah Department's forecast of 120,000. Jewish Agency and government officials began to realize that this was no longer a temporary drop and that *aliyah* was in a state of crisis. Immigration from Morocco, where the Jewish population numbered 230,000, steadily decreased: a total of 5,000 immigrants arrived in 1952, and fewer than 2,000 in 1953. The construction of American military bases in Morocco, which improved the country's economy and provided a source of employment for many Jews; the reduction in political tension; and the rumors circulating about the hardship in the *ma'abarot*—all affected the rate of *aliyah*. As a result, large numbers of Jews preferred to delay their departure from Morocco. A similar situation prevailed in Tunisia.

The Aliyah Department had little choice but to turn its attention to those areas where the prospects for *aliyah* were greater: the rural districts of southern Morocco, the Atlas mountains, and tiny communities in southern Tunisia. Most of the Jews in these places were poor and their political standing was shakier than that of the large communities in the North. Very few met the criteria established by the Jewish Agency. The Aliyah Department warned that, if things continued in this way, *aliyah* might cease altogether.

Moderating Selection Requirements

The Aliyah Department insisted that the elderly and ill (except for mental patients and those suffering from tuberculosis and infectious chronic illnesses) should be permitted to immigrate as long as younger, healthy members of the family promised to take care of them. However, the medical authorities were known to have been deceived dozens of times, sometimes with the cooperation of local immigration officials. More often than not, Aliyah Department *shelihim* (emissaries) turned a blind eye to such instances, causing their superiors endless frustration and embarrassment.[37]

Levi Eshkol, the minister of finance, took the Aliyah Department to task on this score: "There is a kind of trickery going on here. On the one hand, some compassionate person is seeing to it that Jews come on aliyah; on the other hand, someone is trying to bend the law. And the terrible outcome is a growing number of sick and disabled."[38] Eshkol threatened to impose the entire financial burden for absorbing these people on the Jewish Agency, making it responsible, not only for *aliyah,* but also for their care in Israel.

Raphael continued to press for greater *aliyah* from southern Morocco, citing the rise of Arab nationalism there. One of his proposals was to establish a medical-treatment program to serve the remote communities and special transit camps near Cazablanca. The existing camp had been enlarged to accommodate 1,000 persons, but Raphael called for an investment of $360,000 to build and maintain additional treatment camps.

The plan for selective criteria remained on the agenda, although the draft kept being reworded and clauses were periodically added and dropped. At a plenary meeting of the Jewish Agency in March 1952, the Executive's resolve to go ahead with selective immigration was reaffirmed, but with certain changes. The Jewish Agency now stipulated that no restrictions would be imposed on *aliyah* from the Arab League countries and Eastern Europe.[39]

Doubts and Misgivings

Meanwhile, the debate continued and pressure was exerted both for and against selective immigration. In May 1952, the Zionist Actions Committee expressed concern over the decline in *aliyah* since the beginning of the year and ordered the Jewish Agency Executive to take measures that would increase the flow as much as possible.[40] In so doing, the Actions Committee in effect supported the Aliyah Department and its attempts to circumvent the new rules. These intentions were not lost on the Kelitah Department, which protested vociferously against this deviation from the Jewish Agency's statement in March 1952: "Our previous decisions regarding selective immigration remain in force . . . In all countries where selection is possible, up to 80 percent of the immigrants will be made up of families with a breadwinner below the age of 35. Families in which the breadwinner is older will constitute the remaining 20 percent, on condition that [the breadwinner] has no illness . . . which prevents him from working."[41]

That summer, *aliyah* emissaries reported a further decline in the number of prospective immigrants. According to Raphael, the *aliyah* potential from Eastern Europe (Romania, Hungary, etc.) was close to one-quarter of a million; the figure from North Africa, Iran, and Arab countries was similar. However, the actual number of arrivals would depend on the results of the medical examinations and the scope of treatment: "In Morocco, 80 percent of the Jews are being detained due to their own illness or the illness of those accompanying them."[42] The restrictions imposed by the immigration authorities were not relaxed in the wake of this report about the high percentage of disease, even though the obvious implication was a drastic reduction in the number of suitable applicants. On the contrary, supporters of restricted immigration saw these figures as proof of their claim that the majority of *aliyah* candidates in Morocco were in poor physical condition.

In March 1952 the Aliyah Department decided to admit without selection six thousand Jews from small villages in southern Morocco and southern Tunisia. Both this decision and the compromise reached with the JDC were roundly criticized. The JDC apparently had agreed to bring the neediest welfare cases to urban centers in their home country and care for them there. The Aliyah Department disregarded the criticism and rushed to implement the agreement. The Ministry of Health was furious; it charged the Aliyah Department with assuming responsibility for large numbers of Jews who had in fact been disqualified as *aliyah* candidates by ministry-appointed physicians. Dr. Sheba accused Raphael of knowingly ignoring the orders of the Jewish Agency Executive and the Coordinating Committee. Moving the sick to suburbs of the large cities was an illogical and harmful arrangement as far as he was concerned. It separated families and created a body of "refugees" uprooted from their natural surroundings and confined to a ghetto. Moreover, the upkeep of patients and families was an expense that would eventually shrink the JDC's budget in Israel.[43]

From health authority reports reaching Israel it became clear that 10 percent of the candidates for *aliyah* were ailing and nearly one-half the family heads were elderly. If selection were enforced, 60 percent of these people would be dropped from the immigration lists. Lying to the authorities and shipping the seriously ill to Israel under false pretenses had become a common practice. According to Dr. Sheba, the Aliyah Department and the JDC cooperated in circumventing the restrictions. Raphael countered that *aliyah* would reach an unprecedented low unless the criteria were revised.[44] By February, *aliyah* from Morocco would be down to one hundred immigrants for lack of healthy candidates. "If I abide by the rules," said Raphael, "that is all I will find."[45]

Ben-Gurion was livid. He acknowledged that the slump in *aliyah* was a matter for concern, but he would not hear of Jewish Agency officials disobeying government orders: "Is that what you call *aliyah*—bringing in cripples just to inflate the figures? . . . Is that what this country needs? . . . Aside from all our other problems, to take care of cripples and blind people? I understand that if we are emptying out an entire Diaspora community, we cannot leave a single family, but to begin with that? . . . There are 250,000 Jews in Morocco . . . Must our first step be the evacuation of the lame and the blind?"[46]

Ben-Gurion agreed with Sheba that the arrangement with the JDC was not a wise one and would only create more problems. Because of the lack of hospital beds, Health Minister Yosef Burg was opposed to issuing visas to families with a critically ill family member. He insisted that the immigration of such families should not be handled by the Jewish Agency at all but by special Ministry of Health doctors acting under his orders.[47]

Flexibility

As the number of immigrants dropped sharply and grave dissatisfaction was voiced over the composition of the groups that did arrive, the Jewish Agency Executive reviewed its previous decisions concerning selection criteria. At its meeting of 17 November 1952, the Executive reaffirmed the importance of selectivity but agreed to several changes. The possibility of increasing the scope of medical treatment at transit camps in Israel would be looked into; the maximum age of breadwinners would be raised from thirty-five to forty years in the case of immigrants from southern Morocco and villages in Iran; all the Jews of southern Tunisia would be evacuated except for welfare cases, for whom arrangements would be made in the large cities; and the selection of immigrants from remote parts of Iran would be liberalized.

The Jewish Agency Executive promised the Coordinating Committee that its decision regarding the relaxation of selection criteria would be the final one. Meanwhile, the deliberations over the composition of *aliyah* groups continued, leading to further changes in 1953. The maximum age of breadwinners was raised to forty-five years, and it was decided to apply greater flexibility. However, a more serious problem, which was not affected in the least by the drop in *aliyah*, was keeping out those suffering from serious terminal diseases. Relative to the number of immigrants, the percentage of sickly newcomers remained alarmingly high.

Israeli emissaries and *aliyah* activists in North Africa continued to disregard the government restrictions. Dr. Sheba told of families who applied for *aliyah* without their sick family members and, once in Israel, pressed for these relatives to be brought over as part of the "family reunification" program.[48] Raphael tried to persuade the Coordinating Committee to relax the medical requirements to some extent, repeating his contention that growing nationalism placed the Jews of North Africa in jeopardy. Most of his colleagues on the Jewish Agency Executive disagreed on this point. Moshe Sharett admitted that North Africa might be jolted somewhat by the rise of nationalism, but he did not believe it necessary to take the same steps to rescue the Jews as in Iraq or Iran. Moshe Kol was of the same view: "Today the Jews of Morocco have jobs and a source of livelihood. They receive disheartening letters from here; there is no work. Apart from that, the French are in control of the situation, so the Jews feel more secure and are in no hurry to leave. Those who do want to come here are the most wretched beggars." [49]

Aliyah from India

Anxious to increase the volume of *aliyah,* the Jewish Agency and the Coordinating Committee explored the situation in other countries, one of them India. Although many of the Indian Jews brought to Israel in 1951-fifty-two had trouble adjusting and demanded to be sent home, the Aliyah Department was not deterred and its officials continued to promote *aliyah* there. This situation was upsetting to the Kelitah Department. Giora Josephthal complained about the high rate of illness among the arrivals from India. Considering that the lives of the Jews there were in no special danger, he could see no justification for the continued promotion. [50]

The question of *aliyah* from India came up again toward the end of 1952. Naftali Bar-Giora, an Aliyah Department emissary, mainly examined the prospects of *aliyah* from Cochin. Of 1,400 Jews living there in small communities, approximately 1,000 were believed to be suitable for *aliyah*—on condition that elephantiasis, a disease that was common among the Jews of Cochin, would not be viewed as a disqualifying factor. Dr. Sheba proposed treating sufferers on the spot and arranging passage to Israel only after they were cured. [51] Medical reports from Cochin were not encouraging. Dr. Sternberg wrote that the disease was present in nearly 100 percent of the Jews living along the coast. Ambulatory care was virtually impossible, and it would take years to develop an inspection program to keep the disease from spreading. The Ministry of Health claimed it could not take responsibility for such an undertaking due to the shortage of funds, hospital beds, and manpower.

In the long run it was the Jewish Agency Settlement Department, which handled the placement of immigrants in agricultural settlements, that brought groups of Jews from Cochin. These Jews were sent to *moshavei olim* in the Jerusalem corridor, the Negev, and the Galilee. The doctors' concern about the spread of elephantiasis turned out to be unfounded, and most of the *olim* settled down with no problems.

Changes in Government: Effect on Immigration Policy

In 1952 Ben-Gurion's government was again beset by crisis. Agudat Israel resigned on 19 September and the coalition disintegrated shortly thereafter. In

December the ministers representing Ha-Poel ha-Mizrachi and Ha-Mizrachi resigned, too. Later that month Ben-Gurion assembled a new administration incorporating the General Zionists. The platform of this administration was not radically different from that of the previous one, except for two features: it supported state education in all elementary schools and reforms in Israeli election law (the latter were not carried out due to opposition). After the Knesset installation, Ha-Poel ha-Mizrachi's Moshe Shapira and Yosef Burg rejoined the coalition. The General Zionist delegates were Israel Rokach, who took over the Interior Ministry, and Yosef Serlin, who took over health. These changes left their mark on Israel's immigration policy.

For the first time, Rokach and Serlin sat in on the deliberations of the Coordinating Committee. They expressed their dissatisfaction with the current immigration policy and demanded more stringent medical screening. Having served in the past as mayor of Tel-Aviv, Rokach knew what a burden sick and disabled immigrants could be on municipal health and welfare bureaus. There was no question that education and other services required by the newcomers were a major expense. *Aliyah* activists in the Diaspora should make an effort to target the middle and upper classes, he argued.[52] To further Serlin and Rokach's proposals, it was decided to establish a joint Jewish Agency-government council to work out a plan of action.[53] The Coordinating Committee and others involved in the sphere of immigration had few expectations in this regard.

The Coordinating Committee came up with another proposal to counter the sharp decline in the number of immigrants; it suggested that groups of young people, age seventeen to twenty years, be brought from Morocco and Tunisia under the auspices of Youth Aliyah and placed in two-year academic and vocational training programs. The youngsters would also undergo agricultural training similar to that offered by the Nahal. Ben-Gurion was excited about this proposal but the results were disappointing. Only small groups of young people signed up. Surveys done in North Africa to assess the willingness of middle- and upper-class Jews to come on *aliyah* found that attitudes in this part of the world were not much different from those of prosperous Jews everywhere.[54]

Yeridah

The absorption authorities could not ignore the growing phenomenon known as *yeridah* (literally "going down" or leaving the country).[55] The ratio of people leaving the country in 1952–53 as opposed to entering it was worrisome indeed. In 1952, for example, there were 24,000 arrivals compared with 13,571 departures. This trend became more pronounced each year.[56] At the time, *yeridah* was looked upon by the Israeli public as desertion or even treason. Because it was generally the stronger, better qualified immigrants who left, this negative feeling concerned not only the wasted investment in immigration and absorption but also the loss of the nation's "cream of the crop." The majority of those leaving Israel were young people or skilled professionals who were convinced that their prospects for economic advancement were greater in other countries than in Israel; most of them went to the West. Their gloomy accounts of life in Israel scared off many potential immigrants, particularly those in whom the immigration authorities were most interested—the younger generation and those likely to succeed economically and socially. So *yeridah* continued, to the point where there was actually a negative migration balance. In 1953, Israel took in 10,347 persons and lost as many as 13,015. While newcomers ceased to arrive, former immigrants packed their bags, and efforts to attract a better class of immigrant failed, it became clear that Israel's immigration policy needed to be reexamined. The authorities again cast their eyes toward the indigent Jews of southern Morocco and Tunisia, and a decision reached in early 1954 allowed them to obtain visas more easily than before.

As the political tension in North Africa escalated in 1954, *aliyah* began to increase. The Jews no longer felt secure and, with the help of the Jewish Agency, many resettled in Israel. The struggle for independence in Morocco and Tunisia set off another surge of immigration. More than 50,000 Moroccan Jews and 13,000 Tunisian Jews reached Israel in 1955–56. This wave of *aliyah* was very different from previous waves in terms of organization and demographic makeup. Immigration from Eastern Europe also suddenly resumed in 1957. Together, these constituted the second stage of the Great Aliyah, which quantitatively and otherwise bore little resemblance to the first stage.

The steep drop in *aliyah* in the early years of the state was not entirely due to Israel's immigration policy. The primary source of potential immigrants—Holocaust survivors and Jews living in Arab lands—had been practically exhausted during the first wave of the Great Aliyah in 1948–51. Of the large Jewish communities, those in North Africa seemed to present the next great potential. However, the political situation appeared to be stabilizing in 1952–53, and many of the Jews believed that they would be safe under French rule. There had also been some improvement in the economy. After hearing about the absorption difficulties in Israel and the growing tide of *yordim*, the Jews of Morocco and Tunisia decided to stay home; if they moved, it was to France or other countries. The efforts by the Jewish Agency and the Coordinating Committee to encourage middle-class *aliyah* and attract families with means were unsuccessful at this time. The situation was similar in Iran, where the wealthier members of the Jewish community were again reluctant to leave.

The End of an Era

The first wave of mass immigration was over by 1951 and the country experienced a major slump in *aliyah* in 1952–53, but the challenge of absorption was still very much alive. The number of homeless immigrants reached a peak in 1951, and the array of social and economic problems was daunting. The authorities experimented with new approaches to the job of immigrant absorption. An effort was made to eliminate the *ma'abarot* and implement "ship-to-farm" immigration, or sending newcomers directly from the port to their permanent homes in agricultural settlements and development towns, which were established at a rapid pace beginning in 1954.

During late 1953 and early 1954, Israel underwent changes in several spheres. In the sociocultural sphere, it was realized that the "melting pot" concept was not working. The gap between newcomers and veteran Israelis was widening, and the two groups were becoming increasingly alienated. Isolating the immigrants in development towns only promoted the emergence of a "second Israel." In the political arena, the rise of the centrist parties coupled with divisiveness in the Labor camp led to a weakening of the socialist Zionists' sociocultural hold. This debate was signaled by the debate over anthems and flags, which erupted when the country prepared for the introduction of a state educational system. Although all ideological and political trends in education had been canceled, Mapai demanded that, in those schools where the majority of parents and children approved, a red flag be flown alongside the Israeli flag and the "Internationale" be sung after "Hatikva" on the First of May and Histadrut Day. This demand precipitated a government crisis. Four General Zionist ministers resigned on 25 May 1953, insisting that a total ban be imposed on the use of ideological symbols in state schools. Ben-Gurion capitulated to the General Zionists on 3 June 1953, averting a showdown and further clipping the wings of political-ideological beliefs that were held over from the prestate period.[57]

On a personal level, too, 1954 marked the end of an era and the beginning of a new one for the State of Israel. On 7 December 1953, Ben-Gurion announced that he was retiring from the premiership. In a letter to the president, he explained that he needed a rest from the enormous tension and stress involved in leading the state.[58] In effect, the Labor movement was left red-faced and grasping for some theory to account for this surprising move. One of the main hypotheses was that Ben-Gurion was sorely disappointed with Israeli society and the manner in which immigrant absorption was progressing. Ben-Gurion's retirement to Sdeh Boker, an isolated kibbutz in the heart of the southern Negev unaffiliated with any settlement movement, was interpreted as a protest against his own party and the Israeli public for disregarding his call to volunteer for national causes and activities connected with immigrant absorption. Ben-Gurion's continued exhortations on the subject of volunteering and helping the masses of newcomers to integrate socially, even from his home in Sdeh Boker, would seem to reinforce this theory.[59] The departure of Ben-Gurion, who had been such a dominant figure in molding Israel's immigration policy, symbolized the end of the era of mass immigration.

When Moshe Sharett established a new government on 25 January 1954, the change went beyond personality and style; it could be felt in every department of the administration. Sharett was not Ben-Gurion, whose strength and determination had an impact on policy decisions in every sphere. As a member of the cabinet and Israel's foreign minister, Sharett had been involved in shaping and implementing immigration policy since the founding of the state, especially on a diplomatic level. However, *aliyah* and the problems of absorption were not his main concern. Israel's relations with the great powers had entered a critical juncture with the commencement of the Slansky Trials in Prague (November 1952) and the incarceration of Jewish physicians, accompanied by the spread of anti-Semitic propaganda in Russia (February 1953). The bombing of the Soviet consulate in Israel, also in February, provided Russia with an excuse for severing its diplomatic ties with Israel. All these events pointed up the precarious nature of Israel's relations with the Communist bloc, which had immediate repercussions on *aliyah*. American-Israeli relations also suffered a setback that year, when Dwight D. Eisenhower won the presidential elections and brought the Republican Party back to power for the first time in two decades. President Truman's pledges of friendship between the United States and Israel were replaced by courtship of the Arabs; American aid to Israel was even withheld for a certain period of time. As clouds gathered on the international horizon and a military confrontation brewed on Israel's borders, all other problems were shunted aside.

When Sharett assumed the premiership, the handling of *aliyah* and especially the Kelitah Department became the prerogative of the Jewish Agency and those government ministries that were directly involved. These matters no longer took central stage in the mind of the Israeli public. *Aliyah* during the second half of the 1950s was of another breed compared with that of the first half. Volume, demographic features, circumstances of arrival—all were different. Mass immigration during the early years of the Jewish state thus stands out as a unique phenomenon, bearing little resemblance to other throngs of immigration that either preceded or followed it.

Afterword: Birth of a New Society—Veterans and Newcomers

The era of Israel's establishment saw not only the creation of a state but also the birth of a new society.

The throngs of immigrants who made their way to the Jewish state during its first three years, doubling the population, came from lands of distress. The diversity of immigrants was great; Israel was inundated by Jews from many different countries and cultures who brought with them a broad array of languages, customs, and beliefs. In some cases, such as with the Jews of Yemen, Libya, and Iraq, entire communities were transplanted to Israel. The newcomers hailed from dozens of lands and hundreds of towns and villages, yet the wealthy classes were hardly represented. There were some monied Jews for whom participating in building the Jewish state took precedence over a life of ease, but such idealists were clearly in the minority.

From the Western countries, where the largest concentration of Jews remained, no more than a handful made their way to Israel. Of the six million Jews living in the United States during this period, approximately three thousand chose *aliyah*. Of the three million Jews in Western Europe, less than one percent moved to Israel. Even among the Holocaust survivors interned in DP camps in Europe, there were some who sought their fortunes elsewhere. On the other hand, out of a total of one-half million Asian Jews, 240,000 immigrated to Israel, more than half of them from Iraq. Of the 600,000 North African Jews who made *aliyah,* only 16 percent reached the country between 1948 and 1951.

This demographic profile affected the absorption process. The great majority of immigrants who arrived after the founding of the state, both from Europe and from Arab countries, were destitute and lacked skills that would facilitate their employment in Israel. Their dependence on the government was to determine the manner of absorption and the relationship between newcomers and veterans, which was clearly patronizing.

Both the immigrants' dependence and the circumstances of their arrival shaped the attitude of the host society. The great wave of immigration in 1948 did not occur spontaneously: it was the result of a clear-cut foreign policy decision that taxed the country financially and necessitated a major organizational effort. Many absorption activists, Jewish Agency executives, and government officials opposed unlimited, nonselective immigration; they favored a gradual process geared to the country's absorptive capacity. Throughout this period, two charges resurfaced at every public debate: one, that the absorption process caused undue hardship; two, that Israel's immigration policy was misguided. These issues were related because absorption difficulties, it was argued, were the direct consequence of a nonselective mass immigration policy. In any case, criticizing the handling of the immigrants while urging the government to bring in more was a contradictory argument.

Israel's inability to regulate the flow of immigration was particularly harmful to the absorption process. The initial plan was to take in 100,000 to 120,000 newcomers a year, but the actual figure was twice as high. As early as the summer of 1948 there was already talk of restricting the number of arrivals and the subject was discussed again from time to time. On several occasions, resolutions were passed to limit immigration from European and Arab countries alike. However, these limits were never put into practice, mainly due to the opposition of Ben-Gurion. As a driving force in the emergency of the state, Ben-Gurion—both prime minister and minister of defense—carried enormous weight with his veto. His insistence on the right of every Jew to immigrate proved victorious. He would not allow himself to be swayed by financial or other considerations. It was he who orchestrated the large-scale action that enabled the Jews to leave Eastern Europe and Islamic countries, and it was he who effectively forged Israel's foreign policy. Through a series of clandestine activities carried out overseas by the Foreign Office, the Jewish Agency, the Mossad le-Aliyah, and the Joint Distribution Committee, the road was paved for mass immigration.

"Ingathering" and "Integration"

Security and political considerations were not the only factors motivating Ben-Gurion. His outlook was solidly based on the vision of the "ingathering of the exiles" as being the sacred mission of the State of Israel. Ben-Gurion's dream was to spark a double revolution: to change the demographic profile of the Jewish people and to turn Israel into a major spiritual and cultural center that would affect the lives of Jews all over the world. Hence the crucial importance he attached, not only to the "ingathering," but also to the "integration of the exiles," that is, molding the sociocultural character of the new entity evolving in Israel. "The Melting Pot" was his great target.

This development was not left to chance. Ben-Gurion worked tirelessly to steer social and cultural development in the desired direction, enlisting government and public bodies to help him. He perceived the immigrants as objects that required shaping, and he was not alone in such thinking. For those involved in absorption, the rich cultural heritage of the newcomers meant nothing. In many circles, even among intellectuals and academics, ethnic diversity was regarded as a historical fluke that could soon be made to disappear if Israel adopted the appropriate cultural and educational policies. With the need for social reform acknowledged by a broad sector of the population, the patronizing attitude became even more entrenched. The fact that the government and the Jewish Agency were responsible for organizing the immigration enterprise led them to believe they had the right to modify the immigrants' behavior and insure that their development followed certain standards.

The host society in Israel was not necessarily patronizing toward the immigrants from a position of strength. In fact, it was feared that under the burden of mass immigration the Yishuv might literally collapse. A widespread opinion was that "Immigration does not come before the state and must not harm it. If immigration constitutes a threat to the state, it should be restricted lest it break our country's backbone." [60] The concern was for not only the physical and economic welfare of Israel, but also its social and cultural future; would the Yishuv be able to absorb the newcomers or be devoured by it? It is doubtful that any of the immigrants sensed the trepidation of the Yishuv as it stretched its hand out to take in others, all the while trembling at the thought of its own downfall.

Contradiction and Paradox

The ethos of the "ingathering of the exiles" was not an empty slogan. There was a genuine conviction that Israel was the home of the Jewish people and that any Jew who chose to settle in the country had the historical right to do so. But if Israel was the home, the Yishuv nevertheless saw itself as landlord—not only in terms of rights but also in terms of obligations. In contrast to other countries open to immigration, Israel's leadership felt it was their duty to insure that the newcomers were provided with a roof over their heads, food, and vital services. The sense of commitment was all the more intense in view of the role of the Jewish Agency and the government in organizing the immigration enterprise. The national institutions thus took responsibility for absorption as well, assuming that it was their job to decide where and how the immigrants would be integrated in their new home. It was this notion of duty that seemed to legitimize a paternalistic attitude. The emphasis was on Jewish solidarity and the national obligation of helping the arrivals settle in—a phenomenon unknown in any other country—yet it was paradoxically responsible for the immigrants' feeling that they were not being treated fairly.

The great wave of *aliyah* was suffused with contradiction and perplexity. In no small measure, the pangs of absorption were sharpened by fierce political wrangling over the immigrants during the early years of the state. The parties competed viciously among themselves to win the support of the newcomers, seriously questioning the wisdom of conferring citizenship on these people as soon as they disembarked. A component of citizenship was the right to vote, thereby granting considerable political clout to a public that was wholly uninitiated in the intricacies of Israeli politics. Before they knew what was happening, the immigrants found themselves enmeshed in power struggles and the target of manipulation from all sides. On the other hand, withholding citizenship was unthinkable; this was an inalienable right embedded in Israel's constitution. Once again, the paradox is that the battle over the immigrants from the moment they set foot in the country accelerated their integration in the Israeli political scene.

Certain issues connected with absorption aroused major controversy from the start; others became a bone of contention as time went on. One example of the latter was the practice of forcing new immigrants into the role of pioneers by sending them to development and border towns regardless of their wishes. The outcome of this policy of population dispersal and the absorption program based on it was that newcomers were expected to bow to the development and security needs of the country. True, this dispersal policy applied to all Israeli citizens. However, old-timers were given free choice whereas the immigrants did as they were told. There was nothing new in setting up stipulations with regard to immigrant employment and areas of residence. Many countries open to immigration made such demands and no one thought to complain. Yet in Israel this approach was at odds with the right of every Jew to settle in the country as provided by the Law of Return. The socio-spatial plan devised by the government was also intended to prevent the clustering of immigrants in urban centers near Israel's ports of entry; in other countries, it was common for such concentrations to become slums.

Scanning the map, we see that Israel was highly successful in the area of population dispersal during the great wave of immigration just after the establishment of the state. The Negev and the Galilee, in particular, registered an impressive spurt of growth. Nevertheless, the policy of sending immigrants to far-flung locations conflicted with the declared aim of encouraging them to integrate socially and culturally. The outcome was the emergence of the "other" Israel, which lagged behind the Yishuv in social and economic advancement, perpetuating a sense of isolation and alienation from the core of Israeli life.

The mass immigration of the late 1940s and early 1950s descended upon Israel like a fury. Yet, after a panic-stricken flight from their countries of birth, the immigrants found themselves in a land that was no less in turmoil—a land fatigued by war, plagued by financial debt, and torn by political enmity. The absorption endeavor unfolded as an interplay of opposites: lofty ideals alongside pettiness, courageous decisions and heroism alongside organizational disputes and rivalry. On the one hand, the Yishuv demonstrated tremendous devotion, the capacity for endless hours of work, a spirit of voluntarism, and a willingness to extend itself when needed; on the other hand, manifestations of prejudice, separatism, and indifference were not uncommon. It was in the dramatic confrontation between the Yishuv and the immigrants during the early years of statehood that the character of the veteran community began to lose its hard edges and the newcomers were able to leave their mark.

In retrospect, the bewildering array of hardships confronted during this period of immigration do not detract from the glory of the achievement. This was an enterprise that transformed the history of the Jewish people and shaped the development of the Jewish state. The Great Aliyah contained within it the roots of the new Jewish society about to emerge in Israel, a society that was conceived and born in a raging tempest.

CHAPTER EIGHT

Immigration During 1948–98 and Its Ramifications on Israeli Society

THE STATE OF ISRAEL, which arose by virtue of the Zionist movement, expressed its deep connection to immigration from its very inception. Israel's Declaration of Independence states that "The State of Israel shall be open to Jewish immigration and to the ingathering of the exiles." [1] This approach guided the state's immigration policy and is reflected in the Law of Return, which categorically declares that "every Jew has the right to immigrate to the Land of Israel." [2] The Law of Return firmly established the legal right of every Jew to immigrate to Israel.

Mass immigration to Israel during the early years of statehood, which doubled the nation's Jewish population, had a dramatic impact on both the size of the population and its composition. No aspect of the new State of Israel was left untouched, and a unique sociocultural mosaic came into being. The policies established at that time had far-reaching repercussions on the formation of social realities in the state over the following years. During the first decade of Israel's existence, the formative years of Israeli society, about one million immigrants came from all over the world. [3] The relationship developed at that time between the immigrants and the veteran population was to have long-range implications, leaving an indelible mark on the new state's social and cultural makeup as well as on its political system. It was then that the rifts within Israeli society, which deepened further over the years, were born: the ethnic rift between Jews of European extraction and those from Islamic countries; the friction between religious and secular Jews; and the socioeconomic polarization.

During the 1960s immigrants continued to arrive from many different countries, but not to the extent seen in the first decade. [4] Particularly prominent in the last thirty years has been the large number of immigrants from the Soviet Union. About a million immigrants came, all told, in two waves; the first wave of immigration began in the early 1970s and continued intermittently for about twenty years, while the second wave of immigration came in the 1990s.[5] While other immigrants also came to Israel during this period, two immigrant groups were especially conspicuous: those from the Soviet Union and those from Ethiopia—the former were conspicuous because of their large number and the latter because of their cultural distinctiveness. The large waves of immigrants arriving in Israel during the fifty years of its existence constitute the most remarkable aspect of Israeli society, and their impact is apparent in every aspect of the country's life.

Even before the establishment of the state, from the early twentieth century on, immigration was a central feature in the rapid increase in the Jewish population of Palestine. This was not a static population of people who lived in the country over many generations; rather, it was a constantly growing society of immigrants. In 1882 the Jewish population of Palestine was estimated at 24,000 people. By the time the Ottoman rule in Palestine came to an end after World War I (1917), the number of Jews had reached 56,000. During the thirty years of British rule in Palestine, between 1918 and 1947, the Jewish population of Palestine grew by a factor of eleven or more.[6] When the state was established in May 1948, there were about 650,000 Jews in the country.[7] By 1998, fifty years after the establishment of the State of Israel, the Jewish population of Israel was close to five million people.[8]

The demographic revolution that began upon the establishment of the state is evident, not only in the large dimensions of immigration but also in its social and cultural composition. The change in the relative proportions of *Ashkenazim,* who originated in Europe, and *Mizrahim,* who had come from Islamic lands, was the clear result of this process. *Mizrahim* composed about half the immigrants who arrived in Israel during the first decade,[9] while the majority (about 81 percent) of the immigrants who had arrived during the fifty years preceding the establishment of the state had come from Europe. The percentage of immigrants born in Africa or Asia stood at that time at 9.6 percent.[10] This change was partly because during the nineteenth century some 80 percent of the Jewish world lived in Eastern Europe, which was where the Zionist movement was conceived.[11] The homogeneity of the Jewish Yishuv in Palestine was also evident in terms of its sociodemographic composition. Before the establishment of the state the majority of immigrants were young singles or small young families. Most had secondary, and sometimes higher, education. Even though the foundations for economic, cultural, and political differentiation were laid during this period, the Yishuv society was far more homogeneous—socially, culturally, and economically—than were the waves of immigrants during the 1950s.

The State of Israel, which served as the apex of the achievements of the Zionist movement in realizing its national political aims, sought to accomplish its goals in the social and cultural arenas as well. In this respect, Israel differed from other countries that absorbed immigrants and refugees. It saw itself as being responsible for absorbing immigrants, a responsibility that went beyond the physical plane. Israel aimed to design its new, developing society, and this was one of the sources of the tensions that accompanied the absorption process and caused conflicts between the veterans' desire to continue developing the social structures as had been done prior to the establishment of the state and the immigrant population, which brought with it diverse social and cultural traditions that they wished to retain. The wide variety among immigrant groups, the differences in social and cultural backgrounds, and the varying expectations exacerbated the gap between the Yishuv and the new immigrants, especially those who came from a different social and economic background than the European immigrants. During the mass immigration that followed the establishment of the state, the question of absorption became a central issue in Israel's social and cultural design.

The two principle groups of immigrants during the first decade were the remnants of European Jewry, upon whom the imprint of the Holocaust was still visible—expelled from their homes and robbed of their assets, without families, and many battered physically and mentally; and those who had come from Islamic lands, their cultural background alien to that which had arisen in Israel under the influence of European migration. At the time, all of these immigrants had a bad image; negative stereotypes of immigrants who were Holocaust refugees and those who had come from Islamic lands were widespread among veterans. Their lifestyles, traditions, and traits were criticized. These negative images caused concern among the veterans that the sociocultural legacy that had been forged during the Yishuv period would be damaged. The dominant elite that sought to prevent the subversion of cultural and political stability and of the continuity that they had forged adopted, in the words of Moshe Lissak, a "strategy of patronage." [12]

Absorption was characterized by the large-scale involvement of state institutions, especially during the large waves of immigration in the first decade of the state's existence. [13] Immigrant absorption took place in a bureaucratic, administrative context. Veterans of the Yishuv were involved in immigration absorption as part of their role in the establishment, in local or central government institutions, or in the Jewish Agency. This involvement had many implications on the relationship that came into being between immigrants and the veteran residents who manned the government institutions. The dependence of the immigrants upon absorption institutions further emphasized the distance between them and the veterans.

The centralist ruling structure in Israel, along with the control of absorption institutions, enabled policymakers to execute their absorption plans in several areas. As part of a population-dispersal policy, immigrants were sent to development areas far from the center of the country, both towns and agricultural settlements. During the first decade, dozens of development towns and hundreds of immigrant villages sprung up around the country in peripheral areas.[14] To overcome high unemployment among immigrants, a policy of public work projects was developed; the government and such public bodies as the Jewish National Fund set aside public funds for the employment of immigrants in road paving, building, and forestry. This situation also emphasized the immigrants' dependence on the establishment[15] and strengthened the image of immigrants as a burden on the state's economy, clouding over the relations between veterans and immigrants.[16] Absorption policy greatly influenced the process of absorption and determined the actual placing of immigrants on the map of social dispersal in Israel. The majority of the population in development towns today are immigrants from Islamic countries who arrived in the 1950s.

Immigrants hoped to be given the opportunity to move closer to the social and political center. Hence they perceived as unjust the plan to send them to peripheral areas. A further characteristic of the absorption process in Israel was the creation of socioeconomic polarization and an overlap between this polarization and the makeup of the population, whereby groups at the bottom of the socioeconomic scale were comprised mostly of emigrants from Islamic lands. This situation increased the ethnic problem. The claim was made that absorption policy was not fair and that it discriminated between migrants from Europe and those from Islamic countries. The subject of ethnic tension became one that was to agitate Israeli society continuously, from the state's inception on.

Political scientists have pointed to the characteristics of immigrants as a factor in the situation that developed in Israel. In their view, the social and demographic composition of these waves of immigration weighed heavily on the ease with which they were absorbed. Among immigrants from Islamic countries, there was a considerable increase in the average size of families. The age of immigrants was also an influence; there was a majority of babies, young children, and old people. These factors had significant consequences upon the scope of cooperation in the workforce, which was reflected in turn in the reduction of the number of breadwinners and an increase in the number of dependents. Political scientists also noted other components, such as educational level and professional training, and their importance in the economic and social mobility of immigrants.[17]

Apart from the composition of immigrant groups, the size of these groups and the timing of their immigration also influenced their absorption. The large streams of immigrants that arrived in Israel during the first years of statehood, when Israel was suffering from an economic crisis, gave rise to the formation of a significant delay between the arrival of immigrants and their absorption in employment, housing, and other services. The fact that during the first few years after their immigration most immigrants were housed in transit camps separated them in a kind of ecological, sociocultural isolation in which contacts with the veteran population were limited and consisted of interaction mostly with people involved in the absorption process.

The character and process of absorption may also be seen in the order in which immigrants arrived. Most of the immigrants who arrived during the first year of the state's existence came from Europe. They succeeded in integrating themselves into the central part of the country, mainly in cities that had been abandoned by Arabs. Immigrants from Arab lands started to arrive in the summer of 1949 and continued coming until 1952. Most of these immigrants were housed in transit camps. During this same period, immigrants continued to arrive from Romania and Poland. The latter, however, managed to leave the transit camps quickly because they had smaller families and, thanks to the aid and support that they received from social networks in the veteran Yishuv, more easily found housing and employment in the center of the country. Many immigrants from Iraq, who were well educated and trained in professions required in Israel or who had capital, also succeeded in integrating themselves rapidly into the veteran economy and society. On the other hand, those immigrants who had no strong social networks or who had large families to look after, together with those who suffered from health problems and lack of employment, remained in the transit camps for a long time and soon became destitute. Most members of this group came from Islamic countries.

Sociologists also have noted the influence of the immigrants' cultural background on the process of their absorption. They believe that the gap between different groups of immigrants was affected both by demographic considerations such as family size, professional training, and formal education and by social attributes—cultural molds that are usually linked with modernity: enterprise, resourcefulness, and the ability to postpone gratification. Other personal attributes, such as common language and similar style of behavior, and personal contacts in social networks based on one's country of origin, also facilitated comfortable accessibility to the Israeli establishment, to strong social networks, and to the elite.[18]

Critical sociologists have claimed that the development of rifts in Israeli society was due to discriminatory policies. In their opinion, economic and social gaps were not only the result of the immigrants' own constraints. Rather, they argue, the moving of immigrants to development areas remote from the country's center was the result of conscious ethnic discrimination by *Ashkenazic* veterans, who wished to prevent the immigrants from entering the employment market, thereby reducing the potential competition from immigrants in employment and in the demand for services. These sociologists further claim that the veterans did not provide the immigrants with equal opportunities and prevented them from accessing social and political power centers, thereby sealing their fate economically as well. They blamed the elite group that had arisen in Palestine during the period of the Yishuv, most of whom were former Europeans,[19] with intentionally preventing Asian Jews from joining their institutions and leaving them on the social and political periphery. Sociologists also criticized the incumbent paternalism and desire that these immigrants be assimilated into the culture of the veteran Yishuv.[20]

The tension that arose as a result of the "melting pot" policy enhanced the feeling of discrimination against migrants from Islamic countries. This tension was expressed in sporadic outburts of violence. The ethnic tension that arose in the 1950s did not dissipate for many years, and protest movements were founded.[21] The anger increased when the composition of immigration to Israel changed.

Immigration Beginning in the 1970s

Throughout the 1960s many immigrants continued to pour in from North Africa,[22] while only a relatively small number of immigrants arrived from Western Europe and the number of immigrants from the United States was low.[23] However, toward the end of the 1960s this trend changed with the onset of waves of immigration from European countries, in particular from the Soviet Union. Immigration to Israel during the past three decades has not been as varied as it had been in the past. Most immigrants (more than 80 percent) in the later period came from European countries and the Americas. This turnaround was the result of a decline in immigration from Asian and African countries and the large rise in immigration from the Soviet Union.

Immigration from CIS

A substantial change occurred in the social makeup of Israel upon the arrival of the large immigration wave from the USSR beginning at the end of 1989, reaching its peak in the years 1991–94, and continuing today. During this wave, some million immigrants arrived in the country. The change is most visible in the composition of this wave of immigrants, characterized in the main by a large proportion of academics and others in the technological and free professions. There were a large number of scientists—physicists and chemists—of doctors and engineers, as well as of all kinds of other technological professionals, writers, journalists, intellectuals, artists, teachers, musicians, and others. Families were generally small, with few children, and there was a high percentage of mixed marriages (Jews married to non-Jews). Another aspect that stood out was the large number of single-parent families.[24] The social and economic orientation of these immigrants was influenced by the socialization process they had undergone under the communist regime and as a result of the encounter with the Western world after the *Perestroika*.[25]

Immigrants who came to Israel from the USSR in the 1970s were moved to do so mainly by Zionist ideological reasons, while those who arrived in the 1990s were motivated more by pragmatic reasons.[26] Attitudes that became apparent during the absorption of immigrants from the Commonwealth of Independent States (CIS) demonstrated that they were not interested in giving up their former identity and culture. Although these immigrants made serious efforts to learn Hebrew quickly, they tended not to assimilate into Israeli society.[27] While most of them do not isolate themselves from Israeli culture, they see themselves as a sector of the public with an emphatic cultural identity.[28]

The character of absorption in Israel was determined not only by its principles but also by social considerations. In absorbing immigrants from the CIS, it was considered desirable to prevent excessive interference by government authorities; thus a policy of "direct absorption" was adopted. Direct absorption intended to do away with the need for transit camps and to enable every immigrant to choose where he would live and to find employment by himself immediately upon arriving in Israel; the state granted each immigrant an "absorption package"—a sum of money to cover basic costs during the first year after immigration. The aim was to transfer the centralized absorption system that had been in place since the establishment of the state so that instead of a single or dual center of absorption (the government and the Jewish Agency), run by the dominant cultural and political center, immigrants would enjoy optimal decentralization of powers. However, it seems that, in the reality of this large immigration wave, this system had only limited success. The reduced dependence of immigrants on absorption authorities did not necessarily lead to a free choice in their manner of absorption. Even exposing them to the free market did not contribute to their making social contacts with veterans or to the advancement of integration among them. Institutionalized bureaucracy was not abolished

Soviet Jews disembark at Ben-
Gurion Airport after a direct
El Al flight from Moscow.
Photograph by Tsvika Israeli

and, although it affected immigrants less in their daily lives, the consequences
were that they were in fact limited in almost every aspect of their lives. The large
demand for housing led to a scarcity in apartments, causing prices to rise. As a
result, immigrants were forced to turn to underprivileged areas where housing
was cheaper. There they were received with reservation by their veteran neighbors as potential competitors for housing and work. The readiness of immigrants with higher education and professional skills to take on nonprofessional
work made the tensions between them and their neighbors in the poorer areas
even worse. It became clear that the encounter with veterans from weaker strata
created tensions on a sociocultural level, sharpening the rifts in Israeli society
that had been thought to be dissipating.[29]

The second generation of immigrants who arrived in the 1950s began to feel
the threat of competition from new immigrants for places of employment, and
the threat in the social and political sectors revived the tensions between immigrants and veterans; ironically, there was a switch in the dynamic between these
groups. When immigrants arrived from the European Soviet Union, some of the

veterans, especially those who had themselves arrived from Islamic countries in the 1950s, tried to marginalize them and stamp them with a negative image.[30]

Immigration from Ethiopia

Other kinds of difficulties arose with the arrival of immigrants from Ethiopia, the most obvious of which was the cultural uniqueness of these people. These immigrants arrived in two waves, in 1984 and in 1991, and numbered approximately 25,000 people.[31] This migration was completely different from the migration from the former USSR and presented special problems for absorption authorities. Ethiopia was considered one of the most backward countries in the world. The level of education of the immigrants from Ethiopia in the first wave was generally low, and most of them were in poor health. The majority of the Jews of Ethiopia had lived in villages, where they had been shepherds, kept cattle, or engaged in agriculture and other professions, living in extended families under a patriarchal system.[32] Their motivation for coming to Israel was, for the most part, religious.

The demographics of these groups of immigrants gave rise to special difficulties. Ethiopian immigrants were characterized by split families, and about one third of the immigrant families were single-parent households.[33] Many were in poor health, a situation that worsened during their escape from Ethiopia and during the time they spent in refugee camps before arriving in Israel.[34] The circumstances of the secret and hasty organization of their migration to Israel was for most of them a traumatic experience, and they suffered difficulties in striking roots in Israeli society. Difficulties also arose because of their low level of education.[35] Doubts about the method of absorbing the Ethiopians related to the physical aspects of absorption, but the question of social and cultural absorption was the most important. Absorption authorities wished to avoid making the mistakes that had been made during the first years of the state, yet they were also aware that the retention of this community's traditions could sentence them to isolation.[36]

For years there was harsh criticism among absorption authorities regarding mistakes and slip ups that had been made in absorbing immigrants who arrived in the large waves following the establishment of the state. From the 1970s onwards, the goal was to set up a pluralistic cultural framework, bestowing legitimacy upon the unique traditions of any group of immigrants. The intention was not merely to accept the folklore, as had been done in the past, but also to encourage various forms of artistic creativity and devise educational treatment of the traditions. With the immigration from Ethiopia—which in many ways presented an image similar to that of groups of immigrants who had arrived at the time of the establishment of the state—absorption workers attempted to adopt a method that would aim to find the balance between retention of the community's identity, linking it to its past and to certain traditions, and modernization and integration into Israeli society.[37]

Political Aspects

Because Israel's political culture is characterized by a high level of public involvement, the waves of immigration to Israel throughout the years held a central place in public awareness. The growth of Israeli society as a result of immigration placed great importance on the process of political socialization of the immigrants.[38] Therefore, during periods of quick change, whenever a large wave of immigrants arrived, tensions rose and the struggle to win them over politically increased.

A unique situation developed in Israel because immigrants were given a special status that had many implications on their political importance. Pursuant to the Citizenship Law and the Residents Register Ordinance, which are connected to the Law of Return, automatic citizenship is granted to every immigrant immediately upon his or her arrival in Israel.[39] This right includes the right to vote for municipal and central government without any limitation whatsoever, such as knowledge of the Hebrew language or length of period of residence in Israel. As a result, every large wave of immigrants has very strong electoral potential to change the power relations between parties and overturn the political system. Coalition parties that were worried about letting immigrants participate freely in political life worked to regulate the processes of political integration of immigrants, with government personnel simultaneously acting as agents for the parties. This situation led to a struggle for control over those institutions that had influential power over immigrants and their socialization processes.[40] The political struggle did not diminish at party level but was also expressed in the economic sphere.[41]

When immigrants began to be absorbed into the economy and their dependence on bureaucracy lessened, the public atmosphere changed. As a result, the parties that had been dominant in the first decades of the state became weaker. In 1977 a political turnabout took place, in which the Labor Party, which had been in power for the first three decades, lost the elections. This change in the political map strengthened the influence of religious and ultra-religious parties. This change in turn strengthened the phenomenon of populism that was assisted by traditional ethnic symbols, which to this day exerts considerable influence on Israeli political life. A situation arose whereby, despite its being a new society, Israel once again needed to deal with the problems of tension between modernization and tradition, with the traditionalist groups in the society working off the model of the political culture that had been dominant in the Jewish Yishuv in Palestine during the British mandate and that had influenced the institutional structure of the state at its founding.

The waves of immigrants arriving from various social and cultural backgrounds over the years created a pluralistic mosaic of ethnic groups in Israel. The wide spectrum of heterogeneity that they created was expressed in many social and cultural aspects. Some of these ethnic groups adapted themselves over the years to the new social system that developed in Israel, while in other groups the change occurred at a slower rate. The new waves of immigrants that kept coming throughout the years helped to broaden the dimensions of this heterogeneity. This dynamic, which created conflicts between immigrant groups that arrived in different periods and between immigrants and the veteran population, has been in operation since the establishment of the state. This situation was the reason for attempts at political organization on an ethnic basis.[42]

The waves of immigration to Israel gave rise to the development of a social structure that is not so much the result of a continual historical process covering many generations as it is the result of new, short-lived developments whose source is to be found in the process of Jewish settlement in Palestine. The modes of behavior and value relations of each of the groups that make up Israeli society did not develop organically from cultural or social traditions but were mostly imported from the immigrants' country of origin. The various traditions were expressed in many different aspects of life, in lifestyle and manner of behavior, in Jewish religious tradition, and in the preservation of local rituals belonging to people coming from various communities.[43]

The encounter between the veterans' values and culture and that of the immigrants who retained their links to traditional cultures did not take place in conditions of equal power. The absorption authorities were dominant, both politically and socially. Consequently, during the period of speedy growth in Israeli society (in the 1950s and early 1960s) the specific traditions of immigrants' countries of origin did not strongly affect the development of Israeli society. However, this situation changed, and the influence of particularistic traditions on the nature of public life in Israel began to increase with the growing sense of self-assurance among traditionalist groups in Israeli society. These groups began to free themselves from their marginal position in society, opting for a more central stance.[44] Certain folkloric phenomena that were less visible in the 1950s, such as folk medicine, experienced a revival in the 1970s; since that time folk medicine has operated in certain circles of society in parallel with and in competition to conventional medicine.[45] Another striking feature is the rise of the cult surrounding the tombs of holy men and sages, which have become cultural centers more than mere pilgrimage sites.[46] Recently, the phenomenon of belief in the mystical powers of Kabbalists and amulets has grown, and use has been made of this fact to recruit support in the political sphere as well.[47] Sociologists have pointed to the fact that in Israel, as in other countries, traditional ties negating Western-style modernization are more vigorous than might have been expected during the period when the institutional infrastructure was laid down for this sovereign state.[48] Groups that in the past had experienced difficulties integrating into the dominant modern culture are now living an independent existence.

The religious factor that burst onto the scene at the end of the 1960s, accelerating after the Six Day War in 1967, greatly assisted this development. This factor is noticeable in the emergence of religious groups, including those affiliated with the religious Zionist movement, that in earlier years had been compliant and had adopted a centralist compromise position.[49] Their intense involvement in the political debate surrounding the Jewish-Arab conflict, together with their political organization, strengthened their social unity and increased their tendency to create symbols of a unique religious cultural identity. The growth in political strength of the ultra-religious community increased, and its attempt to enforce its standpoints in various areas in general public life[50] was part of the whole process of replacing the central national Zionist ethos with a number of other messages from groups claiming legitimacy for their religious and cultural uniqueness.[51]

The criticism leveled against the centralist system that controlled Israel during the first years of the state, along with the public tendency for more pluralism, caused the veteran elite to reduce their social and cultural dictates. The strength of the secularist ideal that was disseminated in the past by the political center diminished, and there is now a greater tendency to amalgamate it with religious-traditional components. The establishment was no longer able to present a single ideology acceptable to everyone. Prime ministers and politicians began kowtowing to the religious leaders of various ethnic groups and cultural personalities who had been ignored entirely in the past. Although this change was primarily the result of coalition considerations, the phenomenon strengthened the legitimacy of the cultural particularism that had begun to spread throughout Israeli society.

The organization of immigrants from the Commonwealth of Independent States into separate political units, together with the dressing up of their cultural heritage, is an expression of the general trend toward a continually increasing societal split at the expense of the weakened politico-cultural center. There is no

longer a single definition of identity in Israel acceptable to a majo
ulation. Similarly, no single national group or political framework
cultural authority on the whole of society.

As a society of immigrants, Israel is afflicted with economic pro
ficulties, with conflicting lines of policy, with rifts between the expectations of
immigrants and veterans, and with the development of large cultural and social
gaps. Israeli society also has been influenced by the goals of modern Western societies that encourage pluralism and support individualism—a fact that has
played an important role in loosening societal consolidation, in increasing cultural disintegration, and in blurring the boundaries of collective identity in Israel.

Israeli society is an immigrant society. The bulk of the Israeli population is
made up of immigrants, who arrived in waves over the course of the fifty years
since the establishment of the state. While each wave of immigration had its own
unique characteristics, together they created a human mosaic that is both complex and fascinating. Yet, in addition to their contribution to the creation of a
new Israeli society, these waves of immigration brought about a demographic
revolution, one that reshaped the Jewish Diaspora throughout the world.

Appendixes

Notes

Glossary

Bibliography

Index

Appendix A

Aliyah to Israel by Country of Origin and Year of *Aliyah,* 14 May 1948-31 December 1953

Country of Origin	Year of *Aliyah*					
	1948	1949	1950	1951	1952	1953
All Countries	102,879	239,576	169,405	173,901	23,375	10,347
Eastern Europe						
Romania	17,678	13,595	47,041	40,625	3,712	61
Poland	28,788	47,331	25,071	2,529	264	225
Bulgaria	15,091	20,008	1,000	1,142	461	359
Czechoslovakia	2,115	15,685	263	150	24	10
Hungary	3,463	6,842	2,302	1,022	133	224
Yugoslavia	4,126	2,470	427	572	88	14
Soviet Union	1,175	3,230	2,618	689	198	216
Total	72,436	109,161	76,104	46,247	4,682	937
Western Europe						
Germany	1,422	5,329	1,439	662	142	100
France	640	1,653	1,165	548	227	117
Austria	395	1,618	746	233	76	45
Greece	175	1,364	343	122	46	71
Great Britain	501	756	581	302	233	140
Italy	530	501	242	142	95	37
Belgium	-	ª615	297	196	51	44
Holland	188	367	265	282	112	95
Total	3,851	11,588	5,601	2,672	1,058	733
Asia						
Iraq	15	1,708	31,627	88,161	868	375
Yemen	270	35,422	9,203	588	89	26
Turkey	4,362	26,295	2,323	1,228	271	220
Persia (Iran)	43	1,778	11,935	11,048	4,856	1,096
Aden	-	2,636	190	328	35	58
India	12	856	1,105	364	49	650
China	-	ª644	1,207	316	85	160
Other Countries	-	ª1,966	931	634	230	197
Total	4,702	68,695	58,548	102,668	6,430	2,793
Africa						
Morocco	-	-	4,980	7,770	5,031	2,990
Tunisia	6,821	17,353	3,725	3,414	2,548	606
Algeria	-	-	506	272	92	84
Libya	1,064	14,352	8,818	6,534	1,146	224
South Africa	178	217	154	35	11	33
Egypt	-	ª7,268	7,154	2,086	1,251	1,041
Other Countries	-	ª382	5	6	3	9
Total	8,063	39,190	25,425	20,117	10,082	4,990
Unknown	13,827	10,942	-	-	-	-

Source: Based upon data of the Publications and Statistics Department of the Jewish Agency and from Moshe Sikron, *Immigration to Israel, 1948–1957* (in Hebrew) (Jerusalem: Machon Falk and Israel Central Bureau of Statistics, 1957), Table A32.

a. Includes immigrants who came in 1948–49.

Appendix B

Immigrants by Country of Origin and Year of *Aliyah*, 1948–53 (by percentage)

Country of Origin	Year of *Aliyah*						
	1948	1949	1950	1951	1952	1953	1948–53
All Countries	100.0	100.0	100.0	100.0	100.0	100.0	100.0
Asia	5.3	30.5	34.4	59.5	28.7	27.8	35.3
Turkey	4.8	11.2	1.4	0.7	1.5	2.6	5.0
Iraq	0.0	0.7	19.3	51.3	4.1	4.1	17.8
Iran	0.1	0.8	6.3	5.4	17.9	10.6	3.9
Yemen & Aden	0.3	16.3	5.4	0.6	0.6	0.8	6.9
Other	0.1	1.6	2.0	1.5	4.6	9.7	1.7
Africa	9.1	16.7	15.2	11.5	42.9	67.3	15.4
Tunisia, Algeria & Morocco	7.6	7.4	5.6	6.5	32.3	35.1	8.0
Libya	1.2	6.1	5.2	3.8	5.1	2.3	4.6
Other	0.3	3.2	4.3	1.2	5.5	9.9	2.8
Europe	85.1	52.1	49.8	28.6	26.2	19.6	48.6
Soviet Union	1.3	1.4	1.6	0.4	0.8	2.1	1.2
Poland	32.0	20.2	15.8	2.0	2.7	3.8	15.3
Romania	19.6	5.8	27.6	23.1	15.5	0.8	17.4
Bulgaria	16.8	8.6	0.6	0.7	1.9	3.3	5.4
Yugoslavia	4.6	1.1	0.2	0.4	0.4	0.1	1.1
Germany & Austria	2.0	3.0	0.8	0.4	1.1	1.8	1.6
Czechoslovakia	2.3	7.6	0.4	0.2	0.4	0.3	2.7
Hungary	3.9	2.0	1.6	0.7	0.9	2.2	2.1
Other	2.6	2.4	1.2	0.7	2.5	5.2	1.8
America & Oceania	0.5	0.6	0.6	0.4	2.2	5.3	0.7
United States	0.3	0.2	0.2	0.1	0.4	0.7	0.2
Other	0.2	0.4	0.4	0.3	1.8	4.6	0.5

Source: Moshe Sikron, *Immigration to Israel, 1948–1957* (in Hebrew) (Jerusalem: Machon Falk and Israel Central Bureau of Statistics, 1957), Table 33A, and the Publications and Statistics Department of the Jewish Agency.

Appendix C

Immigrants in Camps and *Ma'abarot,* May 1950–May 1952

	Number of Camps	People in Camps	Number of *Ma'abarot*	People in *Ma'abarot*	Total
May 1950	58	108,057	4	1,700	109,757
December 1951	42	77,366	123	179,140	256,506
May 1952	19	[a]	129	[a]	[a]245,599

Source: Publications and Statistics Department of the Jewish Agency.

a. Lacking Division Between Camps and *Ma'abarot*

Appendix D

Immigrants by Place of Absorption, 15 May 1948–1 August 1954

	5-15-48– 5-15-50	5-15-50– 5-15-52	5-15-52– 8-1-54	Total	Percentage of Total *Aliyah*
Total No. Immigrants	393,197	304,457	30,057	727,711	
Abandoned Neighborhoods & Villages	123,669			123,669	41
Housing in Cities & Villages	53,000	54,160	58,218	165,378	23
Relatives & Private Arrangements	36,497	57,165	26,467	133,627	18
Moshavei Olim	35,700	22,825	9,980	68,505	9.5
Kibbutzim	16,000	10,474	3,307	29,781	4
Youth Aliyah	6,000	13,209	2,413	21,622	3
Other[a]	10,316	13,080	4,390	27,786	
Camps and *Ma'abarot*	109,757	245,559	170,747	526,063	[b]

Source: Publications and Statistics Department of the Jewish Agency.

a. Immigrants in institutions of Malben and others for whom details of their absorption is unavailable

b. There was constant change among the inhabitants of the camps and *ma'abarot*.

Appendix E

Number of Immigrants to Israel, 15 May 1948–31 December 1951
(by month)

Month		Year of *Aliyah*		
	1948	1949	1950	1951
January	-	27,530	13,011	13,300
February	-	24,467	10,920	14,900
March	-	31,914	13,347	21,696
April	-	23,275	8,183	30,283
May	6,055	23,196	12,700	26,202
June	1,372	16,358	14,380	22,342
July	17,266	16,315	17,981	15,276
August	8,451	13,470	18,803	7,180
September	10,786	20,254	16,190	8,524
October	10,691	19,206	19,356	5,246
November	20,369	13,470	12,029	5,640
December	2,888	14,341	12,265	3,907
Total	102,879	239,576	169,405	173,901

Source: Based upon data of the Aliyah Department of the Jewish Agency.

Note: In 1952, 23,375 immigrants; in 1953, 10,347 immigrants.

Notes

Introduction

1. Chaim Barkai, *The Beginnings of Israeli Economy* (in Hebrew) (Jerusalem: Bialik Institute, 1990), 21–31.

2. Moshe Sikron, *Immigration to Israel, 1948–1957* (in Hebrew) (Jerusalem: Machon Falk and Israel Central Bureau of Statistics, 1957), 20.

3. Zionist Organization Executive, *The 22nd Zionist Congress Protocols* (Basel: WZO, 1946), 7.

4. Michel Abitbol, *North African Jewry* (in Hebrew) (Jerusalem: Machon Ben Zvi, 1980),

273

385; Eric Cohen, "Black Panthers and Israeli Society," *The Jewish Journal of Sociology,* 14 (1972):70.

5. Cohen, "Black Panthers," 22–68; Michael M. Laskier, *North African Jewry in the Twentieth Century* (New York: New York Univ. Press, 1994), 94–107.

6. Cohen, "Black Panthers"; Michel Abitbol, "The Jews and their Surroundings in North Africa prior to World War II" (in Hebrew), in *History of the Jews in Islamic Countries* (in Hebrew), ed. Shmuel Ettinger (Jerusalem: Merkaz Zalman Shazar, 1986), 2:411–28; 3:9–30; Yosef Tobi, "Jewish Centers in Asia" (in Hebrew), in *History of the Jews in Islamic Countries,* 3:74–90; Jacob Barnai, "The Legal and Social Status of the Jews" (in Hebrew), in *History of the Jews in Islamic Countries,* 3:230–37.

7. Malcolm Jarvis Proudfoot, *European Refugees: 1939–1952* (London: Faber and Faber, 1956), 340–46; David Shaari, *Deportation to Cyprus, 1946–1949* (in Hebrew) (Jerusalem: The Zionist Library, 1981), 155.

8. Jacob Kellner, *The First Immigrant Groups to Eretz Israel: Myth and Reality* (in Hebrew) (Jerusalem: Magnes Press, 1984), 13–34.

9. L. Motzkin at 10th Zionist Congress, in Margalit Shilo, "Changing Attitudes in the Zionist Movement Towards Immigration to Eretz Israel, 1904–1914" (in Hebrew), *Cathedra* 46 (1987):109–22.

10. Hofshi, "Pioneers of Zion," in *The Book of the Second Aliyah* (in Hebrew), ed. Bracha Habbas (Tel Aviv: Am Oved, 1947), 137.

11. Zvi Yehuda, ed., *From Babylon to Jerusalem: Studies and Documents on Zionism and Aliyah from Irag* (in Hebrew) (Tel Aviv: Ha-Mahon le-Heker Yehudei Bavel, 1981), 11–14.

12. Appeal of Actions Committee of World Zionist Movement signed by Nahum Sokolow and Chaim Weizmann, and Julius Simon of the Palestine Office. See *Hapoel Hatzair,* 12, 13 (22 Iyar 1919).

13. The Fourth Aliyah reached Palestine in 1924–31. See Sikron, *Immigration to Israel,* 14; Dan Giladi, *Jewish Palestine During the Fourth Aliyah Period, 1924–1929* (in Hebrew) (Tel Aviv: Am Oved, 1973), 38–39.

14. Giladi, *Jewish Palestine,* 231–35.

15. Sikron, *Immigration to Israel,* 14.

16. Ruth Bondi, *Pinchas Rosen and His Time* (in Hebrew) (Tel Aviv: Zmora Bitan, 1990), 255–63; Yoav Gelber, *New Homeland: Immigration and Absorption of Central European Jews, 1933–1948* (in Hebrew) (Jerusalem: Yad Izhak Ben Zvi and Leo Baeck Institute, 1990), 64–77.

17. Remarks at Zionist Congress, 24 Aug. 1933; David Ben-Gurion, *Memoirs* (in Hebrew) (Tel Aviv: Am Oved, 1971), 2:661.

18. ISA, Standing Committee File, Unit 41.

1. Policy in the Making

1. Zvi Ganin, *Truman, American Jewry, and Israel: 1945–1948* (New York: Holmes and Meier, 1979), chapter 10.

2. Minhelet ha-Am, Protocols, ISA 38–119; Moshe Sharett, *In the Gate of the Nations* (in Hebrew) (Tel Aviv: Am Oved, 1958), 238; Foreign policy documents, ISA 503, 504; Yehuda Slutzky, *Book of the History of the Haganah* (in Hebrew) (Tel Aviv: Am Oved, 1973), 3:1344–56.

3. Meir Pa'il, "From National Home to the State of Israel" (in Hebrew), in *History of Eretz Is-*

rael, vol. 10, *The War of Independence, 1947–1949,* ed. Yehoshua Ben Arieh, (Jerusalem: Keter, 1983), 58–72; Sharett, *In the Gate of the Nations,* 280–90.

4. Slutzky, *History of the Haganah,* 3:2, 1070–81; Zerubavel Gilad and Mati Meged, *The Book of the Palmah* (in Hebrew) (Tel Aviv: Hakibbutz Hameuchad, 1955), 821–29; Israel Defense Forces Archives.

5. Shadmi to-Eliyahu Tamkin, March 1948, IDFA.

6. Slutzky, *History of the Haganah,* 3:2, 1460–61; David Ben-Gurion, *Israel at War* (in Hebrew) (Tel Aviv: Am Oved, 1957), 157; Yoav Gelber, *The Emergence of a Jewish Army* (in Hebrew) (Jerusalem: Yad Izhak Ben-Zvi, 1986), 153–54.

7. Meir Pa'il, "The Military System" (in Hebrew), in *History of Eretz Israel,* vol. 10, *The War of Independence, 1947–1949,* ed. Yehoshua Ben Arieh (Jerusalem: Keter, 1983), 162.

8. Gelber, *Emergence of a Jewish Army,* 162.

9. The precise number of Mahal volunteers is unknown because their arrival in Israel and military recruitment stretched over several months. A census taken in June 1949 ("Mifkad Smadar") counted 270 persons, but this figure is not realistic. Many of the volunteers had already returned to their home countries; others had changed their status to *olim* and were no longer in the Mahal category. Some Mahal volunteers disguised the purpose of their visit to avoid a tangle with the authorities. The United States, for example, threatened to revoke the citizenship of Americans who volunteered their services to the Israeli air force. According to various estimates, the actual number of volunteers was between 700 and 800. Many thanks to Yaakov Hayun for this data, compiled from documents in the Israel Defense Forces and Israel Air Force Archives. See also Leonard Sliter, *Ha-Neemanim* (The Trustees) (Tel Aviv: Maarachot, 1971).

10. Sharett, *In the Gate of the Nations,* 265–71.

11. Ben-Gurion, *Israel at War,* 161–63.

12. Sharett, *In the Gate of the Nations,* 254.

13. Meeting of provisional government, 28 Sept. 1948. David Ben-Gurion, *The Reborn State of Israel* (in Hebrew) (Tel Aviv: Am Oved, 1969), 247; Ben-Gurion, *Israel at War,* 227.

14. Pa'il, "From National Home to the State of Israel," 72; Sharett, *In the Gate of the Nations,* 290.

15. See chapter 3.

16. Pa'il, "From National Home to the State of Israel," 72–78; Sharett, *In the Gate of the Nations,* 280–90.

17. Ezra Danin of the Foreign Ministry; Zalman Lif (Lifshitz), an Israel Electric Corporation engineer and a former government advisor on land and borders; Yosef Weitz of the Jewish National Fund, formerly a member of the "Transfer Committee." See Yaakov Sharett and Gershon Rivlin, *Ezra Danin: A Zionist at All Times* (in Hebrew) (Jerusalem: Kidum, 1987), 310.

18. The "transfer" of Arabs from the Jewish state to the neighboring countries was one of the central issues discussed by the Zionist Congress in Zurich (August 1937) in response to the recommendation of the Peel Commission to divide the country into two states. The commission also spoke of transferring Arabs living within the borders of the Jewish state to the Arab state. In order to study the political and practical implications of this proposal, the Political Department of the Jewish Agency appointed a panel of experts known as the Transfer Committee (November 1937). See Yossi Katz, "Deliberations of the Jewish Agency's Committee on Transfer of Population, 1937–1938" (in Hebrew), *Zion* 53, no. 2 (1988):167–89; Shabtai Teveth, *Kin'at David* (Tel Aviv: Schocken, 1980); "Gilgulei ha-transfer bemahshava ha-tzionit," *Ha-Aretz,* 25 Sept. 1988.

19. Y. Schectman, Zionist Actions Committee, 24 Aug. 1948; CZA S5/324; Sharett, *In the Gate of the Nations,* 269–82.

20. Danin, in Sharett and Rivlin, *Ezra Danin,* 310.

21. The memorandum contained thirty-four pages plus sixty pages of additions. See David Ben-Gurion, Diary (manuscript), 21 Oct. 1948, BGA, Sdeh Boker. Sharett and Rivlin mistakenly claim that the memorandum was submitted on 31 October 1948 *(Ezra Danin* 297).

22. Ben-Gurion Diary, 21 Oct. 1948.

23. Ibid.

24. Ben-Gurion Diary, 6 Nov. 1948.

25. Ibid.

26. Ben-Gurion speaking to Gahal and Mahal units, *Ha-Aretz,* 4 Nov. 1949.

27. Uri Bialer, *Between East and West* (Cambridge: Cambridge Univ. Press, 1990), 59; Michael Bar-Zohar, *David Ben-Gurion* (in Hebrew) (Tel Aviv: Am Oved, 1977), 2:897.

28. Tom Segev, *1949: The First Israelis* (in Hebrew) (Jerusalem: Domino Press, 1984), 109.

29. Ibid., 110.

30. See pages 69–70.

31. Bialer, *Between East and West,* 124.

32. See pages 96–99.

33. Bialer, *Between East and West,* 64–65.

34. See pages 31–32.

35. *22nd Zionist Congress,* 610; Zionist Organization Executive, *The 23rd Zionist Congress Protocols* (Jerusalem: WZO, 1951), 178.

36. Zionist Actions Committee, 23 Aug. 1948; see also Dvora Hacohen, "Political Aspects of the Absorption of the Great Aliyah upon the Establishment of the State" (in Hebrew), *Ha-Zionut* 11 (1986):387–89.

37. Jewish Agency Executive, 22 June 1948, Central Zionist Archives 45/2, Jerusalem.

38. Ibid. See also Emanuel Neumann, *In the Arena* (New York: Herzl Press, 1976), 288–291; JAE, 18 Aug. 1948, CZA 45/2.

39. JAE, 19 Aug. 1948, CZA 45/2.

40. Ibid.

41. Yosef Gorni, *The Quest for Collective Identity* (in Hebrew) (Tel Aviv: Am Oved, 1990), 61–75.

42. JAE, 19 Aug. 1948, CZA 45/2; Zionist Actions Committee, 23 Aug. 1948, CZA S5/323.

43. Zionist Organization Executive, 19 Aug. 1948, CZA S5/323.

44. Ibid.

45. Ibid.

46. Neumann, *In the Arena,* 291.

47. The Zionist executive members who resigned were Ben-Gurion, Bernstein, Meirson (Meir), Fishman (Maimon), Shapira, and Shertok (Sharett). The new members were Goldstein, Grossman, Werfel (Raphael), Zerubavel, Luria, Zuckerman and Skolnik (Eshkol). Braginsky, Herman (Hermon), and Schectman were elected as deputy members.

48. Zionist Actions Committee, Sept. 1948, CZA S5/323.

49. The Zionist Actions Committee debated whether to include Mapam in the Zionist executive. The tendency was to exclude both Mapam and the Revisionists. Mapai found it difficult to

turn down Mapam, but was fiercely opposed to bringing in the Revisionists. The General Zionists, Mizrachi and Ha-Poel ha-Mizrachi, presented an ultimatum: they would accept Mapai only together with the Revisionists. Under pressure from this group, the committee finally decided to include both parties in the Zionist Executive.

50. Zionist Actions Committee, Sept. 1948, CZA S5/324.

51. *23rd Zionist Congress,* 264.

52. Ibid., 264–74.

53. Anita Shapira, ed., *Ha'apalah: Studies in the History of Illegal Immigration and the Remaining Remnant* (in Hebrew) (Tel Aviv: Am Oved, 1990); Dalia Ofer, *Escaping the Holocaust: Illegal Immigration to the Land of Israel, 1939–1944* (New York: Oxford Univ. Press, 1990).

54. JAE, 12 June–23 July 1949, CZA S/100/58b.

55. Zionist Actions Committee, 30 Aug. 1948, CZA S5/324.

56. Anita Shapira, *From the Dismissal of the Head of the National Staff until the Disbanding of the Palmah: Issues in the Struggle for Security Leadership, 1948* (in Hebrew) (Tel Aviv: Hakibbutz Hameuchad, 1985); Gelber, *Emergence of a Jewish Army.*

57. On Ben-Gurion's relationship with the Mossad, see Zeev Tzahor, "Ben-Gurion and Illegal Immigration, 1934–1948" (in Hebrew), in *East European Jewry: Between Holocaust and Rebirth* (in Hebrew), ed. Benyamin Pinkus (Kiryat Sede Boqer: Ben-Gurion Univ. and The Ben-Gurion Research Center, 1987), 422–47. See also below, note 61.

58. Yitzhak Raphael, *Lo Zakhiti be-Or Min ha-Hefker* (in Hebrew) (Tel Aviv: Yidanim, 1981), 50–51.

59. The Mossad worked clandestinely in those countries where the Zionist Organization was unwelcome and no Palestine office could be opened. From 1945 until the establishment of the state, 18,998 immigrants arrived legally, compared with 83,807 illegal immigrants. See *23rd Zionist Congress,* 180–89.

60. Raphael, *Lo Zakhiti be-Or Min ha-Hefker,* 50–55.

61. Zionist Actions Committee, Sept. 1948, CZA S5/323.

62. Raphael, *Lo Zakhiti be-Or Min ha-Hefker,* 51. At a meeting of the Zionist executive, Moshe Kolodny (Kol) remarked, "All matters pertaining to aliyah [are determined] not by immigration officers or by Jewish Agency emissaries but by the Mossad." See ZOE, 19 Aug. 1948, CZA 45/2.

63. Zionist Actions Committee, Sept. 1948, CZA S5/323; Merkaz Mapai, 24 Aug. 1948, Labor Party Archives 25/48, Beit Berl.

64. *23rd Zionist Congress,* 190; Comptroller's report, Aug. 1951, 86.

65. Raphael, *Lo Zakhiti be-Or Min ha-Hefker,* 56–61.

66. Raphael was accused of violating the agreement by choosing someone else to head the department instead of the agreed-upon candidate.

67. Raphael, *Lo Zakhiti be-Or Min ha-Hefker,* 51.

68. ZOE, 23 July 1949, CZA S100/58b; Zionist Actions Committee, Sept. 1948, CZA S5/323.

69. Merkaz Mapai, 10 Oct. 1948, LA 25/48.

70. *22nd Zionist Congress,* 159–60.

71. Ibid., 157–159.

72. ZOE, 4 Apr. 1949, CZA 46/2.

73. ISA 855/c, 3901, 1900/c, 13, 1901/d, 6600, Jerusalem.

74. Meir Gottesman, *Youth Aliyah: Continuity and Change* (in Hebrew) (Tel Aviv: Cherikover, 1987), 15–20.

75. Zionist Actions Committee, see note 61 above; Gottesman, *Youth Aliyah*, 20–22.

76. A total of 440,095 persons, or 87 percent of the electorate, cast their ballots for the Constituent Assembly. Twelve out of twenty-one lists won a seat. Mapai received the largest number of seats (46); followed by Mapam (19); the United Religious Front, representing four religious parties (16); Herut, established by the Jewish military organization, Etzel (14); the General Zionists (7); the Progressive Party (5); the Communist Party (4); the National Unity Party of Sephardim and Oriental Jews (4 each); the Lohamim party, led by Natan Friedman-Yellin (1); the Association of Yemenites, led by Zecharia Gluska (1); and WIZO, led by Rachel Cohen (1).

77. Ben-Gurion Diary, 25 Dec. 1948.

78. Ben-Gurion Diary, 8 Jan. 1949.

79. David Ben-Gurion, *The Missions of the Pioneering Spirit* (in Hebrew) (Jerusalem: Ayanot, 1952), 414.

80. David Ben-Gurion, "Uniqueness and Destiny" (in Hebrew), in *Israel Government Yearbook* (Jerusalem: Government Printing Office, 1951), 36.

81. *Divrei ha-Knesset* 1 (8 Mar. 1949).

82. On obedience to Ben-Gurion, see Teveth, *Kin'at David,* 2:243 and following. On Ben-Gurion's attitude towards military discipline, see Shapira, *Issues in the Struggle for Security Leadership,* 12.

83. Ben-Gurion Diary, 25 Dec. 1948.

84. Michael Keren, *Ben-Gurion and the Intellectuals: Power, Knowledge, and Charisma* (Dekalb, Ill.: Southern Illinois Univ. Press, 1983).

85. Mapai had forty-eight mandates, including two Arab delegates from the Nazareth Democratic party; the United Religious Front, sixteen; the Progressives, five; and the Sephardim, four.

86. In his letter to the president, Ben-Gurion cited this as the main reason for excluding Mapam. See Natan Yanai, *Political Crises in Israel* (in Hebrew) (Jerusalem: Keter, 1982), 76–77.

87. See above, note 56.

88. There were twelve cabinet members. Mapai held seven portfolios: Ben-Gurion, prime minister and minister of defense; Dov Joseph, minister of rationing and supply; Golda Meir, minister of labor and insurance; Eliezer Kaplan, minister of finance; David Remez, minister of transport; Zalman Shazar, minister of education and culture; and Moshe Sharett, minister of foreign affairs. The National Religious Front held three portfolios: Rabbi Hacohen-Maimon Fishman, minister of religion; Moshe Shapira, minister of immigration; and Rabbi Yitzhak Meir Levin, minister of welfare. The Progressives held one portfolio: Pinhas Rosen, minister of justice; and the Sephardim, one portfolio: Bekhor Shitrit, minister of police.

89. Prime minister's presentation of his cabinet and its policy, *Divrei ha-Knesset* 1 (8 Mar. 1949):60–63.

90. Merkaz Mapai, 3 Dec. 1947, LPA 23/47; see also Hacohen, "Absorption of the Great Aliyah," 383.

91. Hacohen, "Absorption of the Great Aliyah"; see also Dvora Hacohen, "The Law of Return as an Embodiment of the Link between Israel and the Jews in the Diaspora," *Journal of Israeli History* 19, no. 1 (1999):61–89.

92. David Ben-Gurion, *The Eternity of Israel* (in Hebrew) (Tel Aviv: Ayanot, 1964), 37.

93. The Law of Return–1950 was passed on 5 July 1950. See *Sefer ha-Hukim* 51 (6 July 1950); see also Hacohen, "The Law of Return" 1998, 61–89.

94. *23rd Zionist Congress,* 189–90.

95. ISA 17/kaf.

96. Ibid.

97. The Aliyah Committee was established by the Provisional State Council on 9 Sept. 1948. Its members, representing the different parties, were: Berl Repetor, committee chairman—Mapam; Binyamin Mintz—Poalei Agudat Yisrael; Zvi Segal—Revisionists; Eliyahu Dobkin and Mordechai Shattner—Mapai; Moshe Kol—General Zionists; Zerah Warhaftig—Ha-Poel ha-Mizrahi.

98. Raphael, Zionist Executive, 10 Jan. 1949, CZA 46/2.

99. Aliyah Committee, Sept.-Oct. 1948, ISA 17/kaf.

100. *Ha-Aretz,* 7 Nov. 1948; *Ha-Tzofeh,* 7 Nov. 1948.

101. *Ha-Mashkif,* 7 Nov. 1948.

102. Zionist Actions Committee, 23 Aug. 1949, CZA S5/323.

103. Ibid., 6 Dec. 1948.

104. JAE, 10 Oct. and 22 Nov. 1948, CZA 46/1.

105. *Davar,* 15 Nov. 1948.

106. ZOE, 20 Dec. 1948, CZA 46/1.

107. ZOE, 10 Jan. 1949, CZA 46/2.

108. On the health of the immigrants, see chapter 4.

109. Mossad le-Aliyah Bet in Paris to Raphael, 21 Apr. 1949, CZA S6/6523; Raphael to Mossad le-Aliyah Bet, 25 Apr. 1949, CZA S6/6523.

110. Shimon Barad, "Zionist Activity in Egypt, 1917–1952" (in Hebrew), *Studies in the Zionist and Pioneering Movements in the Islamic Countries* 2 (1989):118.

111. Raphael to Berl Locker, 13 May 1949, CZA S6/6523.

112. Letter from Rabbi Frank, 29 May 1949, CZA S6/6523.

113. Raphael to Rabbi Gold and S. Z. Shragai, 10 June 1949, CZA S6/6523.

114. JAE, 19 June 1949, CZA S6/6523.

115. Weinstein to Raphael, 20 July 1949, CZA S6/6523.

116. Nahum in Rome to Raphael, 6 Nov. 1949, CZA S6/6523; Raphael to Rome, 7 Nov. 1949, CZA S6/6523.

117. Mossad le-Aliyah Bet in Paris to Raphael, 4 Dec. 1949, CZA S6/6523.

118. Ben-Zvi to Raphael, 4 Dec. 1949, CZA S6/6523.

119. Zionist Actions Committee, 23 Aug. 1948, CZA S5/324.

120. See appendix E.

2. Policy Put to the Test

1. *23rd Zionist Congress,* 197–201.

2. See appendix 1.

3. *23rd Zionist Congress,* 214.

4. See appendix A.

5. CZA S6/6502.

6. *23rd Zionist Congress,* 208–09.

7. Yosef Tzadok, *In the Storms of Yemen* (in Hebrew) (Tel Aviv: Am Oved, 1956).

8. JAE, 5 June 1949, CZA S100/58.

9. JAE, 18 July 1949, CZA S100/59.

10. Ibid.

11. Ibid.

12. Joint Distribution Committee aid to Israel-bound emigrants was directed by Joseph Schwartz; Harry Vitales was the Middle East supervisor; both were Americans.

13. JAE, 18 Aug. 1949, CZA S100/59b.

14. Avraham Sternberg, *When the People Gathers* (in Hebrew) (Tel Aviv: Hakibbutz Hameuchad, 1973), 82.

15. Dr. Meir, memorandum dated 20 Sept. 1949, ISA 4264/57.

16. Most of the country's newspapers, 8 Nov. 1949.

17. Ben-Gurion, *Divrei ha-Knesset* 3 (7 Nov. 1949):1.

18. Yeshayahu to Ben-Gurion, 22 Nov. 1949, ISA 5558/c, 3885.

19. Ben-Gurion Diary, 17 Sept. 1949.

20. Ben-Gurion Diary, *Divrei ha-Knesset* 3 (21 Nov. 1949):128.

21. Barzilai to Foreign Minister, 19 Sept. 1949, ISA 5556/c.

22. Ibid.

23. JAE, 6 Oct. and 8 Nov. 1949, CZA S100/60.

24. JAE, 4 Oct. 1949.

25. JAE, 9 Oct. 1949.

26. Ibid.

27. JAE, 26 Dec. 1949; 27 Mar. 1950.

28. Ibid.

29. Ben-Gurion Diary, 20 Sept. 1949.

30. Ben-Gurion to Gruenbaum, 28 Mar. 1950, ISA 5556/c.

31. Report of Polish Aliyah Committee, CZA XII/362.

32. Report of Aliyah Committee to 23rd Zionist Congress, 198.

33. See note 31 above.

34. Ibid.

35. *23rd Zionist Congress,* 198.

36. Raphael to Shragai, 30 May 1950, CZA S59.

37. Coordinating Committee, 4 June, 9 July, 6 and 28 Aug. 1950, CZA S43/17.

38. Avriel to Josephthal, 17 June 1950, CZA S43/236.

39. Shragai to JAE, 11 July 1950, CZA S43/236.

40. Coordinating Committee, 6 Aug. 1950, CZA S43/17.

41. Ibid.

42. Ibid.

43. Shlomo Hillel, "The Steps that Brought about the Mass Aliyah from Iraq" (in Hebrew), in *From Babylon to Jerusalem* (in Hebrew), ed. Zvi Yehuda (Tel Aviv: Ha-Mahon le-Moreshet Yehudei Bavel, 1981), 35; Shlomo Hillel, *Operation Babylon* (London: Fontana, 1989).

44. Estimates vary from one report to another. Also see ISA 5556/c.

45. Reports of Mossad le-Aliyah Bet from Iraq beginning in March 1950, CZA S6/6533.

46. Mossad operatives in Iraq, 5 Mar. 1950, CZA S6/6533.

47. Ibid., 7, 9, and 10 Mar. 1950.

48. Ibid., 11, 13, and 16 Mar. 1950.

49. Ibid., 28 May 1950; Hillel, *Operation Babylon.*

50. Ben-Gurion Diary, 6 May 1950.

51. *Yediot Aharonot,* 21 May 1950.

52. Ibid., 23 May 1950.

53. Mossad le-Aliyah Bet to Raphael, 14 Mar. 1941, CZA S6/6531.

54. Ibid.

55. 22 Mar. 1951, CZA S48/17.

56. CZA S6/5531.

57. 12 Aug. 1949, ISA 5558/c, 3899.

58. Immigrant hostels were opened in Kiryat Shmuel, Atlit, Bat-Galim, Tel-Aviv, Ra'anana, Rehovot, Kfar Azar, Netanya, Hadera (Neve Haim and Agrobank), and Holon. See *23rd Zionist Congress,* 292–93.

59. Zionist Actions Committee, May 1949, 10.

60. Jewish Agency Kelitah Department, *Eleven Years of Absorption* (Tel-Aviv, 1959).

61. Chaim Darin-Drabkin, *Housing and Absorption in Israel* (in Hebrew) (Tel Aviv: Gadish, 1955), 19.

62. Kelitah Department report to 23rd Zionist Congress, 269.

63. Ibid.

64. Ibid.

65. See above, chapter 1.

66. *Ha-Aretz,* 1 Dec. 1948.

67. Ibid,

68. Kelitah Department report to 23rd Zionist Congress, 298.

69. Ibid., 299.

70. Kiryat Eliyahu accommodated 2,250 olim; Kiryat Motzkin, 1,200; Kiryat Shmuel, 1,100; Bat-Galim, 1,000, Atlit, 3,900; Netanya, 2,900; Binyamina, 2,700; Ra'anana, 2,100; Beit Lid, 1,500; Rehovot, 1,250. The other camps had fewer than 1,000 olim.

71. At the end of March 1949, there were forty buildings and 1,056 cabins for 32,000 immigrants (57 percent of all camp residents). Another 24,000 immigrants (43 percent of all camp residents) were put up in tents.

72. Y. Weissberger, *The Gate of Aliyah: Diary of Mass Immigration, 1947–1957* (in Hebrew) (Jerusalem: n.p., 1986), 75.

73. Ibid., 77.

74. Ibid., 75.

75. Ibid., 71.

76. Aliyah Department report to 23rd Zionist Congress, 208–10.

77. Ibid.

78. The kitchen at the Agrobank camp in Hadera had supplied food to 400 persons; at Kiryat Eliyahu, to 2,000 persons; and at Rehovot, 1,000 persons.

3. Financial Crisis and Policy Implications

1. Barkai, *Beginnings of Israeli Economy,* 21–32.

2. Menachem Kaufman, *An Ambiguous Partnership: Non-Zionists and Zionists in America, 1939–1948* (Jerusalem: Magnes Press, 1991); Menachem Kaufman, "The Jewish Community of Palestine as Viewed by Non-Zionist American Jewry During the Holocaust and Pre-State Period" (in Hebrew), *Cathedra* 19 (1981):205–06.

3. Neumann, *In the Arena,* 292.

4. Kaufman, *Non-Zionists and Zionists in America,* 44–50.

5. Ben-Gurion Diary, 21 Oct. 1948.

6. Zionist Actions Committee, Aug. 1948; Neumann, *In the Arena,* 288–95.

7. JAE, 19 Aug. 1948, CZA 45/2.

8. Ben-Gurion Diary, 22–25 Oct. 1948.

9. Ben-Gurion Diary, 25 Oct. 1948.

10. JAE meetings in October, November, and December 1948; January and February 1949, CZA 45/2, 46/2.

11. Neumann continued to serve as the president of the Zionist Organization of America until the summer of 1949.

12. Report of Finance Department to Zionist Actions Committee, May 1949.

13. Ibid.

14. CZA S43/42.

15. Landauer, 2 May 1950, CZA S41/101.

16. Barkai, *Beginnings of Israeli Economy,* 35–39.

17. Foreign policy documents, vol. 6, 1951, 3.

18. Ben-Gurion, 2 Aug. 1950, CZA S43/17.

19. Coordinating Committee, 27 Aug. 1950, CZA S43/17.

20. Dvora Hacohen, *From Fantasy to Reality: Ben-Gurion's Plan for Mass Immigration Between 1942 and 1945* (in Hebrew) (Tel Aviv: Ministry of Defense Press, 1994); Dvora Hacohen, "Ben-Gurion and the Second World War: Plans for Mass Immigration to Palestine," in *Jews and Messianism in the Modern Era: Studies in Contemporary Jewry,* ed. Jonathan Frankel, (Oxford: Oxford Univ. Press, 1991), 247–68.

21. P. Eliezer Shinar, *Emburdened with Feelings: Israel-German Relations, 1951–1966* (in Hebrew) (Tel Aviv: Schocken, 1967), 16–17.

22. Adenauer to Nahum Goldmann, chairman of the Conference on Jewish Claims against Germany, 6 Dec. 1951. See Shinar, *Israel-German Relations,* 22.

23. *Divrei ha-Knesset,* 9 Jan. 1952.

24. JAE, 20 Dec. 1948, CZA 46/1.

25. Ibid.

26. 20 Dec. 1948, Aliyah Committee, Provisional Council of State.

27. *Yediot Aharonot,* 22 Mar. 1949.

28. *Ha-Mashkif,* 25 Mar. 1949.

29. *Ha-Aretz,* 11 Feb. 1949; *Yediot Aharonot,* 17 Feb. 1949; *Ha-Mashkif,* 22 Mar. 1949.

30. M. Kremer, *Ha-Aretz,* 8 Apr. 1949.

31. *Ha-Mishmar,* 16 Mar. 1949.

32. *Ha-Aretz,* 8 and 15 Apr. 1949; *Yediot Aharonot* and *Ma'ariv,* 26 Apr. 1949.

33. A. Gelblum, *Ha-Aretz,* 13 Apr. 1949.

34. *Ha-Aretz,* 14 Apr. 1949.

35. Ibid., 24 Apr. 1949.

36. Ibid., 25 and 28 Apr. 1949.

37. JAE, 29 Mar. 1949, CZA 46/2. See also Hacohen, "Absorption of the Great Aliyah," 396.

38. JAE, 4 Apr. 1949.

39. In April-December 1949, the Aliyah Department anticipated the arrival of 46,000 persons from DP camps in Germany and 30,000 from North Africa. See its report to Zionist Actions Committee, May 1949, 11.

40. Zionist Federation in Munich to Israeli government, 22 Apr. 1949, ISA 5557/43c, 3872.

41. JAE, 21 Mar. 1949, CZA 46/2.

42. Mossad le-Aliyah Bet in Paris to Raphael, 17 and 21 Apr. 1949, CZA S6/6459.

43. Ibid., 17 Apr. 1949.

44. Raphael to JAE, 21 Apr. 1949, CZA S6/6459.

45. Mossad le-Aliyah Bet in Paris to Raphael, 21 Apr. 1949, CZA S6/6459.

46. Raphael's reports to JAE, 16 and 24 May 1949, CZA S6/6459.

47. Raphael's announcement to the press, 21 June 1949.

48. Reports of Mossad le-Aliyah Bet in Paris, CZA S6/6459.

49. *Divrei ha-Knesset* 1 (26 Apr. 1949):399–400.

50. Ibid.

51. Ben-Gurion Diary, 22 Sept. 1949.

52. Ben-Gurion Diary, 28 Sept. 1949.

53. Ben-Gurion Diary, 2 and 30 Sept. 1949.

54. JAE, 4, 6, and 9 Oct. 1949, CZA S100/60.

55. Ibid.

56. Raphael to Mossad le-Aliyah Bet in Paris, 7 Oct. 1949, CZA S6/6459.

57. Telegrams to Raphael, 26 Oct.–7 Nov. 1949, CZA S6/6459.

58. Barfel to Raphael, 29 Oct. 1949, CZA S6/6459.

59. Goldmann to government secretary, 20 Nov. 1949, CZA S6/6459.

60. Raphael to Locker, 16 Oct. 1949, CZA S6/6459.

61. *Divrei ha-Knesset* 1 (26 Apr. 1949):399.

62. These figures relate to the number of immigrants who remained in the country. See Roberto Bachi and Baruch Gil, "Changes in Immigration and in the Yishuv, 1948–1951" (in Hebrew), in *Shivat Zion* 1953:19–28.

63. *Divrei ha-Knesset* 3 (7 Nov. 1949):8.

64. *Ma'ariv,* 17 Oct. 1949.

65. Ruth Guber's report on the immigrant camps, 12 Aug. 1949, ISA 5558/c, 3894.

66. *Divrei ha-Knesset,* 4 (7 Nov. 1949):1.

67. From January 1950, CZA S6/6459.

68. JAE, 15 Jan. 1950, CZA S100/63.

69. Zionist Actions Committee, Apr. 1950, 19–28.

70. Meeting of ministerial committee and chairman of the JAE, 8 May 1950, CZA S41/101.

71. 8 May 1950, CZA S41/101.

72. Letter of protest and telegrams from Sao Paulo (10 May 1950), from New York (9 June 1950), and elsewhere, CZA S41/101.

73. Sharett to Coordinating Committee, 18 June 1950, CZA S43/42.

74. Mossad le-Aliyah Bet in Paris to Raphael, 20 June 1950, CZA S6/6460.

75. Coordinating Committee, 9 July 1950, CZA S43/17.

76. Ibid.

77. Ibid.

78. Notes and letters from Iraq to Aliyah Department, 10 and 23 Aug. 1950, CZA S6/6532.

79. Sharett to Coordinating Committee, 28 Aug. 1950; Hillel, *Operation Babylon,* 313–14.

80. Mossad le-Aliyah Bet to JA, 18 Sept. and 2 Nov. 1950, CZA S6/6532.

81. 22 Oct. 1950, CZA S6/6532.

82. In January 4,000 immigrants arrived, followed by 6,000 in February. See Malben to Raphael, 8 Feb. 1951, CZA S6/6532; Coordinating Committee, 30 Jan. and 22 Mar. 1951, CZA S43.

83. Coordinating Committee, 30 Jan. 1950, CZA S43/17.

84. *Divrei ha-Knesset* 6:2035–48. See Hacohen, "The Law of Return," 61–89.

85. *Divrei ha-Knesset,* 6:2037.

86. *Sefer ha-Hukim* 51 (6 July 1950):159. See Hacohen, "The Law of Return," 61–89.

87. The debate over "who is a Jew" erupted in 1958, in the wake of this law. See Avner H. Shaki, *Who is a Jew in the Laws of the State of Israel?* (in Hebrew) (Jerusalem: Mossad Harav Kook, 1977), 143–72.

88. *Divrei ha-Knesset* 6:2041.

89. Shapira, Zionist Actions Committee, 23 Aug. 1948, CZA S5/324.

90. Dvora Hacohen, "The Plan for Direct Absorption of Mass Immigration During the 1950s and its Consequences" (in Hebrew), in *Studies in Zionism: The Yishuv and the State of Israel,* ed. Pinhas Ginossar (Sde Boker: Ben-Gurion Research Center, Ben-Gurion Univ. of the Negev Press, 1991), 247–68.

4. From Immigrant Camps to *Ma'abarot*: Housing, Employment, and Health

1. Hacohen, "Ben-Gurion and the Second World War," 264–89.

2. Ibid.

3. Report, *22nd Zionist Congress,* 158; *23rd Zionist Congress,* 293.

4. See appendix C.

5. David Zaslavsky, *Immigrant Housing in Israel* (in Hebrew) (Tel Aviv: Am Oved, 1954), 8.

6. Darin-Drabkin, *Housing and Absorption in Israel,* 39.

7. Ibid., 45.

8. ISA 5513/c, 3016.

9. Darin-Drabkin, *Housing and Absorption in Israel,* 42.

10. In January 1953 Amidar became the proprietor and administrator of housing built by the government and the Jewish Agency. It was responsible for rental and sale of these buildings.

11. ISA 5513/c, 3016.

12. Coordinating Committee, S41/101.

13. Sikron, *Immigration to Israel,* 17.

14. In 1932–1938 only 36 percent of the adult immigrants were single. See Sikron, *Immigration to Israel,* 61.

15. Ibid., 42–43, 62.

16. Ibid., 42–43.

17. Zionist Actions Committee, 23 Aug. 1948, CZA S323.

18. JAE, 6 Dec. 1949, CZA 46/1.

19. Report to JAE, 10 Jan. 1949, CZA 46/2.

20. Report of medical delegation in Marseilles, 1949, CZA S43/118.

21. OSE—Russian acronym for *Obshchestvo Zaravookhraneniya Yevreyev* (Society for the Protection of the Health of the Jews), launched in St. Petersburg in 1912. Over the years OSE developed into a multibranched health and welfare organization; it was active in the ghettos of Europe during and after the Holocaust.

22. CZA 46/1.

23. Aliyah Department report to Zionist Actions Committee, 5–15 May 1949, 6.

24. Report of Dr. Meir, director-general of the Ministry of Health, 23 May 1949, ISA 5558/c.

25. See chapter 2.

26. JAE, 29 Mar. 1949, CZA 26/2.

27. ISA 5558/c.

28. Roberto Bachi, "The Demographic Development of Israel" (in Hebrew), *Riv'on le-Kalkala* 2 (1955):379–92.

29. Y. Rokah, 18 May 1949, *Divrei ha-Knesset* 1:35.

30. Weissberger, *The Gate of Aliyah,* 80.

31. I am indebted to my friend, Professor Yitzhak Halbrecht, a pioneer of medicine in the early years of the state, for data on the health of the immigrants.

32. Ruth Bondi, *Sheba: Everyman's Doctor* (in Hebrew) (Tel Aviv: Zmora Bitan Modan, 1981), 127.

33. Weissberger, *The Gate of Aliyah,* 91–93.

34. Aliyah Department report to Zionist Actions Committee in Jerusalem, May 1949.

35. *Ha-Aretz,* 17 and 19 Apr. 1949.

36. *Divrei ha-Knesset* 2 (10 Aug. 1949):1302.

37. Ibid.

38. *Ha-Boker,* 7 Aug. 1949.

39. Bondi, *Sheba,* 132.

40. *Divrei ha-Knesset* 1 (18 May 1949):536–37.

41. *22nd Zionist Congress,* 159–60.

42. Bondi, *Sheba,* 126.

43. This agreement was reached at a Jewish Agency meeting on 16 March 1948. Among the participants were Dr. Meir of Kupat Holim Klalit, Melamdovitz of Kupat Holim Leumit, Katzenelson of Kupat Holim Amamit, Josephthal of the Kelitah Department, and Dr. Grushka of the Immigrant Health Service. See ISA 5558/c, 3899.

44. Bondi, *Sheba,* 117–65.

45. Yitzhak Raphael, "The Struggle over Mass Immigration" (in Hebrew), in *Yidan, Immigrants and Ma'abarot,* ed. M. Naor (Jerusalem: Yad Izhak Ben-Zvi, 1987), 19–30.

46. Dr. S. Zalodkovsky to Ben-Gurion, 30 Nov. 1951, ISA 5558/c, 3902.

47. Public Services Committee, 2 Nov. 1951, ISA 5558/c, 3902.

48. Coordinating Committee, 18 Apr. 1951, CZA S43/117.

49. JAE, 27 Mar. 1950; Alex Bein, *Immigration and Settlement in the State of Israel* (in Hebrew) (Tel Aviv: Am Oved and Ha-Sifria ha-Zionit, WZO, 1982), 67; Levi Eshkol, *Be-Hevlei Hitnahalut* (The travails of settlement) (Tel Aviv: Ayanot, 1958), 218–23.

50. Zaslavsky, *Immigrant Housing in Israel,* 74.

51. Knesset Working Committee, 18 July 1950, ISA 17/kaf.

52. Coordinating Committee, 25 June 1950, CZA S43/17.

53. Ibid., 23 July 1950.

54. In August 18,803 immigrants arrived, followed by 16,190 in September and 19,356 in October.

55. Josephthal, Knesset Working Committee, 28 Nov. 1950, Knesset Archives.

56. Ibid.

57. Ibid.

5. The Conflict over Education

1. Rachel Elboim-Dror, *Hebrew Education in Eretz Israel* (in Hebrew) (Jerusalem: Yad Itzhak Ben-Zvi, 1986), 42–50; Dan Horowitz and Moshe Lissak, *Origins of the Israeli Polity: Palestine under the Mandate* (Chicago: Univ. of Chicago Press, 1978), 120–27; Yonathan Shapiro, *The Organization of Power: The Historical Ahdut ha-Avodah* (in Hebrew) (Tel Aviv: Am Oved, 1975), 9–10; Zvi Lamm, "Ideological Tensions: Struggles over the Goals of Education" (in Hebrew), in *Education in Israel,* ed. Chaim Ormian (Jerusalem: Ministry of Education and Culture, 1973), 71–84.

2. Lamm, "Struggles over the Goals of Education," 71–84; Yosef Bentwich, *Education in the State of Israel* (in Hebrew) (Tel Aviv: Y. Chachik, 1960), 35–38; Walter Ackerman, Arik Carmon, and David Zucker, eds., *Education in an Evolving Society* (in Hebrew) (Jerusalem: Hakibbutz Hameuchad, Mossad Van Leer, 1985), 120–30; Eliezer Don-Yehiya, "Cooperation and Conflict Between Political Camps" (in Hebrew) (Ph.D. diss., Hebrew Univ. of Jerusalem, 1977), 422–68.

3. Just before the state was established, Agudat Israel was promised that its schools would remain intact. See letter of Jewish Agency, 19 June 1947. See also Menahem Friedman, "The Chronicle of the Status Quo: Religion and State in Israel" (in Hebrew), in *Transition from "Yishuv" to State, 1947–1949: Continuity and Change* (in Hebrew), ed. Varda Pilovsky (Haifa: Herzl Institute for Research in Zionism, Haifa Univ., 1990), 66–67.

4. Hazan, *Divrei ha-Knesset* 9:1664.

5. Ben-Gurion, *Divrei ha-Knesset* 1:136. Also see Shimon Reshef, "Ben-Gurion and State Education" (in Hebrew), *Cathedra* 43 (1987):91–114.

6. Testimony of B. Ben-Yehuda to Committee of Inquiry on Immigrant Education, ISA 5543/c, 3631.

7. Ibid.

8. Ibid.

9. Sikron, *Immigration to Israel,* 47; *Israel Government Yearbook* (Jerusalem: Government Printing Office, 1950), 159–61.

10. ISA 43, 5558/c, 3901; *Israel Government Yearbook* 1951, 311.

11. ISA 1171/C.

12. Ibid.

13. *Israel Government Yearbook* 1949, 98–101.

14. Cultural Absorption Department survey, Ministry of Education and Culture, 1951, government bulletins, ISA 10/950/12.

15. Ibid.

16. Protocol, Committee of Inquiry on Immigrant Education, 333–34, ISA 5543/c, 3631.

17. Protocol, Knesset Education and Culture Committee, 28 Dec. 1949, KA.

18. Ibid.

19. Zerah Warhaftig asked the minister of education to address the Knesset on the issue of coercion and pressure on religious parents. Protests and disputes on that matter were reported in newspapers.

20. Report, Committee of Inquiry on Immigrant Education, ISA 5543/c; Don-Yehiya, "Cooperation and Conflict Between Political Camps," 525–55; Moshe Unna, *In Separate Ways: The Religious Parties in Israel* (in Hebrew) (Alon Shevut: Yad Shapira, 1984), 187–221; Zvi Zameret, *The Melting Pot: The Frumkin Commission on the Education of Immigrant Children (1950)* (in Hebrew) (Kiryat Sdeh Boker: Ben-Gurion Research Center, Ben-Gurion Univ. of the Negev Press, 1993).

21. ISA 5543/c, 3631. Judge Gad Frumkin was chairman, and the committee members were Abraham Elmaleh, Itzhak Ben-Zvi, Rabbi Kalman Kahana, and Rabbi Abraham Shaag. MK Israel Yeshayahu served as secretary.

22. Ibid.

23. Ibid.

24. Report, Committee of Inquiry on Immigrant Education, 1950, 113–14.

25. *Divrei ha-Knesset* 8:1037–1102.

26. Knesset session, 7 June 1950.

27. ISA 43, 5543/c.

28. Interview with Moshe Ben-Nachum, March 1982. See also Eyal Kafkafi, "The Lost Prospect of a Religious Labor School Network" (in Hebrew), *Medina Mimshal ve-Yehasim Benleumiyim* 31 (1990):77–100.

29. Ben-Gurion, *Divrei ha-Knesset* 8 (14 Feb. 1951):1101.

30. Don-Yehiya, "Cooperation and Conflict Between Political Camps," 769.

31. Unna, *Religious Parties in Israel,* 219–20.

32. ISA 43, 5543/c, 3631, II.

33. Eliakim Rubinstein, "From Yishuv to State: Institutions and Parties" (in Hebrew), in *The Jewish National Home: From the Balfour Declaration to Independence,* ed. Binyamin Eliav (Jerusalem: Keter, 1979), 234–41; Shevach Weiss, *Local Government in Israel* (in Hebrew) (Tel Aviv: Am Oved, 1986), 16–17.

34. Giora Goldberg, "Local Elections" (in Hebrew), in *Local Government in Israel* (in Hebrew), ed. Daniel J. Elazar and Chaim Kalchaim (Jerusalem: Jerusalem Center for Public Affairs, 1987), 90.

35. Based on figures in *Israel Government Yearbook* 1952, 370, Table 9.

36. Goldberg, "Local Elections," 90, note 33.

37. Immigrant camp residents, immigrants who did not meet the minimum residency requirements, and immigrants who had died or left the country.

38. J. Sapir, *Divrei ha-Knesset* 2 (27 July 1949):1174.

39. Ibid.

40. Z. Warhaftig, *Divrei ha-Knesset* 3 (17 Jan. 1950):547–73.

41. Goldberg, "Local Elections," 91.

42. *Israel Government Yearbook* 1951, 12.

43. Ibid., 3–4.

44. Those eligible for the vote were immigrants over the age of eighteen who had reached Israel before 1 Mar. 1951.

45. The law was passed on 12 Apr. 1951.

46. *Divrei ha-Knesset* 9:1772–2096.

47. 19 June 1950, ISA 1900/c.

48. Dov Rosen, *Ma'abarot and Immigrant Settlements from the Viewpoint of the Interior Ministry* (in Hebrew) (Jerusalem: Misrad Ha-Pnim, 1985), 36, 56; 22 June and 30 July 1950, ISA 1900/c.

49. 5 Jan. 1951, ISA 1900/c.

50. 17 Oct. 1950, ISA 50, 1900/c.

51. 27 Oct. and 17 Nov. 1950, ISA 50, 1900/c.

52. Kelitah Department to Interior Ministry, ISA 50, 1900/c.

53. *Ha-shilton ha-Mekomi be-Yisrael* 14, 1951.

54. 8 Dec. 1950, ISA 50, 1900/c.

55. 13 Feb. 1950, ISA 50, 1900/c.

56. Interior Ministry circular to local councils, 1 and 4 Dec. 1950, 8 Jan. 1951.

57. Interministerial committee report, ISA 43, 5558/c, 3903.

58. CZA S41/281; *Ma'ariv,* 7 Dec. 1950.

59. Ha-Poel ha-Mizrachi—8 mandates; Ha-Mizrachi—2; Agudat Israel—3; Poalei Agudat Israel—2.

60. Report, 10th Convention of Ha-Poel ha-Mizrachi, 167–68; Unna, *Religious Parties in Israel,* 218.

61. David Ben-Gurion was the prime minister and minister of defense; Levi Eshkol, minister of agriculture and development; Joseph Burg, minister of health; Ben-Zion Dinaburg, minister of education and culture; Dov Joseph, minister of commerce and industry and minister of justice; Rabbi I. M. Levine, minister of welfare; Golda Meir, minister of labor; Peretz Naftali, minister without portfolio; D. Z. Pinkas, minister of transport; Eliezer Kaplan, minister of finance; Bekhor Shitrit, minister of police; Moshe Shapira, minister of the interior and minister of religion; and Moshe Sharett, foreign minister.

6. Confronting the Old-Timers

1. Eliezer Brutzkus, "Dreams that Became Cities" (in Hebrew), in *Immigrants and Maabarot* (Hebrew), ed. Mordechai Naor (Jerusalem: Yad Ben-Zvi, 1987), 133–34.

2. Ibid., 140.

3. Jewish Agency Kelitah Department, *Eleven Years of Absorption,* 41.

4. Zaslavsky, *Immigrant Housing in Israel,* 12; Darin-Drabkin, *Housing and Absorption in Israel,* 32.

5. See notes 3, 40.

6. Brutzkus, "Dreams that Become Cities," 135.

7. Interministerial report, ISA 43, 5558/c, 3903.

8. ISA 109, 2348/c, 6143.

9. ISA 50, 1964/c, 6361; 1900/c; 109; 2348/c, 6143.

10. ISA 22 Mar. 1950.

11. ISA 1900/c, 600; 702; 57.

12. Iraqi immigrants totaled 14,326 in March, 20,340 in April, 22,000 in May, and 14,661 in June. Based on figures of Central Bureau of Statistics, *Israel Government Yearbook 1952–53,* 177.

13. ISA 2348/c; 1900/c, 6600.

14. Zaslavsky, *Immigrant Housing in Israel,* 90; Darin-Drabkin, *Housing and Absorption in Israel,* 75.

15. ISA 50, 1900/c.

16. See pages 213–16.

17. ISA 50, 1900/c.

18. 24 Jan. 1951, ISA 50, 1900/c, 6600.

19. ISA 50, 5558/c; 1900/c.

20. 10 Apr. 1951, Knesset Public Services Committee, ISA 60/kaf.

21. ISA 1900/c, 6500.

22. 2 Apr. 1951, ISA 1901/c.

23. 9 May 1952, ISA 1900/c.

24. ISA 5558/c, 3902.

25. 26 Oct. 1951, IDF Survey Committee Report, IDFA, DH 8.

26. 17 July 1950; ISA 2348/c, 6143.

27. File of telegrams and letters, Kfar Saba Archives 1951.

28. 18 Apr. 1951, Coordinating Committee, CZA S43/117.

29. 10 Apr. 1951, Knesset Public Services Committee, ISA 60/kaf; Kfar Saba Archives, 13 Feb. 1950.

30. Municipal convention, 13 Dec. 1951, BGA.

31. Zeev Tzur, *Kibbutz Ha-Me'uhad in the Settlement of Eretz Israel* (in Hebrew) (Tel Aviv: Hakibbutz Hameuchad, 1982), 2:368–69; Chaim Gvati, *A Century of Settlement: The History of Jewish Agricultural Settlement in Israel* (in Hebrew) (Tel Aviv: Hakibbutz Hameuchad, 1981), 1:9–19; 2:53–54, 139.

32. Gvati, *A Century of Settlement,* 2:137–38; Tzur, Hakibbutz Hameuchad, 2:350; Baruch Kanari, *Hakibbutz Hameuchad: Mission and Reality* (in Hebrew) (Tel Aviv: Hakibbutz Hameuchad, 1989), 393–95.

33. Knesset Public Services Committee, Nov. 1950.

34. Yitzhak Koren, *Ingathering of Exiles in their Inheritance: A History of the Immigrant Moshavim in Israel* (in Hebrew) (Tel Aviv: Am Oved, 1964), 64–66; Gvati, *A Century of Settlement,* 2:28–32, 53.

35. Smadar Ottolenghi and Rachel Wilkansky, *Legal and Organizational Problems in the Structure of the Public Council* (in Hebrew) (Tel Aviv: Tel Aviv Univ., Merkaz Pinhas Sapir, 1985), 5–6.

36. Arie Sharon, *Physical Planning in Israel* (in Hebrew) (Tel Aviv, 1951), 13.

37. ISA 50, 1900/c, 6500.

38. Ibid.

39. ISA 50, 1902, 33.

40. 25 June 1951, ISA 1900/c, 6600.

41. ISA 1902, 15.

42. Dec. 1950, ISA 1902, 15.

43. Ottolenghi and Wilkansky, *Legal and Organizational Problems*, 2.

44. Ibid., 6; Law Codes 1950, 149, clause 8.

45. Knesset Internal Affairs Committee, 28 Mar. 1950, Knesset Archive.

46. Ibid., 27 Mar. 1951.

47. Department of Local Government, Misrad Ha-Penim to Josephthal, 26 Feb. 1951, ISA 1900/c.

48. 29 Jan. 1952, ISA 1900/c.

49. 12 Jan. 1952, ISA 1900/c.

50. ISA 5558/c.

51. Interministerial Committee's report, July 1954, ISA 5558/c, 3903.

52. ISA 5558/c, 3903, 24.

53. ISA 1901/c; Kfar Saba Archives, Hadera Archives, Petah Tikva Archives.

54. Rosen to Interior Minister, 2 Apr. 1952, ISA 1900/c.

55. Leonard Pye, "Armies in the Process of Political Modernization," in *The Role of the Military in Underdeveloped Countries*, ed. James T. Johnson (Princeton, N.J.: Princeton Univ. Press, 1962), 69–91.

56. Amos Perlmutter, *Military and Politics in Israel: Nation Building and Role Expansion* (London: F. Cass, 1969), 54–68; Yoram Peri, *Between Battles and Ballots: Israeli Military in Politics* (Cambridge: Cambridge Univ. Press, 1983), 19; Mordechai Bar-On, *Education Process in Israel Defense Forces* (Tel Aviv, 1966), 8.

57. Ben-Gurion, *The Eternity of Israel*, 7–41, 42–78.

58. Ben-Gurion, Zionist Actions Committee, April 1950, CZA S5/327; Ben-Gurion, *The Reborn State of Israel*, 262–67, 389–99.

59. Peri, *Israeli Military in Politics*, 10–11.

60. Ben-Gurion, *The Eternity of Israel*, 7–41.

61. Ben-Gurion, "Uniqueness and Destiny," 43.

62. Ben-Gurion, *The Reborn State of Israel*, 390.

63. Ben-Gurion, *The Reborn State of Israel*, 391. Also see Ben-Gurion, *Divrei ha-Knesset* 2:1563–72.

64. National Security Service Law, 1949, *Divrei ha-Knesset* 2:1646–51.

65. Survey Committee Report, 10 Nov. 1950, IDFA, DH 6, 247.

66. Knesset Committee for Ma'abara Affairs, 16 Jan. 1951, ISA 70/kaf.

67. Raanan Weitz to Settlement Department counselors, 22 Nov. 1950, ISA 1900/c, 6600.

68. Knesset Committee for Ma'abara Affairs, 16 Jan. 1951, ISA 70/kaf.

69. Order for Operation Ma'abara, 7 Nov. 1950, IDFA, DH 6.

70. Medical Corps Report, 31 Mar. 1951, IDFA, DH 6, 119.

71. Rabbi I. M. Levine to Ben-Gurion, 22 Nov. 1950, BGA.

72. Binyamin Mintz to Ben-Gurion, 27 Nov. 1950, Histadrut Poalei Agudat Yisrael, BGA.

73. Actions Committee of Ha-Poel ha-Mizrachi to Ben-Gurion, 4 Dec. 1950, BGA.

74. P. Rosen to Chief of Staff, 18 Dec. 1950, BGA.

75. Residents of Kessalon *Ma'abara* to rabbis, 28 Dec. 1950, BGA.

76. Protocol, Jisr inquiry, 20 Dec. 1950, ISA 5543/c, 3631.

77. Rabbi I. M. Levine and Golda Meirson, 26 Dec. 1951, ISA 5543/c, 3631.

78. Order for Operation Frontier Settlements, 1 Apr. 1951, IDFA, DH 6, 119.

79. 29 June 1951, IDFA, DH 6, 119.

80. 25 July 1951, IDFA, DH 6, 119.

81. August 1951, IDFA, DH 6, 119.

82. "Mivtza Ma'abara 2," 26 Oct. 1951, IDFA, DH 6, 119.

83. Knesset Public Services Committee, 28 Nov. 1951.

7. Changes in Immigration and Absorption Policy

1. Shalom Worm, *Giora Josephtal: His Life and Work* (in Hebrew) (Tel Aviv: Mifleget Po'alei Eretz Israel, 1963), 139.

2. Ibid.

3. 26 Oct. 1950, ISA 1900/c; 23 Dec. 1951, Kfar Saba Archives.

4. Worm, *Giora Josephtal*, 160.

5. 10 July 1952, ISA 1900/c.

6. Worm, *Giora Josephtal*, 148.

7. 31 Oct. 1951, ISA 1900/c.

8. Ibid.

9. 29 Nov. 1951, ISA 1900/c.

10. 10 Dec. 1951, ISA 1900/c.

11. 9 Jan. 1952, ISA 5429/c, 1294.

12. 9 Jan. 1952, ISA 5429/c.

13. 5 Feb. 1952, ISA 5429/c.

14. Director General of Interior Ministry to R. Weitz, Jewish Agency Settlement Department, 26 Feb. 1952, ISA 5429/c.

15. JAE, 21 Aug. 1951, CZA S43/51.

16. Raphael to Mossad le-Aliyah, 3 May 1951, CZA S6/6523.

17. JAE, 13 Mar. 1952, CZA S6/6384.

18. 5 Feb. 1952, CZA S6/6523.

19. Proposed guidelines for the work of the Council for Aliyah Affairs, 4 May 1952, CZA S6/6523.

20. Darin-Drabkin, *Housing and Absorption in Israel,* 81–82.

21. Summary of meeting at office of the minister of labor, 21 July 1952, ISA 2348/c.

22. Notice of Kfar Saba Local Council to tenants, 18 Feb. 1952, Kfar Saba Archives.

23. Proposals of Ministerial Committee on Budgetary Affairs (undated), ISA 2348/c. See also appendix 4.

24. The forecast was 13,500 immigrants from Iran, 15,000 from Egypt, 3,000 from Syria and Lebanon, and 2,500 from India.

25. Raphael to Eshkol, 8 Oct. 1951, CZA S6/6462.

26. 15,276 immigrants arrived in July, after which the figures declined drastically: 7,810 in August, 8,524 in September, and 5,246 in October.

27. Raphael, press conference, 8 Nov. 1951, ISA 5556/c.

28. Ibid.

29. The members of the committee were Josephthal, Kol, Raphael, and Braginsky.

30. Raphael to Beit Arieh, 18 Nov. 1951, CZA S6/6462.

31. The government was approved on 7 Oct. 1951. There were thirteen cabinet members: nine from Mapai, two from Ha-Poel ha-Mizrachi, one from Mizrachi, and one from Agudat Israel.

32. The selection rules were to be applied in Morocco, Tunisia, Algeria, Turkey, Iran, India, and Central and Western Europe.

33. JAE, 18 Nov. 1951, CZA S6/6384.

34. JAE, 22 Nov. 1951, CZA S6/6384.

35. JAE, 4 Feb. 1952; Coordinating Committee, 7 Feb. 1952, CZA S6/6384.

36. The immigrant total for December 1951 was 3,907; from 1952 on the figures steadily declined: January—3,719, February—1,486, March—4,221, April—1,656, and so on. See Aliyah Department files, CZA S6/6462, and appendixes 1 and 2.

37. Worm, *Giora Josephtal,* 174.

38. Coordinating Committee, 15 Mar. 1953, CZA S6/6384.

39. The Arab League countries were then Egypt, Syria, Lebanon, and Iraq. 13 Mar. 1952, CZA S6/6462.

40. Zionist Actions Committee, May 1952, CZA S6/6462.

41. D. Tene to Raphael, 25 Apr. 1952, ISA 5556/c.

42. Aliyah Department reports, June 1952, CZA S6/6462.

43. JAE, 29 Jan. 1952; Raphael, *Lo Zakhiti be-Or Min ha-Hefker,* 157.

44. Aliyah Department reports, June 1952, CZA S6/6462.

45. JAE, 29 Jan. 1952, CZA S6/6462.

46. Coordinating Committee, 14 July 1952, BGA.

47. Ibid.

48. 15 Mar. 1953, BGA.

49. 15 Mar. 1953, BGA. On the situation of North African Jews at that time, see M. Laskier, *North African Jewry in the Twentieth Century,* 117–57.

50. Josephthal to Raphael, 10 Dec. 1951, CZA S6/6149.

51. Bar-Giora to Raphael, 27 Oct. 1952, CZA S6/6149.

52. Coordinating Committee, 15 Mar. 1953; Sharett to Locker, 30 July 1953, CZA S41/101.

53. Coordinating Committee, CZA S41/101.

54. Report of Dr. Y. Amir, Ministry of Defense, 15 Mar. 1953, BGA.

55. During 1948–49, when immigration was at its peak—340,000 arrivals—only 5,776 left the country. In 1950, when the number of *olim* totaled 170,000, as many as 10,599 left. The figures for 1951 are similar.

56. Bachi, "Demographic Development of Israel," 385–86; Sikron, *Immigration to Israel,* 28, Table 3. According to Sikron, 80 percent of the *yordim* (emigrants from Israel) during the early days of the state were recent immigrants. The remainder were native-born Israelis or persons who had come in the pre-state period.

57. *Divrei ha-Knesset*14 (3 June 1953) 1480–1730.

58. Bar-Zohar, *David Ben-Gurion,* 2:953.

59. Ibid., 954–55; Ben-Gurion, *The Reborn State of Israel,* 2:453–59.

60. A. Granott, *Gesharim,* May 1950.

8. Immigration During 1948–98 and Its Ramifications on Israeli Society

1. Declaration of the Establishment of the State of Israel, Tel Aviv, 5 Iyyar, 5708, 14 May 1948.

2. The Law of Return 5710—1950 was approved by the Knesset on 20 Tammuz 5710 (5 July 1950), *Hukkei Yisrael,* 1950, 174. Although the law contained two caveats intended to prevent the immigration of persons who acted against the Jewish people and those who might endanger public health or the security of the state, there have in fact been very few cases where a Jew has been refused permission to enter the country. See Hacohen, "The Law of Return," 61–89.

3. The second wave of immigration to Israel arrived between 1955 and 1957. See *Israeli Statistical Annual 1994,* no. 45, Jerusalem, Israel Central Bureau of Statistics.

4. During the 1960s, approximately 370,000 immigrants came to Israel. Ibid.

5. During the first wave in the 1970s and 1980s, some 180,000 immigrants came to Israel; during the 1990s, about 800,000 immigrants arrived.

6. Sikron, *Immigration to Israel,* 17.

7. Ibid.

8. At the end of 1998, the population of Israel stood at 6,037,000, of whom 4,783,000 were Jews (the remainder belonging to other ethnic groupings—Moslems, Christians, Druze, and others). Based on figures from the ICBS, December 1998.

9. See *Israeli Statistical Annual 1994,* no. 45, Jerusalem, ICBS.

10. The remaining immigrants were unidentified as to their country of origin. See Moshe Lissak, "Immigration, Absorption, and the Building of a Society in Palestine During the 1920s (1918–1930)" (in Hebrew), in *History of the Jewish Yishuv in Palestine, from the First Aliya* (in Hebrew), ed. Moshe Lissak (Jerusalem: The Israel Academy for Sciences and Humanities and Bialik Institute, 1995), 191–92.

11. Ibid.

12. Moshe Lissak, "Images of Immigrants: Stereotypes and Stigmatization in the Period of Mass Immigration to Israel in the 1950s" (in Hebrew), *Cathedra* 43 (1987):129.

13. Yair Aharoni, *The Political Economy in Israel* (in Hebrew) (Tel Aviv: Am Oved, 1991), 69–79.

14. Elisha Efrat, *Development Towns in Israel: Past or Future?* (in Hebrew) (Tel Aviv: Ahiasaf, 1987); Amiram Gonen, "Dispersal of Population in Israel During the Transition from Yishuv to State" (in Hebrew), in *The Transition From Yishuv to State, 1947–1949: Continuity and Change* (in Hebrew), ed. Varda Pilovsky (Haifa: Herzl Institute for Research into Zionism, Haifa Univ., 1990), 157–72; Hacohen, "Plan for Direct Absorption of Mass Immigration," 359–78; Dvora Hacohen, *The Grain and the Millstone: The Settlement of Immigrants in the Negev in the First Decade of the State* (in Hebrew) (Tel Aviv: Am Oved, 1998), 70–123.

15. On the involvement of government institutions in the economic sector, see Barkai, *Beginnings of Israeli Economy,* 33–48; Aharoni, *The Political Economy in Israel,* 87–142.

16. This image continued to exist for a long time despite the fact that economists pointed to the contributions made by various immigrant groups to an increase in employment and the tremendous growth in the economy. See Yoram Ben-Porat, ed., *The Israeli Economy: Growing Pains* (in Hebrew) (Tel Aviv: Am Oved, 1989), 9; A. Alexander, "The Economies of Absorption in the First Decade of the State of Israel" (Hebrew), in *Independence* (in Hebrew), ed. A. Shapira (Jerusalem: Merkaz Zalman Shazar, 1998), 89–104. Economists also emphasized the contribution

of immigration from the Soviet Union to the state's economy. See Zvi Zusmann, "The Influence of Immigration from the USSR on the Economic Situation of the Veteran Society" (in Hebrew), in *Portrait of an Immigration* (in Hebrew), ed. Moshe Sikron and Elazar Leshem (Jerusalem: Magnes Press, 1998), 182–206.

17. Moshe Lissak, "The Social Demographic Revolution During the 1950s: Absorbing Mass Immigration" (in Hebrew), in *Independence* (in Hebrew), ed. A. Shapira, 13–55; Ben-Porat, ed., *The Israeli Economy*, 162–68.

18. Dan Horowitz and Moshe Lissak, *Trouble in Utopia* (Albany: SUNY Press, 1989), 64–69.

19. On the composition of the elite, see Moshe Lissak, *The Elites of the Jewish Community in Palestine* (in Hebrew) (Tel Aviv: Am Oved, 1981), 36–44.

20. Sami Smooha, *Israel: Pluralism and Conflict* (London: Routledge, 1978); Sami Smooha, "Critique of the Modern Institutional Version of the Cultural Approach in the Sociology of Ethnic Relations in Israel" (in Hebrew), *Megamot* 29 (1985):73–92; S. Svirsky, *Not Backward but Forced Backward* (in Hebrew) (Haifa: Mahbarot le-Mehkar u-Bikoret, 1981).

21. The violent demonstrations that took place in 1959 in Wadi Salib—a neighborhood in Haifa—in protest against ethnic discrimination were widely publicized. Wadi Salib had been abandoned by its former Arab residents and was subsequently populated by immigrants. The living conditions there were terrible. Initially, Holocaust refugees were housed there—emigrées from Poland and Romania who arrived at the time of the establishment of the state. After a while, most managed to leave the neighborhood to find more comfortable residences. In their place came immigrants from Moslem countries, mostly from North Africa. See *Report of Committee of Public Inquiry into the Events of July 9, 1959 at Wadi Salib* (in Hebrew) (Haifa: The Government of Israel, 1959). On other protest movements, see Shlomo Hasson, *The Protest of the Second Generation: Cultural Municipal Movements in Jerusalem* (in Hebrew) (Jerusalem: Jerusalem Institute for Research of Israel, 1987); Cohen, "Black Panthers," 93–109.

22. In the second decade of the state's existence, some 340,000 immigrants arrived in the country—about one third of the number that arrived in the first decade. Between 1961 and 1964, many of the immigrants, some 115,000, came from North Africa, while approximately 67,000 came from Romania. Immigration from Argentina was the most distinguishable of the waves from other countries. Data gleaned from publications of the Immigration and Absorption Department of the Jewish Agency, Tel Aviv, September 1970; *Israeli Statistical Annual* no. 45, 1994, Jerusalem, ICBS.

23. During the first twenty years following the establishment of the state, the total number of immigrants from the United States was only about 10,000. By the end of the 1960s, immigration from the United States had somewhat increased. During 1969–70, 12,000 immigrants arrived in Israel from the United States. See Chaim A. Waxman, "Immigration from the United States: Religious, Cultural, and Social Characteristics" (in Hebrew), in *Ingathering of the Exiles: Myth and Reality* (in Hebrew), ed. Dvora Hacohen (Jerusalem: Merkaz Shazar, 1998), 343–62.

24. Moshe Sikron, "Demography of Immigration" (in Hebrew), in *A Portrait of Immigration: The Absorption Process of Immigrants from the Former Soviet Union, 1990–1995* (in Hebrew), ed. Moshe Sikron and Elazar Leshem (Jerusalem: Magnes Press, 1998), 13–40.

25. Zvi Gitelman, *Immigration and Identity: The Resettlement and Impact of Soviet Immigrants on Israeli Politics and Society* (Los Angeles, Calif.: Wilstein Institute of Jewish Policy Studies, 1995); Tamar T. Horowitz and Elazar Leshem, "Emigrants from the Soviet Union in the Cultural

Expanse in Israel" (in Hebrew), in *Portrait of Immigration,* ed. Moshe Sirkon and Elazar Leshem (Jerusalem: Magnes Press, 1998), 291–333.

26. Gitelman, *Immigration and Identity;* Horowitz and Leshem, "Emigrants from the Soviet Union"; see also Tamar T. Horowitz, "Valued Inputs for the Immigration and Absorption Processes in the Wave of the 1990s" (in Hebrew), in *Israel Towards the Year 2000: Society, Politics, and Culture* (in Hebrew), ed. Moshe Lissak and Barukh Knei-Paz (Jerusalem: Magnes Press, 1996), 369–87.

27. There are a large number of Russian-language newspapers available to immigrants from the CIS, as well as literary and poetic publications in Russian. They have their own theater and some of them send their children to courses in Russian language and culture as a supplement to their studies in Israeli schools. See G. Zilberg, Elazar Leshem, and Moshe Lissak, *The Community of Emigrants from the Former Soviet Union Between Hints of Seclusion: Integration or Assimilation* (in Hebrew) (Jerusalem: Silbert Center for Jewish Studies, Hebrew Univ., 1995).

28. Gitelman, *Immigration and Identity;* Eilit Ulstein and Eliezer Ben-Raphael, *Aspects of Identity and Language in Absorption Immigrants from Former Soviet Union* (in Hebrew) (Jerusalem: Jerusalem Institute for Research into Israel, 1994); Horowitz, "Valued Inputs," 369–87.

29. Hacohen, *Shitat HaKlitah HaYeshira ve-Hashlahotea* ("Direct Absorption"—Sociocultural Absorption of Immigrants from the Former Soviet Union), Discussion Paper no. 28 (Jerusalem: The Jerusalem Institute for Israel Studies, 1994).

30. Ibid.

31. In Operation Moses (November 1984) some 6,700 immigrants from Ethiopia were brought to Israel during one and one-half months on flights via Sudan. In Operation Solomon (May 1991) the larger group of Ethiopian Jews arrived—about 14,000 in one week. Both of these waves were the climax of immigration from Ethiopia. In the year following the operation, a further 4,500 immigrants arrived from Ethiopia. See *Youth Aliya Report to Trustees* (in Hebrew) (Jerusalem: The Jewish Agency, 1995).

32. The extended family was augmented by people adopted into the family apart from relatives, such as servants or the children of poor families who were sent to a wealthier family. See Dany Bodovski et al., *Ethiopian Jewry in Inter-Cultural Transit: The Family and Circle of Life* (in Hebrew) (Jerusalem: Beitachin, 1994), 13–14; Shalva Weil, "Collective Designations and Collective Identity among Ethiopian Jews," *Israel Social Research* 10 (1995):25–40.

33. See above, note 31; Shalva Weil, *Single-Parent Families Among Ethiopian Immigrants in Israel* (in Hebrew) (Jerusalem: NCGW-Research Institute for Innovation in Education, Hebrew Univ., 1992).

34. Jacob Nahmias et al., "Health Profile of Ethiopian Immigrants in Israel: An Overview," *Israel Journal of Medical Science* 29, no. 6–7 (1993):338–43.

35. See above, notes 20, 31.

36. Gila Noam, ed., *Achievements and Challenges in the Absorption of Immigrants from Ethiopia* (Jerusalem: Joint-Brookdale Institute, Ministry of Absorption and the Jewish Agency, 1994), 3–10.

37. Ibid.

38. Horowitz and Lissak, *Origins of the Israeli Polity,* 120–56.

39. Citizenship is granted pursuant to the Law of Return to every immigrant arriving in Israel who declares his or her desire to settle in Israel. See Hacohen, "The Law of Return," 61–89.

40. See above, chapter 1.

41. Aharoni, *The Political Economy in Israel,* 87–142.

42. Parties that have been set up on ethnic grounds include The Black Panthers, 1973; Tami, 1977; Shas, 1984; and Yisrael Be-Aliya, 1996. See Chana Herzog, *Political Ethnicity: Image Versus Reality* (in Hebrew) (Tel Aviv: Yad Tabankin, Hakibbutz Hameuchad, 1986).

43. Shlomo Deshen and Moshe Shokeid, eds., *Jews of the East: Anthropological Studies of Past and Present* (Jerusalem and Tel Aviv: Schocken, 1984).

44. Horowitz and Lissak, *Trouble in Utopia,* 8–9.

45. Yoram Bilu, "Traditional Medicine Amongst Immigrants from Morocco" (in Hebrew), in *Jews of the East,* ed. Shlomo Deshen and Moshe Shokeid (Jerusalem and Tel Aviv: Schocken, 1984), 75–166.

46. Yoram Bilu and E. Ben-Ari, "Saint Sanctions in Israeli Development Towns: On a Mechanism of Urban Transformation," *Urban Anthropology* 15, no. 2 (1987):243–72.

47. The Shas Party used Rabbi Ovadia Yosef in its election campaign in 1996 and distributed amulets from the Kabbalist Rabbi Kadouri in order to woo potential voters.

48. Horowitz and Lissak, *Trouble in Utopia,* 8–9.

49. Amnon Rubinstein, *From Herzl to Rabin: 100 Years of Zionism* (in Hebrew) (Jerusalem and Tel Aviv: Schocken, 1998); Zvi Ra'anan, *Gush Emunim* (in Hebrew) (Tel Aviv: Sifriat Hapoalim, 1980).

50. Menahem Friedman, *The Haredi Orthodox Society: Sources, Trends, and Processes* (in Hebrew) (Jerusalem: Jerusalem Institute for Israel Studies, 1991).

51. Barukh Knei-Paz, "Israel Towards the Year 2000: A Changing World" (in Hebrew), in *Israel Towards the Year 2000: Society, Politics, and Culture* (in Hebrew), ed. Moshe Lissak and Barukh Knei-Paz (Jerusalem: Magnes Press, 1996), 408–28.

Glossary

Agudat Israel: a non-Zionist Orthodox party founded in 1912 in Eastern Europe

aliyah: literally, "ascent"; the Hebrew term for immigration of Jews to the land of Israel

Aliyah Bet: Organized illegal immigration of Jews to Palestine in violation of British regulations

Ashkenazim: Jews of European origin

Eretz Israel: the Land of Israel; Palestine

Gadna: abbreviation of *Gedudei No'ar* (youth corps); youth who undergo paramilitary training in preparation for their service in the Israel Defense Forces (IDF)

Gahal: acronym of *Giyyus hutz la'aretz* (foreign recruits); young people who underwent training abroad before their *aliyah* in order to join the IDF during the 1948 war

Haganah: paramilitary organization of the Yishuv

Ha-Poel ha-Mizrachi: a religious Zionist workers' party, formed by the left wing of the Mizrachi in 1921

Ha-Vaad ha-Leumi: the executive council of the Yishuv

Herut: a right-wing nationalist political party founded in 1948 by the former leaders of Irgun Zvai Leumi (IZL), a paramilitary organization associated with the revisionist movement

kibbutz (pl. *kibbutzim*): communal settlement based on collective ownership of means of production

Knesset: the Israeli parliament

ma'abara: (pl. *ma'abarot*): temporary immigrant camp

ma'apilim: illegal Jewish immigrants to Palestine, organized by the Mossad le-Aliyah Bet

Mahal: acronym of *mitnadvei hutz la'aretz* (foreign volunteers); professional soldiers who volunteered to fight in the IDF in the 1948 war

Mapai: acronym for *Mifleget Po'alei Eretz Israel* (Land of Israel Workers Party); a socialist Zionist party founded in 1930

Mapam: acronym for *Mifleget Po'alim Meuhedet* (United Workers Party); left-wing Zionist party founded in 1948

Mizrachi: abbreviation for *Merkaz Ruhani* (Spiritual Center); religious Zionist party founded in 1902

mizrahim: Jews whose origins are in the Islamic countries.

moshav (pl. *moshavim*): cooperative smallholders' settlement based on self-labor

moshav olim: a *moshav* for immigrants

Mossad le-Aliyah Bet: literally, "Organization for Aliyah Bet"; organized for *ma'apilim*

Nahal: acronym of *no'ar halutzi lohem* (pioneering fighting youth); special army units for graduates of pioneering youth movements, who spend part of their army service working on new agricultural settlements

oleh (pl. *olim*): immigrant to Israel. See *aliyah* above

Palmah: acronym for *Plugot Mahatz*; shock troops of the Haganah

Po'alei Agudat Israel: an Orthodox religious party with Zionist inclinations and social awareness

shelihim (sing. *shaliah*): *aliyah* emmisaries

ulpan (pl. *ulpanim*): special Hebrew language school for immigrants

yerida: literally, "going down"; the Hebrew term for emigration of Jews from the Land of Israel. An emigreé is known as a *yored* (pl. *yordim*)

Yishuv: literally, "settlement"; used to refer to the Jewish community in prestate Palestine

Bibliography

Abitbol, Michel. "The Jews and their Surroundings in North Africa prior to World War II" (in Hebrew). In *History of the Jews in Islamic Countries* (in Hebrew), edited by Shmuel Ettinger, 2: 411–28; 3: 9–30. Jerusalem: Merkaz Zalman Shazar, 1986.

———. *North African Jewry* (in Hebrew). Jerusalem: Machon Ben Zvi, 1980.

Ackerman, Walter, Arik Carmon, and David Zucker, eds. *Education in an Evolving Society* (in Hebrew). Jerusalem: Hakibbutz Hameuchad, Mossad Van Leer, 1985.

Aharoni, Yair. *The Political Economy in Israel* (in Hebrew). Tel Aviv: Am Oved, 1991.

Alexander, A. "The Economies of Absorption in the First Decade of the State of Israel" (Hebrew). In *Independence* (in Hebrew), edited by A. Shapira, 89–104. Jerusalem: Merkaz Zalman Shazar, 1998.

Alterman, Natan. *Ir ha-Yonah* (The City of the Dove). Tel Aviv: Mahbarot le-Sifrut, 1957.

Amir, Yehuda. "The Effects of Interpersonal Relationships on the Reduction of Ethnic Prejudices" (in Hebrew). *Megamot* 16, no. 1 (1968): 5–25.

Avineri, Shlomo. *David Ben-Gurion as a Labor Leader* (in Hebrew). Tel Aviv: Am Oved, 1988.

Bachi, Roberto. "The Demographic Development of Israel" (in Hebrew). *Riv'on le-Kalkala* 2 (1955): 205–11.

Bachi, Roberto, and Baruch Gil. "Changes in Immigration and in the Yishuv, 1948–1951" (in Hebrew). In *Shivat Zion* 2–3 (1953).

Bar-On, Mordechai. *Education Process in Israel Defense Forces.* Tel Aviv, 1966.

Bar-Zohar, Michael. *David Ben-Gurion* (in Hebrew). Tel Aviv: Am Oved, 1977.

Barad, Shimon. "Zionist Activity in Egypt, 1917–1952" (in Hebrew). *Studies in the Zionist and Pioneering Movements in the Islamic Countries* 2 (1989): 11–66.

Barkai, Chaim. *The Beginnings of Israeli Economy* (in Hebrew). Jerusalem: Bialik Institute, 1990.

Barnai, Jacob. "The Legal and Social Status of the Jews" (in Hebrew). In *History of the Jews in Islamic Countries* (in Hebrew), edited by Shmuel Ettinger. 3: 230–37. Jerusalem: Merkaz Zalman Shazar, 1986.

Bein, Alex. *Immigration and Settlement in the State of Israel* (in Hebrew). Tel Aviv: Am Oved and Ha-Sifria ha-Zionit, WZO, 1982.

Ben-Gurion, David. Diary (manuscript). Ben-Gurion Archives, Sdeh Boker.

———. *The Eternity of Israel* (in Hebrew). Tel Aviv: Ayanot, 1964.

———. *Israel at War* (in Hebrew). Tel Aviv: Am Oved, 1957.

———. *Memoirs* (in Hebrew). Tel Aviv: Am Oved, 1971.

———. *The Missions of the Pioneering Spirit* (in Hebrew). Jerusalem: Ayanot, 1952.

———. *The Reborn State of Israel* (in Hebrew). Tel Aviv: Am Oved, 1969.

———. "Terms and Values" (in Hebrew). *Hazut* 3 (1957).

———. "Uniqueness and Destiny" (in Hebrew). In *Israel Government Yearbook,* 7–30. Jerusalem: Government Printing Office, 1951.

Ben-Porat, Yoram, ed. *The Israeli Economy: Growing Pains* (in Hebrew). Tel Aviv: Am Oved, 1989.

Bentwich, Yosef. *Education in the State of Israel* (in Hebrew). Tel Aviv: Y. Chachik, 1960.

Bialer, Uri. "Ben-Gurion and the Issue of Israel's International Orientation, 1948–1956" (in Hebrew). *Cathedra* 43 (1987): 145–72.

———. *Between East and West.* Cambridge: Cambridge Univ. Press, 1990.

Bilu, Yoram. "Traditional Medicine Amongst Immigrants from Morocco" (in Hebrew). In *Jews of the East,* edited by Shlomo Deshen and Moshe Shokeid, 75–166. Jerusalem and Tel Aviv: Schocken, 1984.

Bilu, Yoram, and E. Ben-Ari. "Saint Sanctions in Israeli Development Towns: On a Mechanism of Urban Transformation." *Urban Anthropology* 15, no. 2 (1987): 243–72.

Bodovski, Dany, et al. *Ethiopian Jewry in Inter-Cultural Transit: The Family and Circle of Life* (in Hebrew). Jerusalem: Beitachin, 1994.

Bondi, Ruth. *Sheba: Everyman's Doctor* (in Hebrew). Tel Aviv: Zmora Bitan Modan, 1981.

Bondi, Ruth. Felix, *Pinchas Rosen and His Time* (in Hebrew). Tel Aviv: Zmora Bitan, 1990.

Brutzkus, Eliezer. "Dreams that Became Cities" (in Hebrew). In *Immigrants and Maabarot* (Hebrew), edited by Mordechai Naor, 127–40. Jerusalem: Yad Ben-Zvi, 1987.

Cohen, Chaim Yoseph. *The Jews of the East* (in Hebrew). Tel Aviv: Hakibbutz Hameuchad, 1972.

Cohen, Eric. "Black Panthers and Israeli Society." *The Jewish Journal of Sociology,* 14 (1972): 93–109.

Darin-Drabkin, Chaim. *Housing and Absorption in Israel* (in Hebrew). Tel Aviv: Gadish, 1955.

Dayan, David. *Yes, We Are Youth! The History of Gadna* (in Hebrew). Tel Aviv: Ministry of Defence, 1977.

Deshen, Shlomo, and Moshe Shokeid, eds. *Jews of the East: Anthropological Studies of Past and Present.* Jerusalem and Tel Aviv: Schocken, 1984.

Don-Yehiya, Eliezer. "Cooperation and Conflict Between Political Camps" (in Hebrew). Ph.D. diss., Hebrew Univ. of Jerusalem, 1977.

Duer, Yair. *The Book of the Naha'l Settlement Groups: 40 Years, 1948–1987* (in Hebrew). Tel Aviv: Ministry of Defense and Yad Tabenkin, 1989.

Efrat, Elisha. *Development Towns in Israel: Past or Future?* (in Hebrew). Tel Aviv: Ahiasaf, 1987.

Eisenstadt, S. N. "Immigration Absorption: Amalgamation of the Exiles and the Transformation Problems of the Israeli Society" (in Hebrew). In *Amalgamation of the Exiles* (in Hebrew). Jerusalem: Magnes Press, 1987.

———. *Israeli Society: Development and Problems* (in Hebrew). Jerusalem: Magnes Press, 1973.

———. *Israeli Society in Change* (in Hebrew). Jerusalem: Magnes Press, 1989.

Eisenstadt, S. N., et al., eds. *Israel: A Society in Formation* (in Hebrew). Jerusalem: Academon, 1972.

Elboim-Dror, Rachel. *Hebrew Education in Eretz Israel* (in Hebrew). Jerusalem: Yad Itzhak Ben-Zvi, 1986.

Eshkol, Levi. *Be-Hevlei Hitnahalut* (The travails of settlement). Tel Aviv: Ayanot, 1958.

———. *Be-Ma'aleh ha-Derekh* (On the Heights of the Road). Tel Aviv: Am Oved, 1966.

Finer, S. E. *The Man on the Horseback.* Oxford: Pall Mall Press, 1962.

Friedman, Menahem. "The Chronicle of the Status Quo: Religion and State in Israel" (in Hebrew). In *Transition from "Yishuv" to State, 1947–1949: Continuity and Change* (in Hebrew), edited by Varda Pilovsky, 47–80. Haifa: Herzl Institute for Research in Zionism, Haifa Univ., 1990.

———. *The Haredi Orthodox Society: Sources, Trends, and Processes* (in Hebrew). Jerusalem: Jerusalem Institute for Israel Studies, 1991.

Ganin, Zvi. *Truman, American Jewry, and Israel: 1945–1948.* New York: Holmes and Meier, 1979.

Gelber, Yoav. *The Emergence of a Jewish Army* (in Hebrew). Jerusalem: Yad Izhak Ben-Zvi, 1986.

———. *New Homeland: Immigration and Absorption of Central European Jews, 1933–1948* (in Hebrew). Jerusalem: Yad Izhak Ben Zvi and Leo Baeck Institute, 1990.

———. *Why Did They Disband the Palmah?* (in Hebrew). Tel Aviv: Schocken, 1986b.

Gilad, Zerubavel, and Mati Meged. *The Book of the Palmah* (in Hebrew). Tel Aviv: Hakibbutz Hameuchad, 1955.

Giladi, Dan. *Jewish Palestine During the Fourth Aliyah Period, 1924–1929* (in Hebrew). Tel Aviv: Am Oved, 1973.

Gitelman, Zvi. *Immigration and Identity: The Resettlement and Impact of Soviet Immigrants on Israeli Politics and Society.* Los Angeles, Calif.: Wilstein Institute of Jewish Policy Studies, 1995.

Goldberg, Giora. "Local Elections" (in Hebrew). In *Local Government in Israel* (in Hebrew), edited by Daniel J. Elazar and Chaim Kalchaim, 89–110. Jerusalem: Jerusalem Center for Public Affairs, 1987.

Gonen, Amiram. "Dispersal of Population in Israel During the Transition from Yishuv to State" (in Hebrew). In *The Transition From Yishuv to State, 1947–1949: Continuity and Change* (in Hebrew), edited by Varda Pilovsky, 157–72. Haifa: Herzl Institute for Research into Zionism, Haifa Univ., 1990.

Goren, Dina. *Freedom of the Press and National Security* (in Hebrew). Jerusalem: Magnes Press, 1976.

Gorni, Yosef. *Labor Unity, 1919–1930: The Conceptual Bases and Political System* (in Hebrew). Tel Aviv: Tel Aviv Univ. and Hakibbutz Hameuchad, 1973.

———. *The Quest for Collective Identity* (in Hebrew). Tel Aviv: Am Oved, 1990.

Gottesman, Meir. *Youth Aliyah: Continuity and Change* (in Hebrew). Tel Aviv: Cherikover, 1987.

Gruenbaum, A. L. *Economic Development in Israel* (in Hebrew). Tel Aviv: n.p., 1951.

Gutmann, Emanuel, and Jacob M. Landau. "The Political Elite in Israel: Characteristics and Make" (in Hebrew). In *The Israeli Political System* (in Hebrew), edited by Moshe Lissak and Emanuel Gutmann, 192–228. Tel Aviv: Am Oved, 1977.

Gvati, Chaim. *A Century of Settlement: The History of Jewish Agricultural Settlement in Israel* (in Hebrew). Tel Aviv: Hakibbutz Hameuchad, 1981.

Habbas, Bracha, ed. *The Book of the Second Aliyah* (in Hebrew). Tel Aviv: Am Oved, 1947.

Hacohen, Dvora. "Ben-Gurion and the Second World War: Plans for Mass Immigration to Palestine." In *Jews and Messianism in the Modern Era: Studies in Contemporary Jewry*, edited by Jonathan Frankel, 247–68. Oxford: Oxford Univ. Press, 1991.

———. *From Fantasy to Reality: Ben-Gurion's Plan for Mass Immigration Between 1942 and 1945* (in Hebrew). Tel Aviv: Ministry of Defense Press, 1994.

———. *The Grain and the Millstone: The Settlement of Immigrants in the Negev in the First Decade of the State* (in Hebrew). Tel Aviv: Am Oved, 1998.

———. "The Law of Return as an Embodiment of the Link between Israel and the Jews in the Diaspora." *Journal of Israeli History* 19, no. 1 (1998): 61–89.

———. "The Plan for Direct Absorption of Mass Immigration During the 1950s and its Consequences" (in Hebrew). In Iyunim, *Studies in Zionism: The Yishuv and the State of Israel*, edited by Pinhas Ginossar. Sde Boker: Ben-Gurion Research Center, Univ. of the Negev Press (1991): 359–78.

———. "The Policy of Mass Immigration Absorption in Israel During the Years 1948–1953" (in Hebrew). Ph.D. diss., Bar-Ilan Univ., 1984.

———. "Political Aspects of the Absorption of the Great Aliyah upon the Establishment of the State" (in Hebrew). *Ha-Zionut* 11 (1986): 381–402.

Halperin, Sarah. *Dr. A. Biram and his Reali School: Tradition and Experimentation in Education* (in Hebrew). Jerusalem: R. Mass, 1970.

Hasson, Shlomo. *The Protest of the Second Generation: Cultural Municipal Movements in Jerusalem* (in Hebrew). Jerusalem: Jerusalem Institute for Research of Israel, 1987.

Herzog, Chana. *Political Ethnicity: Image Versus Reality* (in Hebrew). Tel Aviv: Yad Tabankin, Hakibbutz Hameuchad, 1986.

Hillel, Shlomo. *Operation Babylon.* London: Fontana, 1989.

———. "The Steps that Brought about the Mass Aliyah from Iraq" (in Hebrew). In *From Babylon to Jerusalem* (in Hebrew), edited by Zvi Yehuda. Tel Aviv: Ha-Mahon le-Moreshet Yehudei Bavel, 1981.

Horowitz, Dan, and Moshe Lissak. *Origins of the Israeli Polity: Palestine under the Mandate.* Chicago: Univ. of Chicago Press, 1978.

———. *Trouble in Utopia.* Albany: SUNY Press, 1989.

Horowitz, Tamar T. "Valued Inputs for the Immigration and Absorption Processes in the Wave of the 1990s" (in Hebrew). In *Israel Towards the Year 2000: Society, Politics, and Culture* (in Hebrew), edited by Moshe Lissak and Barukh Knei-Paz. Jerusalem: Magnes Press, 1996.

Horowitz, Tamar T., and Elazar Leshem. "Emigrants from the Soviet Union in the Cultural Expanse in Israel" (in Hebrew). In *Portrait of Immigration,* edited by Moshe Sirkon and Elazar Leshem, 291–333. Jerusalem: Magnes Press, 1998.

Huntington, Samuel P. *The Soldier and the State.* Cambridge, Mass.: Harvard Univ. Press, 1957.

Janowitz, Morris. *The Professional Soldier.* New York: Free Press, 1971.

Kafkafi, Eyal. *A Country Searching for its People* (in Hebrew). Tel Aviv: Hakibbutz Hameuchad, 1991.

———. "The Lost Prospect of a Religious Labor School Network" (in Hebrew). *Medina Mimshal ve-Yihasim Benleumiyim* 31 (1990): 77–100.

Kanari, Baruch. *Hakibbutz Hameuchad: Mission and Reality* (in Hebrew). Tel Aviv: Hakibbutz Hameuchad, 1989.

Katz, Yossi. "Deliberations of the Jewish Agency's Committee on Transfer of Population, 1937–1938" (in Hebrew). *Zion* 53, no. 2 (1988): 167–90.

Katzburg, Nathaniel. *Nahalat Emunim: Religious Settlement in the Land of Israel* (in Hebrew). Jerusalem: JNF, 1955.

Kaufman, Menachem. *An Ambiguous Partnership: Non-Zionists and Zionists in America, 1939–1948.* Jerusalem: Magnes Press, 1991.

———. "The Jewish Community of Palestine as Viewed by Non-Zionist American Jewry During the Holocaust and Pre-State Period" (in Hebrew). *Cathedra* 19 (1981): 205–26.

Kellner, Jacob. *The First Immigrant Groups to Eretz Israel: Myth and Reality* (in Hebrew). Jerusalem: Magnes Press, 1984.

Keren, Michael. *Ben-Gurion and the Intellectuals: Power, Knowledge, and Charisma.* Dekalb, Ill.: Southern Illinois Univ. Press, 1983.

Keren, Shlomit. *Between the Sheaves and the Sword: Youth Movements and the Founding of the Nahal* (in Hebrew). Tel Aviv: Ministry of Defense Press, 1991.

Knei-Paz, Barukh. "Israel Towards the Year 2000: A Changing World" (in Hebrew). In

Israel Towards the Year 2000: Society, Politics, and Culture (in Hebrew), edited by Moshe Lissak and Barukh Knei-Paz, 408–28. Jerusalem: Magnes Press, 1996.

Koren, Yitzhak. *Ingathering of Exiles in their Settlement: A History of the Immigrant Moshavim in Israel* (in Hebrew). Tel Aviv: Am Oved, 1964.

Lamm, Zvi. "Ideological Tensions: Struggles over the Goals of Education" (in Hebrew). In *Education in Israel,* edited by Chaim Ormian, 71–84. Jerusalem: Ministry of Education and Culture, 1973.

———. "Ideology and Education" (in Hebrew). Ph.D. diss., Hebrew Univ. of Jerusalem, 1967.

Laskier, Michael M. *North African Jewry in the Twentieth Century.* New York: New York Univ. Press, 1994.

Liebman, Charles E., and Eliezer Don Yehiya. *Civil Religion in Israel: Traditional Judaism and Political Culture in the Jewish State.* Berkeley, Calif.: Berkeley Univ. Press, 1983.

Lissak, Moshe. *The Elites of the Jewish Community in Palestine.* Tel Aviv: Am Oved, 1981.

———. "Images of Immigrants: Stereotypes and Stigmatization in the Period of Mass Immigration to Israel in the 1950s" (in Hebrew). *Cathedra* 43 (1987): 125–44.

———. "Immigration, Absorption, and the Building of a Society in Palestine During the 1920s (1918–1930)" (in Hebrew). In *History of the Jewish Yishuv in Palestine, from the First Aliya* (in Hebrew), edited by Moshe Lissak. *Part II: The British Mandate,* 173–302. Jerusalem: The Israel Academy for Sciences and Humanities and Bialik Institute, 1995.

———. "Institution Building in Ben-Gurion's View" (in Hebrew). In *David Ben-Gurion as a Labor Leader* (in Hebrew), edited by Shlomo Avineri. Tel Aviv: Am Oved, 1987.

———. "The Social Demographic Revolution During the 1950s: Absorbing Mass Immigration" (in Hebrew). In *Independence: The First Fifty Years* (in Hebrew), edited by A. Shapira, 13–55. Jerusalem: Merkaz Zalman Shazar, 1998.

Lissak, Moshe, and Barukh Knei-Paz, eds. *Israel Towards the Year 2000: Society, Politics, and Culture* (in Hebrew). Jerusalem: Magnes Press, 1996.

Margalit, Elkana. *Kibbutz: Society and Politics* (in Hebrew). Tel Aviv: Am Oved, 1980.

Nahmias, Jacob, et al. "Health Profile of Ethiopian Immigrants in Israel: An Overview." *Israel Journal of Medical Science* 29, no. 6–7 (1993): 338–43.

Neumann, Emanuel. *In the Arena.* New York: Herzl Press, 1976.

Noam, Gila, ed. *Achievements and Challenges in the Absorption of Immigrants from Ethiopia.* Jerusalem: Joint-Brookdale Institute, Ministry of Absorption and the Jewish Agency, 1994.

Ofer, Dalia. *Escaping the Holocaust: Illegal Immigration to the Land of Israel, 1939–1944.* New York: Oxford Univ. Press, 1990.

Ottolenghi, Smadar, and Rachel Wilkansky. *Legal and Organizational Problems in the Structure of the Public Council* (in Hebrew). Tel Aviv: Tel Aviv Univ., Merkaz Pinhas Sapir, 1985.

Pa'il, Meir. "From National Home to the State of Israel" (in Hebrew). In *History of Eretz*

Israel. Vol. 10, *The War of Independence, 1947–1949,* edited by Yehoshua Ben Arieh, 11–80. Jerusalem: Keter, 1983.

———. "The Military System" (in Hebrew). In *History of Eretz Israel.* Vol. 10, *The War of Independence, 1947–1949,* edited by Yehoshua Ben Arieh, 151–272. Jerusalem: Keter, 1983.

Peres, Yohanan. *Ethnic Relations in Israel* (in Hebrew). Tel Aviv: Sifriat Hapoalim, 1976.

Peri, Yoram. *Between Battles and Ballots: Israeli Military in Politics.* Cambridge: Cambridge Univ. Press, 1983.

Perlmutter, Amos. *Military and Politics in Israel: Nation Building and Role Expansion.* London: F. Cass, 1969.

Proudfoot, Malcolm Jarvis. *European Refugees: 1939–1952.* London: Faber and Faber, 1956.

Pye, Leonard. "Armies in the Process of Political Modernization." In *The Role of the Military in Underdeveloped Countries,* edited by James T. Johnson. Princeton, N.J.: Princeton Univ. Press, 1962.

Ra'anan, Zvi. *Gush Emunim* (in Hebrew). Tel Aviv: Sifriat Hapoalim, 1980.

Raphael, Yitzhak. *Lo Zakhiti be-Or Min ha-Hefker* (in Hebrew). Tel Aviv: Yidanim, 1981.

———. "The Struggle over Mass Immigration" (in Hebrew). In *Immigrants and Ma'abarot,* edited by M. Naor. *Yidan* 8: 19–30. Jerusalem: Yad Izhak Ben-Zvi, 1987.

Raz, Nahman. "On Educational Problems of the Nahal." In *Conversations: Youth in Israel* (in Hebrew), edited by N. Shtrasberg, 229–33. Tel Aviv: Mifleget Po'alei Eretz Israel, 1951.

Reichman, Shalom. *From Foothold to Settled Territory: 1918–1948* (in Hebrew). Jerusalem: Yad Izhak Ben-Zvi, 1979.

Reshef, Shimon. "Ben-Gurion and State Education" (in Hebrew). *Cathedra* 43 (1987): 91–114.

Rosen, Dov. *Ma'abarot and Immigrant Settlements from the Viewpoint of the Interior Ministry* (in Hebrew). Jerusalem: Misrad Ha-Pnim, 1985.

Rubinstein, Amnon. *From Herzl to Rabin: 100 Years of Zionism* (in Hebrew). Jerusalem and Tel Aviv: Schocken, 1998.

Rubinstein, Eliakim. "From Yishuv to State: Institutions and Parties" (in Hebrew). In *The Jewish National Home: From the Balfour Declaration to Independence,* edited by Binyamin Eliav, 129–205. Jerusalem: Keter, 1979.

Saadoun, Chaim. "Aliyah from Tunisia During the Struggle for Tunisian Independence" (in Hebrew). *Pe'amim* 39 (1989): 103–25.

Segev, Tom. *1949: The First Israelis* (in Hebrew). Jerusalem: Domino Press, 1984.

Shaari, David. *Deportation to Cyprus, 1946–1949* (in Hebrew). Jerusalem: The Zionist Library, 1981.

Shaki, Avner H. *Who is a Jew in the Laws of the State of Israel?* (in Hebrew). Jerusalem: Mossad Harav Kook, 1977.

Shapira, Anita. *From the Dismissal of the Head of the National Staff until the Disbanding of the Palmah: Issues in the Struggle for Security Leadership, 1948* (in Hebrew). Tel Aviv: Hakibbutz Hameuchad, 1985.

———. *New Jews, Old Jews.* Tel Aviv: Am Oved, 1997.

———, ed. *Ha'apalah: Studies in the History of Illegal Immigration and the Remaining Remnant* (in Hebrew). Tel Aviv: Am Oved, 1990.

Shapiro, Yonathan. *The Organization of Power: The Historical Ahdut ha-Avodah* (in Hebrew). Tel Aviv: Am Oved, 1975.

Sharett, Moshe. *In the Gate of the Nations* (in Hebrew). Tel Aviv: Am Oved, 1958.

Sharett, Yaakov, and Gershon Rivlin. *Ezra Danin: A Zionist at All Times* (in Hebrew). Jerusalem: Kidum, 1987.

Sharon, Arie. *Physical Planning in Israel* (in Hebrew). Tel Aviv, 1951.

Shefer, Zeev. *A Society in Emergence: The Kibbutz* (in Hebrew). Tel Aviv: Am Oved, 1961.

Shilo, Margalit. "Changing Attitudes in the Zionist Movement Towards Immigration to Eretz Israel, 1904–1914" (in Hebrew). *Cathedra* 46 (1987): 109–22.

Shinar, P. Eliezer. *Emburdened with Feelings: Israel-German Relations, 1951–1966* (in Hebrew). Tel Aviv: Schocken, 1967.

Shomroni, Elik. *Scythe and Sword* (in Hebrew). Tel Aviv: Mayanot, 1953.

Shtrasberg, N., ed. *Conversations: Youth in Israel* (in Hebrew). Tel Aviv: Mifleget Po'alei Eretz Israel, 1951.

Sikron, Moshe. "Demography of Immigration" (in Hebrew). In *A Portrait of Immigration: The Absorption Process of Immigrants from the Former Soviet Union, 1990–1995* (in Hebrew), edited by Moshe Sikron and Elazar Leshem, 13–40. Jerusalem: Magnes Press, 1998.

———. *Immigration to Israel, 1948–1957* (in Hebrew). Jerusalem: Machon Falk and Israel Central Bureau of Statistics, 1957.

Sliter, Leonard. *Ha-Neemanim* (The Trustees). Tel Aviv: Maarachot, 1971.

Slutzky, Yehuda. *Book of the History of the Haganah* (in Hebrew). Tel Aviv: Am Oved, 1973.

Smooha, Sami. "Critique of the Modern Institutional Version of the Cultural Approach in the Sociology of Ethnic Relations in Israel" (in Hebrew). *Megamot* 29 (1985): 73–92.

———. *Israel: Pluralism and Conflict.* London: Routledge, 1978.

Sternberg, Avraham. *When the People Gathers* (in Hebrew). Tel Aviv: Hakibbutz Hameuchad, 1973.

Svirsky, S. *Not Backward but Forced Backward* (in Hebrew). Haifa: Mahbarot le-Mehkar u-Bikoret, 1981.

Teveth, Shabtai. *Kin'at David.* Tel Aviv: Schocken, 1980.

Tobi, Yosef. "Jewish Centers in Asia" (in Hebrew). In *History of the Jews in Islamic Countries* (in Hebrew), edited by Shmuel Ettinger, 3: 74–90. Jerusalem: Merkaz Zalman Shazar, 1986.

Tzadok, Yosef. *In the Storms of Yemen* (in Hebrew). Tel Aviv: Am Oved, 1956.

Tzahor, Zeev. "Ben-Gurion and Illegal Immigration, 1934–1948" (in Hebrew). In *East European Jewry: Between Holocaust and Rebirth* (in Hebrew), edited by Benyamin Pinkus. Kiryat Sede Boqer: Ben-Gurion Univ. and The Ben-Gurion Research Center, 1987.

———. "Sad Victory: Ben-Gurion and Gdud ha-Avoda" (in Hebrew). *Cathedra* 43 (1987): 33–51.

Tzur, Zeev. "The Incident of Shaharyiah in the Lachish Area" (in Hebrew). *Shorashim* 2 (1980): 202–07.

———. *Kibbutz ha-Me'uhad in the Settlement of Eretz Israel* (in Hebrew). Vol. 2, *1939–1949.* Tel Aviv: Hakibbutz Hameuchad, 1982.

———. *Kibbutz ha-Me'uhad in the Settlement of Eretz Israel* (in Hebrew). Vol. 3, *1949–1960.* Tel Aviv: Hakibbutz Hameuchad, 1984.

Ulstein, Eilit, and Eliezer Ben-Raphael. *Aspects of Identity and Language in Absorption Immigrants from Former Soviet Union* (in Hebrew). Jerusalem: Jerusalem Institute for Research into Israel, 1994.

Unna, Moshe. *In the Paths of Thought and Deed* (in Hebrew). Tel Aviv: Moreshet, 1955.

———. *In Separate Ways: The Religious Parties in Israel* (in Hebrew). Alon Shevut: Yad Shapira, 1984.

Waxman, Chaim A. "Immigration from the United States: Religious, Cultural, and Social Characteristics" (in Hebrew). In *Ingathering of the Exiles: Myth and Reality* (in Hebrew), edited by Dvora Hacohen, 343–62. Jerusalem: Merkaz Shazar, 1998.

Weil, Shalva. "Collective Designations and Collective Identity among Ethiopian Jews." *Israel Social Research* 10 (1995): 25–40.

———. *Single-Parent Families Among Ethiopian Immigrants in Israel* (in Hebrew). Jerusalem: NCGW-Research Institute for Innovation in Education, Hebrew Univ., 1992.

Weissberger, Y. *The Gate of Aliyah: Diary of Mass Immigration, 1947–1957* (in Hebrew). Jerusalem: n.p., 1986.

Weiss, Shevach. *Local Government in Israel* (in Hebrew). Tel Aviv: Am Oved, 1986.

Worm, Shalom. *Giora Josephtal: His Life and Work* (in Hebrew). Tel Aviv: Mifleget Po'alei Eretz Israel, 1963.

Yanai, Natan. *Political Crises in Israel* (in Hebrew). Jerusalem: Keter, 1982.

Yehuda, Zvi, ed. *From Babylon to Jerusalem: Studies and Documents on Zionism and Aliyah from Iraq* (in Hebrew). Tel Aviv: Ha-Mahon le-Heker Yehudei Bavel, 1981.

Zameret, Zvi. *The Melting Pot: The Frumkin Commission on the Education of Immigrant Children (1950)* (in Hebrew). Kiryat Sdeh Boker: Ben-Gurion Research Center, Ben-Gurion Univ. of the Negev Press, 1993.

Zaslavsky, David. *Immigrant Housing in Israel* (in Hebrew). Tel Aviv: Am Oved, 1954.

Zilberg, G., Elazar Leshem, and Moshe Lissak. *The Community of Emigrants from the Former Soviet Union Between Hints of Seclusion: Integration or Assimilation* (in Hebrew). Jerusalem: Silbert Center for Jewish Studies, Hebrew Univ., 1995.

Zionist Organization Executive. *The 10th Zionist Congress Protocols.* Basel: WZO, 1911.

———. *The 22nd Zionist Congress Protocols*. Basel: WZO, 1946.

———. *The 23rd Zionist Congress Protocols*. Jerusalem: WZO, 1951.

Zusmann, Zvi. "The Influence of Immigration from the USSR on the Economic Situation of the Veteran Society" (in Hebrew), 182–206. In *Portrait of an Immigration* (in Hebrew), edited by Moshe Sikron and Elazar Leshem. Jerusalem: Magnes Press, 1998.

Index

Italic page number denotes photograph; page number followed by a *t* indicates a table.

absorption: administration of, 30, 228–29,
253–54; characteristics of, 253–54; of
CIS immigrants, 257; of Ethiopian Jews,
259–60; finances and, 94, 98–103, 152;
Great Aliyah and, 57; health of
immigrants and, 61, 135, 147, 200; IDF
and, 210; impact of horror stories of,
71–73, 76, 108, 119–20; Kelitah
Department and, 35–36; lack of
preparedness for, 57–58; Land
Settlement Department and, 36–37;
mass immigration and, 81–84, 122;
near-collapse of network, 83, 85, 222;
number of immigrants by place of, 270t;
overview of, 244–45; paradoxes of,
58–59, 248–50; policies regarding, 24;
Polish *aliyah* and, 70–71; politics and,
162–63; powerlessness of network, 137;
problems relating to, 10–11, 47, 129–30,
246–47, 249–50; public opinion of,
110–12; quotas and, 116; relief attempts,
88–94; restructuring of network, 87;
retirement of Ben-Gurion and, 244–45;
return to homelands, 119, 241, 242–43;
of Russian Jews, 257–59; "trade"
agreements and, 23; Yemenite Jews and,
67–69. *See also* cultural arena; education;
employment; health care; immigrant
camps; *ma'abarot*; social arena
Absorption Department. *See* Kelitah
Department
Aden, 63–69, 139, 267–68t

Adenauer, Konrad, 106
afforestation project: Eshkol's plan for,
151–52; inadequacy of, 118, 125, 199;
as jobs for immigrants, 156, 254
agricultural colonies, 194, 195
agriculture, 135, 156, 158, 199, 231
Agudat Israel: Cultural Absorption
Department and, 171; education and,
175–76, 286n. 3; new cabinet member
from, 292n. 31; resignation of, 241;
schools of, 165, 174
Aharon, Zeev, 16
aliyah. See immigration
Aliyah Committee, 48, 50–53, 56, 279n. 97
Aliyah Department: control of immigration
and, 32–34; function of, 30, 58; health
care of immigrants and, 139, 146;
housing for immigrants and, 130;
immigration requirements and, 237;
Jewish Agency Executive and, 108–9;
Karaite immigration and, 54–55;
Moroccan Jews and, 239; political battles
over, 31–34; projections for
immigration, 283n. 39; provisional
government and, 25; restrictions on
immigration and, 117
American Jewish Conference, 96–97
Amidar, 34, 131, 133, 191, 284n. 10
Anglo-Palestine Bank, 95–96
anti-Semitism: in Egypt, 55–56; impact on
immigration, 7; in Iraq, 80, 82–83, 123;
in Romania, 74; in Russia, 245